IMMERSIVE ENVIRONMENTS SERIES

Virtual Worlds, also known as Multi-User Virtual Environments (MUVEs), have demonstrated remarkable growth during the first decade of the 21st century, largely due to the increased capability of computing technology and telecom networks. This development has effectively opened up a new field for exploration.

Activity in these immersive environments attracts professionals from a wide range of backgrounds, drawn by the richly varied opportunities for practice and research, often resulting in the formation of creative, multidisciplinary teams. Innovations entail both the application of tried and tested methods for research and evaluation and the tailoring of new approaches. It is important that studies advancing our understanding of this rapidly developing field are collated and disseminated in a timely fashion.

In this series we present current knowledge and discussion that explores how people interact with virtual worlds at all levels, what these environments have to offer us, and what their future might hold. The Immersive Environments Series will encompass theoretical perspectives, practical and technical approaches and social issues, including determinants of efficacy, usability and acceptability.

We welcome proposals for monographs, edited volumes, Briefs and other suggested publications.

For further volumes:
http://www.springer.com/series/10095

Anna Peachey • Mark Childs
Editors

Reinventing Ourselves: Contemporary Concepts of Identity in Virtual Worlds

 Springer

Editors
Anna Peachey
Eygus Ltd
69A North Street
Ashburton TQ13 7QH
United Kingdom
anna@eygus.co.uk

Mark Childs
Coventry University
Priory Street
Coventry CV1 5FB
United Kingdom
mark.childs@coventry.ac.uk

ISBN 978-0-85729-360-2   e-ISBN 978-0-85729-361-9
DOI 10.1007/978-0-85729-361-9
Springer London Dordrecht Heidelberg New York

British Library Cataloguing in Publication Data
A catalogue record for this book is available from the British Library

Library of Congress Control Number: 2011931288

Printed on acid-free paper

Springer is part of Springer Science+Business Media (www.springer.com)

Acknowledgments

Images from three virtual worlds are used throughout this book. The authors would like to acknowledge Blizzard Entertainment for the use of images taken from Diablo, Jagex Games Studio for the use of the images of RuneScape and Linden Lab for the Second Life images.

Author Biographies

Anne Adams is a lecturer in the Institute of Educational Technology at The Open University with expertise in social sciences and technology and extensive experience of industrial and cross-disciplinary research in Science, Education, and Technology. Dr. Adams has managed large and small scale projects across disciplines and is particularly interested in situated learning and identity.

Lluïsa Astruc is a Lecturer in Spanish at The Open University. Her main research interest is language acquisition in the first and in the second language.

Jon Cabiria is currently one of only a small number of people worldwide who hold a doctorate degree in Media Psychology and is on the leading edge of this increasingly important field. Dr. Cabiria's interests and research include online social sites, virtual worlds, and augmented reality technologies, where he specializes in the intersection of psychology and media as they relate to identity exploration and development. He is also a media psychology consultant and public speaker, traveling worldwide to present on topics about the positive benefits of online social engagement, online education, and augmented reality psychology. Dr. Cabiria teaches in the Media Psychology master's programme for Walden University, and in the Media Psychology and Social Change programme for Fielding Graduate Institute, where he developed the very popular course "Identity in the Virtual Age".

Diane Carr is a Lecturer in Media and Cultural Studies based at the Institute of Education, University of London. Diane currently teaches digital game studies, film theory and childhood studies. Most of her writing and research focuses on digital games and virtual worlds, with an emphasis on issues of identity, representation and learning. She has led funded research into digital games methodology, learning practices and pedagogy in social worlds and MMORPGs, gendered preferences and games culture, and the notion of games as 'playable texts'. For more information, visit http://playhouse.wordpress.com/

Sanjay Chandrasekharan is a postdoctoral fellow with the School of Interactive Computing at the Georgia Institute of Technology. Previously, he was a postdoctoral fellow with the Cognitive and Motor Neuroscience lab, Faculty of Kinesiology,

University of Calgary, and a faculty member at the Centre for Behavioral and Cognitive Sciences, University of Allahabad, India. Chandrasekharan is an expert in cognitive sciences, specializing in common coding theory and experimentation. He completed his Ph.D. in Cognitive Science from Carleton University, Ottawa, Canada.

Alec Charles is Principal Lecturer in Media at the University of Bedfordshire. He has worked as a documentary programme-maker for BBC Radio and is the editor of *EU Enlargement – One Year On* and *Media in the Enlarged Europe* and co-editor of *The End of Journalism*. He has published widely on new media, cinema, television, literature, politics and journalism. His recent publications include papers in *Science Fiction Studies, Science Fiction Film & Television, Eludamos, Colloquy, British Journalism Review, CEU Political Science Journal, Historia Actual Online* and the *Journal of Contemporary European Research*, as well as chapters in *The Films of Tod Browning* and *The Films of Edgar G. Ulmer*. He has previously held positions at universities in Japan and Estonia, where he also worked as a newspaper journalist.

Mark Childs is the Senior Research Fellow for Elearning at Coventry University, UK. He has worked in Higher Education since 1995 on close to thirty technology-supported learning projects employing a variety of different technologies. His PhD in Education was awarded in 2010 by the University of Warwick and was on the subject of Learners' Experience of Presence in Virtual Worlds, a subject he has been studying since 2005. Although his previous degrees are in astrophysics, media studies and consultancy, the majority of his research projects have been in Theatre and Performance Studies, beginning with telematic performance and 3D modelling at Warwick, and then managing the Theatron Project at King's College London, which involved developing a series of historical theatres in Second Life. His most recent project was working with the Birmingham Royal Ballet, Coventry's Serious Games Institute and Daden Ltd. to develop a simulation of the Birmingham Hippodrome.

Paul Clifton is a Ph.D. student in Digital Media at the Georgia Institute of Technology. His research focuses on the ability of and ways that interfaces bridge the gap between virtual and real spaces. His previous and current projects include embodied Digital Creativity, described in this book, WorkTop, a collaborative design tool for multi-touch tabletop computers, and a smartphone based interactive narrative remote control. He also produces a monthly science fiction radio show, The Science Fiction Lab, on WREK, Georgia Tech's student radio station.

Marc Conrad currently works for the Faculty of Creative Arts, Technology and Science at the University of Bedfordshire as a Senior Lecturer in Computer Science. While being educated as a Mathematician, where he received his PhD, interest in virtual worlds dates back to 1994 when he became engaged with the German MUD Unitopia hosted at the University of Stuttgart. When in 2007 his University acquired the Second Life islands 'Bedfordia' and 'University of Bedfordshire' he utilized both the social and technical aspects of Second Life for his teaching and research. The name of his avatar is Sanf Oh. Other then virtual worlds, he has research interests and publications in areas as diverse as Algebraic Number Theory, Software Engineering, Project Management, Trust, Security and Sound Art.

Simon Evans spent 15 years in advertising, during which he gained an interest in the role of communications in society and consumer behaviour. As a mature student, he has undertaken the Open University Psychology Honours Degree programme and the Master's degree programme in Social and Cultural Psychology at the London School of Economics. During his time at the LSE, he developed an interest in how someone's sense of self arises through social interactions and he was introduced to Second Life, where he has lived since December 2007. During 2009, he conducted research and developed a thesis for the Master's programme, upon which the contribution to this book is based. Simon is currently undertaking a doctoral programme at the LSE, the objective being to develop a theoretical structure for the self in contemporary society and methodological frameworks applicable to all spheres of virtual life including virtual worlds.

Jessica A. Foss received her BA in Psychology at Loyola Marymount University, where she was an active member of the P.R.O.S.E. Project research on personality in Second Life. Her present research is in the area of positive psychology with an emphasis on positive youth development. She is currently attending Fuller Graduate School of Psychology pursuing her PhD in Clinical Psychology.

Ferdinand Francino aka Gwynn (Gunawan) has been playing computer games since 1987, online since 1997. He has been active on, in and with the internet since before HTML got released into the public domain in August 1991. He had an internet design and consultancy agency from 1994 to 2006 and now works as Project Manager Virtual Worlds for Glasgow Caledonian University where he also part time teaches 3D Internet and Virtual Worlds to 4th year students.

Cecilia Garrido is Associate Dean and Senior Lecturer in Spanish in the Faculty of Education and Language Studies at The Open University. She has extensive experience in the teaching of Spanish in different settings. Her research interests lie in the areas of intercultural competence and the use of technologies for language learning and teaching.

Richard L. Gilbert is Professor and Assistant Chair in the Department of Psychology at Loyola Marymount University in Los Angeles, California. He is the Director of The P.R.O.S.E. Project (Psychological Research on Synthetic Environments) (www. proseproject.info), a lab that is conducting a program of in-world behavioral research on the psychology of 3D virtual environments. In addition, he is the Founder of Loyola Marymount Virtual University (LMVU), Loyola Marymount's multidisciplinary campus in the 3D virtual world of Second Life (http://www.youtube.com/watch?v=RD5vkIFjRYk). He received his BA in Psychology from Princeton University and his PhD in Clinical Psychology at the University of California, Los Angeles. In addition to his work in psychology, he has a background in the arts both as a Grammy-award winning songwriter and a published novelist, authoring the book The Third Condition: A Memoir of Freud's Return.

Jane Guiller is a Chartered Psychologist and Lecturer at Glasgow Caledonian University, where she was awarded her doctorate in Social Psychology in 2004 for her thesis on 'Gender, language and online interaction styles in online learning environments'. Her research interests include online discourse, gender and language, online identities and self-presentation, social networking, gender and deception on the internet and learning and teaching in Higher Education (particularly elearning, argumentation and critical thinking). Jane currently runs an honours-level module in Cyberpsychology and is writing her first book on Cyberpsychology and Gender, with her colleague Dr Sarah Williams from the University of Southampton.

Gilly Leshed is a Visiting Assistant Professor in the Department of Communication at Cornell University. Her research examines social and cultural issues within technical systems that challenge the fundamental design assumption of information technologies to help individuals and groups accomplish tasks more productively. For example, although interpersonal social behaviors are important for teams' well-being, too often technologies for teams focus on simply helping them effectively complete tasks. As another example, a growing sense of rush, stress, and overwork is exacerbated by technologies designed to increase efficiency and productivity, resulting in raising the standards of how much one should accomplish, and leading to more stress. She uses quantitative and qualitative studies and designs information technologies to highlight theoretical concepts and as research platforms. Leshed received her Ph.D. in Information Science from Cornell University. Her professional experience includes several years in designing and evaluating commercial flight-deck avionics and military command and control systems.

Christine Liao is a doctoral candidate in art education in the School of Visual Arts at the Pennsylvania State University. Her research focuses on new media, technology and society, contemporary art, pedagogy, identity, and the body. She has published articles in *Visual Culture and Gender, The Journal of Art Education*, and a chapter in the coming book *Digital Visual Culture*.

Nicola Marae Martínez is an assistant professor of digital media at SUNY Empire State College in Saratoga Springs, NY. She has a PhD in Media and Communications from the European Graduate School, Switzerland, a MA from the University of California, Santa Barbara, and a BA from the University of Ottawa / Université d'Ottawa in Canada. Her theoretical research interests include the dynamics of power within the context of taboo and transgression (applied to emergent media such as the virtual world Second Life); virtual citizenry; individual autonomy and human agency within an age of ubiquitous media; and the balance of privacy, security and freedom in the 21st century. Nicola is the author of *Taboo and Transgression in Artificial Lifeworlds*, forthcoming from Atropos Press.

Ali Mazalek is an assistant professor in Digital Media with the School of Literature, Communication and Culture at the Georgia Institute of Technology, where she directs the Synaesthetic Media Lab in the GVU Center. Her research focuses on tangible and embodied interaction technologies for creativity and expression across media arts, entertainment and sciences. Mazalek completed her M.S. and Ph.D. in media arts and sciences from the Massachusetts Institute of Technology, where she worked with the Tangible Media and Media Fabrics research groups.

Poppy Lauretta McLeod is an Associate Professor in the Department of Communication at Cornell University where she teaches courses on social influence and on group communication and decision-making, and an Adjunct Professor at Cornell's Johnson Graduate School of Management where she teaches courses on leadership and on managing teams. Her research interests include linguistic bias in intergroup communication, computer-mediated communication in groups, social influence in group decision-making, information exchange in group decision-making, anonymity and identity in group communication and group interaction within virtual environments. She also taught at the University of Michigan Business School, The University of Iowa College of Business, and the Weatherhead School of Management at Case Western Reserve University. She received her Ph.D. in Social Psychology from Harvard University.

Nora A. Murphy is an Assistant Professor of Psychology in the Department of Psychology at Loyola Marymount University. Her main research interests involve social psychology and first impressions. She has published numerous research articles and book chapters regarding nonverbal behavior, impression formation, and emotions. She is also keen on statistics and meta-analysis, to the great amusement of her students. Her work has appeared various journals including *Cognition and Emotion, Journal of Nonverbal Behavior, Journal of Research in Personality, Personality and Social Psychology Bulletin*, and *Psychology and Aging*. She has taught at Emerson College, Northeastern University, Tufts University, and the University of Florida, where she was a visiting professor of social psychology for two years. She earned her MA and PhD in experimental psychology with a specialization in social/personality psychology from Northeastern University in Boston, MA. She also completed a postdoctoral fellowship at Brandeis University in Waltham, MA.

Jo Neale is Senior Research Fellow in the Institute of Applied Social Research at the University of Bedfordshire. She has worked on projects across a wide range of disciplines (education, health, social care), using both quantitative and qualitative methodology. She is particularly interested in the relationship between psychology and 'culture' (i.e. how one's attitudes and behaviours are influenced by 'culture', and vice versa). Her own research has explored this theme in relation to violence against women. She is currently looking at issues of identity in relation to heterosexual women who have experienced domestic abuse.

Michael Nitsche is an associate professor in Digital Media with the School of Literature, Communication and Culture at the Georgia Institute of Technology. His expertise is in the functionality, design, and presentation of virtual 3D worlds. His current research focuses on borderlines between virtual and physical environments and expressive means available in those worlds. Nitsche completed his Ph.D. in Architecture at Cambridge University.

Anna Peachey (Elsa Dickins in Second Life) spent 4 years (2006-2010) researching identity and community in virtual worlds as a Teaching Fellow with the Centre for Open Learning in Maths, Science, Computing and Technology at The Open University UK. She continues to teach, study and research with The Open University, and manages a small company (Eygus Ltd) delivering learning technology solutions, with a particular focus on virtual world content. This is her second book with Springer, following *Researching Learning in Virtual Worlds* (with Julia Gillen, Daniel Livingstone and Sarah Smith-Robbins) in 2010. Anna is Editor-in-Chief of the Springer series on Immersive Environments.

Ralph Schroeder is Senior Research Fellow at the Oxford Internet Institute. Before coming to Oxford University, he was Professor in the School of Technology Management and Economics at Chalmers University in Gothenburg. He is the author of 'Rethinking Science, Technology and Social Change' (Stanford University Press 2007) and 'Being There Together: Social Interaction in Virtual Environments'(Oxford University Press 2011). He has also edited 'The Social Life of Avatars: Presence and Interaction in Shared Virtual Environments' (Springer 2002) and co-edited (with Ann-Sofie Axelsson) and 'Avatars at Work and Play: Collaboration and Interaction in Shared Virtual Environments'(Springer 2006). He is currently pursuing research on e-Science.

Breen Sweeney is an Associate Lecturer in Mathematics at The Open University. His main research interests are technology enhanced teaching and learning.

Maeva Veerapen is currently undertaking her PhD research at Monash University, Australia. She has been teaching within the Centre of Theatre and Performance and the Centre of Communications and Media for two years. Her research interests centre around the processes of redefining the body and forms of embodiment as a result of new technological progress. Her current research is a phenomenological inquiry into the virtual world Second Life, and how the body is situated within it. She has presented her work at local symposia and international conferences, and has been published in the *International Journal of the Humanities*. In 2009, she was the convener of the Second Life stream at the International Conference *Time Transcendence Performance*. In 2010, she was the co-convenor of a symposium series titled *Performance Studies Melbourne*. She, with a colleague, has also launched a new symposium series titled *Transdisciplinary Performance Forum*, which she is also co-convening.

Tim Welsh joined the University of Toronto in July of 2009 after spending 4 years at the University of Calgary. His primary appointment is in the Faculty of Physical education and Health, but he also has a joint appointment in the Department of Psychology. He focuses on three main areas of research: the interactions between attention and motor processing, cerebral specialization for movement-related processes in average and special populations, and the neural basis of coordinated movement. It is his hope that once a detailed knowledge of the cognitive and neural processes underlying movement has been developed, clinicians and scientists can work together to develop technologies and environments that can facilitate the efficient performance of all members of society.

Contents

Chapter 1
Virtual Worlds and Identity

Anna Peachey and Mark Childs

1.1 Avatars and Virtual Worlds

Virtual worlds in their graphical forms have been used since the mid-1980s (Yakal 1986, p. 32), primarily for social networking. They are computer-generated environments in which participants adopt an avatar to interact with each other and with the virtual environment around them. The word "avatar" in this sense means "a graphical representation of a user within the environment which is under his or her direct control" (Allbeck and Badler 2002, p. 313). It is derived from the Sanskrit *avatârah*, a compound of ava, ("down"), and tarati, ("he crosses"). It means therefore "the crossing down" and traditionally refers to the incarnation of a deity within the physical world (Isdale et al. 2002, p. 530). Taking on the form of an avatar within a virtual world is thus a literacy of crossing down from the real into the digital. The word has been used in this context since it was employed by Farmer and Morningstar in an immersive virtual world called *Habitat* in 1985 (Britt 2008), the first platform that enabled tens of thousands of users to participate in creating aspects of the environment around them, chat with other users, play games and engage in governance of their emerging community.

Interaction with the virtual world, and with the other virtual participants, is conducted via the digital representation of the avatar, since the character is visible to other users who may be simultaneously exploring the same area. If their avatars

A. Peachey (✉)
Eygus Ltd, 69A North Street, Devon TQ13 7QH, UK
e-mail: anna@eygus.co.uk

M. Childs
Coventry University, Priory Street, Coventry, CV1 5FB, UK
e-mail: mark.childs@coventry.ac.uk

A. Peachey and M. Childs (eds.), *Reinventing Ourselves: Contemporary Concepts of Identity in Virtual Worlds*, Springer Series in Immersive Environments, DOI 10.1007/978-0-85729-361-9_1, © Springer-Verlag London Limited 2011

are in close proximity to each other, the two participants may communicate (usually through text, though voice is often also possible, depending on the environment). Avatars also "provide access points in the creation of identity and social life. The bodies people use in these spaces provide a means to live digitally – to fully inhabit the world" (Taylor 2002, p. 40). Through the use of avatars, "users do not simply roam through the space as "mind", but find themselves grounded in the *practice* of the body, and thus in the world" (Taylor 2002, p. 42). Avatars can have their movement blocked by objects, can collide with other users, will fall if they step off the edges of buildings and can pick up and drop objects. Avatar names usually remain constant, conferring a persistent identity upon regular users.

In 2010 there were between 20 and 40 3D virtual worlds depending on how the term is defined. Second Life™ is the most popular of those worlds used primarily for social networking (as opposed to primarily for gaming, such as EVE Online and World of Warcraft), and was launched in 2003 by Linden Lab. Second Life is a virtual land space consisting of a small number of continents and many small islands. Land can be bought on the continents, or for more privacy (and more prestige) an individual or organisation can purchase an island. An inworld currency of Linden dollars can be exchanged for US dollars, with an exchange rate of about 300 Linden dollars to one US dollar. Residents, as Second Life's users are commonly termed, can create their own objects within the space, built from adding together many basic geometric shapes (known as prims – short for primitives). An active economy is driven by the buying and selling of these decorated objects in many forms, including hair, clothes, furniture, vehicles etc.

Despite an open call for the book, and our intent to explore aspects of identity as mediated in a range of virtual world environments, the overwhelming majority of the response and hence the subsequent book has focused on research taking place within Second Life rather than any other social or game world. We see this as confirmation that in recent years Second Life has provided a compelling environment for research, emerging as the most sophisticated of the social virtual worlds. Many academic Second Life users are currently exploring Open Sim, an open source spin off from Second Life, and perhaps this is where the future lies. However as more people move into Open Sim, or other virtual worlds, the experiences taken from Second Life will be transferable (in ways that research into game worlds is often more restrictive), and we see its privileging in this book as a commentary in itself on a snapshot of identity research in virtual worlds of this period.

Since roughly 2006 there has been a rapid increase in virtual world activity across the developed world, for an infinitely diverse range of uses spanning work, rest and play. Millions of us are logging in to our shared environment of choice and acting through our avatars. The identity of the person operating the avatar is usually theirs to reveal according to their preference, and the avatar itself is completely malleable – one step removed from our offline selves. Because of this flexibility the act of representing ourselves through an avatar, of having choices about how to present visually and act through this medium, have made virtual worlds into social laboratories for identity study (Peachey 2010, p. 37).

1.2   Reinventing Ourselves

It is this opportunity that virtual worlds provide, for exploring identity in new and exciting ways, which formed the genesis of this book along with our observation that despite a rapid rise in research interest, indicated by the range of journal articles and papers on the subject of identity in virtual worlds, there are very few books available dealing specifically with this focus.

In selecting the chapters for the book, the editors were aware that identity itself is a broad subject, and is also understood to mean different things to different parts of the academic community. To address these issues two editorial decisions were made. One was to select submissions that were directly concerned with identity, and exclude those that dealt with connected fields, such as the communities and cultures that exist within virtual worlds. Our focus was very much the *individual*'s perception and development of their own identity within these worlds. This deliberate omission of such an important area will be addressed as a separate topic in future publications. The second issue was addressed by the inclusion of an introductory chapter that defines our view of identity; this chapter also provides a background to many of the concepts that are explored in more depth within the main body of the book. Despite the goal of being very focused in its remit, this book aims to represent a variety of approaches to the exploration of identity in virtual worlds. The chapters included here are drawn from a range of disciplines, as well as many that are cross-disciplinary. They also reflect an array of research paradigms; some are case studies, others are theoretical overviews and some are very discursive reflections on personal experience.

To structure the book, these chapters have been grouped into four themes: the first of these is a general introduction to the concepts, while the others are more wide-ranging in their remit.

1.3   Introduction: Identities, Avatars and the Relationship Between Them

This section contains a series of chapter intended to set the scene for the rest of the book. The chapters take a variety of approaches, from a basic introduction to the key concepts, through analyses of the various stages that development goes through, to a personal account of the author's own development of an inworld identity.

1.3.1   Identity: A Primer – Mark Childs

The first chapter in *Reinventing Ourselves* provides an introduction to the wider range of literature exploring our understandings of physical identity, and subsequently identity in virtual worlds. It begins by acknowledging the range of contexts in which identity can be defined, and placing self-informative identities at the core of this book.

Childs considers the literature around how the self is conceptualised, and how aspects of this self are presented to others. From theories of physical identity we are moved into self-representation and avatars, and explore a range of perspectives on understanding aspects of embodiment in the virtual environment. With a virtual body comes the creation of an online identity, and the merging or separation of aspects of the physical reality of self. This is often explored in representation or re-representation and role-play, and Childs references this before describing the process of evolving a persistent online identity and how this impacts on issues such as reputation and relationships within an inworld environment. Finally, through a discussion on self-presence and embodiment, describing levels of connection between the physical and phenomenal body, we are led to the question, "What purpose does identity in virtual worlds serve?". Childs replies by referencing a range of debates and perspectives that lead into the significance of the rest of the book.

1.3.2   The Self and Second Life, A Case Study Exploring the Emergence of Virtual Selves – Simon Evans

Evans develops the argument for investigating identity in virtual worlds by exploring how living within these environments is "changing notions of who we are". The stated position of the chapter is "to highlight that virtual worlds are places where people live lives, form relationships and explore what it means to be a person", reflecting on how people are using virtual worlds to actively explore and construct who they are as "selves". The chapter begins with a detailed literature review focusing on theories of self and the underpinning of theories of self in virtual worlds, before moving into the Second Life case study. Evans provides a detailed rationale for, and outline of, the research methodology including rationale, context, questions and design as well as ethical considerations. He describes his interviewing recruitment, schedule and procedure and then his approach to the thematic analysis of the subsequent data. This analysis of 40 interviews identifies four themes arising from the variety of complex relationships between the self experienced in the physical world and Second Life. Evans concludes by relating his findings back into the wider research literature and offering a critique on how research practice may be improved.

1.3.3   Liminal Phases of Avatar Identity Formation in Virtual World Communities – Nicola Marae Martínez

After Evans' overview of the self in virtual worlds, Martínez examines the early phases of entrance into virtual worlds as a "newbie" avatar within the framework of Gennep and Turner's liminal phases of neophyte initiation rituals (van Gennep 1960;

Turner 1974). The introduction relates the author's position as a resident of Second Life and her relationship with and to the three avatars that she employed during the active study period of this research. She then describes her methodology and the context of the role-play community in which her analysis was conducted. The case studies are contextualised by a discussion of the literature relating to rites of passage and liminal states, before an in-depth exploration of the preliminal, liminal and post-liminal rites of Martínez's case studies and how this relates to the defining of an avatar's identity. This analysis of the avatar in liminal states examines how, even in seemingly anarchistic virtual worlds such as Second Life, social norms and sanctions emerge to influence avatar identity formation and persistence, and Martínez concludes that "The avatar joins Second Life communities at will, and yet, once she joins a community, her liminality ends and early stage freedoms become restricted within the bounds of the consensual social norms."

1.3.4 Encountering Oneself and the Other: A Case Study of Identity Formation in Second Life – Maeva Veerapen

The first section of the book concludes with Veerapen's personal and discursive narrative of the development of the creation of her own identity within Second Life, focusing on the context or "situated experience" within which virtual identity emerges. Veerapen begins by describing the positioning of existing identity research and placing her own work as a shift in focus towards "investigating how the physical user shapes the inworld experience in order to better comprehend why online identity construction differs from the present processes in the physical world.". Popular culture as well as academic literature is referenced in an argument for moving away from a discourse of disembodiment in discussions of virtual identity. Veerapen then describes her entry into Second Life as a process of symbembodied experience structured with and by encounters with Others, supporting a conclusion that it is "the nature of the virtual world embodiment, through the user-avatar relation, [that] informs how the user constructs his/ her inworld identity."

1.4 Factors That Support the Development of Identity in Virtual Worlds

The development of an inworld identity depends upon a range of factors, dependent upon the technology, the characteristics and intentions of the participants. Four aspects are explored here: the role of clothing in developing an identity, the use of movement, the role of gender role-play and the inclusivity and exclusivity of the technology with particular respect to the support of participants with disabilities (specifically hearing impairments).

1.4.1   Virtual Fashion Play as Embodied Identity Re/Assembling: Second Life Fashion Bloggers and Their Avatar Body Images – Christine Liao

This empirical research looks at identity in virtual worlds though popular fashion practices, recognising the significant role that fashion plays in external representation of identity and body image. Through a qualitative study and by engaging with theories that challenge notions of identity as immutable, Liao provides different perspectives on online identity. She begins by establishing a theoretical framework for understanding bloggers' identity play through virtual bodies, exploring technological bodies and the experience of embodiment and introducing Deleuze and Guattari's (1987) theories of the Body without Organs (BwO) This notion of BwO is used to conceptualise how an avatar may become free of identity categories, a space in which multiplicities happen and transformations take place. Through a study of fashion blogs and interviews with the bloggers Liao explores their identity re/assembling, embodied becoming and self-invention. She concludes, "Though formed by the very social and political forces that they express, these bloggers' avatar body images are capable of creating a new assemblage of the self, one in which the self is always becoming."

1.4.2   Embodying Self in Virtual Worlds – Ali Mazalek, Sanjay Chandrasekharan, Michael Nitsche and Tim Welsh

The research presented in this chapter builds on and integrates the fields of cognitive science, virtual environments and tangible/embodied interaction. Mazalek et al. use the avatar as the common reference for intentions, expressions and movements in virtual worlds, and examine how physical body movements may be mapped onto a virtual self using experiments to explore self-recognition. The chapter begins by drawing attention to the standardised nature of avatar movement in most virtual environments, meaning that aspects of physical identity expressed through movement cannot be replicated in any personal or meaningful way inworld. Through an exploration of this position, the authors hypothesise that "players would identify and coordinate better with characters that encode their own movements.", and set out to test this through empirical research. A second experiment tests a full body puppet interface with a virtual environment for personalising an avatar's movements. The ideomotor theory explored in this chapter provides the theoretical and experimental basis for developing technological tools to support effective self-projection into the virtual space, thereby opening up possibilities for enhancing human imagination and action.

1.4.3 Is That Your Boyfriend? An Experiential and Theoretical Approach to Understanding Gender Bending in Virtual Worlds – Ferdinand Francino and Jane Guiller

This chapter combines the elements of Francino's extended gaming and gender bending role-playing experience, presented as first person narrative, with Guiller's theoretical analysis drawing on psychological and sociological concepts of self and identity to mediate the relationship between Francino's online and offline selves. It begins by introducing the perspectives of the authors and providing references to a theoretical background to online gender experimentation. The methodology of the work covered in the chapter is laid out as a phenomenological, case-study approach. The first scenario in the case study takes place in the game world Diablo, and Francino describes his experience of a specific relationship within this environment where he mediated through a female avatar. Guiller then provides the analysis and discussion, exploring motivation the ethics of deception, gender performance and the development of the inworld relationship. In total four scenarios are presented and reviewed. Francino and Guiller conclude that their study, although limited in scope, "questions previous conclusions in this area that gender-swapping does not impact significantly on the offline self and that such experiences do not lead us to learn anything about gender."

1.4.4 Constructing Disability in Online Worlds; Conceptualising Disability in Online Research – Diane Carr

In this chapter Carr investigates the online construction of and considers the implications for educators working in virtual worlds, based on her analysis of data collected through interviews with Deaf residents of Second Life. The chapter argues that educators need to recognise the power relations that can lurk within practices of provision or accessibility support. It begins by relating the introduction of a speech facility into the previously text-based communication options within Second Life, and explains the significance of this change to the Deaf community within the environment. Carr then provides a theoretical background to the wider context of disability issues in virtual worlds, and the risks inherent in a focus on theorising accessibility. She moves from this into a review of core literature relative to the terminology and construction of Deaf experience in virtual worlds before describing her own research strategy and methods for data collection from 5 interviews. Excerpts from these interviews are embedded in an analysis relating to a strong theoretical background of Disability Studies. Carr concludes that "online worlds and their various communities do demonstrate in new, clear ways, just how pervasive inequitable practices and discourses can be, and how difficult it can be to articulate and hence resist the power relations that are embedded within, and disseminated by, these same practices."

1.5 Managing Multiple Identities Across Different Environments

Creating additional identities also leads to issues with managing this multiplicity. In this section the issues relating to managing an inworld identity across three different boundaries are explored: from a virtual identity to a physical identity, with other inworld identities and with identities in other online technologies. The findings in these chapters are that users differ widely in how closely their virtual and physical identities match and that how people relate to their primary avatars and their alternative avatars or "alts" also differs.

1.5.1 As Long as They Don't Know Where I Live – Poppy McLeod and Gilly Leshed

In Chap. 9, McLeod and Leshed explore the different ways in which people cross the boundaries between the physical world and the virtual, and whether people choose to disclose or conceal their offline identities when online. This chapter recounts some of the strategies people use for maintaining this boundary. It begins with a review of literature around online anonymity prior to the use of graphical avatars and moves into present day context with an example to illustrate the difference and connection between anonymity and identifiability. In order to understand these connections and the strategies people use to manage boundaries between physical and virtual worlds, McLeod and Leshed conducted interviews with 30 s Life residents. They report on these interviews under several groupings relating to issues such as self-disclosure and self-expression. The authors raise issues for future work (under "questions we wish we'd asked"), before concluding that participants who use virtual worlds to explore different aspects of identity are also those that have a more defined boundary between their virtual world and physical world lives.

1.5.2 Multiple Personality Order – Richard Gilbert, Jessica Foss and Nora Murphy

The next chapter, from Gilbert, Foss and Murphy, examines a different aspect of the boundary crossing between the physical self and avatars. They explore how closely these identities conform to each other, and how the characteristics of the avatars differ from each other and from the physical selves of the participants. They also offer a further analysis of the reasons why people create alts and the uses to which they are put. The chapter begins with a literature review that reflects on the range of ways and purposes for which anonymity can be manipulated online. They set out the method for their own study, recruiting 104 participants to complete an inworld questionnaire, and then present the results using statistical sampling in three sections: physical and activity characteristics; personality and social-emotional characteristics; and alt usage characteristics. From this focus, the authors step back to consider "the broadest implications of the self being composed of multiple offline and inworld identities", finding that as virtual worlds continue to proliferate, "Individuals will manage their multiple personality orders in a manner analogous to a choreographer managing a company of dancers [...] and the operation of personality will increasingly take on [...] a quality of performance art."

1.5.3   Comparing Avatar and Video Representations – Ralph Schroeder

In Chap. 11, Schroeder makes comparisons between the formation of identity in virtual worlds and the formation of identity across a range of other virtual environments. He also draws comparisons between the uses to which webconferencing and virtual worlds are put, and how these contribute to the formation of identities across a range of media. The chief distinctions are that virtual spaces are useful for spatial interactions, video-based communication comes into its own when visual closeness is required. It is the purposes to which the different technologies are put, rather than the relative "richness" or otherwise of the two media that determines which technology is employed. Schroeder also examines how these different technologies support the experience of copresence, but this too can mean different things for different people. The role of the environment across is also different for video or for virtual worlds, in a videoconference the environment rarely has a function, in a virtual world interactions where the environment is irrelevant are rare. In both, interacting with large numbers of others is problematic. Ultimately, however, Schroeder predicts that as these technologies converge, the distinction between video-based and avatar-based representations will become less.

1.6   Creating an Online Identity for a Physical World Purpose

This section explores the ramifications of developing an inworld identity when there is intent to fulfil a purpose in the physical world through the development of that identity. Three very different examples are explored by the authors in this section: the intention to develop a means to conduct project management, the need to have a platform from which to conduct elearning activities and the use made of inworld identities as safe harbours for identity exploration.

1.6.1   What Is My Avatar? Who Is My Avatar? The Avatar as a Device to Achieve a Goal: Perceptions and Implications – Marc Conrad, Alec Charles and Jo Neale

In Chap. 12, Conrad, Charles and Neale report on a case study carried out with an undergraduate computing class at the University of Bedfordshire, UK. In this study students were asked to take on avatar identities inworld to support their learning activities within this programme. The authors asked the students about their choices of human or non-human avatars, gender, ethnicity and name of avatar. The students differed to a large extent in the role they saw this avatar as having in relationship to their learning; some seeing it solely as a means to interact with the software, others seeing it as an extension of themselves. For all of the students the appearance of the avatar functioned as a device to facilitate communication and interaction, but differed on whether they saw this as a means of self-expression, a platform for social interaction, or merely a pragmatic necessity for moving within a virtual world.

The study conducted by Conrad, Charles and Neale indicates that how we perceive the purpose of virtual worlds influences how we behave within them, and therefore how we develop and enact our identities within them, or even whether we develop an identity at all. It identifies the complexity and range of users' experiences and draws attention to the role of motivation and values to the creation of a virtual identity.

1.6.2   Situated Learning in Virtual Worlds and Identity Reformation – Anne Adams, Lluisa Astruc, Cecilia Garrido and Breen Sweeney

In Chap. 13, Adams, Astruc, Garrido and Sweeney relate more case studies in an educational setting, these taking place at the Open University in the UK. One of these studies was of a Spanish language learning class; the other was of a tutorial class for Mathematics. In the former study, students interacted with others in a Spanish home and a Spanish bar simulation in Second Life and were interviewed regarding their experiences. In the latter, students created avatars in both RuneScape and Second Life and the direction of their gaze was observed using eye-tracking data, in order to gain an insight into their degree of immersion. The environments to which the students were exposed ranged from realistic to surreal, enclosed to open and formal to informal.

Students recorded a range of responses, running from experiencing claustrophobia within some environments to anxiety over whether some of the avatars had human controllers or were computer-controlled and the embarrassment of certain social faux pas. These environmental factors also had an impact on the development of the students' inworld identities but indicate the degree to which the students' were immersed. Adams, Astruc, Garrido and Sweeney also identify the students' identity of themselves as learners as stereotyped to some extent and see virtual worlds as a potential tool for exploring and challenging some of the preconceptions that learners may have.

1.6.3   Virtual Worlds and Identity Exploration for Marginalised People – Jon Cabiria

The final chapter of the book explores another rationale for which many people enter virtual worlds, that is as "a means of self-exploration, emotional support, identity affirmation, belongingness, and strong communities that may have eluded them in physical life". Cabiria reports on a case study he conducted in which he surveyed a group of lesbian and gay people who had indicated that they felt marginalised in their physical world lives, and explored with them comparisons between their physical world experiences and their virtual world ones.

Cabiria found that the experience of the physical world experienced by the people in his study led to "the expected emerging themes of loneliness, isolation, depression, low self-esteem, withdrawal and lack of authenticity" caused largely by "developmental obstruction, negative psychological effect of being marginalised, the power of hetero-normative forces and identity compartmentalisation". Themes typifying their virtual world experiences were "belongingness, connectedness, improved well-being, higher self-esteem, optimism, sense of authenticity, and evidence of transferable positive benefits". Cabiria concludes that the virtual world provided "a sense of belonging, provides marginalised people with the tools they needed to redirect their developmental paths and to reform their identities. Second Life provides the place, safety, and relationship opportunities for that development to occur." For people marginalised within the physical world, virtual worlds provide an opportunity for people to be themselves, and forge a stronger sense of their own identity.

1.7   A Note on Keeping It Real

Throughout the book we have sought to refer to the *physical world* in distinction to the virtual world, despite the common inworld use of "real life"(RL) (for example in a text chat: "have to go in a sec, RL calling"). We argue that on many levels the impact of activity and relationships that take place within virtual worlds is no more or less real than those that occur in the physical world, and that the literary separation of virtual life from real life when reflecting on virtual world issues in an academic context often indicates a passive disregard for that significance. The exception to this consistency is in Chap. 9, where McLeod and Leshed argue a positive case for referencing the *material world*.

References

Allbeck, J.M., Badler, N.I.: Embodied autonomous agents. In: Stanney, K.M. (ed.) Handbook of Virtual Environments; Design Implementation and Applications, pp. 313–332. Lawrence Erlbaum Associates, Mahwah (2002)

Britt, A.: On Language. Avatar, New York Times Magazine, August 8th (2008)

Deleuze, G., Guattari, F.: A Thousand Plateaus: Capitalism and Schizophrenia. (Massumi, B. Tran.). University of Minnesota Press, Minneapolis (1987)

Gennep, Av: The Rites of Passage. University of Chicago Press, Chicago (1960)

Isdale, J., Fencott, C., Heim, M., Daly, L.: Content design for virtual environments. In: Stanney, K.M. (ed.) Handbook of Virtual Environments; Design Implementation and Applications, pp. 519–532. Lawrence Erlbaum Associates, Mahwah (2002)

Peachey, A.: Living in immaterial worlds: Who are we when we learn and teach in virtual worlds? In: Sheehy, K., Ferguson, F., Clough, G. (eds.) Virtual Worlds: Controversies at the Frontier of Education, pp. 33–51. Nova Science Publishers Inc, New York (2010)

Taylor, T.L.: Living digitally: Embodiment in virtual worlds. In: Schroeder, R. (ed.) The Social Life of Avatars, pp. 40–62. Springer, London (2002)

Turner, V.W.: Dramas, Fields, and Metaphors; Symbolic Action in Human Society. Cornell University Press, Ithaca (1974)

Yakal, K.: Habitat: A look at the future of online games, Compute! Oct, 1986, 77, 32, http://www.atarimagazines.com/compute/issue77/habitat.php (1986). Retrieved 30 Aug 2008

Chapter 2
Identity: A Primer

Mark Childs

Abstract This chapter is intended to provide a background for readers unfamiliar with the concept of identity, or familiar with it in different contexts than that employed within this book. It is intended both as a general introduction and to preclude the need for the authors of the following chapters to cover the basic concepts and hence reduce repetition and redundancy within the book as a whole.

The chapter defines different uses of the word identity, discusses different theories of self-informative identity (the sense in which the disciplines represented here use it), particularly social identity theory and role identity theory, and how identity can be seen as something to be performed. Finally it examines the role that virtual worlds have played in shaping the concept of identity, and how identity influences our experiences of virtual worlds.

2.1 Introduction

On preparing a book such as this, authors are faced with a dilemma: the extent to which the reader must be prepared with background information, and a theoretical perspective, before the intended subject of the chapter can be begun. For the reader too, there is the possibility that the texts can become repetitive in places, since much of this preliminary material is repeated across the chapters. Discussing identity also requires an understanding of how it plays out in the physical world before investigating its place in the virtual, and therefore runs the risk of appearing off-topic, especially in a book in a series on Immersive Environments. The intention of this

M. Childs (✉)
Coventry University, Priory Street, Coventry, CV1 5FB, UK
e-mail: mark.childs@coventry.ac.uk

A. Peachey and M. Childs (eds.), *Reinventing Ourselves: Contemporary Concepts of Identity in Virtual Worlds*, Springer Series in Immersive Environments, DOI 10.1007/978-0-85729-361-9_2, © Springer-Verlag London Limited 2011

first chapter is therefore to place much of this introductory content in one place and provide some explanation of the terminology. The separate authors will expand upon these ideas where more background is required, or may take an alternative viewpoint; identity is a field in which there is far from a consensus. However, it is intended that the following will support both readers and authors in establishing a basis from which to read and learn from the remainder of this book.

2.2 Different Definitions of Identity

One difficulty with the use of the word "identity" is that different disciplines use the word to mean very different things. Within philosophy, the concept of identity is concerned with the factors that establish the differences or similarities between two entities. The philosophical discussions regarding identity within the Habitat project for example (Cormier et al. 2009, p. 43), consider qualitative and numerical identity concepts that apply little, if at all, to the subjects considered here.

The term "identity" is also used in the context of the name, labels, identification numbers, and a whole set of other metrics, that identify and establish who a person is, i.e. the identity that is stolen in identity theft, or controlled through identity management systems. Again this is not (on the whole) the meaning in which it is used within these texts, and we find this more usefully referenced as a "construct of credentials" (Peachey and Withnail 2011).

Identity here is used in the sense of a person's conceptualisation of self; the ways in which subjectively people perceive or experience themselves as individuals. Manders-Huits (2010, p. 46) identifies these two definitions of identity as self-informative and nominal. Nominal identity is the set of attributes assigned to a person by society and which need to be fixed, so that a person can be identified and re-identified consistently (Manders-Huits 2010, p. 48). Self-informative identity is a person's conceptualisation of their self, which can be fluid. These two concepts do relate to each other but are quite different, in that self-informative identity usually draws on nominal identity, but nominal identity typically omits self-informative identity.

Identity does not exist in isolation, of course, and attempts have been made to develop frameworks deconstructing the ways in which it can link to other factors. One of these frameworks is Wenger's community of practice model, in which communities are defined in terms of social groups that develop around a common practice, and in which interaction with the group can be seen in terms of learning the practice of that group, and in contributing to the common learning of the group. Wenger links the theories of social learning that define the group with theories of identity, theories of social structure, theories of practice and theories of situated experience and describes identity as the "social formation of the person, the cultural interpretation of the body, and the creation and use of markers of membership such as rites of passage and social categories" (1998, p. 13). Childs (2010) develops a synthesis of Wenger's model and that of Activity Theory (Engeström 1999, p. 31) to build the Mediated Environments Reference Model, which identifies links between identity and the following factors:

- The characteristics of the individual.
- The community.
- The rules and conventions of the group.
- The object or practice of the group.
- The roles or division of labour within the group.
- The tools and implements that mediate interactions.
- The situated experience of the interaction, within virtual worlds this is specifically the experience of presence and embodiment.

2.3   Self-Informative Identity

As described above, the meaning of "identities" most commonly employed within this book is that of self-informative identities, i.e. the collection of a person's self-conceptualisations and attribution of meanings to their self, usually with respect to a certain role or social milieu (Stets and Burke 2008, p. 130).

> In general, the self-concept is the set of meanings based on our observations of ourselves, our inferences about who we are, based on how others act toward us, our wishes and desires, and our evaluations of ourselves (Stets and Burke 2008, p. 130).

In fact, not only are these different identities informed by the social roles or groups to which we already belong, but also "the values, attitudes, and behavioural intentions of the social group to which they aspire to belong" (Cabiria 2008, p. 3). Because people have many roles and live within many different milieux, they therefore have many identities, each one constructed from a particular role or social groups that they encounter within their lives. The consequence of this is that "The overall self is organized into multiple parts (identities), each of which is tied to aspects of the social structure." (Stets and Burke 2008, p. 131).

These separate parts are usually defined in terms of the role one adopts in the group or in terms of the social group with whom one interacts. These two approaches, looking at the role or looking at the social grouping, lead to two main theoretical threads through the literature; that of role identity theory and social identity theory respectively. In "A Sociological Approach to Self and Identity", Stets and Burke recognise that these are two different aspects of the same process, arguing for a synthesis of these two theoretical positions. However, role identity theory and social identity theory still predominate as separate approaches to the understanding of identity.

Identifying further facets to the perspective of how an individual interacts within a social group has given rise to two main subdivisions to a role or social identity, which are:

- Those that conform or represent affiliation to the role or group and
- Those personal aspects of identity with which the person individuates him or herself from that group.

These two forms are called "conventional" and "idiosyncratic" by McCall and Simmons in role identity theory (Stets and Burke 2008, p. 133) and Idem and Ipse by Ricouer in social identity theory (Macfadyen 2008, p. 563). Idem or conventional identities are those aspects of identity that identify the ways in which we adhere to a group or a nation, or ethnicity, for example (Macfadyen 2008, p. 564). Ipse identities are the aspects that define us as separate from those groups, i.e. our idiosyncrasies (Macfadyen 2008, pp. 564–565). These ipse and idem identities are in tension with each other, but they can be held simultaneously, for example "I live in San Francisco but am English" or "I am a vegetarian but still have cravings for bacon sandwiches" and so on.

However, these multiple identities do not exist as discrete parts of a person. They must be balanced and synthesised to form a person's sense of self; an individual's self-concept "embodies both content and structure" (Stets and Burke 2008, p. 129). The structure of identities provides the internal dynamics by which these various meanings within identities, and the various identities, are brought together into a whole (Stets and Burke 2008, p. 135) and it is this overall structure that informs how a new identity is formed when a new social group or role is encountered (Stets and Burke 2008, p. 142). Other parts of identity will then be structured differently, and accrue meaning differently, around these core values. For example, someone who identifies him or herself most closely with their nationality, rather than their home, would not conceptualise their self by the phrase "I live in San Francisco, but am English", but rather "I am English, but live in San Francisco". Furthermore "this self is not a static entity but an entity that is dynamic and can change, it is important to examine how these different identities change over time and come to shape a new self-concept" (Stets and Burke 2008, p. 145). This dynamic nature of self means that we are constantly changing our identities through choice or through circumstance, for example as an émigré returning to one's native country, or making the transformation from a failing vegetarian to a lapsed one.

Identity is therefore an amorphous, dynamic, faceted and sometimes fragmented thing. How we conceptualise ourselves is a difficult process, and far more complex than space allows to be fully described here. However, our own view of ourselves is only part of the picture. In addition there is the aspect of ourselves which we present to others, explored below.

2.4 Masks and Faces: Presenting Ourselves to Others

A seminal work in the field of this presentation of ourselves to others is that by Goffman (1959). Like Park before him (1959, p. 30), Goffman draws on the etymology of the word persona (which is derived from per sonare or "sound through" i.e. a mask through which sound emerges in theatrical performances) as a basis for an extended metaphor to describe all interaction as a performance. Although acknowledging the limits of this metaphor (1959, preface), Goffman contends that in interactions, individuals consciously contrive to give off particular expressions in order to create particular impressions in the others around them (Goffman (1959), p. 18). The social environment then becomes a stage in which these various performances interact, and other people are an audience for these personae.

Certain rules and conventions operate to maintain these performances, for example, during first encounters with others, "Society is organized on the principle that any individual who possesses certain social characteristics has a moral right to expect that others will value and treat him in an appropriate way" (Goffman 1959, p. 24) and this creates a definition of that situation for all involved. Mistakes in the performance, ("faux pas", "gaffes", "bricks" or "boners", Goffman (1959), p. 204) or "definitional disruptions" will be covered up by those who have made them (in which they are referred to as "defensive practices"), or by others, in which case they are known as "protective practices" or "tact" (Goffman (1959), p. 25). These definitional disruptions are what we mean by "losing face" (Goffman 1967, p. 9); avoiding them is an act of "maintaining face" (Goffman 1967, p. 5) and recovering from them is "saving face" (Goffman 1967, p. 39). When those who should be in dramaturgical co-operation break out of their assigned performances, this is described as "creating a scene" (Goffman 1959, p. 205).

Although these roles are artificially adopted, and we may not initially believe in them (Goffman 1959, p. 28), Goffman claims we can eventually incorporate them into our identities. Quoting Park, Goffman states:

> In so far as this mask represents the conception we have formed of ourselves – the role we are striving to live up to – this mask is our truer self, the self we would like to be. In the end, our conception of our role becomes second nature and an integral part of our personality. (Goffman 1959, p. 30)

Goffman's view of interactions is simultaneously both a pessimistic view of social interaction (in that he views people as engaging in a perpetual level of deceit and self-conscious enough to be constantly considering what impression they make on others) and optimistic (in that he believes that people could maintain this constant level of performance). In addition, Park and Goffman's concept of "the true self" being that which we display and then aspire too, seems less accurate than it being the hidden self we feel we can only display when our nominal identities are not attributable (the meaning in which it is used later in this chapter). The idea of tact and etiquette being employed to maintain a shared dramaturgical activity, and individuals' definitions of a situation being respected, is very much of its time and may carry less weight now. However, the idea of a persona as a deliberate and constructed mask one puts on for a role, as distinct from personality or identity, is a very useful clarification of the distinction between how we conceptualise ourselves and what we project. The metaphor of social interaction as drama (since at times within social interactions we are putting on a performance to fulfil a requirement of our role) is a useful one, and much of Goffman's work remains relevant.

The function of appearance in forming identity (and performing personae) is also of importance.

> Since appearance can often be interpreted by other people, bodies can be used as a way of presenting a particular identity to the world, and for some bodies can become conscious

"body projects" to manipulate this means of representing identity to others .... Foucault describes this process of altering ones body to create an identity as a "technology of self" (Phoenix 2007, pp. 49–50).

In her discussion on body and identity Phoenix then states, "Of course, no body is entirely malleable." (2007, p. 50). This last statement is, of course, less applicable when one is considering the role of appearance in virtual worlds, which are discussed in the following section.

2.5   Self-Representation and Avatars

Since these environments enable interaction between people to be conducted entirely online, the absence of direct visual and (usually) audio contact and the flexibility the technology provides for creating digital representation, enables users to adopt new identities without physical constraints, becoming an idealised "body project".

> Ultimately, digital bodies tell the world something about your self. They are a public signal of who you are. They also shape and make real how users internally experience their selves. Taylor (2002, p. 51)

The body projects in a virtual world are not necessarily entirely unconstrained however. There may be technological, design or financial constraints in making an avatar's appearance just as one would wish. Choice in these worlds is important, though. In the virtual world "Active World", developers found that increasing the availability of different avatar designs was the most common request by users (Schroeder 2002, p. 7). Limiting the choice therefore, as the developers of Active Worlds discovered, creates frustration amongst the users, since it denies them the opportunity to inform the community about who they are, and also to fulfil an act of reification of their own conception of self.

Other immersive virtual worlds differ in the amount of flexibility users have over their appearance. Within the research into a mediated environment (Microsoft V-Chat), Cheng, Farnham and Stone chose to group their categories for describing avatars as human-male, human-female, animal, object abstract and child (2002, p. 99). Active Worlds Europe provides citizens (subscribers to the service) with between 10 and 20 avatars from which to select at any one time. As a user moves from space to space within the environment they are given a choice of avatars appropriate to the space which can be male, female or neither. Second Life has male or female shapes for all of its users that can be personalised by manipulating approximately 150 different metrics. Clothes can be added and more sophisticated skin and hair acquired to create a more individual look, and also demarcate users as more experienced in (and more prepared to spend money on) their inworld lives. In addition, looks can be more radically adapted by adding extra objects to parts of the avatar's body, and changing the underlying shape, to create appearances that range from simple inanimate objects (such as cardboard boxes) to detailed recreations of figures from mythology or popular culture. However, estimates are that only around 6% of users choose a non-human look (Au 2007).

Annetta et al. (2008) conducted a study that took place in Active Worlds, in which users can either be "residents", in which case they have a choice of "100 different avatars ranging from humans to abstract objects such as a motorcycle, helicopter, or animal", or "tourists", in which case the choices are just male or female. Half of their students were given resident status, half were given tourist status. The students in the tourist group reported that their lack of choice reduced their experience of social presence. Those in the residents group changed avatars until they found one they felt suited their mood on the day, the roles they had been assigned within the tasks they had been set and how they wanted to be perceived in those roles. The students were also asked to complete a Jung-Myers-Briggs personality inventory, which attributes personality types to respondents to a questionnaire based on four dichotomous scales. No correlation between avatar choice and psychological profiles was detected, and indeed the students reported that they saw no correspondence between these psychological profiles and their own perceptions of self.

Participants in Multi-User Dungeons (MUDs) have the ability to label themselves with a set of descriptions regarding their appearance, assigning settings to gender, artefacts carried, and movement descriptors (White 2001, p. 130). Even though MUDs are purely text-based environments, these labels can be used to create a body image. Gender classifications can be more flexible than in real life, or in immersive virtual worlds. White (2001, p. 129) reports a MUD with ten genders available for participants to choose from ("neuter, male, female, splat, Spivak which is named after a programmer, royal, plural, second, either and egotistical"). Participants may also attempt to convey gender through the use of language perceived to be gender-stereotypical (Tompkins 2003, p. 202).

Performance of idem and ipse aspects of identity occur in text-based communication through specific self-attesting statements (Macfadyen 2008, p. 563). Macfadyen notes that there are stages through which this self-attestation occurs; the first is demonstrating affiliation or membership of a particular nation, or ethnicity, (Macfadyen 2008, p. 564). This is then followed by a more individuated set of statements in which the elements that make them an individual are stated (Macfadyen 2008, p. 564–565). After this, learners will then attest their new group-identities as part of the new group in which they are taking part (Macfadyen 2008, p. 566) and then attest to how they may be individuated within this new identity (Macfadyen 2008, p. 565).

The constraints on the choice of appearances are not only external ones. There are also unconscious assumptions that lead to a more limited range of choices that people make when creating an avatar.

> Users were not involved in progressive explorations of self-construction but instead relied on stereotype and caricature that allowed a kind of unreflective appropriation. Underlying these performances were assumptions about what kinds of bodies and identities were deemed as legitimate. (Taylor 2002, p. 58)

Dumitrica and Gaden (2009, p. 13) note that even with the non-human avatars, choices are limited to the binary of male and female during the initial entry into Second Life. This gender binary can be subverted through the acquisition of hermaphroditic genitalia, or setting metrics to such that one appears androgynous, but the basic forms remain male and female. Furthermore, the tendency within this virtual world is to reproduce the masculine and feminine ideals as body images, which can feel constraining (Dumitrica and Gaden (2009, p. 11). Resisting these pressures, even within a virtual world, can lead to lack of integration. As Dumitrica and Gaden observe:

> Looks – and particularly bodies – are significant mechanisms for social integration: we are positioned as male or female according to our visible physical features, and we are judged as feminine/masculine based on our abilities to exhibit and perform the cues associated with them. We carried over these norms and criteria for successful performance of 'femaleness'/ 'maleness' in our SL journeys. (2009, p. 12).

2.6   The Creation of an Online Identity and the "True Self"

As already stated, identity changes depending on the roles, or the social milieu, in which we find ourselves. The question then arises, how different are our identities in the virtual world from the physical world in which our roles and milieux are likely to be very different?

There is some suggestion that the identity adopted in virtual worlds is actually a closer reflection of the self than many of identities we have within the physical world. As McKenna et al. (2001, p. 304) note:

> In general, individuals tend to express more aspects of their true selves when they interact with others on the Internet than when they interact in person

McKenna et al. (2001, p. 304) define "true self" as:

> comprised of those attributes an individual feels he or she possesses and would like for others to perceive but, for whatever reason is generally unable to express and have acknowledged …

Taylor (2002, pp. 54–55) records that avatars can be truer reflections of a person than their offline selves.

> In this (digital) form, users suggest that the corporeal can no longer "corrupt" the truth about who they are and people often say it was through their avatars that they found a "better" version of themselves, one that felt even more right than their offline body.

Hence, these participants may not see the reality of their offline selves to be relevant. Indeed, insisting on participants being "true" to their offline identity may even negate their reason to enter a virtual world. This is reflected in the comments of Bailey (2007), an active participant within Second Life.

> there are people who create an avatar that is completely unlike them … They basically create a whole new person, so role-playing is a natural part of their Second Life. Then there are people (including myself), who are staying true to themselves as much as possible, who are maybe even more honest than in First Life, as this world is not as tied up as the one we live in, and it gives us opportunity to become more brave to express ourselves. (Bailey 2007, p. 20)

These discrepancies may be attributed to people suppressing aspects of their identity while offline due to those elements being marginalised or stigmatised within their physical world relationships; the pseudonymous nature of their virtual relationships then enables them to express these aspects of their self (McKenna et al. 2001, p. 303).

However, the discrepancies may instead (or also) be due to a difference between their actual body and their body identity: the virtual world then enables them to express their body identity and hence reflect how they "truly" see themselves.

This discrepancy between actual body and body identity occurs because, although the development of an identity is informed by one's physical body (Phoenix 2007, p. 49), it is not constrained by it; individuals may have a conceptualisation of self that is quite different from their physical bodies. This is often referred to as body-identity dysmorphia disorder (BDD), but disorder is perhaps less accurate a term than dichotomy, since this dichotomy is, to some extent, something we all share. Milder forms of these body-identity dichotomies are to conceptualise one's true self as being that of someone taller than the physical self, or slimmer, or looking more like Johnny Depp, or having green eyes instead of blue. In some cases, however, people may have a gender identity that is different from their own, or they may have an identity that does not have a gender at all. As a consequence of this, some may wish to change their physical body to match their self-conception (Roberts et al. 2008). Other examples of this mismatch are for people to see themselves as an amputee despite not physically being an amputee (Lawrence 2006); or they may feel that they belong to a different species, or are dead (or even both a different species and dead [Nejad and Toofani 2005, p. 250]). Although these latter examples are perhaps more extreme cases of conflicts between self-conceptualisation and physical reality, they do illustrate the problematic nature of identity being associated with physical reality, and that the manner in which people conceptualise their identities may be disconnected from their physical appearance.

2.7   Re-Representation and Role-Play

Virtual worlds then offer an opportunity for people to express the self they feel they "truly" are. However, they also provide an opportunity to try out a different identity, and test the extent to which this connects with their conception of self. Experimenting with experiencing interaction as a person of different age, race or gender is an activity known as "identity tourism" (Taylor 2002, p. 58) or "avibending" (Amdahl 2007). Lee and Hoadley (2007) also note that this experimentation may be part of an exploration of possible selves, a process by which aspects of identity are tested out before being rejected or incorporated into one's concept of self.

To some extent this may also be part of an uncoupling of their conceptualisation of self from any one specific physical form:

> The ease of creating and modifying virtual identities encourages players to think of themselves as "fluid, emergent, decentralized, multiplicitous, flexible and ever in process" (Turkle 1995 pp. 263–264)

Of course, there is also the potential to try out different appearances and behaviours, not to explore different aspects of oneself, or discover one's "true" identity, but simply to role-play. Certain domains within immersive virtual worlds are specifically set aside for role-playing and in these the role-playing aspect is made explicit. These role-play domains are often based around science fiction and fantasy worlds from books, television programmes or films. Within these dedicated spaces, participants take on different avatars, act out roles and create narratives. Whereas the purpose of the virtual worlds in general are primarily socialising and meeting people (Becker and Mark 2002, p. 29), within role-playing areas the purpose may be quite different. Newman (2007, p. 27) notes that

> There are some similarities between online role-playing and improvisational theatre. In both activities, participants are collaborating to produce a story in real time. Söderberg, Waern et al. (2004, p. 1) note this similarity but also note that online role-playing is done for the benefit of the participants whereas improvisational theatre is done for an audience. It is not hard to see this distinction becoming less significant in role-playing within an extended online community, where there may indeed be an audience.

In fact, role-play could be said to always be for an audience, in that the other participants in the role-play become the audience for one's own performance.

However, the in-character roles and out-of-character roles are kept quite separate (Bailey 2007, p. 24). Even though the out-of-character role is still a virtual identity, the implication is that this is the "real" virtual identity. Since some participants never role-play at all, we therefore have three levels of adoption of different identities within a virtual environment;

- Those for whom their online identity is congruent with an aspect of their "real selves".
- Those for whom their online identity when out-of-character is congruent with their real self, but will play roles within designated domains.
- Those for whom the entire online experience is role-play.

For clarification it should be noted that within these categories, a transgender male (i.e. someone who is physically male, but self-conceptualises his/herself as female) who takes on a female avatar, is not role-playing, since they are being their "true self", even though this is not congruent with their real physical self. In fact, if they are performing the role of male in the physical world, being female inworld would be the only time they are not role-playing. Making judgments about what constitutes role-play and identity tourism may therefore not be a simple matter.

2.8   Persistent and Evolving Online Identity

The "real" virtual identity described above is the identity by which we become known within the virtual world; it is our constant unchanging aspect and is therefore known as a "persistent" identity. Despite the malleability of identity within online worlds, "there exists a social pressure in virtual worlds to maintain a stable primary identity" (Jakobsson 2002, p. 74). Participants must maintain a persistent identity in order to build and maintain connections to people and to their communities, since this stable identity is both how the software identifies us, and also how we can be recognised by others within the virtual world. This constant identity also means that

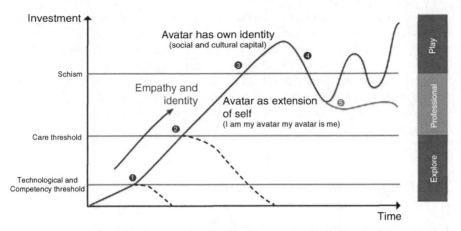

Fig. 2.1 Development of avatar identity in virtual worlds. Image provided by permission of Steve Warburton (2008)

the interactions within a virtual world are not anonymous (even though they may be different from our physical world name), but are pseudonymous, in that there is a single name by which we are always known. Within Second Life, each person has a surname (which is selected from a list provided during registration) and a forename which is an open choice of the user. Other virtual worlds use physical world names, or allow complete freedom of choice. This persistent identity then constrains behaviour, since this mean that there are social consequences for antisocial behaviour.

> We are held responsible for our actions. All societies, physical or virtual, demand that we contribute something in order to benefit from being part of it, and, to keep tabs on our contributions, there have to be identifiers, and without an identifier, and identity, there will be no payback (Jakobsson 2002, p. 74)

And these consequences of the actions, even in a virtual world, can be emotionally real.

> virtual actions can work as causes of effects on my mental state that are as real as anything I might experience in the physical world. (Jakobsson 2002, p. 70)

Cheng, Farnham and Stone also note that this process also "works in the other direction, offering participants the opportunity to retain a persistent identity will encourage them to invest more in their online representation" (2002, p. 95).

These constraints are not only limiting in the sense of preventing antisocial behaviour, they also limit the extent to which a variety of self-informative online identities can be explored, since some consistency of behaviour within one's social group is expected. This leads some people to develop a range of online presences, called alts. Each alt then has a separate nominal identity (a separate name and other identifying data), and hence the potential for a separate self-informative identity.

This investment in an online persistent identity mentioned by Cheng, Farnham and Stone above will often result in a growing association with, and attachment to, that avatar. Warburton (2008) maps the gradual development of inworld identities (Fig. 2.1).

In these stages, the first stage is one of learning the environment. If this threshold is passed, then users will continue to work within the environment and become more familiar with it, however it is only when the second threshold is passed (the "care threshold") that users will identify with their avatar and see it as an extension of themselves. There is a third threshold, in which the extended identity may become distinct from the physical identity often in response to social and cultural interactions within the virtual world. Over time, multiple identities, and therefore multiple avatars, may be created.

2.9   Responses to Representation

The choices of some users to represent themselves as a gender other than male or female can be resisted by other members of the online environment, with responses to choices to remain neuter being, for example, "So, r u a male it, or a female it?" (White 2001, p. 141). Participants representing themselves as non-human have "been a source of controversy" due to the belief that they are "exhibiting an inauthentic self in a virtual context that expects authenticity" (Boellstorff 2008, p. 184–185), although as seen above, representing oneself as an animal may not be inauthentic, if that is how someone sees their "true self".

This clash can be due to different communities within the space coming into contact with each other, through participants being unfamiliar with the conventions of the environment or, as in this quote from a participant in the study by Bayne (2008) there may be cultural reasons for these controversies.

> Choice of animal heads for avatar faces may send a terribly wrong message in my culture. Such an avatar may be considered a sorcerer or witch/wizard. Who would want to interact with such a person'?

The responses to a particular choice of avatar also can be imported from real world prejudices.

> Remarkably, an avatar's design, behaviors, and speech still cause stereotyping, prejudice, and preferential treatment (Kolko 1999). For example, studies have shown that female characters receive more assistance, freebies, and handouts than male characters (Lee and Hoadley 2007).

Wallace and Marryott (2009) found that students given the choice between choosing an ethnicity that matched their own or was different, tended to choose one that looked like them. In their study, students were given a choice of four ethnicities for their avatars (European, Chamorro, Filipino and Micronesian) and were asked a set of questions to identify the closeness of their collaboration with other avatars within Second Life. They found that regional ethnic tensions were reproduced within the environment, with Chamorro students being least willing to collaborate with European avatars, and Filipino students being least willing to collaborate with Micronesian avatars. Wallace and Marryott also noted that all participants were willing to collaborate with Filipino avatars, which they attribute to the attractiveness of the appearance of the avatars that had that ethnicity. This does indicate that choice of avatars is significant in its bearing on virtual world relationships.

2.10   Self-Presence and Embodiment

The relationship a person has with their avatar can go beyond that of creating an avatar and using that avatar to explore and communicate aspects of their identity. After a degree of time interacting within the virtual world, the sense of connection with that avatar becomes very strong, to the extent that what happens to the avatar, and the space within which it moves, can have an emotional or physical reaction on the person whose avatar it is. This level of connection is referred to as embodiment. Embodiment is only possible because of the distinction between the phenomenal body and the physical body (Loomis 1992; Biocca 1997). The phenomenal body is "the mental representation of the body" (Biocca 1997) which, according to Biocca, is not necessarily in our physical body, but can be within an extended body, such as an image on the screen. Our sense of "self" resides wherever the phenomenal body is placed and it is this transfer of our phenomenal body on to an external agent gives rise to embodiment (Biocca 1997). Thomas (2006) refers to this process as "metaxis" which is "the state of belonging completely and simultaneously to two different, autonomous worlds: the image of reality and the reality of the image", although Biocca would argue that this is not a state of complete belonging, the "self" is actually located in one space; either the physical or the virtual.

These distinctions are clarified by Knudsen (2004, pp. 42–43) in which she classifies three different types of body:

- Physical body – the physically real body.
- Extended body – the representation of the body as mediated through technology and displayed at a remote site. This extended body is also a function of the mediating technology in that it can be deliberately manipulated by the technology, or its representation can be unintentionally curtailed by the constraints of the technology.
- Mental body – "the internal mental representation of a real or imagined body" (Knudsen 2004, p. 43). This is equivalent to Biocca's concept of the phenomenal body.

According to Murray and Sixsmith (1999, p. 315), embodiment is a function of the sensorial (i.e. the realness of the environment) and the morphological, (i.e. the plasticity of body boundaries). They state that an understanding of how the "corporeal boundaries" of physical bodies are malleable (through transformation such as amputation and prosthesis use) may inform the degree to which body boundaries may be malleable in virtual worlds. Some of the ways in which body boundaries can be malleable are described below.

Within the physical world, the sense of the ownership of one's body has two aspects, that of body image (which emphasises visual aspects (de Vignemont 2007, p. 439)) and body schema (which emphasises proprioception, i.e. the body in action (de Vignemont 2007, p. 443)). The body schema of physical bodies is informed by interaction with the world around us, and can be adapted through training (Murray and Sixsmith 1999, p. 324). Body schema is related to the spatial representation one has of one's body, and gives rise to the sense of ownership of the body. It is "an unconscious functional sensori-motor map of the body based on the information one needs in order to move one's own body (e.g. bodily posture and position, bodily constraints like size and strength of the limbs, kinematical constraints like the degree of freedom of the joints, etc.)" (de Vignemont 2007, p. 439). Body schema is malleable, however, and does not necessarily match the physical limits of the body (de Vignemont 2007, p. 436). This mismatch gives rise to a variety of different phenomena, for example tactile sensations can be altered so they appear to belong outside of the physical limits of the body (de Vignemont 2007, p. 437), anaesthetised limbs are still experienced as part of the body by most people, even though they cannot be felt (de Vignemont 2007, p. 434), in asomatognosia, parts of the body are felt to not belong to the person and may explain the body-identity dichotomy described earlier (de Vignemont 2007, p. 429), amputees can feel the prosthesis to be part of their body (de Vignemont 2007, p. 431) or even one can extend the feeling of spatial representation to include that of the tools one uses (de Vignemont 2007, p. 441).

Body image is different from body schema in that it "is a set of beliefs, attitudes and perceptions that are about one's body" (Carruthers 2009, p. 124) although some authors (e.g. Murray and Sixsmith 1999) use the term "body image" for both. Body image informs the body projects and technology of self described earlier in the chapter. According to de Vignemont, "body schema is for action and body image is for identification" (2007, p. 439).

Embodiment within one's physical body is stated by Carruthers (2009, p. 130) to be "the experience [of] the body as what I am. I experience my body as me. This is the properly self conscious sense of being an embodied self" as opposed to "the experience of the body as a thing that belongs to me. I experience my body as mine."

The relevance to the experience of virtual worlds arises through the suggestion by Carruthers that the sense of embodiment can arise through a mapping of the body schema to include an object or image; which is an alternative version of Biocca and Knudsen's description of the phenomenal/mental self transferring to the extended body. Carruthers states that this may be generated through a conscious sense of agency that includes that object or image (Carruthers 2009, p. 132) even though tactile information is not fed back to the person.

Not all avatars are humanoid (or anthropomorphic), however, some may be polymorphic and opinions differ as to whether embodiment is greater for anthropomorphic avatars. The pro-anthropomorphic argument is that "for a sense of "presence" in virtual environments, the virtual body must closely resemble (both visually and sensorially) the body of the user" (Murray and Sixsmith 1999, p. 325). Anthropomorphism supports presence in two ways:

- "Geometric mappings" of the body from the virtual to the physical (Sheridan 1992)
- Identification through a similarity in the visual appearance of the person and the virtual body (Held and Durlach 1992).

The argument for polymorphism is that

the represented body in VR does not have to closely map the person's body in real life. In effect, it is envisaged that people could experience a radically reconfigured body, say from their usual anthropoid experience, to that of a lobster. It is not that you experience yourself through the lobster; rather, you experience the architecture of the body as that of a lobster. (Murray and Sixsmith 1992, p. 325–326).

Murray and Sixsmith (1992, pp. 328–329) quote Penny regarding his mapping of a virtual body with extra limbs to that of the physical body: "The mind maps to this new body almost effortlessly… (suggesting) that the mind can quickly draw a new internal body representation to allow control of the new body" (1994, p. 262).

2.11 What Purpose Does Identity in Virtual Worlds Serve?

There, however, a question that hangs over any such discussion about identity, body schema, body image and so on, and that is, "so what?" So a body schema is extensively malleable, to the degree that it can map to that of a lobster, what value can this serve? In response, two possible answers figure. The first of these is from the field of education.

The various types of teaching approach adopted can be categorised into three main forms, these are associative, cognitive and situative (Mayes and de Freitas 2004, pp. 7–9). In general terms, associative techniques approach learning as an acquisition of knowledge; facts are read and memorised, tasks are repeated by rote and so on. Cognitive approaches attempt to build on the learners' prior experience, usually through tasks and activities that they take part in, such as problem-based activities or experiential learning. Situative approaches encourage learners to co-create knowledge through discussion and collaboration. Any of these approaches can be appropriate depending on the subject being learnt, and each draw on different pedagogical models of learning.

Learning activities conducted with students in virtual worlds employing each of these approaches indicate that their success depends to a large extent on the amount of time learners have spent inworld, and consequently the degree of presence and embodiment they have been able to form (Childs and Kuksa 2009). In learning activities tried inworld, associative approaches required the students to only have acquired the technical competence to move within the world and observe the objects they saw there. Situative approaches, in which students were required to communicate with their peers, and interact with the virtual world as a whole, met the barrier of the learners' self-awareness. Creating a proper body image was paramount to the majority of the learners in these situations, and having the right look, not standing out as "newbies" but being individually identifiable, preceded even the acquisition of competence at navigating and communicating. Since their avatars were both the tools through which the learning activities took place, and their social capital within the group (and the wider world), spending time developing a body image (and as educators, supporting the process by which they did this) became an essential precursor for any subject-based activity.

Furthermore, cognitive approaches, in which students were asked to explore and report on their feelings and impressions about the virtual spaces they travelled through, demanded further time spent inworld. Learners' ability to respond with an emotional connection to these space required a capacity described by Rowe as "proprioception" (Childs and Rowe 2009), i.e. the development of an extended body schema connecting the learner with their avatar.

The conclusion of these activities is that learning and teaching within a virtual world makes greater demands upon the participants than merely learning to use a piece of software; it also requires the development of a virtual body with which to learn.

This link between embodiment within the virtual world and learning is not unexpected, however, since within the physical world, cognition can be seen as embodied. Wilson (2002) reviews embodied cognition, describing its essential elements.

> Cognition is situated. Cognitive activity takes place in the context of a real-world environment, and it inherently involves perception and action
> Cognition is time pressured. ... cognition must be understood in terms of how it functions under the pressures of real-time interaction with the environment.
> We off-load cognitive work onto the environment. Because of limits on our information-processing abilities ... we make the environment hold or even manipulate information for us ...
> Cognition is for action. The function of the mind is to guide action, and cognitive mechanisms such as perception and memory must be understood in terms of their ultimate contribution to situation-appropriate behaviour (Wilson 2002, p. 626)

Wilson also concludes that "off-line cognition is body based", however, within the context of virtual worlds, where online bodies and online spaces can fulfil all of the requirements above, online cognition too could be seen to be body-based, and until the learners has acquired that sense of body within those spaces, cognition can be impaired.

The concept of embodied cognition has its roots in the nineteenth century in the work of Husserl and in the 20th in the work of Merleau-Ponty. Both of these authors focused on the role of perception in the experience of the world, developing the idea of phenomenology, though for Husserl the focus of this was the role of sight, and movement through the world, in the conceptualising of that world;

> For Husserl, the body – the 'lived' body (Leib) not the 'objective' body (Körper) – is essential for perception of the world and for being in the world ... Sensible appearances can be appearances of physical things – or even as of physical things – only as they are co-ordinated with our bodily movements. (Smith 2007, p. 5).

For Merleau-Ponty it was the relationship of the body with the tasks or the objects that was important. For example, for Merleau-Ponty the idea of grasping things is meant both in its literal and figurative senses simultaneously; to fully grasp something figuratively requires grasping it literally (Smith 2007, p. 16).

> The spatiality of the body is not one of 'location' but of 'situation'. The 'here' of the body is its 'situation in face of its tasks' and a situation is delimited in terms of objects offering themselves as 'poles of action'. To have a body-schema is to be in the world. And conversely: the body is what it is by being 'polarised' in the face of objects, by its tasks; which is the same has having (or being) an 'existence towards objects'. (Smith 2007, p. 16).

The distinction between "location" and "situation" identifies the essential difference between the experience of the virtual world as simply a space to be viewed, and that of it as an environment in which to be lived. Inhabiting those spaces through interaction (with others or with the spaces) can develop a sense of embodiment, and conversely, when feeling more embodied, the potential for experiencing and learning is greater. As an educator working in virtual worlds, it is important to be aware of, and be able to support the development of learners' identity, body image and body schema within the virtual world.

Although virtual worlds are proving to be a valuable resource for educators, there is another, greater reason why understanding the role of identity in virtual worlds is important. Essentially, virtual worlds are not simply about the creation of a 3D computer world; the use of avatars means they are about the creation of a 3D computer-generated us. When asked about the importance of virtual worlds in a changing society, Bill Thompson (a UK-based commentator on the role of technology in society) stated that their real benefit is that they provide an opportunity to "rethink our fundamental assumptions about what personality is, what identity is, what it is to be a human being" (Thompson 2008). The experimentation and exploration of identity that virtual worlds permit, which has been touched on in this chapter and is explored in far more depth in the remainder of this book, is a chance to work out who and what we are on a far wider arena than in virtual worlds alone. As technology evolves, society evolves, and we evolve alongside them. We can challenge previous preconceptions; about gender, sexuality, physicality. We can redefine our roles in society or invent new ones. We can change how we view our bodies, or even modify them to adapt to our desires. These are changes that society as a whole will be facing in the ensuing century and these are issues that those exploring virtual worlds are already encountering. The debates encountered here will be ones that not only have relevance to the role of identity in virtual worlds, but will eventually challenge the meaning of identity for everyone.

References

Amdahl, K.: New world, new words!, The winged girl blog, 23rd May, 2007, http://kateamdahl. livejournal.com/13121.html, (2007)

Annetta, L., Klesath, M., Holmes, S.: V-learning: How gaming and avatars are engaging online students. Innovate 4(3). http://www.innovateonline.info/index.php?view=article&id=485 (2008). Accessed 16 Feb 2008

Au, J.W.: Furry Plateau, New World Notes. http://nwn.blogs.com/nwn/2007/07/furry-plateau.html (2007). Accessed 16th Nov 2008

Bailey, T.: Role-playing: The third life within second life. Konstrukt **10**, 20–24 (2007). May 2007

Bayne, S.: Uncanny spaces for higher education: Teaching and learning in virtual worlds. ALT J. **16**(3), 197–205 (2008)

Becker, B., Mark, G.: Social conventions in computer-mediated communication: A comparison of three online shared virtual environments. In Schroeder, R. (ed.) The Social Life of Avatars, London: Springer-Verlag, 19–39 (2002)

Biocca, F.,: The Cyborg's dilemma: Progressive embodiment in virtual environments. J. Comput. Mediat. Commun. **3** (2), http://jcmc.indiana.edu/vol3/issue2/biocca2.html (1997). Accessed 15 Oct 2006

Boellstorff, T.: Coming of Age in Second Life: An Anthropologist Explores the Virtually Human. Princeton University Press, Princeton (2008)

Cabiria, J.: Virtual world and real world permeability: Transference of positive benefits for marginalized gay and lesbian populations. J. Virt. Worlds Res.: Past Present Fut. **1** (1), 1–13 (July 2008)

Carruthers, G.: Is the body schema sufficient for the sense of embodiment? An alternative to de Vignemont's model. Philos. Psychol. **22**(2), 123–142 (2009)

Cheng, L., Farnham, S., Stone, L.: Lessons learned: Building and deploying shared virtual environments. In: Schroeder, R. (ed.) The Social Life of Avatars, pp. 90–112. Springer, London (2002)

Childs, M.: A conceptual framework for mediated environments. Educ. Res. **52**(2), 197–213 (2010). June 2010

Childs, M., Rowe, K.: Virtual Theater History: Teaching with Theatron. Modern Languages Association Convention, Philadelphia. Monday, 28 Dec 2009

Childs, M., Kuksa, I.: Why are we in the floor? Learning about theatre design in second life. In: Proceedings of the Edulearn 09 International Conference on Education and New Learning Technologies, pp. 1134–1145, Barcelona, 6–8th July 2009

Cormier, D., Gardner, M., Hibbert, G., Le Cornu, A., Perez-Garcia, M., Talbot, M., Truelove, I., Warburton, S., White, D.: Open Habitat, Bristol: JISC (2009). http://magazine.openhabitat.org/sites/magazine.openhabitat.org/files/OpenHabitatFullImages.pdf. Accessed 22nd Aug, 2010

de Vignemont, F.: Habeas corpus: The sense of ownership of one's own body. Mind Lang. **22**(4), 427–449 (2007)

Dumitrica, D., Gaden, G.: Knee-high boots and six-pack abs: Autoethnographic reflections on gender and technology in second life. J. Virt. World. Res., **1** (3) Cultures of Virtual Worlds Feb 2009.

Engeström, Y.: Activity theory and individual and social transformation. In: Engeström, Y., Miettinen, R., Punamäki, R.-L. (eds.) Perspectives on Activity Theory, pp. 19–38. Cambridge University Press, Cambridge (1999)

Goffman, E.: The Presentation of Self in Everyday Life. Penguin, London (1959)

Goffman, E.: Interaction Ritual; Essays in Face-to-Face Behavior. Transaction Publishers, New Brunswick (1967)

Held, R.M., Durlach, N.: Telepresence. Presence Teleoper. Virt. Environ. **1**(1), 102–112 (1992)

Jakobsson, M.: Rest in peace, bill the bot: Death and life in virtual worlds. In: Schroeder, R. (ed.) The Social Life of Avatars, pp. 63–76. Springer, London (2002)

Knudsen, A.C.: Presence production. Published doctoral thesis, Royal Institute of Technology, Stockholm (2004)

Lawrence, A.: Clinical and theoretical parallels between desire for limb amputation and gender identity disorder. Arch. Sex. Behav. **35**(3), 263–278 (2006). June 2006

Lee, J.J., Hoadley, C.M.: Leveraging identity to make learning fun: Possible selves and experiential learning in massively multiplayer online games (MMOGs). Innovate **3** (6). http://www.innovateonline.info/index.php?view=article&id=348. Accessed 31 July 2007

Loomis, J.M.: Distal attribution and presence. Presence, **1**(1), 113–118 (1992)

Macfadyen, L.P.: Constructing ethnicity and identity in the online classroom: Linguistic practices and ritual text acts. In: Hodgson, V., Jones, C., Kargidis, T., McConnell, D., Retalis, S., Stamatis, D., Zenios, M. (eds.) Proceedings of the Sixth International Conference on Networked Learning, pp. 560–568, Halkidiki, 5th & 6th May 2008

Manders-Huits, N.: Practical versus moral identities in identity management. Ethics Inf. Technol. **12**, 43–55 (2010)

Mayes, T., de Freitas, S.: Review of e-learning frameworks, models and theories: JISC e-learning models desk study, JISC (1999)

McKenna, K.Y.A., Green, A.S., Smith, P.K.: Demarginalizing the sexual self. J. Sex Res. **38**(4), 302–311 (2001)

Murray, D.C., Sixsmith, J.: The corporeal body in virtual reality, ethos. Body Self Technol. **27**(3), 315–343 (1999). Sep 1999

Nejad, A.G., Toofani, K.: Co-existence of lycanthropy and Cotard's syndrome in a single case. Acta Psychiatr. Scand. **111**, 250–252 (2005)

Newman, K.: PhD thesis, An investigation of narrative and role-playing activities in online communication environments. Griffith University, Queensland (2007)

Peachey, A., Withnail, G.: A sociocultural perspective on negotiating digital identities in a community of learners. In: Warburton, S., Hatzipanagos, S. (eds.) Digital Identity and Social Media. IGI Global, Hershey (2011)

Phoenix, A.: Identities and diversities. In: Miell, D., Phoenix, A., Thomas, K. (eds.) DSE212 Mapping Psychology Book 1. The Open University, Milton Keynes (2007)

Roberts, L.F., Brett, M.A., Johnson, T.W., Wassersug, R.J.: A passion for castration: Characterizing men who are fascinated with castration, but have not been castrated. J. Sex. Med. **5**, 1669–1680 (2008)

Schroeder, R.: Social interaction in virtual environments: Key issues, common themes, and a framework for research. In: Schroeder, R. (ed.) The Social Life of Avatars, pp. 1–18. Springer, London (2002)

Sheridan, T.: Musings on telepresence and virtual presence. Presence Teleop. Virt. Environ. **1**(1), 120–126 (1992)

Smith, A.D.: The Flesh of Perception: Merleau-Ponty and Husserl. In Thomas Baldwin (ed.), Reading Merleau-Ponty: On Phenomenology of Perception, 1–22, (1999)

Stets, J. E., Burke, P.J.: A sociological approach to self and identity. In: Mark Leary, June Tangney (eds.), Handbook of Self and Identity, Guilford Press, pp. 128–152, http://www.people.fas.harvard.edu/~johnston/burke.pdf. Accessed 13th Aug 2008

Taylor, T.L.: Living digitally: Embodiment in virtual worlds. In: Schroeder, R. (ed.) The Social Life of Avatars, pp. 40–62. Springer, London (2002)

Thomas, A.: Heterotopia and My Second Life (2006). http://anya.blogsome.com/2006/05/27/heterotopia-and-my-second-life/. Accessed 23rd Aug 2010

Thompson, W.: Chaired debate, Anna Peachey, Roo Reynolds, Edward Castronova, Claudia L'Amoreaux, Bill Thompson, Ren Reynolds, *ReLIVE08*, 21st Nov 2008, Open University. Available at http://stadium.open.ac.uk/stadia/preview.php?whichevent=1248&s=31&schedule=1468 (2008).

Tompkins, P.S.: Truth, trust and telepresence. J. Mass Media Ethics **18**(3&4), 194–212 (2003)

Turkle, S.: Life on the Screen: Identity in the Age of the Internet. Simon & Schuster, New York (1995)

Wallace, P., Maryott, J.: The impact of avatar self-representation on collaboration in virtual worlds. Innovate **5** (5). http://www.innovateonline.info/index.php?view=article&id=689. Accessed 31 May 2009

Warburton, S.: Loving your avatar: Identity, immersion and empathy. Liquid Learning, 28th Jan 2008. http://warburton.typepad.com/liquidlearning/2008/01/loving-your-ava.html. Accessed 1st Jan 2009

Wenger, E.: Communities of Practice; Learning, Meaning and Identity. Cambridge University Press, Cambridge (1998)

White, M.: Visual pleasure in textual places. In: Green, E., Adam, A. (eds.) Virtual Gender: Technology, Consumption and Identity. Routledge, London (2001)

Wilson, M.: Six views embodied cognition. Psychon. Bull. Rev. **9**(4), 625–636 (2002)

Chapter 3
The Self and Second Life: A Case Study Exploring the Emergence of Virtual Selves

Simon Evans

Abstract Using the virtual world Second Life™ as a case study, the chapter begins a social psychological exploration of how living in virtual worlds may be transforming the experience of the self in contemporary society, from the 'insider viewpoint' of virtual world residents. The relationship between the virtual self and the 'real life' self is explored using data collected and key themes elicited from 40 textual interviews conducted inworld and inductive thematic analysis. The findings indicate a variety of complex relationships between the self experienced in the physical world and Second Life. First, the degree of similarity between the actual and virtual self varies according to experience. Second, the avatar tends to be seen as a separate entity. Finally, social processes within Second Life affects how the self is experienced, by allowing exploration of aspects of the self not possible in the physical world.

3.1 Introduction

This chapter has a trajectory beginning in November 2007 and a programme broadcast on BBC4, *Visions of the Future*. Presented by physicist and futurist Dr Michio Kaku, it included a piece on Second Life.[1] The article was intriguing on a number of levels: that people created lives alternate to or alongside their real lives; the potential for exploration of one's identity through creation of avatars; the conflicts that such alternatives and explorations can cause in relation to real lives and

---

[1] An outline of the series that included the article may be found on http://www.bbc.co.uk/bbcfour/documentaries/features/visions-future.shtml.

S. Evans (✉)
Social and Cultural Psychology, London School of Economics and Political Science, London, UK
e-mail: s.evans@lse.ac.uk

A. Peachey and M. Childs (eds.), *Reinventing Ourselves: Contemporary Concepts of Identity in Virtual Worlds*, Springer Series in Immersive Environments,
DOI 10.1007/978-0-85729-361-9_3, © Springer-Verlag London Limited 2011

'real life' identities; and implications for the (Western) common sense notion of the self as being 'unique and bounded' (Geertz 2000). Inspired by the programme, the author, then a social psychology master's level student, became a Second Life resident. It is in the context of his own 'second life', that the author undertook a research programme making a social psychological investigation of being a virtual self in virtual worlds, which is described in this chapter. Agger (2003) uses the term 'virtual self' to describe the experience of being a person in contemporary post-modern society, which among its characteristics are virtual interactions via computer mediated communication (CMC). In particular, this chapter considers how the self or virtual self is affected by experiences within virtual worlds, using Second Life as a case study. The need to understand how the rise of virtual worlds may be affecting how the self is experienced is becoming ever pressing, since most recent figures indicate the number of registered accounts in virtual worlds has reached one billion, with almost half being among 10–15 year olds ("Virtual world" 2010).[2]

The chapter serves a number of functions within the context of this book. It provides a social psychological exploration of how living within virtual worlds is changing notions of who we are, by outlining research that shows how people are using such worlds to actively explore and construct who they are as selves. It also contributes to the development of good practice in research in virtual worlds by providing a detailed rationale for, and outline of, a research programme that was undertaken by the author, and by offering critique on how research practice may be improved. Finally, it provides insight into how Second Life specifically is being used to explore the nature of the self by the people who live there. In particular, the stance of the chapter is to highlight that virtual worlds are places where people live lives, form relationships and explore what it means to be a person.

To this end there are four main sections. The first provides a brief review of the existing literature, exploring existing theoretical conceptions of the self. The second provides details of the case study itself, including the research context, questions and design, methodology for data collection and analytic approach. The third presents an outline of the findings, relating them to the research questions posed and some case histories outlining the particular experience of specific residents. The final section provides a discussion of the findings, highlighting implications for theoretical conceptions of the self and providing recommendations for future research. Given the author's context as a resident in Second Life, the final section also contains a brief reflexive analysis of the implications on the research procedure and interpretation.

---

[2] One billion accounts does not necessarily signify one billion individuals, since it is possible to have accounts across different worlds and more than one account within a given world.

3.2   A Review of Existing Literature

3.2.1   Theoretical Background: The Self

It has been claimed that "it is at the level of human interaction and interpersonal relationships that the fabrication of the self arises" (Elliot 2001, pp. 22–23). However, how the self may be conceptualised is a contested issue. Geertz (2000) argues that the western notion of the person as a "bounded, unique, more or less integrated motivational and cognitive universe, a dynamic centre of awareness, emotion, judgement and action, organised into a distinctive whole and set contrastively both against other such wholes and against its social and natural background, is, however ... a rather peculiar idea within the context of world cultures" (p. 59). This western conception has its roots in the Cartesian mind-body separation, where the "visual and sensual aspects of human nature are subordinated to faculty of reason" (Bolter 2003, p. 129). It is against this backdrop of a unitary bounded person, that traditional theories of the self have been developed, but against which post-modern theories of the self pitch themselves. This section reviews these theories.

Traditional theories propose a self that is reflexive and arises through mind and body together, the mind being "inseparably associated with and dependent upon the physical organism known as the body" (Hintz 1960, cited in Barnes 2003, p. 239). Primary among these is that of Mead, who proposes that the self "can arise only where there is a social process within which this self has had its initiation" (Mead 1956, p. 41). It is through interactions with others in what he calls 'the conversation of gestures' that one adopts the perspective of the other, becomes an object of observation to oneself and hence through reflexivity becomes conscious and aware of the self. Crucial to the development of self is awareness of a 'generalised other', initially arising through childhood play, and defined as "the organized community or social groups that gives the individual his unity of self" (Mead 1962, p. 154); the conversation of gestures is key to this. This term is adopted by Berger and Luckmann (1966) who claim that "a person's experience of himself always hovers in a balance between being and having a body" (p. 68). For them, both the organismic development and the social environment as mediated by significant others are crucial for the formation of self.

Like Mead, Goffman (1959) considers the self to be arising in a social environment and to be a reflexive agent. For him, presentation of the self is a salient part of everyday life, and involves the management of information intentionally or unintentionally given off to others (Papacharissi 2002). He proposes a theatrical metaphor for the development of the self and, while everyday interactions are crucial, he envisions a self that is more situated and fragmentary. For him, people can be likened to actors on a stage, using scripts and props to portray convincing performances according to the social environment they are in. Hence, a sense of self arises from "an awareness of the multiplicity of roles that are performed in various situated contexts" (Elliot 2001, p. 31).

In contrast to these earlier theories of the self, post-modern theorists emphasise a self that is fragmented, empathetic and 'anti-Cartesian' (Bolter 2003). In this vein, Gergen (1991) proposes that the self in contemporary society is saturated by multiple voices, typified by multiple disconnected relationships and roles which result from a cast of 'significant others' in "continuous motion" (p. 67). He proposes that these myriad relationships, which arise through technologies of saturation such as telecommunications, facilitate a self that is inauthentic and unknowable and that a "fully saturated self becomes no self at all" (Gergen 1991, p. 7). This influence of new communications technologies on the self is supported by Cerulo (1997), who proposes that they have expanded the range of 'generalised others', changing the context in which the self arises. Hence because the postmodern view proposes a self that is subject to external constraints and lacks agency and coherence, it implies a self that is non-reflexive. This is contrary to the traditional view for which reflexive "turning back of the experience of the individual upon himself" (Mead 1962, p. 134) is crucial to the development of the self.

Postmodern theorists have also considered specifically how the arrival of CMC has had influences on the contemporary self. According to Poster (1990), when electronically mediated exchange replaces oral and written exchange there are four implications: there are new possibilities of playing with identities; gender cues are removed; existing hierarchies in relationships are destabilised; and "the self is decentred, dispersed and multiplied in continuous instability" (p. 6). Moreover, Baym (2006) claims that CMC allows a self that is divorced from bodies, time and space and a "multiplicity of identity ... with no one of these selves necessarily more valid than any other" (p. 41). As with Gergen's view, this indicates a self that is uprooted and unfocused. However, contrary to this, Turkle (2005) proposes that the computer is a medium for 'getting things done', working through personal concerns and thinking through issues to do with the self. Rather than being saturated by uncontrollable myriad influences, people may become the "masters of self-presentation and self-creation" (Turkle 1996, p. 158). Consequently, this indicates that while the selves mediated by computer technologies could indeed be divorced from bodies, time and space, they may still be characterised by the reflexivity characteristic of more traditional conceptions of the self. It is in this context that the author developed a research programme designed to explore further the experience of the self in contemporary times.

3.2.2 The Self in Virtual Worlds

In addition to the consideration of the impact of changes in society on the experience of self, there has also been specific research on the effects of participation in virtual worlds. These can be argued to group around certain themes.

Firstly, there is the potential for self-exploration. The clinical and ethnographic investigation of the textual MUDs conducted by Turkle (1995, 1996) reveals a blurring between the boundaries between the self and game, the self and role and the self and simulation, with the self being experienced as a "composite of characters" (Turkle 1996, p. 157). She proposes that such virtual worlds offer the opportunity for 'parallel lives'. More recently, Boellstorff (2008) conducted an ethnographical study of Second Life and explored all aspects of social life, including what he terms 'personhood'. While he found a tendency for people not to consciously role play but to be themselves in some way, he also found it was possible for the self experienced in Second Life to be different from that experienced in the physical world. He proposes that the possession of alt avatars or avatars of a different gender to that in the physical world allows the exploration of aspects of the self.

There has also been research conducted into the role of avatars in offering an embodied experience of the self. Following his ethnographic study of the virtual world The Dreamscape, Taylor (2002) proposes that it is through the use of a body, in the form of an avatar, that users gain a sense of 'being real' and of immersion in virtual worlds. This has parallels with Mead's emphasis on the role of the body in social interactions facilitating a sense of self. Taylor also found that some people identify with their avatar as being 'more them' than their physical world body. The effects of embodiment via an avatar on behaviour and perceptions of self have been explored by Yee and Bailenson (2007). Using experimental studies, they propose the Proteus Effect, i.e. individual's behaviour conforms to the appearance of their avatar. Those with avatars that were 'more attractive' or taller, acted more intimately or confidently respectively. Likewise Boellstorff (2008) found that an avatar can take on a 'role' that fits their appearance, outside of what its user would necessarily take on themselves in the physical world. Ducheneaut et al. (2009) used questionnaires to investigate the rationale for avatar depiction in three graphical virtual worlds (Maple Street, Second Life and Worlds of Warcraft), which reveals a tendency to use avatars to explore embodiment rather than facets of personality or self.

Finally, there are findings that suggest physical world benefits that the virtual life has on the self. Turkle (1996, 2005) proposes that it is possible for participants in the textual MUDs to work through 'real life issues',[3] through exploration of different aspects of the self and personality. Boellstorff (2008) found similar benefits in Second Life but proposes the potential for aspects of personality in the physical world to be changed in ways not possible in MUDs. This is because it offers a closer approximation to the physical world through its graphical format that the textual MUDs cannot.

---

[3] While this chapter will most often use the expression 'physical world', on occasion the term 'real life' will be adopted when in the context of taking the viewpoint of virtual world residents or in understanding various aspects of being a virtual self. This is because 'real life' (or RL) is the expression used by virtual world residents when referring to the physical world.

3.2.3   A Note: Social Psychological Research in Virtual Worlds

It is interesting to note that, while there has been deliberation on the effects of CMC generally and virtual worlds particularly on the experience of the self, much of this comes from without the discipline of psychology, for example, anthropology (Boellstorff 2008) and communications (Yee and Bailenson 2007). Where research has been conducted by psychologists, it has been with an eye on its clinical applications (Turkle 2005; Gorini et al. 2008). This suggests that there is potential to consider more than the social psychological implications of the virtual self.

3.3   The Case Study: Second Life

3.3.1   The Research Rationale, Context and Questions

While theorists concerned with virtual worlds have begun to explore the experience of being a self in them, there is an opportunity to consider this from the perspective of social psychology and from an 'insider viewpoint'. This chapter seeks to do this through research in the form of a case study based on the residents of Second Life. It explores the tensions, similarities and differences between the self as experienced within Second Life and in 'real life'. Because of the variety of existing theories and assumptions with respect to the self, but limited insight into the social psychological phenomena involved, the case study takes an inductive approach. It explores the range of experience of being a Second Life self and then considers how present theories may or may not be applied.[4]

Boellstorff (2008) provides a very detailed account of the history and workings of Second Life. At the time of writing, there are 1,360,030 accounts[5] that have been active in the 60 days to 13th October 2010,[6] with the number of accounts active at any one time ranging from 40,000 to 80,000 depending on the time of day, day of week and time of year. An important consideration for current purposes is that it

---

[4] As a relatively new area of study for the discipline of social psychology, a grounded theory approach, as outlined by Flick (2009), could provide the basis of a new social psychological 'theory of the self'. A grounded theory is one that is developed inductively from data, via a cycle of data collection, coding, analysis, writing, design and theoretical categorisation, rather than being a pre-developed theory tested by data. While a new grounded 'theory of the self' is outside the scope of this chapter, it is believed that the procedures and findings from the research discussed here could form the basis of a more extensive piece of research that develops a grounded theory.

[5] As with the current universe of virtual worlds detailed above, this does not necessarily indicate 1,360,030 different users, since it is possible for one person to have more than one avatar, i.e. more than one account.

[6] The numbers of residents who have logged in the previous 60 days and who are online at the time of logging are presented every time an account holder logs into Second Life. This is the source of the statistics presented here.

may be argued that there is a demarcation between the physical world and Second Life for many residents. While it is possible to make public physical world information through the avatar profile, in practice many residents choose to keep this information private or reserve it for those they feel they can trust. At the same time, residents are conducting 'second lives' that may be private from people known to them in the physical world and involve experiences, relationships, interests and employment that are separate from that realm. Another key consideration is the researcher's experience of virtual life generally and Second Life specifically. This is because it can inform the research questions that are posed and the appropriateness of transferring methodologies from the physical world to virtual worlds, as well as allow potential insight into others' experience. The researcher has been a resident in Second Life since December 2007 and has two homes, one a modern beach house, the second a small terraced home in an area of Second Life devoted to Victorian-inspired lifestyles. He has a large number of friends, is a member of a number of groups and has had a wide variety of experiences, including attending weddings, exploring simulations of physical world cities, attending night clubs and parties. Throughout the research period, he identified as a white human male (his appearance in the physical world also). This makes him well placed to understand the issues that may arise with respect to the self within Second Life and to have empathy and appreciation for the situations and experiences of other residents.

The research outlined here focuses particularly on the relationship between Second Life and the physical world, with respect to the experience of the self. The questions it seeks to address are:

- To what extent are Second Life selves the same or different from 'real life' selves, in terms of characteristics, capabilities, motivations and traits?
- To what extent are Second Life selves independent of or dependent on the 'real life' selves operating the keyboard?
- To what extent does a Second Life self emerge as a result of social processes within Second Life, separate from 'real life'?

3.3.2 Research Design

The research presented many new and unique challenges not normally experienced when conducting research in the physical world. These challenges were present in all aspects of the research process and shaped the research design, the methodology and procedures. In terms of the design, there were a number of influencing factors. Second Life is a place with unique practices, rituals and environments, and the experience of it is in the privacy of the residents homes and potentially private from others in the physical world. Additionally, residents are located worldwide, with a tendency to keep their identity in the physical world private from those in Second Life. Coupled with the subject matter of the virtual self potentially being a personal one, this meant that utmost confidentiality and sensitivity would be needed in approaching participants. Finally, it was not the 'average' or 'usual' experience of being a person in

Second Life that was of interest for the purpose of the research, but the range of experiences that are found among Second Life residents and their 'insider viewpoint' of that experience. To address these challenges and the research question, a programme of individual interviews was devised, the format and questions informed by the researcher's experiences as a Second Life resident, with the interviews providing the data by which to address the research questions. However, it was important that researchers own experience did not influence or determine the outcome of the research, so a semi-structured interview approach was undertaken, allowing flexibility in the discussion according to the participants' own experiences.

All interviews were conducted inworld. There were a number of specific benefits to this. It allowed research participants irrespective of location and cultural background, not necessarily possible if conducting physical world interviews. Additionally, it potentially overcame any concerns participants might have in keeping the physical world and Second Life private from each other. Moreover, the fact that the researcher had already been a resident for several months could ease the recruitment and research process, because of access to individuals and groups comprising potential participants. This also afforded the researcher ready-made credentials and experience as a genuine resident, providing a basis for rapport with participants.

3.3.3   Methodology: Format, Data Collection, Sampling, the Topic Guide and Ethical Considerations

Although Second Life provides a 'voice' facility,[7] all interviews were conducted in text. This was because not all residents have English as a first language, and may feel more confident in written rather than verbal formats. Moreover, some residents specifically choose text-only communications, for example, if they represent themselves as another gender, have hearing difficulties, or wish to protect other physical world privacies. A by-product of textual interviews is the option to download textual communications to the computer hard drive, which is built into the Second Life programme, facilitating raw data for analysis.

For this research, it was assumed that the data produced in a single textual interview of comparable length to a verbal interview would produce less data. This is because a typed response usually takes more time than a verbal one. Also experience suggested that textual communication in Second Life is more truncated, so it was believed that textual responses could be shorter than verbal. Hence, to gather as much data as possible, the interview programme comprised 40 h-long interviews.

Participants were from a number of sources. The majority were recruited from the Second Life help group New Citizens Inc. (NCI), with the remainder recruited from Monkey Channel (a group used to advertise services), opportunity recruitment

---

[7] i.e. where users can use a microphone to allowing verbal communicate rather than being limited to text only.

Table 3.1 Numbers of participants, detailed by source

Source of recruitment	Number of participants
New Citizens Inc. (NCI)	34
Monkey channel	2
Opportunity recruitment	2
Referral by another participant	2

from chance encounters, and referrals by participants. Table 3.1 details the sources of participants. No physical world demographic recruitment controls were exercised, since in virtual worlds, physical world age and location controls cannot be easily applied as people commonly keep such information confidential or can deceive. Any demographic controls based on the avatar (for example, how long the avatar had been in Second Life, and its gender) risk being invalidated, since individuals may have alts of different ages or have an avatar of different gender to their physical world status (both situations occurred during the course of this research).

A topic guide was used, aiming to provide "an easy and comfortable framework for a discussion" (Gaskell 2000, p. 40). It addressed four main areas: arrival and 'settling into' Second Life; the balance between 'real life' and Second Life; similarities and differences between 'real life' and Second Life; the relationship with their avatar.

Ethics were a consideration that presented particular challenges, because the process involved interviews conducted virtually and between avatars. One challenge concerned informed consent, which in the physical world is indicated by participant signatures notifying their awareness of and consent to participate in the research procedure. In Second Life, signatures are not possible, so to address this, an 'Information and Consent Notecard' was given to all prospective participants. This detailed the research purpose and interview topics, with a request to Instant Message (IM) their informed consent with the phrase "I agree to participate in your study". Another challenge, concerns anonymity and confidentiality. While theoretically all avatars represent an 'alias' that cannot be tracked to the physical world, all text is downloaded onto Linden Lab logs, and it is the researcher's experience that residents guard their privacy. Hence, the researcher assured anonymity in the final report, that physical world identities would never be requested and guaranteed that avatar names would only be stored on the researcher's personal computer hard drive. A third challenge concerned the unknown physical world status of participants, which impacted on the normal procedures of verification. Consequently participants were asked to verbally verify that they were considered adults in the physical world country they lived in, at the beginning of each interview.

3.3.4   Interviewing: Recruitment, Schedule and Procedure

Participants were recruited from the NCI group via a group IM and the Monkey Channel through a group notice, where the research was outlined very briefly and a call for participants made. Anyone expressing interest in participating were given

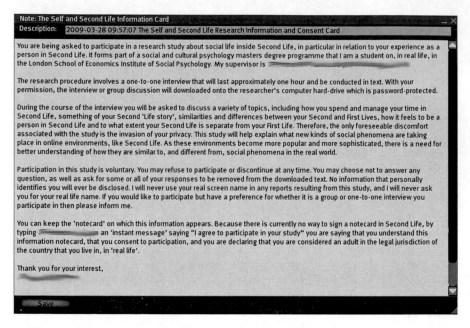

Fig. 3.1 Information and consent notecard

a copy of the 'Information and Consent Notecard' and appointments for interviews made, confirmed via an appointment notecard. Figure 3.1 demonstrates how the 'Information and Consent Notecard' appeared in Second Life.

Forty interviews were conducted over the period March 3–April 19, 2009, held at times convenient to both participant and recruiter and dependent on the participant location. Participants were given a choice of location for the interview; 38 of the 40 interviewees elected one of the researcher's homes and two their own homes. All interviews were conducted in IM, allowing privacy and aiding analysis by downloading the interview into a dedicated participant file. All interviews commenced with a welcome, thanks for participating and sought permission for the conversation to be in IM. Before questioning began, the researcher asked for confirmation of adult status, reminded of the right to refuse questions or to terminate the interview, and advised them of arrangements should either participant or researcher 'crash'[8] (a relatively common occurrence in Second Life, although only experienced a few times during the interview programme). Although each interview was due to be an hour's duration, participants were often willing to converse beyond this. To monitor the interview experience, each concluded with an enquiry into participants' experience of the interview, their reason for participating and willingness to recommend to others.

---

[8] This means to be unexpectedly logged out of the Second Life program, usually due to data overload.

3.3.5   The Approach: Thematic Analysis

The research here does not seek to work within a particular epistemological frame-work, nor build on a particular theory. Its purpose is to understand the range of experiences of being a virtual self in Second Life and from this understand how existing theories of the self may relate to virtual worlds. Hence a thematic analysis method is used because, according to Braun and Clarke (2006), it is "a method for identifying, analysing and reporting patterns (themes) within data. It minimally organises and describes your data in (rich) detail" (p. 79) and is argued to be an approach to qualitative analysis independent of theory and epistemology.

Given the exploratory nature of the research, an inductive thematic analysis was undertaken, with themes purely derived from the data without applying any predeter-mined frames. The procedure provided by Attride-Stirling (2001) was used as a guide-line. There is a systematic classification of data into 'basic themes' based on semantic meanings, which is then used to construct hierarchies of 'organising themes', which groups the 'basic themes' together based on abstract common principles, and 'global themes', which represent the principle underlying themes. Relationships can then be identified between the hierarchies to conceptualise a 'thematic network'.

The thematic analysis was undertaken with the assistance of Computer-Aided Qualitative Data Analysis Software, in the form of NVivo (version 8). The data set was analysed twice, the first to provide a coding framework identifying potential 'basic themes' arising from the data, the second to refine it. This derives 75 'basic themes', clustered then into 14 'organising themes', in turn grouped into four 'global themes'.

3.4   The Themes and Thematic Network

The four global themes arising from the data analysis are: 'The Second Life Experience'; 'The Real Life – Second Life Relation'; 'Relationships with Others'; 'The Second Life Self'. Each global theme encapsulates a number of organising themes as detailed in Table 3.2.

Figure 3.2 outlines the structure of thematic network constructed from the data and indicates the relationships between global, organising themes and basic themes, a summary of which follows.

3.4.1   Global Theme: 'The Second Life Experience'

This encapsulates areas of experience by Second Life residents that may reflect and impact on their sense of self. The relationship between organising and basic themes is shown in Table 3.3.

Table 3.2 A summary of the global and organising themes derived from interview data

Global theme	Organising theme
The second life experience	Introduction to second life
	Socialisation
	Second life as a game
	Second life as a place for activities
The real life – second life relation	Real life – second life division
	Real life – second life time relation
	Real life – second life mutual influences
	Second life as a place in its own right
Relationships with others	Social interactions
	Everyday relationships
	Intimate relationships
The second life self	Avatar and real life self relations
	Stability and instability of second life self
	Real life v second life relationship

Fig. 3.2 Thematic network
from data

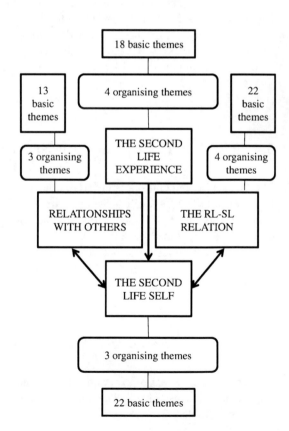

Table 3.3 The relationship between organising and basic themes as associated with the global theme 'The Second Life Experience'

Organising theme	Basic theme
Introduction to SL	Professional introduction
	Friend introduction
	Introduction through media coverage
	Long-term online resident
	Stuttered start
Socialisation	Assistance in settling
	Help of friends in settling
	Learning
	Easy adjustment to SL
	Helping people
	Self-adjustment to SL
SL as a game	Role-play
	SL is a game
	SL as 'not real'
	SL as a 'place to play'
SL as a place for activities	Creativity
	Exploration
	SL business

There were several ways in which participants were introduced into Second Life but for some it was a natural progression from and enhancement of their involvement in other textual or graphical virtual worlds. For example:

> I had experienced online affection in the use of chat programs before, that were all text ... and the thought of a visual seemed to me that it would enhance the experience. (VL)[9]

How they came to Second Life had influences on how well they were socialised into it, for example those introduced by friends were helped by the same friends to understand how to make the most of the experience and to understand etiquette, how things are 'done', etc. Participants were not passive in the socialisation process and show active determination in joining and understanding how to be part of Second Life:

> .. so I became frustrated ... and was screaming in local[10] ... asking for help ... and then someone came across and helped me to a noob[11] place. (LM)

---

[9]All quotes in this section have been amended to be grammatically correct for ease of reading. Initials parenthesised after each quote represent the participant from whose interview the quote is taken. Moreover, the quotes adhere to the convention of abbreviating Second Life and 'real life' as SL and RL respectively, which is commonly used by residents.

[10]The terms 'local', 'local chat', 'open chat' or 'open' are used to denote conversations that occur in public making it possible for anyone within in a given distance (typically 20 'metres') to hear or read what is said verbally or textually. In this context LM means that she was continuously asking for help via text in 'local chat'.

[11]The term 'noob', 'noobie', 'newb' or 'newbie' is an expression used to denote someone who is relatively new and/or inexperienced in Second Life.

> **Case History Box 1**: MN's Second Life Experience
>
> MN, a graphic designer in the physical world, discovered Second Life through its coverage on You Tube and search engines and was intrigued by its creative and networking possibilities. She gave herself a 'crash course' on socialisation into the virtual world and, with the help of those she met in Second Life, in her first extended session learned about 'freebie shopping', searching, navigation, flying, teleporting, purchasing new skin and hair, and sex. She now has an active and busy social and business life in Second Life, having a large group of friends she has fun with and a nightclub designed as a place for men and women to find potential sexual partners. While she does not role-play in Second Life, she does see her virtual self as being a teenage version of herself in the physical world.

Once in Second Life, while seeing it as a place to socialise and meet people from all walks of life and nationalities, participants also engage in all kinds of activities, although the capacity for exploration and creative expression is an important aspect of people's experience:

> I love exploring in here, wandering around by myself, late at night, you get to peek inside people's heads. (MD)

> SL really brings out a creative side in me - I love seeing how others make this world their own. (LN)

Whether Second Life is a game is a contested issue. While some do engage in role-play games within Second Life or even see themselves as role-playing a character during their everyday lives within it, the sentiment that it is important to recognise that 'real people' are involved is stressed:

> I think there are two types of people in SL. Those who are themselves and retain their own character and treat others as if they are too. And those that think it's a game and forget that there are other people behind the av. (RW)

An example of a particular participant's experience is outlined in Case History Box 1.

3.4.2 Global Theme: 'The Real Life – Second Life Relation'

This theme reflects concerns, opinions and experiences that participants expressed with respect to how the physical world relates to Second Life, which in turn influences, and was influenced by, their experience of being a person within it. The relationship between organising and basic themes is shown in Table 3.4.

A division between 'real life' and Second Life is alluded to, with the privacy of 'real life' being important and with 'real life' taking priority, for as one participant said:

> No one knows me, no one will be at the grocery store, so I am free to do what I want. (ZD)

> I prefer the term First Life to real life, as when it comes down to it, in general, "RL" has to come first. (MT)

Table 3.4 The relationship between organising and basic themes as associated with the global theme 'The Real Life – Second Life Relation'

Organising theme	Basic theme
RL-SL division	RL as priority
	RL privacy from SL
	RL and SL similarity
	RL and SL difference
	RL and SL self difference
	RL and SL self similarity
	SL as an alternative to RL
	RL and SL separation
	SL as part of RL entertainment portfolio
RL-SL division	Addiction
	Balancing time
	Difficult balance RL v SL
	Immersion
	Passage of time differences
RL-SL mutual influences	RL sickness and RL
	RL v SL blurring
	RL v SL overflow
	SL burnout
	SL improvement of RL
SL as a place in its own right	Achievements not possible in RL
	SL as an escape and place to be
	SL as 'real'

Despite this, some participants indicate that Second Life is a place in its own right and just as real as the physical world. Being a person in Second Life is seen as both different and similar to 'real life'. Participants indicate that it offers the opportunity for activities and self-expression not possible in the physical world, although perhaps still subject to the same social structures found in the physical world:

I saw how one could do many things here that they were unable to do in RL and that excited me. (KM)

It's more a realisation that RL and SL are more similar than different ... in both places there are social norms and expectations, in both places I worry about wearing the right thing. (EZ)

Time spent in Second Life is expressed as being intense: much happens in a short time period, and this experience is often described as compulsive and addictive, meaning that participants differ on how well they manage to balance time spent in Second Life with that in the physical world:

... but the balance thing was hard, I have an addictive personality anyway and playing a minor god in your own little world is mighty enticing. (MD)

RL has gone neglected. However, the past few weeks, I have HAD to do something about it, so I do what I have to in RL although .. my mind ... my brain ... see to be here. (LE)

This illustrates that, despite there being indications that the physical world and Second Life are considered separate, participants also acknowledge that there are

Case History Box 2: Relationships Between DP's 'Real' and Second Lives

When DP discovered Second Life, he was recovering from stress related ill-ness and a failed marriage in the physical world. By reading about Second Life he taught himself to build but due to his anxiety did not make any friends in the virtual world until 1 year had passed. He found being in Second Life therapeu-tic, giving him the opportunity to express himself creatively and build relation-ships with people, things that he would have been even more difficult in his physical world environment. He feels that being a resident in Second Life has helped improve his mental health such that he has reduced from being on heavy medication to none. His view is that Second Life gives everyone, despite any disabilities they might have, the freedom to express themselves.

influences between the two lives. On a basic level, Second Life, their friends and activities within Second Life occupy some participants' thoughts when in the physi-cal world. However, more significant influences are also indicated. Some partici-pants related how being in Second Life helped them cope with, and overcome, physical world sickness and disability, while others spoke of 'burn out' and the physical ramifications of continual presence inworld. Some also indicate how expe-riencing themselves as a person in Second Life, enable them to improve their physi-cal world self by exploring new attitudes and behaviours or learning new skills:

> I came into SL it helped my RL. Well, I was in abusive life. I learned you can be treated
> well. An abused person has abuse as focus, see, and SL helped give me focus away from
> abuse. So I didn't go back. ☺ (SC)

An example of a particular participant's experience is outlined in Case History Box 2.

3.4.3   Global Theme: 'Relationships with Others'

This concerns the importance that participants placed on relationships, which in turn influenced and was influenced by their sense of self. The relationship between organising and basic themes, and explanation of the basic themes, is shown in Table 3.5.

Social interaction with people from all over the world is indicated by some to be one of the key drivers of their participating in Second Life. However, communica-tions are not necessarily straightforward, with language differences and lack of verbal tone and body language often the source of misunderstandings:

> I think people have huge drama in SL that wouldn't fly in RL because the missing cues and
> body language, facial expressions, etc. are in RL to get more information and meaning
> across. (KV)

	Organising theme	Basic theme
Table 3.5 The relationship between organising and basic themes as associated with the global theme 'Relationships with Others'	Social interaction	Communication
		Internationality
		Social interactions
	Everyday relationships	Friendship
		Community
		SL as reuniting separated friends
		Trust and deception
	Intimate relationships	SL relationships
		SL families
		SL relationship pain
		SL sex
		SL relationships as real
		RL emotions in SL

Some participants indicate the value of friendship and community within Second Life, and in particular how being in Second Life gives them a sense of place and offers the potential to be in contact or be reunited with people in ways that otherwise would be difficult:

> But I think what SL was for me in the beginning, and probably still is, is a way of being with the people I love and care about. And it's almost as if I'm right there, right here, seeing us together, or even chatting in the same window. Out there, anywhere, but online. :p (KW)

Because of anonymity issues and the risk of 'alts', trust is indicated by some to be a fundamental part of relationships, because the potential is always there to be hurt and deceived by others:

> In RL you have to trust to a certain degree. In SL you have no choice BUT to trust, unless you let it drive you crazy. (LE)

Despite this risk, close and intimate bonds are formed by participants, including sexual and familial relationships.[12] Moreover, intense 'real life' emotions are experienced by participants within Second Life. While some indicate that Second Life relationships are a source of emotional pain, the experience of the physical world emotions are seen as valuable and important:

> I like RL feelings and emotions ... even if they hurt. (LE)

An example of a particular participant's experience is outlined in Case History Box 3.

---

[12] In Second Life relationships occur that reflect those that occur in the physical world. Residents may have sexual partners, which may not become realised in the actual world, but occur intensely within virtual space. These relationships may involve role-playing sexual activity through animations available within Second Life and/or describing it through text or voice. Additionally, Second Life families may be constructed by the residents, so that they may be consider themselves to be husband, wife, mother, father, brother, sister, etc. to other selected residents. While this may involve child avatar role-play, it is not necessarily the case.

Case History Box 3: GU's Relationships with Others

GU is a successful businessperson in Second Life, running a sim that has activities and shops. Through her business she makes many acquaintances and has become aware that, as in the physical world, being seen to be in a position of influence, as she is, can impact on how others interact with her. She is also aware that being such a person means that many people are aware of her behaviour within Second Life, which means that she cannot always be open in her thoughts and opinions as they may reflect negatively upon her. An important part of her Second Life is her relationship with her virtual partner with whom she fell in love. She has found that 'real life' emotions are involved in Second Life and, in her words, "… there is definitely a RL psychological effect from SL stuff".

3.4.4   Global Theme: 'The Second Life Self'

This global theme encapsulates participants' viewpoints on being a person in Second Life. The relationship between organising and basic themes, and explanation of the basic themes, is shown in Table 3.6.

A key aspect of their experience is their avatar. For participants this may be both a representation of who they are as a person, reflect some kind of ideal self that they wish to portray, represent a younger self, or even reflect a desire for exploring the potential to be non-human:

> Well this is how I see myself a couple of years ago. Since my operation I have gained weight so this is how [I] intend to be in the near future, more like my original self.(KM)

Some participants indicate how the avatar is seen as separate from them, expressing admiration or a need to protect them from bad experiences within SL. Some discuss how the avatar is a puppet or doll that can be manipulated by them, while others claimed avatars can have a life of their own:

> It's more like when I was little and playing with dolls. I would control the doll, the movement, how the doll acted, and the personality behind the doll were me, but I was not the doll. (LQ)

> The alt has developed its own life … things happen and you react to the situation, people you meet. (IC)

Participants reiterate that despite this, it is important to remember that there are real life people operating the avatars:

> They are from blood and bones behind that doll. (MD)

The opportunity for changing appearance and using alts reflects some participants' views that Second Life allows them to explore aspects of themselves,

Table 3.6 The relationship between organising and basic themes as associated with the global theme 'The Second Life Self'

Organising theme	Basic theme
Avatar and RL self relations	Alting
	Avatar and self disassociation
	Avatars as controllable
	Avatars as 'idealised me'
	Avatars as representations of the self
	Real people behind the avatar
	Relation with avatar as separate entity
	SL self as younger or non-human
Stability and instability of SL self	Consistency of self
	Different selves
	Contentment with self
	Evolution of self
	Exploration of self and identity
	Second lifestory
	SL as a 'try out' for self
	Transgender avatar
RL v SL self relationship	RL misfit
	SL as a reflection of RL self
	SL as 'me'
	SL as a version of RL self
	SL as the real 'inner me'
	SL as an extension of the RL self

including those more difficult to outwardly change in the physical world such as another gender:

> They have different personalities and also have the same as RL. I have several personalities I have found out since being here. (IC)

> She is also me. I didn't know what to make of that or what to do with her at first, but I realised slowly that she is transgender version of me. She's gay, she's more sub than [TC]. (TC)

Because of such explorations, most participants feel that their time in Second Life has a sense of history, and that over time they have evolved, both as a person in Second Life, and sometimes as a person in the physical world:

> She has become more understanding.... more open eyed to who people really are … and has become hard in some ways and softer in others. (RW)

Some participants feel that who they are in Second Life is almost the same as who they are in the physical world, a reflection or version of themselves, while others feel it enables them to extend themselves and add different aspects to their 'real life' personality and attributes. Many participants claim that the personality and characteristics they have in Second Life are the same as in the physical world, irrespective of how they appear or what avatar they use:

> … I am who I am. The avatar is more a lens than an aspect. (PS)

> **Case History Box 4**: LW's 'Second Life Selves'
>
> LW, a resident in Second Life since 2006, has seen his experience of being a
> person in Second Life change over time and has taken the opportunity to
> explore various aspects of himself. His representation of himself in the vir-
> tual world has evolved over time and his avatar has been adapted to circum-
> stance and the community he has been involved in (which include those
> involving such themes as steampunk, Star Trek and dragons) and he has also
> explored aspects of gender and spending a few hours a month as a female alt.
> However, while in the 35–50 age bracket in the actual world, he currently
> represents himself for the majority of the time as an older man and in his
> words, "[LW] is old on the SL timeline … maybe I'm playing at being old".
> He sees himself in Second Life as being quite similar to who he is in the
> actual world. However, he admits his behaviour and character traits change
> according to the type of avatar he has in ways that are different to that in
> the physical world. He views his male avatar as being "comfortable with
> being old" while he is not, and that he "looks dignified, intelligent, wise, a
> guy I'd want to have living next door".

However, some participants express that who they are in Second Life is the person
who they are inside, the person that few or no people see in the physical world:

There are great differences in behaviour, but in many ways, I feel that [EZ] much more
accurately portrays who I am inside. (EZ)

An example of a particular participant's experience is outlined in Case History
Box 4.

3.5   Relating the Findings to the Research Questions

The research questions were related and focused on the relationship between the
self in Second Life, compared to that experienced in the physical world. This section
provides a summary of the related findings. They suggest that the relation between
the experience of self in Second Life and that in the physical world is not straight
forward and there are a variety of experiences.

*To what extent are 'Second Life selves' the same or different to 'real life selves', in
terms of characteristics, capabilities, motivations and traits?*

The extent to which there is similarity or difference between the self in the physical
world and Second Life varies according to the individual. Some participants claim
to be the same person in both lives. Others indicate that that who they are in Second

Life is a representation of who they are 'inside', their 'real self' which they feel they cannot reveal in the physical world. Others suggest their self in Second Life is a version of themselves in the physical world, similar but with 'modification' (without disability for example).

To what extent are 'Second Life selves' independent of, or dependent on, the 'real life selves' operating the keyboard?

The use of an avatar as a mediator for being present in Second Life has a significant effect on how the self is experienced, irrespective of whether the user feels they are being the same person as they are in the physical world. The avatar is the person's representative in Second Life and, whether it represents them as they are in the physical world or some other form, indications are that people have an attachment to and relationship with their avatars. Some people find that avatars take on a life of their own, and begin to exhibit behaviours and personality traits not necessarily evidenced in the physical world. Even if this is not the case, people recognise that the avatar may be a separate entity from them and are able to make observations on how they appear and behave from an external perspective.

To what extent does a Second Life self emerge as a result of social processes within Second Life, separate from 'real life'?

Social processes within Second Life are fundamental to the overall experience of being within it, and to the experience of being a person in Second Life. From receiving or giving help in becoming fully participating residents, to all the interactions and relationships that occur and are formed with other people, there are many social influences on the self within Second Life. Such interactions help people explore different aspects of their personalities or offer opportunities for personal relationships and emotional experiences potentially difficult in the physical world. Nevertheless, such processes are not necessarily responsible for the emergence of a Second Life self that is separate from 'real life', for as described above, there is a complex relation between the experience of self in Second Life and that in the physical world.

3.6   Reviewing the Present Research

3.6.1   Relating This Case Study to the Theoretical Context

With respect to the self in virtual worlds, supporting the findings of Turkle (1995, 1996) and Boellstorff (2008), this research shows that virtual worlds such as Second Life offer the opportunity to explore aspects of the self and parallel lives not possible in the physical world, with benefits for 'real life'. However, the research also underlines how the experience of virtual worlds is a personal one, and can vary between people. Some explore parallel lives, others take the opportunity to be the person who they feel they are 'inside', while others see virtual worlds as somewhere to be the person they are in the physical world, but in a different environment with different experiences. Additionally, any benefits of virtual life go beyond exploration of the self in the physical world, but also include ways of coping with physical world difficulties, such as illness. This research also supports the observations offered by Taylor (2002), Yee and Bailenson (2007), Boellstorff (2008) and Ducheneaut et al. (2009) by confirming that the avatar is used to embody the self and can affect experience in Second Life. However, it also indicates that people may develop an attachment to them and also remind themselves that other avatars are representatives of other people. By exploring many facets of what it means to be a self in Second Life by understanding the 'insider perspective', the research discussed here is able to add texture to previous research.

Turning to theories of the self in general, traditional theories such as those of Mead (1962) and Goffman (1959) emphasise the role of social environment in the construction of the self, with an emphasis on the ability of the self to be reflexive. More contemporary postmodern theories suggest traditional theories over-emphasise the singularity and reflexivity of the self and that contemporary society saturates the self with myriad responsibilities and voices (Gergen 1991), with new communications technologies promoting a self that is "decentred, dispersed and multiplied" (Poster 1990, p. 6). However, the research outlined here indicates that while multiple selves may be facilitated through new technologies, those partici-pating in them are neither saturated, decentred nor non-reflexive. Residents of virtual worlds take the opportunity to reflect on themselves and actively explore different aspects of their personalities and capabilities and use this experience to bring benefit to being a person in the physical world. Rather than being saturated, they are taking new opportunities and enhancing their 'real' lives. Rather than being decentred, residents have a strong sense of self and its relation to who they are in the physical world, whether their self in the virtual world was their 'real life' self, a part of it, an addition to it, or a reflection of who they believed themselves to be 'inside'.

This indicates that experience of being a self in virtual worlds may have more in common with traditional views of self than contemporary theories suggest. Being resident in a virtual world gives unique opportunities to have a mind in a virtual rather than physical body, to actively take on new roles in situations not possible in the physical world, and to take an outsider viewpoint to observe one-self in those roles by witnessing events on the computer screen. These factors add a new twist to conventional theories, where being able to interact with a virtual body rather than a physical one, the notion of physically being able to take on the view of others, or the ability to take on new roles to the extent that is possible in virtual worlds, were never envisaged. Overall, this research indicates that contem-porary views of the self may overemphasise its potential for instability and neglect the potential for a self that is active and reflexive. As Adler and Adler (1999) sug-gest "[The] postmodernists' most pessimistic view of the demise of the self has not been borne out; rather, the core self has adapted to contemporary conditions and thrived" (p. 54).

3.6.2   Assessing the Present Research

Besides addressing the questions posed, this research also raises considerations related to the fact that it concerned an area relatively new to social psychology specifically and research as a whole. Although research has taken place in virtual worlds, there are still uncertainties with regard to appropriate methodologies. With respect to this particular study, a bespoke approach was developed that revealed that the experience of being a person in a virtual world is very varied and complex, demonstrated by the scale of the thematic network. This validates the taking of a qualitative approach that emphasises the 'insider viewpoint'. Despite this, in hindsight, its structure may have placed limitations on the findings. For example, the strategy meant that all data was textual, which may have restricted the nuance of insight it could offer. Going beyond individual interviews and conducting group discussions would have added greater depth to the understanding of how the self arises through social interactions within virtual worlds and 'in situ'. As Gaskell (2000) suggests, group discussions are more representative of what occurs in reality, since they encapsulate the processes occurring in society. Additionally, the scale of the findings suggests it would have been more beneficial to have a deeper focus on just one aspect of being a self in a virtual world. Nevertheless, the fact that so much varied experience was captured in any case indicates the potential for further fine textured analysis of the data or even develop the basis of a grounded theory.

There is also potential for further research in the area of understanding and conceptualising the self both in Second Life and other virtual worlds, and hence in contemporary society generally. Within Second Life, further research amongst residents who participate in specific activities, groups or cultures, such as role-play, 'age play',[13] or who take on non-human forms, for example, will offer further understanding of how the self is being expressed and constructed within virtual worlds. Meanwhile, replicating the research in other virtual worlds, which may have different raisons d'être, such as Worlds of Warcraft, may provide alternative findings.

The role of the researcher – While the months spent as a participant observer bore fruit in terms of being able to understand the insider viewpoint of participants and to quickly build rapport with them, it was not without its risks. Boellstorff (2008) indicates that the term participant observation is intentionally oxymoronic as one cannot fully participate and fully observe at the same time. Consequently, as a participant, in the time prior, during and subsequent to, the interview phase, the researcher became socialised and fully immersed within Second Life and experienced some of the issues with respect to self that were the purpose of the research. As an observer of others' experiences, the experience of being a participant informed the research questions and the interview topic guide.

---

[13] That is, having an avatar appearing of a different age to their 'real life' self and acting in accordance with that age.

Consequently this approach offered a fine-textured understanding and analysis of the issues at stake in being a self in contemporary society. As a participant in Second Life, the researcher observed and became aware of research taking an outsider viewpoint of the processes that occur within Second Life, in the areas of marketing, education and psychological therapy, for example. It can be argued that such approaches take risks: they risk underestimating the complexities of life in virtual worlds and misconstruing virtual worlds as places of utility, rather than in their own right. Places such as Second Life are not just tools to be exploited by the physical world but for many people they are a fundamental part of 'real life' itself.

3.7 Conclusion

This chapter has outlined research that offers both theoretical illuminations and methodological challenges. In terms of theoretical illuminations, it indicates that the postmodern theory of a self that is saturated by social influences, dissipated and decentred may be exaggerated. By using Second Life as a case study, the research has been able to take an 'insider viewpoint' to consider how CMC, and the phenomena of virtual worlds in particular, is influencing the sense of self that people in contemporary society are experiencing. While it indicates there are a wide variety of experiences among people who are residents of virtual worlds, it also shows that they are taking the opportunity to explore new aspects of themselves and even to improve their lives in the physical world. It indicates that traditional theories that emphasise the role of reflexivity in the emergence of self may continue to be relevant, albeit in modified form.

The methodological challenges are based on the relatively 'youthful' nature of research in virtual worlds. While research and theorising has begun, the time involved in the research process, the variety of disciplines and epistemological perspectives mean that insight is in its infancy. The research outlined here involved bespoke recruitment and executional procedures. As a result, in addition to 'current' insight being attained from the present research, it could be said that more expertise in the area of research in virtual worlds has been gained.

References

Adler, P.A., Adler, P.: Transience and the postmodern self: the geographical mobility of resort workers. Sociol. Q. **40**(1), 31–58 (1999)

Agger, B.: The Virtual Self: A Contemporary Sociology. Wiley-Blackwell, Malden (2003)

Attride-Stirling, J.: Thematic networks: an analytic tool for qualitative research. Qual. Res. **1**(3), 385–405 (2001)

Barnes, S.: Cyberspace: creating paradoxes for the ecology of the self. In: Strate, L., Jacobson, R., Gibson, S.B. (eds.) Communication and Cyberspace: Social Interaction in and Electronic Environment, 2nd edn, pp. 229–253. Hampton, Cresskill (2003)

Baym, N.K.: Interpersonal life online. In: Lievrouw, L.A., Livingstone, S. (eds.) The Handbook of New Media: Updated, Student edn, pp. 35–54. Sage, London (2006)

Berger, P., Luckmann, T.: The Social Construction of Reality: A Treatise in the Sociology of Knowledge. Penguin, London (1966)

Boellstorff, T.: Coming of Age in Second Life: An Anthropologist Explores the Virtually Human. Princeton University Press, Princeton (2008)

Bolter, J.D.: Virtual reality and the redefinition of self. In: Strate, L., Jacobson, R., Gibson, S.B. (eds.) Communication and Cyberspace: Social Interaction in and Electronic Environment, 2nd edn, pp. 123–137. Hampton, Cresskill (2003)

Braun, V., Clarke, V.: Using thematic analysis in psychology. Qual. Res. Psychol. 3, 77–101 (2006)

Cerulo, K.: Identity construction: new issues, new directions. Ann. Rev. Sociol. 23, 385–409 (1997)

Ducheneaut, N., Wen, M., Yee, N., Wadley, G.: Body and mind: a study of avatar personalisation in three virtual worlds. In: Proceedings of the 27th International Conference on Human Factors in Computing Systems, pp. 1151–1160. Association for Computing Machinery, New York (2009)

Elliot, A.: Concepts of the Self. Polity, Cambridge (2001)

Flick, U.: An Introduction to Qualitative Research, 4th edn. Sage, London (2009)

Gaskell, G.: Individual and group interviewing. In: Bauer, M.W., Gaskell, G. (eds.) Qualitative Researching with Text, Image and Sound, pp. 38–56. Sage, London (2000)

Geertz, C.: Local Knowledge: Further Essays in Interpretive Anthropology, 3rd edn. Basic Books, New York (2000)

Gergen, K.J.: The Saturated Self: Dilemmas of Identity in Contemporary Life. HarperCollins, New York (1991)

Goffman, E.: The Presentation of the Self in Everyday Life. Penguin, Harmondsworth (1959)

Gorini, A., Gaggioli, A., Vigna, C., Riva, G.: A second life for e-health; prospects for the use of 3-D virtual worlds in clinical psychology. J. Med. Internet Res. 10(3), e21 (2008)

Mead, G.H.: The Social Psychology of George Herbert Mead. University of Chicago Press, Chicago (1956)

Mead, G.H.: Mind, Self and Society. University of Chicago Press, Chicago (1962)

Papacharissi, Z.: The presentation of self in virtual life: characteristics of personal home page. Journalism Mass Commun. Q. 79(3), 643–660 (2002)

Poster, M.: The Mode of Information. Polity, Cambridge (1990)

Taylor, T.L.: Living digitally: embodiment in virtual worlds. In: Schroeder, R. (ed.) The Social Life of Avatars: Presence and Interaction in Shared Virtual Environments. Springer, London (2002)

Turkle, S.: Life on the Screen: Identity in the Age of the Internet. Simon & Schuster, New York (1995)

Turkle, S.: Parallel lives: working on identity in virtual space. In: Grodin, D., Lindolf, T.R. (eds.) Constructing the Self in a Mediated World, pp. 156–175. Sage, London (1996)

Turkle, S.: The Second Self: Computers and the Human Spirit, Twentieth Anniversary edn. The MIT Press, Cambridge (2005)

Virtual world registered accounts breakthrough 1bn. Retrieved 22 Oct 2010 from. http://www.kzero.co.uk/blog/?p=4448

Yee, N., Bailenson, J.: The proteus effect: the effect of transformed self-representation on behavior. Hum. Commun. Res. 33, 271–290 (2007)

Chapter 4
Liminal Phases of Avatar Identity Formation in Virtual World Communities

Nicola Marae Martínez

Abstract This chapter examines the early phases of entrance into virtual worlds as a "newbie" avatar within the framework of van Gennep and Turner's liminal phases of neophyte initiation rituals. This analysis of the avatar in liminal states examines how, even in seemingly anarchistic virtual worlds such as Second Life™, social norms and sanctions emerge to influence avatar identity formation and persistence. Observations on avatar identity development in liminal phases are drawn from the author's research studies of avatars becoming initiated into dragonhood conducted on the Isle of Wyrms in Second Life from 2007 to 2009. Theoretical underpinnings of the chapter are illustrated using case studies highlighting key liminal phases of avatar development.

4.1 Introduction

This chapter focuses on the early phases of entrance into virtual worlds as a "newbie" avatar within the framework of van Gennep and Turner's liminal phases of neophyte initiation rituals (van Gennep 1960; Turner 1974). This analysis of the avatar in liminal states examines how, even in seemingly anarchistic virtual worlds such as Second Life, social norms and sanctions emerge to influence avatar identity formation and persistence. The theoretical underpinnings of the chapter will be illustrated using case studies highlighting key liminal phases of avatar development within the context of van Gennep and Turner's liminal stages and Habermas' theory of symbolic interaction (1971).

Primary participant observation research for this study had a strong focus on older, well established fantasy communities of Second Life. The Isle of Wyrms (a dragon realm), the Elf Circle lands, and Gorean city states adhere to various

N.M. Martínez (✉)
SUNY Empire State College, Saratoga Springs, NY, USA
e-mail: nicola.martinez@esc.edu

A. Peachey and M. Childs (eds.), *Reinventing Ourselves: Contemporary Concepts of Identity in Virtual Worlds*, Springer Series in Immersive Environments,
DOI 10.1007/978-0-85729-361-9_4, © Springer-Verlag London Limited 2011

forms of modified medieval fantasy.[1] These communities share the following characteristics: a cohesive citizenry; a strict covenant; longevity in Second Life; and perhaps most importantly, they attract residents in search of cultured community with a common set of values and aesthetic principles. The methodology section of this chapter (4.2) includes a detailed description and analysis of the Isle of Wyrms citizenry and steps leading up to avatar identity transformation into adult dragons.

The author has been a resident of Second Life since May 2006, active in research, education, and community analysis. I created three research avatars for the purpose of exploring liminal phases of avatar identity development from a phenomenological perspective. Section 4.3 on Research Avatars provides a description of the avatar identity development of these embodiments. The primary research avatar used for the study is Ragitake Takakura, born in May, 2006, a participant in immersive education efforts and a dragon guardian on the Isle of Wyrms, a leading fantasy community. Section 4.6 provides the first case study of Ragitake Takakura as an avatar in various stages of liminal identity development, followed by a section on postliminal stages (4.7) that includes Habermas' Theory of Symbolic Interaction (1971). Section 4.8 presents the case study of the second avatar, Vick Dragonash, created to explore fantasy role-play communities within a male embodiment. Section 4.9 examines the experience of the third avatar, Atea Aeon, created to experience the liminal path of an avatar designed without design, to see what shape she would take given freedom to self-actualise as an avatar. Atea Aeon conducted secondary research in BDSM territory,[2] by attending a series of lectures on the Isle of Shadows and observing avatar interactions in open, broadly visited BDSM communities in Second Life such as Bondage Ranch.

The avatar Ragitake Takakura most resembles the physical characteristics of the author, a petite blonde female with blue eyes. In the early stages of Ragitake's development, I took great pains to create an avatar that realistically represented who I am in the physical world. In the beginning, Ragitake was my "I" in the avatar. I closely identified with Ragitake as an extension of myself. However, perhaps due to the research nature of my work with Ragitake, as I created new avatars to analyse various aspects of "being in the world", each of them became less of an "I" and more of a "him or her" as they developed more as "characters", to investigate research elements, than "self" to represent me as Nicola to residents of the virtual world. Ragitake remains the avatar most closely aligned with my identity in the physical world. I continue to consider the other avatar embodiments as instrumental persona with specific tasks and roles within the scope of the study. I have therefore chosen to present each of the avatars in this study in the third person "him, her or they",

---

[1]Gorean city states are based on a series of science fiction fantasy novels by John Norman, in which a majority of the women are slaves serving male masters. Some Gorean city states are purported to capture female visitors in order to enslave them. However, during the period of this study, the author only observed voluntary slaves in consensual role play within the Gor storyline. Most Gorean cities are exceptionally well designed by Second Life standards, with a formal community organisational structure. For more about Gor in SL, see Sixma (2009).

[2]Bondage and Discipline (BD), Dominance and Submission (DS), Sadism and Masochism (SM).

rather than the accepted convention of using the "I" Avatar, as in Meadows work on the topic (2007). This also reflects the interesting phenomenon that each of these avatars seemed to embody specific characteristics unique to that particular embodiment – whether the characteristics be physical (red hair rather than blonde for Atea and Vick, different types of dress than Ragitake), or attitudinal (Atea displayed a disinterest in joining communities and Vick developed an interest in architecture and building). As the "avatar driver", I had previously had no strong interest, for example, in either architectural building prior to Vick, who built Cathedrals and Castles, or in skin creation and avatar artistry, which became a skill I acquired within the Atea embodiment that neither Ragitake nor Vick had previously possessed.

4.2 Methodology: The Isle of Wyrms

This chapter is drawn from the author's larger work on the relationship between taboo, power, and transgression and its impact on avatar autonomy and agency in the artificial lifeworld (Martinez 2011). The larger work draws from anthropological studies, media philosophy, a phenomenological and ontological analysis of Heidegger's Dasein, as avatar, emergent literature in virtual worlds studies, and participant observation as a resident of Second Life. In addition, observations on avatar identity development in liminal phases are drawn from the author's research studies of avatars becoming initiated into dragonhood conducted on the Isle of Wyrms in Second Life from 2007 to 2009 (Martinez et al. 2007; Martinez 2008a, b).

My findings on the role of social interaction and community restraints in the defining of avatar identity while moving the avatar from a preliminal to post liminal state is based on longitudinal observation of Isle of Wyrms citizens as they passed through various stages of identity development in becoming fully-fledged dragons, and community engagement as official citizens of the Isle. Becoming dragon on the Isle of Wyrms is a formal and complex process, in which the avatar has clearly selected to embrace a new identity by divesting his or herself of the former identity and participating in a formal dragon hatching ceremony. During the period of study, adult dragons were not available by regular purchase. Dragons (wyrms) were only released four times yearly, at solstices and equinoxes, in a formal ceremony. Second Life residents desiring to become dragons participated in a limited drawing during which only a selected few would become eligible to join the Council of Wyrms, and carry the avatar and title of dragon. Throughout the study, Ragitake Takakura assisted hundreds of potential initiates in the important process of embracing a new avatar identity. I witnessed the transformation of these avatars from residents in various forms of preliminal states to fully post-liminal avatars initiated into dragonhood, and mentored to become contributing members of the community. During this period I had access to inworld and external resources for the Isle, citizen meetings, and meetings of the governance bodies of the Isle (High Council; Isle of Wyrms Guardians). The Isle of Wyrms citizenry and councils counted approximately 2,500 members throughout the period of the study.

Many of these members were active in community festivals and events throughout the period of the study, and a number of them continue to have an active presence in the Isle of Wyrms in 2010.

The Isle of Wyrms Citizenry is founded upon a complex governance structure and volunteer management system to greet, guide and mentor new visitors to the isle as potential citizens. This period of research included participatory observation of the neighboring Elf Circle community activities and approaches, which utilises a similar volunteer management system and high council governing structure. As researcher and community participant, I self-disclosed my role and nature of my research to the Isle of Wyrms leadership, and shared results with the community. Key members of the community know my physical world identity, and several Isle leaders have collaborated with me on academic projects in Second Life (having also disclosed their physical identities). In the course of the study, however, I did not disclose details of my research to Second Life residents at large. Rather, my profile contained a note that I was active in Second Life research, and I provided details to any avatar who asked. In respect for the privacy of community members and avatars observed during the study, I did not collect avatar-specific information on dragon aspirants, though avatar names and dragon type are reported and collected in the Isle of Wyrms databases, to which I contributed.

The Isle of Wyrms leadership has carefully established practices, processes and events that nurture an international citizen participation that keeps visitors engaged and enthused. They have an organised volunteer development programme in which citizens are recruited and developed as volunteers, guides, mentors and ambassadors to mentor their peers and perform community outreach. In addition, they present all educational and informational materials in a wide range of media: an updated wiki; active forum; note cards; holograms; virtual books; an immersive space; and one-to-one live assistance. The community leadership makes a concerted effort to recruit guides from among the native speakers of nine language groups, including Japanese.

The Isle of Wyrms Citizen Group includes the following roles that are only attainable though sustained volunteerism and mentorship by a more advanced citizen staff member: guest (trial citizenship), citizen (full citizenship), volunteer (citizen helper, non staff), guide (citizen helper, first level staff), mentor (citizen leader, chosen from the guide pool), advocate (a bridge between citizens and high council members), mayor (elected by citizens from among the citizens), and ambassador (which is not a citizen group role but a bridge to the higher councils and a citizen representative at large). The community has a number of communication channels, both in world and on the World Wide Web. These include the Isle of Wyrms Help Forum, with open membership, which provides 24-h live assistance drawing from international citizenry. Any active community member may assist, whether or not they are part of the official volunteer staff. Membership in the Isle of Wyrms Citizen's Group is closed. Aspirants must request an invitation from a staff member ranking at guide or above. The various avatar councils are accessible by invitation only, after authentication of their purchased Isle of Wyrms avatar by a high ranking staff member, and by a formal registration process. The Isle of Wyrms Conference

Hall is the staff communications channel, which includes all staff roles from guides to guardians. This channel provides staff with immediate access to each other and to the highest levels of leadership, and is most active during periods preceding and during the hatching ceremonies. During the research period hundreds of aspirants gathered on the Isle to participate in the initiation rituals during these times, joined by citizen volunteers to assist them in the process.The volunteer citizen staff is recruited from among citizens and citizen volunteers, mentored by a mentor, and attend regular staff meetings. They are provided with "staff tools" and information, attend required training, and managed by the community manager from amongst the guardian staff. Gradually given increased responsibilities as trust is built, aspirants must prove themselves capable of managing a project or event in order to be promoted to the rank of mentor. Regular promotions at every level are used as motivators for rise in rank, along with public staff recognition and staff appreciation parties. A staff forum entry matches aptitudes and interests to potential assignments, all on a volunteer basis. The community uses the following types of inworld communications:

- live one-to-one assistance;
- inworld staffing of the Cathedral and the Sandbox, the two places new visitors are most likely to visit;
- a 24 h Live Help Forum;
- multilingual note cards;
- posters that give out information kits;
- the Herald, a monthly newspaper.

Web based information resources include the Isle of Wyrms Wiki,[3] and the Isle of Wyrms Forums, with public, open access area as well as closed, staff only section for project management, membership registration, and issue resolution.[4]

Throughout the research period of participant observation within the Isle of Wyrms community, Ragitake Takakura served in the following citizen helper roles: volunteer, guide, mentor, ambassador, guardian, and elder guardian. These roles included the following duties: greet newcomers and introduce them to the community in the process of becoming dragon; assist visitors with the selection of a dragon avatar that would best reflect the identity of their choice; assist residents in the transformation process from one avatar form to a full bipedal or quadruped dragon form; invite and initiate newcomers into the Isle of Wyrms and citizen group, including the communication of community rules and regulations along with sanctions for transgression. In addition, at the mentor level and beyond I was responsible for verifying the authenticity of an avatar prior to initiating them into community council groups, and at the guardian level, participating in a formal honour guard to receive new adult dragons into the community.

---

[3] http://www.daryth.com/draconica/index.php/Main_Page
[4] http://www.daryth.com/council/index.php

4.3   Research Avatars

In addition to participant observation on Isle of Wyrms, in which I had the opportunity to witness avatar identity development, liminal phases, and social interaction among Second Life residents choosing to embrace a dragon identity, I present case studies of cases of identity development in my own avatars. I recognise that this approach is limited in scope in analysing a combination of liminal stages of identity development and the role of social interaction and community constraint on avatar identity. My analysis of the experiences of my primary avatar and alts is based on the larger phenomenological study of the avatar and artificial lifeworlds using Heidegger's method and placing the avatar as Dasein in the virtual world. My reflection on the liminal phases of the development of these avatars is only a slice within a much larger work that also examines avatar autonomy, taboo, transgression, and power dynamics in artificial lifeworlds (Martinez 2011).

The biggest challenges in presenting the case studies, if I present each avatar of mine as a separate individual, are that the level of self-awareness of the avatars varied greatly, and that the first person analysis may or may not be representative of a larger avatar experience. Ragitake, my first avatar and primary identity in Second Life, the one that most resembles me in the physical world, did not begin the period of study until after she had spent time acclimatising herself to the New World and acquiring the necessary skills to transact successfully in Second Life. The avatar Vick Dragonash, however, started in Second Life with all of Ragitake's knowledge, and fully cognizant of his role in conducting participant observation research in Gorean cities. Atea Aeon possessed the skill sets and knowledge acquired by both Vick and Ragitake, but entered Second Life as a blank slate, with the intention of resisting community membership and heightened social interaction throughout the period of study, in order to analyse identity definition in the absence of community constraints. A next step in this research would be to interview avatars on parallel paths in the Isle of Wyrms and related communities and conduct a comparative analysis of the avatar experience. My observations and conversations with other alts on the Isles would suggest that their paths were parallel – two of them reported similar experiences of an alt developing separate interests, identity, and friends from the primary avatar, and becoming creators, in a similar manner to the Atea embodiment reported below.

4.4   The Avatar as Liminal Being

The avatar enters the virtual world as a liminal being, analogous to Turner's neophyte in a state "betwixt or between". The neophyte is born into a world of possibility. Unbound by earthly physics, given flight as an inherent ability, free to transport anywhere in the worlds, Second Life affords the avatar a chance to create a new identity. Mary Douglas (1966) has argued that there is power in ambiguous states, in places where boundaries have not yet been set at the margins of power and places; in the absence of sacred spaces, or the as yet to be sacred, the to be determined. The virtual world of Second Life in its early predefined stages, and the unformed state of the newly born avatar both reside within this state of ambiguity, in potentiality-for-power.

At the turn of the twentieth Century, Arnold Van Gennep (1960) theorised rites of passage across the human lifespan, with particular attention paid to key transitional phases and rites associated with territorial passages and the crossing of thresholds. Van Gennep states:

> Territorial passages can provide a framework for the discussion of rites of passage which follows.... it is this magical-religious aspect of crossing frontiers and that interests us (p. 15).

Van Gennep describes neutral territories, those accommodating in between states, as follows:

> Because of the pivoting of sacredness, the territories on either side of the neutral zone are sacred in relation to whoever is in the zone, but the zone, in turn, is sacred for the inhabitants of the adjacent territories. Whoever passes from one to the other finds himself physically and magico – religiously in a special situation for certain length of time: he wavers in between two worlds. It is a situation which I have designated a transition, and one of the sole purposes of this book is to demonstrate that this symbolic and spatial area of transition may be found in more or less pronounced form in all the ceremonies which accompany the passage from one social and magical – religious position to another (p. 12).

If we consider the passage from the "physical world" into the "virtual world" to be territorial, then these territorial crossings encompass the following rites and stages:

1. The rites of separation from a previous world: *preliminal rites*
2. Those executed during the transitional stage: *liminal, or threshold rites*
3. Ceremonies of incorporation into the new world: *postliminal rites.* (van Gennep 1960, p. 21)

4.4.1 Preliminal Rites

In the rites of separation from a previous world, the human agent must first pass a series of initiative activities in the previous world. In current virtual worlds this means going through an online registration and verification process to acquire an account; the challenging task of choosing a name; and selecting a starter avatar. During the period of this study, limited selections of last names were provided at any given time. The avatar's appearance, profile and gender could change at any time, but the name remained permanently with the avatar and could not be changed unless a new account was created. Once the naming is complete, the agent leaves the physical world behind, and, stripped of identifying factors such as name, gender, appearance, enters the virtual world as a liminal being, in between worlds, no longer belonging to the physical world but not yet a true "resident" of the new world.

The crossing of the threshold begins when the avatar enters the virtual world. The avatar, divested of any previous identity, is free to discover a world anew and reinvent herself as she materialises as a new being. As a liminal, newly born being, the avatar has an opportunity to explore different dimensions of being in the world.

4.4.2   Liminal Rites

Upon arrival into the virtual world, the initiate enters a transitional space in which to receive and prepare a preliminary identity while learning the basic operational rules of the new environment. For most virtual worlds, this involves the receipt of a "starter avatar" from a selection of limited options. Most new avatars spend a considerable amount of their early orientation period "sorting out" the physical characteristics of their virtual body. This is however, only one aspect of avatar identity. Avatar identity in virtual worlds encompasses characteristics within the following categories:

Physical characteristics. This includes species, such as: human, hybrid, furry, feral, bipedal, quadruped, and mythological. The avatar boundary between animal and human, human and machine, and animal – machine has already been obliterated in Second Life. There, dragonkin (avatars of draconic descent or with an affinity for dragons), therians (avatars with a strong affinity and self-association with a particular animal), otherkin (avatars with a strong affinity and self-association with non-human elements and beings, other than animal, often mythological), anthropomorphic avatars blending animal features with human characteristics, hybrid creatures, robots, mesh and cyborgs exist side by side with contemporary human figures. The avatar no longer expresses itself in simply human terms; it stretches the boundaries of identity to embrace a wide range of embodiments, including animal, machine, and mythical variants on being. Most furry avatars are anthropomorphic in design (bipedal and humanoid) as opposed to feral (quadruped with fully animalistic features). Subgroups within the furry community identify with fursona that are cartoon like in nature; others embrace furry fandom related to Anime and wear anime type animal inspired avatars.[5] Some furs wear realistic avatars, or choose to represent themselves as mythological creatures such as dragons, gryphons, or a phoenix. Tinies include a subgroup of furs who generally refrain from mature and adult activities, and are often completely separate from general furry culture and communities.[6] Many tinies choose to engage in childlike or silly behaviours, generally within PG standards and not related to formal role-play. Physical characteristics of humans and human hybrids are generally subdivided into the following elements: skin, shape, eyes, hair, outfits and accessories. Mythological hybrids generally include

---

[5]Furry + persona. A furry's main character or identity. See http://furry.wikia.com/wiki/Fursona for more details on this topic.

[6]Tiny avatars, usually in the form of small animals, teddy bears, or robots. For more information about the tiny community in Second Life, see: http://raglanshire.com/.

additional core elements such as wings, horns, and tail. Physical characteristic of furries and ferals, whether bipedal or quadruped, include all of the above with the addition of attached objects created in the shape of animal elements such as claws, movable jaw, and animalistic limbs.

1. **Movement characteristics.** The animation of avatars and objects in Second Life very much influences the projection of their appearance. In the case of avatars, newbies are easily identified by the awkward default movement sequence they receive at first log in. Sophisticated avatars select animation overriders that project the types of movement sequence (in walking, flying, standing and sitting) that best fit their chosen identity. Furry and feral avatars generally come fitted with appropriate animations. This is rarely the case for human and hybrid avatars such as fae and elves.
2. **Profile.** In alignment with web 2.0 and social media conventions, current virtual worlds include a written avatar profile, along with space for a photograph, which allows the owners of avatars to present themselves in the world. The profile includes a listing of group memberships, an interests page (in which skills and language may be selected), a link to a web page, picks (which allows an avatar to either share favorite locations in the virtual world, or add commentary on friends, philosophy, role-play character definition, and other identity details). The avatar may also reveal aspects of his or her physical life in a related profile section.
3. **Group Membership.** Group membership is used by sophisticated virtual worlds users to assess the identity of an avatar. Virtual worlds group options in Second Life and similar grids (such as Inworldz) include a wide range of interests.
4. **Conversation Style.** Though at first glance the identity of an avatar is interpreted by impressions from physical characteristics, conversational style is perhaps more telling of avatar identity in itself. The use of complex language, correct grammar, and full sentences, for example, serve to identify a certain avatar type. This type is generally quite different from a resident who communicates in abbreviated text speech. Second Life communities generally consist of group members with similar communication styles. For example, education related groups tend towards a more academic form of communication; high fantasy groups (such as the Elf Circle in Second Life) generally use formal speech conventions in modified Medieval fantasy style; technical groups tend to include a wide range of technical jargon, and so on.

4.5 The Avatar Arrives in the Artificial Life World

In his work *Media Aesthetics in Europe*, media philosopher Wolfgang Schirmacher described four rules of an artificial lifeworld, including the self as the focal point as the first rule. For Schirmacher,

The Self of media is an activity, the process of constantly receiving patterns, destructuring and reconstructuring unities, an "unending struggle with the world"...

This creative Self is an elusive self interrupting the conventions of dominant culture by twisting it around. (Schirmacher 1991, para 14–15).

For the avatar, the care of the self is the primary consideration when entering the new world. A newly born avatar generally begins his journey in the virtual world in pursuit of the right look: whether human, hybrid, furry or scaly, the neophyte pursues avenues to either purchase or create the right hair, skin, shape, eyes, and clothing to project the sense of self, or personhood. A typical scene at the initial arrival point in virtual worlds is one in which arms outstretched, riveted in place, newborn avatars focus on setting parameters for their appearance. Once the avatar has created the desired look, then s/he begins to explore, may or may not purchase or rent land, create a home, start a business, and join communities.

In many ways this care of the self is not just an extension of the avatar, but rather a caring that reflects back to the human being driving the avatar. Avatars often reflect that they were quite taken aback by the vulnerability they feel in Second Life, and that the irony of this Second Life is that, while masked, they feel able to unmask their true selves to the world in ways that are less restricted and more accessible than in the "real world"(Boellstorff 2008).

4.5.1   The Nascent Human Being in the Aesthetic Dimension

In *Eco-Sophia: the Artist of Life*, Schirmacher (1989) describes the journey of the nascent human being in the aesthetic dimension:

> Eco-Sophia takes seriously precisely that which is concealed, the nascent human being, still, and perhaps always, in concealedness. Moments of true humanness burst forth suddenly, briefly. This "flashing" (Aufblitzen) in the aesthetic experience as in the ethical process of fulfilling cannot be accommodated in a one-dimensional determination, in a definition of the human being that is, which includes only the obvious about us or what has been cleverly raised to a conscious level (p. 133)

The nascent human being, concealed behind an avatar, has perhaps more access to three-dimensional determination in a 3D virtual world than can be afforded in most physical world environments. Masked and yet unmasked, the avatar is free to be and to become the being of her choosing; more often than not revealing far more of that which is concealed that she intended. In many ways the early phases of being a newbie in Second Life are similar to Victor Turner's neophyte. Turner expanded on Van Gennep's work on liminality, and then continued to develop his ideas on liminality in several subsequent writings.

In the following passage, Turner elaborates on van Gennep's first two stages of separation and liminal phase:

> The first phase, separation, comprises symbolic behaviour signifying the detachment of the individual or the group from either an earlier fixed point in the social structure or from an established set of cultural conditions (a "state"). During the intervening liminal period, the state of the ritual subject (the "passenger," or "liminal,") becomes ambiguous, neither here nor there, betwixt and between all fixed points of classification; he passes through a symbolic domain that has few or none of the attributes of his past or coming state (Turner 1974, p. 232).

How long does this state of grace, the liminal state, last? How much time transpires before the avatar's lifeworld begins to take shape, and before the possibility for power becomes either diminished or defined? At what point does the transitional state transform into a defined identity? The following case studies describe the liminal phases of 3 S Life avatars in habited by the author at various stages of the study.

4.6 First Research Avatar: Ragitake Takakura

The first and primary Second Life research avatar for this study, Ragitake Takakura, enjoyed a much longer liminal state than my second and third avatars. Entering the new world on March 15, 2006, Ragitake had an extended learning curve, and spent the first months visiting orientation islands and welcome areas for newbies; taking Second Life classes inworld; learning to navigate and transact in the world, and customising avatar appearance. She entered the world as a thoroughly post modern Ragitake, and, like many other avatars before her, was enraptured with the many aspects of Second Life that replicated physical life experiences while enhancing them with Second Life capabilities (Fig. 4.1).

For the first several months of "non-belonging", Ragitake wandered across the virtual worlds in a state of being betwixt and between, gradually acquiring enough knowledge and skill to be competent in the world, yet still unsettled in both identity and place, going through multiple levels of changes to her avatar appearance, and temporary rentals in various communities. Ragitake became fully, "a resident" of the

Fig. 4.1 Ragitake Takakura

virtual world when she purchased a Second Life land parcel and thus took ownership of a designated space. This is also when the boundaries between Second Life and Real Life began to blur, and how Ragitake Takakura's identity in Second Life began to take form. Blurring of boundaries included the arrival in Second Life of several colleagues, friends and family members, who came to visit Ragitake on her island home. It also occurred with the discovery that while living on the tropi-cal island, her nearest Island neighbour was a native Hawaiian. I had chosen the tropical island because it reminded me of my childhood home on the island of Tahiti, and I had created an authentic looking Tahitian beach home and garden for Ragitake's home. Ragitake had begun to experiment with non-human avatars in this phase, and the reaction of physical world associates and island neighbours reminded me of the importance of fixed, reliable identity to the comfort levels of newcomers to the virtual world as well as residents of the wholly human domains in Second Life.

Integration into a given community, or society as a whole, fits the final stage of territorial and transitional passage described by Van Gennep and Turner:

> In the third phase the passage is consummated and the ritual subject, the neophyte or ini-tiand reenters the social structure, often, but not always at a higher status level. Ritual deg-radation occurs as well as elevation (Turner 1974, p. 232).

This entrance into the final phase was only the beginning for Ragitake Takakura. After several months of being thoroughly human and fully millennial, she ventured out in search of community outside of the island neighbourhood. This journey led the avatar Ragitake to the elven lands, recognised in Second Life for an emphasis on the aesthetic experience and a cultivated approach to community and communications. Here she discovered the sophisticated fantasy communities at the heart of Second Life, along with furry and other alternative communities, with residents who had moved into Second Life from MUCKS, MOOS, MUDS, MMORPGS, and MUVES.

The Second Life fantasy continent is comprised of the elven lands, mer cities, dragon worlds and fae communities. The fantasy sims form a neighbourly coalition sharing PG standards and offering a safe haven in Second Life for residents seeking an aesthetic experience; friendly and open communities; and cultured conversations. The residents of the fantasy continent are recognised in Second Life for their creativ-ity, high skill in building and scripting, and friendliness to newcomers.[7] Prominent members of the Second Life higher education community are also members of the dragon worlds, the elven community, or both. The fantasy community celebrates ceremonies and ritual in a heightened manner, honouring the cycles of the physical world while creating a new existence n the virtual world. Every summer, Elf Circle member and Second Life educator Lyr Lobo hosts a mystical festival to raise funds for cancer research. Lyr Lobo is the avatar of Dr. Cynthia Calongne, a pro-fessor of gaming design, software engineering and robotics at Colorado Technical University. This is where Ragitake encountered the dragon ambassador Skylarian Isachenko, an emissary from the Isle of Wyrms – the dragon worlds of Second Life.

---

[7] See my earlier comments on community organisation, volunteer staff ranks, and avatar orienta-tion for newcomers to the Isle of Wyrms.

Skylarian presented Ragitake with the Isle of Wyrms Herald (an inworld newspaper); a guidebook to becoming dragon; and a series of notes on joining the Isle of Wyrms community. Shortly thereafter, Ragitake Takakura became a dragon during a ritual hatching ceremony.

During the period of this study Isle of Wyrms dragon artist Daryth Kennedy only released her full adult dragons for sale during hatching rituals at solstices and equinoxes, and in limited numbers released per species. This created a scarcity of full dragons and seats on the Council of Wyrms, making both dragon ownership and council membership coveted privileges. Maintaining exclusive membership in councils and citizen groups provided the Isle of Wyrms leadership with ongoing authority over both neophyte and older dragon avatars, furthering the societal and community role in exerting influence over avatar identity formation within a mandated set of rules, principles, and covenants.

4.7 Postliminal Rites – The Defining Moment of Avatar Identity

This was the defining moment of the avatar identity, and one in which Ragitake's liminal state ended. Ragitake quickly rose in ranks among the dragon volunteers and citizenry – before long, inducted into the very select High Council of the Isle of Wyrms, the leaders of the land, and shortly after that into an even smaller select group, the Isle of Wyrms Guardians. Ragitake possessed political power with a position on the high council and as a guardian – power accompanied by hefty responsibility as citizens lobbied for their projects, ideas, or needs to be met; and as fellow leaders from other communities requested Ragitake's involvement in a number of initiatives. The large, quadruped adult dragon guardian Ragitake Takakura has been granted many of the access control powers to the Isle of Wyrms lands given with the land and group tools in Second Life: Ragitake may ban access to land, eject griefers and troublemakers, set media streams, set teleporting points and build anywhere on the lands – a privilege only accorded to guardians. In addition, she may invite and promote citizens and induct young dragons into the Isle Councils, including the coveted Council of Wyrms.

4.7.1 Habermas' Theory of Symbolic Interaction

With these powers, however, comes a fixing of identity that both enables and constraints the avatar. Bound by the covenant and conventions of the community, Ragitake is expected to adhere to a specific set of behaviours and present a fixed, reliable, and recognisable identity. She is expected to fulfil certain duties and obligations to the community; communicate within a defined set of norms; and engage in symbolic interaction.

Habermas' theory of symbolic interaction (1971) is particularly relevant to an analysis of social interaction and community development in Second Life. Habermas discusses social norms forced through sanctions and consensual norms in his work on communicative action and symbolic interaction:

> By "interaction," on the other hand, I understand *communicative action*, symbolic interaction. It has governed by binding *consensual norms*, which define reciprocal expectations about behaviour and which must be understood and recognized by at least two acting subjects. Social norms are enforced through sanctions,... the validity of social norms is grounded only in the intersubjectivity of the mutual understanding of intentions and secured by the general recognition of obligations. Violation of a role has a different consequence according to type. *Incompetent* behaviour, which violates about technical rules or strategies, is condemned per se to failure the lack of success; the "punishment" is built, so to speak, into its rebuff by reality. *Deviant* behaviour, which violates consensual norms, provokes sanctions that are connected with the roles only externally, that is by convention (Habermas 1971, p. 72).

The avatar joins Second Life communities at will, and yet, once she joins a community, her freedom become restricted within the bounds of the consensual social norms. Some communities have very few regulations or policies, and therefore little opportunity for transgression. The majority of successful communities in Second Life are, however, governed by covenants – reflecting consensual norms – the terms of which a resident must agree in order to be accepted, and remain, within the community. Social sanctions are applied to those who violate the covenant, from simple rebuke, to warnings, then banishment. By successful, I mean those that:

1. Maintain a relatively stable yet growing community.
2. Have a reputation in Second Life for being a successful community, through official Linden publications, Second Life press, and blogs related to Second Life.
3. Have a critical mass of resident members, proportionate to their overall membership, that have been in Second Life for longer than 1 year and members of the community for at least 6 months.

Most organised Second Life communities have officers who serve in a security or peacekeeping function. They generally enforce the community regulations and apply punitive measures if deemed appropriate. However, more often than not regular citizens express outrage at an overt rule violation, and are prompt to both chastise the offender and request sanctions from a guardian when transgress occurs (even when the guardians may have decided not to intervene in the case of a minor infraction). This is a frequent occurrence within the Isle of Wyrms, which was a PG community during the period of this study. Visitors and fellow citizens alike are immediately chastised by Isle of Wyrms community members if they use profanity, discuss adult themes, or otherwise violate the PG rules. Ragitake Takakura, Isle of Wyrms guardian, once spent a good part of a guardian meeting calming the outrage of citizens after another citizen accidentally used the group IM to make an explicit comment. It was the citizens who called out for immediate sanctions and who serve to enforce the community consensual norms on a far broader scale than the handful of Isle guardians.

Table 4.1 Habermas' symbolic interaction and purpose-rational action (Habermas 1971, p. 93)

	Institutional framework: symbolic interaction	Systems of purpose-rational (instrumental and strategic) action
Action-orienting rules	Social norms	Technical rules
Level of definition	Intersubjectively shared ordinary language	Context-free language
Type of definition	Reciprocal expectations about behaviour	Conditional predictions conditional imperatives
Mechanisms of acquisition	Role internalisation	Learning of skills and qualifications
Function of action type	Maintenance of institutions (conformity to norms on the basis of reciprocal enforcement)	Problem-solving (goal attainment, defined in means-ends relations)
Sanctions against a violation of rules	Punishment on the basis of conventional sanctions: failure against authority	In efficacy: failure in reality
"Rationalisation"	Emancipation, individual ration; extension of communication free of domination	Growth of productive forces; extension of power of technical control

Habermas (1971) further elaborates on his theory of communicative action and social interaction by distinguishing between:

(1) the institutional framework of a society or the sociocultural life-world and
(2) the subsystems of purposive-rational action that are "embedded" in it (Habermas 1971, p. 93).

The following table provides a detailed analysis of the elements of **Symbolic Interaction and Purpose-Rational Action** (Table 4.1):

It is the column on Institutional Framework: Symbolic Interaction that is of interest to us in this analysis, for each of the elements of social norms, intersubjectively shared ordinary language, reciprocal expectations about behaviour, role internalisation, conformity to norms on the basis of reciprocal enforcement, punishment on the basis of conventional sanctions, and extension of communication free of domination may be observed in the development of successful Second Life communities.

These communities and interactions in Second Life do have the subsystems of purposive-rational action embedded within them, but as with "real" lifeworlds, the framework of symbolic interaction supersedes these actions within the framework. Adherence to community standards and social norms is just as important to the advancement of the avatar being-in-the-virtual world as to the individual in the real world. In fact, failure to adhere to the Second Life community standards can result in the ultimate punishment: banishment from Second Life, which essentially represents the death of the avatar.

4.8   Second Research Avatar: Vick Dragonash
and the Gorean Worlds

Unlike Ragitake, the secondary research avatar (alt) Vick Dragonash has not been defined by the boundaries established within communities. However, the author revealed that Ragitake and Vick shared the same physical life identity to the Isle of Wyrms Guardians, who occasionally communicated with Vick as they would with Ragitake. In addition, Vick often stepped in to assist a citizen, respond to an inquiry, or handle a griefing incident. In this way, Ragitake's powers and responsibilities carried over to the avatar Vick; though he benefited from a less public profile and thus a stronger capacity to freely define his role (and therefore both independence and autonomy) (Fig. 4.2).

The avatar Vick Dragonash was originally created to conduct research as a male avatar exploring Gorean worlds for the author's work on *Taboo and Transgression in Artificial Lifeworlds* (Martinez 2011). Vick's role was to learn about the Gorean slave/master roles and observe Gorean communities in action. Inspired by John Norman's science fantasy novels Chronicles of Gor, Gorean worlds have been the subject of controversy in Second Life because the more radical Gorean communities practice the forced collaring of female avatars to take them into slavery, and have been accused of simulated rape and forcible degradation of women.

Fig. 4.2 Vick Dragonash

Becoming Vick was more of a challenge for the author than becoming Ragitake, partially because at the time there was a dearth of available avatar resources for males compared to the wide range of shapes, skins, clothing, hair and accessories for female avatars. Vick spent a good portion of his early days in Second Life searching for suitable skins, animation overriders to create "male" movements, and appropriate clothing for men. Over time, he discovered that some of the fantasy and role play communities had excellent avatar accessories for men, and shortly thereafter his physical identity emerged.

As a female embodying a male, I was careful to modify communication style to ensure that Vick used text conventions that were more typical of male communication styles. According to Herring & Martison in their study assessing gender authenticity in computer mediated language use (2004),

"scholars have amassed evidence that males and females tend to use language in different ways, presumably unconsciously, online as well as offline (Hall, 1996; Herring, 1993, 1994, 1996, 1998, 2003; Hills, 2000; Kendall, 1998; Thomson & Murachver, 2001): Males make greater use of assertions, self-promotion, rhetorical questions, profanity, sexual references, sarcasm, challenges, and insults, whereas females make greater use of hedges, justifications, expressions of emotion, representations of smiling and laughter, personal pronouns, and supportive and polite language. Unconscious use of gendered discourse styles can reveal one's actual gender even when one is performing a different gender (or trying not to give off any gender cues). Herring (1996) cites examples of individuals attempting to pass as a different gender in asynchronous discussion forums (what Hall [1996] calls "cross-expressing") who were outed as imposters on the basis of inconsistencies between their performed gender and their discourse style (p. 443)".

Cherny (1994), had previously discussed gender differences in online communication. Subsequently, Palomares and Eun-Ju (2010) conducted a study of gender linguistic performance in computer mediated environments examining the influence of avatar gender selection on linguistic performance. These studies provide evidence that there is gender difference in communication in virtual environments, and that when an avatar of one gender "performs" the other, they often make performative conversation mistakes that give away their actual gender identity. With this in mind, I reduced the use of emoticons and overly supportive language favored by Ragitake. As a resident of the fantasy continent, Vick adopted the more formal speech that is the convention of medieval fantasy settings. The use of formal speech, modulated movement patterns, and formal fantasy dress prepared Vick to begin research in the Gorean worlds, which shared characteristics of fantasy and science fiction literature.

Vick Dragonash visited 40 of these worlds during a 6 month period of observation from August 2007 to February 2008. Gorean cities are typically built on islands surrounded by water. Their official landing place consists of a ship docked outside the island/city, containing chests and other sources of information with the rules of role-play and community covenant (often accompanied by an application for membership). These information centres also supply an "observer" tag, which Vick wore at all times while observing the communities in action. During that period, Vick dressed in the Gorean style when visiting Gorean cities, adapted Gorean speech conventions, visited the extensive Gorean libraries to learn about the culture and covenants, and mingled with Gorean role-players. Vick's profile did not reveal that, though in male form and clad as a free Gorean male and master, he was actually a female in the physical world. Vick was addressed as "Lord" and "Master", and treated with friendly respect by both free Goreans and slaves. The avatar Vick was heavily recruited by the warriors of a prominent Gorean community, and invited to join the ranks of their guards. In addition, he was recruited by a more peaceful Gorean community, run by a "free woman", to join as a citizen in open rank.

Vick was quite successful in his community interactions and establishment of a credible identity which persists 3 years subsequent to his initial foray into Gor. Perhaps the most interesting aspect of this avatar identity is that in addition to doing research, Vick experimented with building and created elaborate builds that neither Ragitake nor Atea have any interest in building. He also established a number of friendships with other Second Life residents who are not on Ragitake's friend's list, whereas Atea and Ragitake, over time, came to share a number of friends.

4.9   Third Research Avatar: Atea Aeon, the Autonomous Avatar

The avatar Atea Aeon was established to see what would happen if one "gave life" to an avatar without a pre-determined role and allowed her Second Life to take shape on its own. For the first few months of her existence, Atea explored various worlds, joined a few groups, and spent some time defining her identity. This process included making decisions about avatar appearance, the types of communities she would explore, and the types of activities in which she would engage. For example, early in her development Atea wore contemporary clothing, rather than the medieval fantasy attire favoured by Ragitake, and choose eye and hair colour that differentiated her from Ragitake as well. During the early research period, Atea deliberately limited her friends list, and was therefore unfettered by communications and social expectations. At the time of the research for this project, she was not known to others as a Ragitake alt, and could therefore circulate freely among Isle of Wyrms citizens or in Second Life at large. As time evolved so did Atea's interests. Though initially Atea spent relatively little time in Second Life, what time she spent was condensed, intensive, and highly productive. Atea became active in a group related to Polynesian culture that was founded by a favourite (physical) author. She began taking classes in Second Life, quickly mastering advanced content creation and scripting that Ragitake or Vick hadn't had the time to learn (Fig. 4.3).

Atea had no interest in power and authority of the kind held by Ragitake; she recognised that it is bound by social norms and conventions, tied to responsibilities, and fundamentally linked to whether or not Ragitake fulfils the expectations of the Isle of Wyrms community and leadership. The power that Atea sought was one unfettered by societal norms; the powers to explore, transform, and become as many iterations of the self as she desired. And yet, her identity soon took shape in a fixed form; her interactions with communities leading to the defining of her personality within social contexts, and her choices creating a projection of presence that

Fig. 4.3 Atea Aeon

distinguishes her amongst other avatars. For example, in her research on the Isle of Shadows and in observing avatar interaction on Bondage Ranch, Atea wore classic designer jeans and a top with a contemporary look, with sophisticated hair, shoes, and skin. In contrast, most of the avatars in attendance on the Bondage Ranch, regardless of how long they had been residents of Second Life, were attired in extreme fetish wear or black leather role-play outfits. Many of them performed stereotypical behaviours related to their projected preference (dominant/submissive; master/slave; etc.). In contrast, Atea presented a physical identity projection that was sophisticated and self-assured, comfortable circulating among the leather clad avatars yet resisting the pressure to conform in attire and behaviours. Atea engaged freely in conversation, both in chat and instant messages, with the avatars in attendance, without engaging in role play behaviours or dress. By contrast, Ragitake had adopted the conventions and style of Isle of Wyrms, and Vick Dragonash had adopted the speech conventions, dress, and expected behaviour of a free male Gorean citizen or resident of high fantasy communities. Atea chose to adopt her own style and identity, without conforming to community patterns in dress, speech, behaviours and other identity indicators.

Throughout a period of research for the author's work on taboo and transgression in Second Life, Atea also observed the Isle of Shadows, a BDSM teaching environment, by taking classes on exploring BDSM role play, BDSM Strategy for Submissives, and Domination – Dominant Self Discovery. These classes were offered lecture style in a Second Life amphitheatre style classroom, in which self-titled masters and submissives described their experience with BDSM, their philosophy of dominance or submission, and responded to questions from class attendees.

Their goal for the classes was to provide an educated introduction to BDSM and recommend avenues for a safe entrance into the Second Life BDSM community. All three instructors professed to be BDSM practitioners in the physical world (lifestylers) as well as active in the Second Life BDSM community.

Throughout this research phase and during the course of social interactions with class instructors and fellow students, Atea felt a shaping of the self taking place; as if she were emerging from a liminal state of unfixed selfhood to evolve a set of defining characteristics. Particularly, the extensive discussion of alternative lifestyles in Second Life, and the degree of training required to participate in serious role-play activities reaffirmed Atea's commitment to remain unfettered by community constraints. Rather, she decided to focus on becoming an avatar artist and creator. Of all three primary research avatars, Atea Aeon is the one who, unfettered by community and obligations, has been able to exercise her autonomy, creativity, and independence in Second Life, as a successful avatar creator. Both Ragitake and Vick possessed the same skill sets and a degree of community capital that would have allowed them to make the same decision. However, it was within the Atea embodiment that I felt the interest and inclination to pursue that path, which was largely possible because the Atea avatar, in the early stages of development, possessed time and freedom from communication and constraints that limited the time available to both Vick and Ragitake during the period of study.

Ragitake Takakura's autonomy is constrained by the expectations and obligations towards the Isle of Wyrms community, as well as her active role in representing her physical world institution in Second Life as a researcher and educator. Vick Dragonash and Atea Aeon had equal potential for active autonomy as avatars, but it is Atea Aeon who seized the opportunity to develop artistic and financial autonomy in Second Life.

4.10 Conclusion: Identity Persists Within Community Constraints

Though a nascent avatar is seemingly free to choose actions, behaviours, and identity formation, these are in fact restrained by the Second Life community covenants and terms of service. The avatar enjoys a liminal phase of identity formation prior to initiation and assimilation into given communities, and thus adherence to prescribed rules of social interaction. The avatar may nonetheless cross boundaries and thresholds of acceptable transgressive behaviours, as long as this occurs within a permissive covenant in alignment with Second Life terms of service and US federal regulations.

Avatar agency and autonomy in the virtual world continues to be bound by the covenants of the community standards and Second Life Terms of Service. Violation of these standards and terms may result in immediate and permanent suspension of the user's account. In addition, land rules set by Second Life land, region, and estate owners in Second Life may restrict an avatar's ability to act freely upon and within territorial limits. Group membership, while voluntary, provides another level of restrictions on individual autonomy and action, depending on the community covenant. Some communities, such as the Isle of Wyrms Citizens Group, provide active and ongoing live monitoring of group chat, instant messaging, and citizen comportment on the community lands.

The avatar joins Second Life communities at will, and yet, once she joins a community, her liminality ends and early stage freedoms become restricted within the bounds of the consensual social norms. With community comes a fixing of identity that both enables and constrains the avatar. Bound by the covenant and conventions of the community, the avatar is expected to adhere to a specific set of behaviours and present a fixed, reliable, and recognisable identity. She is expected to fulfil certain duties and obligations to the community; communicate within a defined set of norms; and engage in symbolic interaction. This integration into a given community, or society as a whole, fits the final stage of territorial and transitional passage described by Van Gennep (1960) and Turner (1974).

The influence of community standards and social norms are just as important to avatar identity persistence in the virtual world as to the individual in the real world. In fact, failure to adhere to the Second Life community standards can result in the ultimate punishment: banishment from Second Life, which essentially represents the death of the avatar (and thus, identity termination).

References

Boellstorff, T.: Coming of Age in Second Life: An Anthropologist Explores the Virtually Human. Princeton University Press, Princeton (2008)

Cherny, L.: Gender differences in text-based virtual reality. In: Proceedings of the Berkeley Conference on Women and Language, San Diego (1994)

Douglas, M.: Purity and Danger; an Analysis of Concepts of Pollution and Taboo. Praeger, New York (1966)

Habermas, J.: Toward a Rational Society: Student Protest, Science, and Politics. Beacon, Boston (1971)

Herring, S.C., Martinson, A.: Assessing gender authenticity in computer-mediated language use: evidence from an identity game. J. Lang. Soc. Psychol. **23**(4), 424–446 (2004). doi:10.1177/0261927X04269586

Martinez, N.: Here be dragons: second life community building and citizen engagement on the Isle of Wyrms. In: Sloan-C International Symposium on Emerging Technology Applications for Online Learning. Carefree (2008a)

Martinez, N.: Second Life: The Future of Communications? Society for Technical Communications Annual Summit, Philadelphia (2008b)

Martinez, N.: Taboo and Transgression in Artificial Lifeworlds. Atropos, New York/Dresden (2011)

Martinez, N., Kemp, L., Carnevale, C.: Creating virtual community and engaging a virtual citizenry: lessons in leadership from the Isle of Wyrms. In: The 13th Sloan-C International Conference on Asynchronous Learning Networks, Orlando (2007)

Meadows, M. S. I, Avatar: The culture and consequences of having a second life. Indianapolis, Ind., London, New Riders, Pearson Education [distributor] (2007)

Palomares, N.A., Eun-Ju, L.: Virtual gender identity: the linguistic assimilation to gendered avatars in computer-mediated communication. J. Lang. Soc. Psychol. **29**(1), 5–23 (2010)

Schirmacher, W.: Media Aesthetics in Europe. Association Descartes and the College International de Philosophie, Paris (1991)

Schirmacher, W.: Eco-sophia: the artist of life. research in philosophy and technology 9. In: Carl, Mitcham (ed.) Ethics and Technology, pp. 125–134. JAI Press, Greenwhich/London (1989)

Sixma, T.: The gorean community in second life: rules of sexual inspired role-play. J. Virtual Worlds Res. Vol. 1, 3–18 (2009). doi:February 2009

Turner, V.W.: Dramas, Fields, and Metaphors; Symbolic Action in Human Society. Cornell University Press, Ithaca (1974)

Van Gennep, A.: The Rites of Passage. University of Chicago Press, Chicago (1960)

Chapter 5
Encountering Oneself and the Other: A Case Study of Identity Formation in Second Life

Maeva Veerapen

Abstract The phenomenon of virtual worlds is changing how humans behave and make sense of the world. Working within the paradigm that all human experience is incarnate, this chapter investigates how the processes of inworld identity construction occur within and in relation to the user's body. Ninoo Nansen, my avatar, is the catalyst for this inquiry. Referring to past ethnographic research in Second Life™ and drawing on Merleau-Ponty's (The Phenomenology of Perception. In: C. Smith (Trans.). Routledge, London (Original work published in 1945.)) and Sartre's (1968) theories, I utilise phenomenological analysis to interpret the data. This analysis reveals the intentional structure within which identity is formed in the virtual world, differing from how it emerges in the physical world. I initially analyse how a unified, phenomenal I – from which the world is perceived – is formed from the interaction between the user and avatar during the experience of Second Life. I then consider how the encounter with the Other in Second Life modified the pre-virtual and inworld identities.

5.1 Introduction

This chapter focuses on the context or 'situated experience' within which virtual identity emerges and develops. I utilise my involvement in Second Life as a case study to explore the journey of the creation of an inworld identity. I first joined the community of Second Life residents in March 2009 mainly for research purposes. This was also the first instance whereby I had ever created and become acquainted with an avatar named Ninoo Nansen. In the thick of my research activities in Second Life, the lines between I – Maeva – and Ninoo often blurred.

M. Veerapen (✉)
Monash University, Melbourne, Australia
e-mail: Maeva.Veerapen@monash.edu

A. Peachey and M. Childs (eds.), *Reinventing Ourselves: Contemporary Concepts of Identity in Virtual Worlds*, Springer Series in Immersive Environments, DOI 10.1007/978-0-85729-361-9_5, © Springer-Verlag London Limited 2011

As a result of such inworld occurrences, I was brought to question who I, as a singular identity entity, had evolved into. I used to be one unique individual known by the name of Maeva, who understood how I fit within a community, what my identity was for myself and other members of the community. Ninoo's arrival upset this and invited me to think about who I was in new ways. My encounter and subsequent experiences with Ninoo Nansen act as a catalyst for this chapter. The writing weaves in and out of, on the one hand, theoretical and discursive discussions pertaining to the context of identity formation inworld and, on the other hand, personal narratives relating to Ninoo and I, extracts of fieldwork notes which I collected over the course of nearly 2 years of ethnographic research in Second Life. I facilitate this investigation into the processes leading to identity formation in a virtual world context by using embodiment as a paradigmatic approach and focus.

Research on identity formation in virtual worlds has existed since the early days of the Internet revolution (Turkle 1997). Current research often approaches online worlds as an instance of an emerging societal format within which original methods of creating, maintaining and communicating identity are developed (Boellstorff 2008; Boon and Sinclair 2009; Jones 1998; Schroeder 2002; Winder 2008). Other existing research examines the user(s) in the physical world by studying the user profiles (Cooper et al. 2007; Spence 2008) or the intersection between the physical and virtual worlds (Doyle and Kim 2007; Taylor 2006). This chapter shifts the focus towards investigating how the physical user shapes the inworld experience in order to better comprehend why online identity construction differs from the present processes in the physical world.

All human experience is incarnate. Our body maintains us alive. We perceive our surroundings and live out experiences through the body. This body is also the source of our emotions and desires. Fundamentally, the body acts as grounding in the world: it provides us with the confirmation that our surroundings, actions and ourselves exist. Humans are essentially embodied beings. Hence, it is no wonder that the process of forming an identity is an embodied activity during which the body plays an essential and formative part. However, the manner in which the body is defined and how it consequently shapes experience in the context of virtual worlds differs from what takes place in the physical world: for example, the body cannot directly touch or smell virtual surroundings. Although identity is constructed differently in virtual worlds, it is still created, maintained and performed by the phenomenal body. Hence, an understanding of embodiment in virtual worlds leads to a better grasp of the context within which virtual identity is constituted.

Identity formation is a succession of attempts to initially unveil who I is and then put it in relation to the Other. Accordingly, this chapter will first explore how I is shaped in the context of Second Life, usually through a negotiation between the user and avatar from which a phenomenal body, which acts as grounding in the world, emerges. Then, the focus will shift to the encounter of the Other in Second Life, and the impact it has on the pre-virtual and inworld identities.

5.2 Moving Away from Disembodiment

A discourse of disembodiment has dominated discussions of virtual worlds. Disembodiment is not the opposite of embodiment but rather signifies a specific form of embodied experience during which the body is relegated to the periphery and thereby is not considered an active or essential element of said experience. This approach usually perpetuates a Cartesian tradition, whereby the mind is considered separate from and is privileged over the body.

The concept of disembodiment has a long tradition and is still pervasive in popular culture. The privileging of the mind over the body during the cyberspace experience in science fiction is unmistakable. William Gibson's *Neuromancer* (1984), an influential novel in the field of virtual worlds, traces the story of a hacker who yearns to free himself from the prison of his flesh by jacking into cyberspace. More recently, James Cameron's *Avatar* (2010) maintains this tradition of a disembodied virtual world experience when the avatar becomes 'alive' or active, and consequently able to enter the mystical and wondrous world of Pandora, only after its user reaches an unconscious state.

Such a perception of cyberspace as a disembodied activity originates partly from the impression an outside observer forms when looking at a person involved in virtual worlds and similar activities.

> [Gibson] said that the idea of 'cyberspace' came to him while watching 'the body language' of kids playing early video games in a 1980s arcade, leaning into the consoles and – as Gibson assumed – longing to 'reach right through the screen and get with what they were playing,' to merge with the game, to inhabit the *Tron*-like virtual space behind the glass (Jones 2008, p. 12).

If we consider how the initial understanding of a 'bodiless exultation of cyberspace' originates and apply it to our contemporary virtual worlds, it is not surprising that a discourse of disembodiment is still prevalent nowadays. To an outside observer, the inworld activity consists of a person sitting, seemingly immobile and inactive, and staring at a computer screen while losing awareness of the physical surroundings. As the user becomes increasingly unresponsive to physical stimuli, it seems that by staring at and focusing strongly on a highly active onscreen world, s/he bridges a connection between the mind and the virtual world. As a result, the user seems to be absent, lost in a different world on the other side of the computer screen while the body remains, empty of its essence or mind, in this physical place. Such observations are responsible for discourses of disembodiment's implicit and explicit influence on thinking about and researching virtual worlds, reflected in works that approach the inworld activity as an act of mental engagement and consequently do not grant much attention to the body.

Instead, I argue that the body is still active and engaged when the user is inworld, albeit in a different manner from what we are familiar with in the physical world. My whole body reacts to the events I live out in Second Life by, for example, feeling downhearted or elated as a result of something that happened inworld. In doing so, the body once again acts as grounding during the inworld experience, confirming what is taking place and my presence within the experience, akin to the task it also accomplishes in the physical world. This confirmation in turn permits the user to create a new body schema and identity during the inworld experience. Hence, a focus on the type of embodiment formed during the inworld experience offers a starting point to deciphering how identity is formed in virtual worlds. This chapter places a strong emphasis on comprehending how the body maintains its role as the grounding element of experience. Furthermore, if we consider minutely the virtual world experience, we realise that the physical body is not erased but instead that a new body, in the form of the avatar, is introduced. Analysing how the user manages two bodies in lieu of one reveals how a phenomenal body is re-created and hence elucidates some of the ways in which identity is conceived in a unique way in Second Life and other virtual worlds.

5.3   The Avatar Enters

I can still vividly remember my first encounter with my avatar. In fact I delayed joining Second Life because of the importance I had placed on the would-be avatar; I felt I was not ready to create an account because I could not think of an inworld name. Nonetheless, I eventually went to Second Life's website (www.secondlife.com) to register an account. After having filled in all the sections concerning my personal details, it was time to choose a name. I was stuck and still without inspiration: I felt it was too important a factor to get it wrong. I had never considered using my own name because, from what I had read about Second Life, it was not a common practice. Unable to come up with anything, I stared at the screen blankly when suddenly Ninoo came to mind. I liked it straight away: it was a nice and uncommon name, a bit like my own name in fact. The next step, choosing an avatar from the generic ones on offer, was no easier. I struggled to make up my mind and again took my time. I was concerned about the image of myself I would be projecting onto others: I did not want to be scantily clad; I wished to look respectable and professional (Fig. 5.1).

During my first few sessions, I used a slightly modified version of the generic avatar I had chosen, called 'Female Musician.' I remember feeling, for one of the few times in my life, highly self-conscious during that period. Everytime I entered a place in which other avatars were present, I could not help comparing myself (my avatar) to all the other highly modified and beautiful avatars. As a result, I felt uncomfortable due to my (avatar's) lack of sophistication. Consequently, I was shy and timid during the first few weeks in Second Life, a personality trait that is not part of Maeva's identity (Fig. 5.2).

Despite not being aware of it then, these first points of contact with Second Life had already initiated an active engagement with concerns pertaining directly or indirectly to identity. Furthermore, I was already carving a new identity in very specific ways for this place which I would periodically inhabit. From the moment I registered a Second Life account, notions of how to present myself to others influenced most of the choices that informed the making of the avatar. In other words,

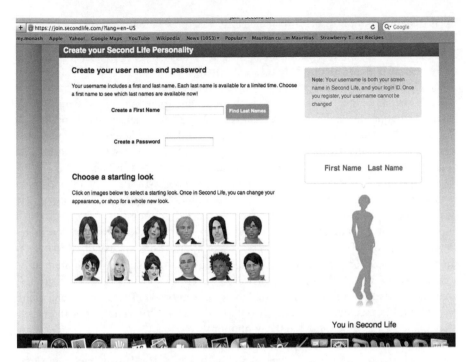

Fig. 5.1   Creating an avatar on the second life website

Fig. 5.2   Ninoo Nansen in the early days

I was thinking about how other residents might assign an identity to me, how I could influence it and implicitly what I conceived my self to be. The qualities of the avatar become quintessential in creating an identity inworld, as the avatar is the only aspect of the user that other Second Life residents engage with.

Firstly, I used several aspects of my own established pre-virtual world identity metrics to assist in the creation of the avatar by, for example, picking an avatar name that had the same qualities as my own name and choosing a female avatar which maintained my physical world nominal and self-informative gender. This behaviour is symptomatic of a pattern whereby one moves from the known to the unknown in an unfamiliar context. Hence, possessing a name with similar characteristics in Second Life to my own assisted me in normalising my perception of my being-in-the-virtual world.

Secondly, I followed the rules and conventions of the group in an attempt to become a member of it, in this case the Second Life community. The process of choosing my avatar name exemplifies my need to fit in with the group by reproducing their normative behavioural patterns. Avatar names were not usually the same as the user's names nor did they have any fantastical qualities such as those in gaming worlds like World of Warcraft and EverQuest. Hence, I perpetuated the group's conventions and norms when I decided to not use my own name and instead chose one with no fantastical undertones. I only asserted my difference from the others after knowing that I belonged to the community.

Thirdly, as I spent more time in Second Life and met other avatars, new layers were added to the process of identity formation. Initially, I evaluated myself by comparing my avatar to other avatars. Although no one said anything about my appearance, I felt judged and consequently the way I interacted within a group was different from how Maeva would operate in a social context in the physical world. In order for this to happen, the self has to be influenced by the avatar.

Based on my experience during these early weeks and confirmed by later inworld occurrences, I argue that the bodies of the user and avatar exist in symbiosis with each other to create the inworld experience, and consequently form a unique unified identity during the duration of the inworld experience. The identity created abounds with tension between the user's pre-virtual world identity, the inworld identity and a combined identity. I qualify the context within which this takes place as being symbembodied, which stands for symbiotic embodiment. I further contend that the state of symbembodiment is characteristic of being inworld due to how the structure of Second Life itself and the user's physical activity of looking both sustain the symbembodied state and allow it to grow.

5.3.1   Being Inworld Is Being Symbembodied

The structure of Second Life enables the creation and maintenance of a symbembodied experience through its set-up which constantly encourages the user to become one with the avatar. During the registration process, the phrasing on the website shows the new user what s/he will look like in Second Life as opposed to what their avatar will look like, as can be noticed in Fig. 5.1. Inworld, the Second

Fig. 5.3 Written chat in second life

Life user does not see the face of the avatar but instead perceives the world from a camera angle placed slightly above and behind the avatar's head. By opting for such a visual set-up, Second Life encourages the user to forget that the avatar is a different body. If the avatar were encountered face on, the user would likely perceive it as existing outside of the body schema.

Furthermore, the visual set-up recreates how my body moves through and perceives the physical world. Firstly, the angle from which I see the world of Second Life is very close to the angle from which I see the physical world, except for a reduced peripheral vision. Secondly, in the physical world I can always see the outline of some body parts, whether my nose or hands for example, on the periphery of my visual field, which ground all the objects around my body in relation to me. The avatar adopts this role because I can always see the back of the avatar's head, which acts as grounding for the world of Second Life. By taking on this role which is usually performed by my physical body, the avatar again merges with the user and his/her body. Thirdly, the very structure of looking is such that "to see an object is either to have it on the fringe of the visual field... or actually [be] concentrating on it" (Merleau-Ponty 1958, p. 78). In the context of Second Life, although the avatar is located within a fairly central position on the screen, it still recedes into the fringe while simultaneously acting as a reference point against which the Second Life world is perceived (Veerapen 2010, p. 110–111). In other words, the avatar integrates itself into the user's body schema and becomes the subjective position from which the world is seen and made sense of, which produces a symbembodied state.

Moreover, the structure of written chat, the most common mode of communication in Second Life, further facilitates the user to amalgamate him/herself with the avatar during the inworld experience. Text chat in Second Life follows the conventions of Internet Relay Chat, whereby the username of the person precedes what the corresponding person types. Hence, as illustrated in Fig. 5.3, if I type "Hello," it

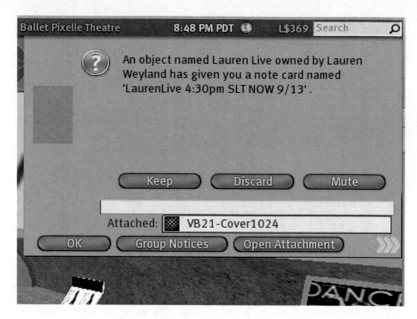

Fig. 5.4 Receiving an object in second life

appears to be written by Ninoo Nansen. After repeatedly seeing something I type presented as being said by Ninoo, the distinction between the two collapses. Thus over time, it becomes easy to incorporate the avatar with the user. Additionally, when an avatar receives an object inworld, Second Life formulates it so it reads that someone 'has given you' something, as exemplified in Fig. 5.4. In this instance too, what happens to the avatar is conflated as also happening to the user, again facilitating the creation of a symbembodied state.

5.4 Being in Symbiosis with the Avatar

The relation between the user and avatar is rarely a simple one where both parties automatically combine into one entity. An investigation into how the user-avatar relation is created reveals some of the complexities of this relation and also indicates the repercussions of this relation on the construction of an inworld identity. I do not aim to produce a reductive analysis but instead approach the relation by considering four meanings of avatar. All four meanings hold true throughout the whole duration of the inworld experience, albeit to varying degrees. Meaning one is implicit within meaning two, which together with the first meaning is implicit within the third meaning, and so forth. Although one meaning might have a stronger influence than the others at a point, the inworld experience never loses the qualities of the other ones.

5.4.1   The Avatar as Object: "I Am Me, and the Avatar Is Mine"

The first meaning understands the avatar as an object. When I first joined Second Life, Ninoo was something outside of me, something upon which I could perform actions. We had a subject to object relation. The avatar presented itself to me with a range of potentialities of actions I could perform upon it. The fieldwork notes I recorded after my first inworld session exemplify this first sense of the avatar within the context of its relation to the user:

> As my avatar arrived there (Avatar Orientation Island), I was able to undertake tutorials that taught me how to control my avatar in order to make it perform certain tasks such as walking around, flying or even sitting, among many others. I tried modifying the appearance of my avatar as part of one of the tutorials but was disappointed to realise there was not much I could do to alter her basic features.

As can be noted in this entry, I view Ninoo as being outside of me, as an object whose movements, actions and appearance I can control. Ninoo has no existence without my presence and our relation exists mainly within the framework of a subject, me, controlling an object, the avatar. Hence, the avatar has no significant influence on the user. Consequently, the identity of the user remains unchanged. The user retains his/her qualities and continues to be the person s/he is within the physical environment. The avatar is not challenging, extending or changing my identity during this initial contact. Instead, the user develops a proprietary relation with the avatar, which acts as an object that belongs to him/her.

More specifically, the avatar should be viewed as an object that serves a specific purpose during the process of identity formation. The avatar acts in a manner similar to a clothing item, an object that allows me to perform my identity and consequently through which I communicate my identity with other people. The design, style, brand and other similar details of the clothing item indicate aspects of a person's identity, such as their job, taste, social class, etc. Similarly, the avatar does not modify the user's identity but permits the latter to express his/her identity within the virtual world context for other residents to interpret.

5.4.2   Avatar as Prosthesis: "The Avatar Extends Me"

The second meaning considers the avatar as a prosthesis. In simple terms, a prosthesis is an object that acts as an extension of the body schema, a phenomenon at work in the blind man's stick.

> The blind man's stick has ceased to be an object for him, and is no longer perceived for itself; its point has become an area of sensitivity, extending the scope and active radius of touch, and providing a parallel to sight (Merleau-Ponty 1958 [1945], p. 165).

The prosthesis acts as an extension of both the perceptual – as applies in the case of the blind man's stick – and motor – as applies with a car – qualities of the human body. As a result, a prosthesis offers new potentialities to the body. Up until now, prostheses have usually been physical in nature, whereby they extend the body schema through direct contact with the body. Hence, reading glasses extend the sense of sight of its wearer after they are placed in front of the eyes which can see better through them. Also, a process of habituation is necessary with any prosthesis. The blind man does not adjust straight away to the stick but becomes used to it through repetitive use of the stick and an assimilation of how it works.

The avatar is a unique type of prosthesis. As it is not physical, it cannot directly enhance the body's potential in the same manner as reading glasses or the blind man's stick do. Rather, it allows the boundary of the user's physical body to extend into the otherwise inaccessible non-physical world of Second Life. The avatar as prosthesis comes forth when the avatar adopts subjective qualities. Instead of being an object upon which the user can perform actions, the avatar interacts with the world of Second Life and its content, including other avatars, as a subject. Hence, the avatar might touch a book or sit on a chair in Second Life. The avatar is the only means for the user to perform such tasks as his/her physical body is unable to directly interact with the virtual world. The avatar is now the one executing the doing as opposed to having actions done upon it. The shift from avatar as object to avatar as prosthesis coincides with a shift away from the stability in the usage of whom the first personal pronouns refer to. This shift occurred during my first inworld session.

> … Most of the other avatars around me were editing their appearances too. An avatar requested to be my friend and I accepted the request.
> I had to move from one room to another, each one covering a different topic within a new tutorial. Hence, I wandered around, following the blue arrows that were on the floor. As I went through the different themed rooms, I did not come across any other avatars.

The first instance whereby a personal pronoun is used within the above fieldwork notes occurs when I position the avatar as a marker against which to compare others, a process I usually do as a subject. The avatar also gains more subjective qualities as she walks through the rooms. At the same time as the avatar acquires subjective qualities, a confusion over the use of personal pronouns develops, whereby they alternatively refer to the user only, the avatar only or the user and avatar together as one. This affects the manner in which the user perceives his/her self and identity. If we consider that a prosthesis means an extension of the body schema, it also implies an extension of the user's identity into the virtual world. Hence, the user's identity does not change but is extended or transposed into the virtual set up, both when undertaking solitary activities and when interacting with other avatars. The avatar does not develop a new identity but allows the pre-virtual world identity to enter the world of Second Life, sometimes through a slight adaptation. This is exemplified when I transferred several of my physical world identity metrics to Second Life during my initial sessions.

However, the meaning of the avatar as object is heavily present within this sense of the avatar as prosthesis. As mentioned, a prosthesis is an object which extends. Hence, the avatar is an object which serves one purpose, that of extending the boundary of the physical body into the virtual world. The implicit presence of the object-ness of the avatar as prosthesis adopting certain subjective qualities creates a tension or resistance within both the user-avatar relation and the formation of identity in virtual worlds. The user perceives the avatar as being both an object outside of the body and an extension of the same body. In terms of identity formation, the avatar oscillates between being an object used to express one's identity and an extension of the user's identity into a new context. In other words, the avatar as prosthesis allows the user's identity to not only exist in the physical world but also be present and embodied within the virtual world. The new set-up of the virtual world is likely to require the user's identity to be slightly modified in order to fit. For example, if someone usually initiates conversation with strangers only after establishing eye contact with said person, s/he will have to adopt another approach in the virtual world. Through repetition and a process of habituation, the identity of the user develops and extends into the virtual setting as well as readjusting itself according to the demands of the new world.

5.4.3   The Avatar as a Phantom Limb: "I Think My Avatar Is Changing Me"

The next meaning of avatar within the context of its symbiotic relation with the user relates to it acting as a phantom limb. "The phantom limb is the presence of part of the representation of the body which should not be given, since the corresponding limb is not there" (Merleau-Ponty 1958, p. 93) and is illustrated in the case of "a man wounded in battle [who] can still feel in his phantom limb the shell splinters that lacerated the real one" (Merleau-Ponty 1958, p. 88). The ambivalent present limb is a reaction against mutilation and "thus what is found behind the phenomenon of substitution is the impulse of being-in-the-world" (Merleau-Ponty 1958, p. 90) or, in other words, an attempt to retain the body's practical field (Merleau-Ponty 1958, p. 94). The phantom limb differs from the prosthesis because it does not extend the body schema but instead it is a quasi-present body part of the person who feels sensations through it as well as attempts to act in the world with it. "But in concealing his deficiency from him, the world cannot fail simultaneously to reveal it to him" (Merleau-Ponty 1958, p. 94).

An experience I once had in Second Life helps to shed some light onto grasping how the avatar works as a phantom limb. Once, after an inworld performance, one of the other audience members invited me to have a look at a small theatre he owned in Second Life. I agreed and we teleported together to the location. As the new locale rezzed up on my computer screen, I could see a relatively small building made out of some type of wood. We walked through a doorway into a small kabuki-styled theatre made out entirely of the texture of bamboo except for small purple cushions for audience members to sit on. I was impressed by the theatre. After a few seconds, I became aware that, sitting at my desk, I could smell bamboo and even feel it under my hand. Although the avatar did not physically exist, its ambivalent presence created the same sensations I would have felt had I been in a physical theatre similar to the one I saw on my computer screen. It should have been impossible for me to perceive the place my avatar was located within. Yet, by reacting against the disablement imposed on me during the inworld experience due to not being able to directly perceive the world, my avatar assumed the role of a quasi component of my body schema and as a result preserved the quality of being-in-the-world within the inworld experience.

The avatar functioning as a phantom limb implies that it operates as a quasi part of me. In terms of identity formation, it signifies that the avatar is seemingly a part of me. Hence, although the user might seem to be identical to the avatar at a quick glance, the latter has picked up some identity markers and features that do not apply to the user. For example, Ninoo does not possess the same physical identity metrics as I do.

Here, I wish to return to my first few sessions in Second Life. During this period, I noted that I was reserved and shy inworld as a result of feeling inferior in comparison to other highly modified avatars. As the avatar is ostensibly a part of me, my behaviour patterns are altered. I became shy. However, at the same time, I was aware of the fabricated-ness of the construct of the avatar, which was in fact an object aiding me to bridge into the virtual world. Although I was acting in a more reserved manner than normal, I instinctually knew this entity was not really me. Furthermore, I regained my pre-virtual world identity in social interactions within the physical world, which were not affected by my inworld experiences. In other words, in its attempt to conceal the deficiency of the inworld experience, whereby I can not perceive the world anymore and have lost the feeling of being-in-the-world, the avatar as phantom limb also reveals this very same deficiency. Just as I was conscious that I was not actually in Second Life, I also realised that I was not the shy individual talking to other avatars. The avatar as phantom limb explains what is really happening when virtual worlds users describe feeling that their avatars overtake them and they become new people during the inworld experience.

5.4.4 The Avatar as Equal: "I = Physical-I + Avatar-I"

The final meaning of avatar in this attempt to better understand the relation between it and the user approaches the avatar as equal to the user within the relation. If human experience is incarnate, then the inworld experience is also incarnate. Within this paradigm the body as is experienced, which is called the phenomenal body, is crucial. This body possesses a few qualities: it is a sensorimotor, perceptual, tactile and visceral body. During the inworld experience, the physical body of the user can no longer perform all the tasks of the phenomenal body. Although it is still a sensorial, perceptual, tactile and visceral body, this body has lost its motor qualities. On the other hand, the avatar body acts purely as a motor body, a quality that the physical body of the user is deprived of. Hence, I contend that through the coming together of the user's and avatar's bodies, a phenomenal body is re-created.

Let us consider how this might apply by evaluating an example from my first inworld session. In my fieldwork notes, I wrote, "An avatar requested to be my friend and I accepted that request." At that specific point in time, my avatar was the body located in the same place as the other avatar and was also the only body able to move through and interact with that place and avatar. However, the avatar could not accept the friendship request on its own and needed the user in order to become a complete phenomenal body that could consider the request. Consequently, the other avatar is the friend of the phenomenal I which consists of both Ninoo and Maeva. The avatar seemingly becomes one and the same with the user, in a similar manner to how a phantom limb would, and allows the user to reach into the virtual world through this object. However, the effect of the phenomenal body differs from the avatar as prosthesis and phantom limb due to a deep-rooted sense of unification in its embodiment absent from the other meanings. The avatar as equal contributes in a manner similar to the physical body towards the formation of the phenomenal body. The avatar has its own legitimate purpose and reason within the embodiment created during the inworld experience instead of a quasi-presence.

In terms of identity, the avatar acquires his/her own identity. A few months after joining Second Life, I was involved in the organisation of a conference track to be held in Second Life. During the lead-up period, I communicated with the performers and presenters both inworld and through email. Outside of the inworld context, yet dealing with Second Life contacts, I struggled to decide which name, Maeva or Ninoo, to use when signing off emails. I realised Ninoo had developed an identity distinctive from Maeva's. She had become a researcher who was herself involved in Second Life and enjoyed the occasional long chat while sipping virtual wine. She had friends who knew her as such. Maeva was a complete stranger for those people. Yet, in all the conference's documents, my name was recorded as Maeva. Ninoo had not only developed a lifestyle, habits, likes and dislikes but also a network of friends, reputation and goodwill that Maeva did not have. Ninoo had become a legitimate identity that was not dependent on Maeva in order to exist for the other Second Life residents. The development of this aspect of Ninoo is also contingent on the interaction with other avatars.

5.5   Preparing for the Encounter with the Other

Identity is not fixed and this is particularly true of inworld identity. As a result of how the avatar oscillates between four meanings during the Second Life experience, the way identity is built for the user and how other avatars perceive it also changes accordingly. The knowledge and awareness of other avatars is present within the user before s/he even first enters the virtual world. This is why I was cautious in my choice of a generic avatar so as not to project a negative image of myself to other Second Life residents.

Identity is also highly performative: our bodies are the means through which we play out a line of actions that determine our role, and consequently our identity. Given the focus of this chapter has so far been on bodies and how they are acting, I wish to consider the performative nature of identity formation in virtual worlds.

When an individual plays a part he implicitly requests his observers to take seriously the impression that is fostered before them. They are asked to believe that the character they see actually possesses the attributes he appears to possess, that the task he performs will have the consequences that are implicitly claimed for it, and that, in general, matters are what they appear to be (Goffman 2004, p. 59).

Such an approach to identity takes on new dimensions in the context of virtual worlds. The small details of body language, usually crucial to any performance context, are lost. Instead, the user needs to rely on other features. The avatar's body image becomes quintessential, from the body size and colour to the clothes or hair the avatar is wearing. On one level, it is generally easy to gage if someone is new or does not spend much time in Second Life based on the appearance of the avatar. This explains my reaction during my first week or two in Second Life when my avatar was not very different from a generic one. Although other avatars had not made any comments about my appearance, I felt that I was recognised purely as a 'noob,' which made me feel uncomfortable, as if I was lacking in respect to other avatars. The performance of identity within virtual worlds also adopts features significantly similar to those of a theatre performance. During a play at the theatre, the audience is aware that they are watching a character played by an actor as opposed to a permanently existing entity. However, they willingly suspend their disbelief and accept the existence of the character presented onstage. Similarly, the virtual world user knows that the avatar s/he meets inworld is a role performed by the avatar's user. Contrary to a play, the user does not know where the boundary between the performer (user) and character (avatar) lies. Nevertheless, s/he still believes the performance they witness. One must be careful to maintain coherence in the performance of identity in virtual worlds such as Second Life in order to maintain a quality of 'authenticity.'

The concept of 'front' offers a starting point when considering how the inworld identity is presented to and for others.

It will be convenient to label as "front" that part of the individual's performance which regularly functions in a general and fixed fashion to define the situation for those who observe the performance (Goffman 2004, p. 61).

The 'front' of the avatar in Second Life would likely consist of several identity features unique to virtual worlds that include the group tag and avatar's profile. The profile can reveal the avatar's and perhaps aspects of the user's identity without the user being aware of it. List of groups the avatar is a member of, their favourite locations in Second Life, the avatar photo as well as the short bio a user writes all offer information about the identity of the Second Life resident. It is expected that the user would make the avatar act according to these identity markers and not against them.

When I first joined Second Life and mainly perceived my avatar as an object, I spent some time experimenting with different clothes, hairs and skins for purely aesthetic reasons. However, this did not last long. Ninoo quickly became what would allow me to conduct the necessary ethnographic research by extending my body schema into the virtual world. I chose short hair, jeans and a top for her; they represented my perception of what an ethnographer entering a remote tribe might be dressed like. In order to ensure I was undertaking ethical research, my profile biography outlined the research I was conducting in Second Life. I also activated the

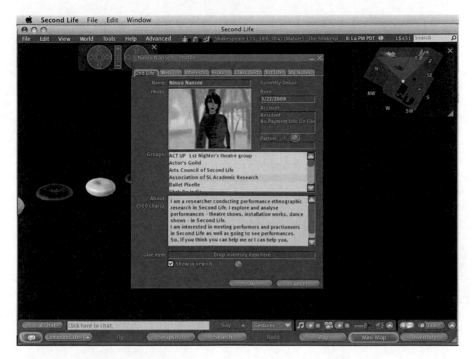

Fig. 5.5 The 'front' of Ninoo Nansen

Second Life Researchers title, which appeared as the title "SL Researcher" above my avatar name, as can be seen in Fig. 5.5. I had created a front for Ninoo, a character description that provided me with the framework within which to perform my identity.

However, when Ninoo also acted as a phantom limb and equal to the human body, the created identity became more fluid. I made friends in Second Life and we adopted behaviour patterns that we often repeated. I also became a dancer with the LaPerformance Company, initially for research purposes but then remained with them for my own pleasure. Ninoo was no longer my way into Second Life purely to collect data for my research project. Ninoo had developed friends and activities, some of which she was good at. Her appearance also moved away from the ethnographer look to a professional but pleasing look, as illustrated in Fig. 5.6. I did not change her skin and body, as I feel lost when the body that acts as grounding for the world of Second Life changes and becomes an object again, breaking the feeling of being there in Second Life.

Still, as my avatar became more fluid and sometimes was not aimed at purely being an ethnographer, one element guided all the choices I made when creating and changing my inworld identity. The main concern regarded how other residents would perceive and judge me. This might not seem different from what takes place in the physical world. However, in virtual worlds, the relation between I and the Other is not as clear cut. Everytime I am inworld, I feel that the Others are judging

Fig. 5.6 Non-ethnographer Ninoo Nansen

Maeva based on what Ninoo is doing. However, interestingly I think of the other residents in terms of the avatars instead of their users. If I do consider other users, I think of him/her as the avatar's user instead of the other user's avatar and realise how little I know about who the user behind another computer in the world is. This situation creates an unequal relation whereby the user feels that how s/he is judged depends on the avatar's actions while the user does not judge other users based on their avatars.

5.6 Facing the Other

A manner to approach the meeting of the Other is by looking at the face-to-face encounter. The face allows the relation with the Other to come into being. Understanding how this applies to the case of virtual worlds such as Second Life offers us an insight into how the relation with other residents is formed.

> The relation with the face, the Other absolutely other which I can not contain, the other in this sense infinite, is nonetheless my Idea, a commerce. But the relation is maintained without violence, in peace with this absolute alterity. The "resistance" of the other does not do violence to me, does not act negatively; it has a positive structure: ethical (Levinas 1969 [1961], p. 197).

The manner the Other is apprehended consolidates the symbiotic relation between the user and avatar. The capacity to see another avatar's face is dependent on the location of one's avatar within the world. Yet, the response to the face takes place within the physical body and is translated through the actions of the avatar. Hence, within an I-Other conjecture, both the avatar and user work together to constitute the I. Furthermore, the user does not usually see the face of his/her avatar. Consequently, it is abnormal for one's avatar to become an Other with whom one can have a relation with. Although the avatar as object exists outside of the user's I and body schema, it remains an object and does not transform into a subject independent of the user, or an Other with whom the user can have an I-Other relation.

In regards to the other avatar, his/her face presents itself to the user. The face manifests itself through the other avatar, implicitly understood to be controlled by a person. The user allows the face to appeal to him/her in a similar fashion to what happens in the physical world. The face seen by the user belongs to the avatar and not the other avatar's user, who exists on the periphery of the inworld experience. The relation with the Other is initiated through the encounter with the face of the avatar. If one encounters the Other and establishes a relation with him/her through the face, an interesting situation occurs in virtual worlds. A virtual world user encounters the avatar's face and not the user's. Consequently, the user entertains an ethical relation with the avatar and not the user. This explains why I perceive the Other user as being the avatar's user instead of the user of the avatar: I know, relate to and consequently position the avatar over the user. Similarly, the Other does not relate to me, Maeva, but to my avatar. Thus, when adopting both perspectives, a symmetry appears within the relation among avatars. However, I still feel that Maeva is being defined by how the Others (avatars) judge Ninoo and make sense of who she is. Hence, an inequality is created in the relation between the user and other residents, whereby a user values other avatars over their users despite feeling that the other residents might perceive him/herself through his/her avatar.

Keeping in mind the inequality of the relation with the Other and its potential impact on the user, the next and last section of this chapter tackles the question of how the established pre-virtual world identity of the user can be modified as a result of the encounter with the Other in Second Life.

5.7 Being-for-Others

"The Other is not only the one whom I see but the one who *sees* me" (Sartre 1958, p. 228). Hence, the Other engages in a similar relation with me as I do with him/her. The relation with the Other also influences my state of being and consequently my identity. The Other looks at me, passes judgment on me, and assigns to me objective qualities, a process I will later perpetrate.

By the mere appearance of the Other, I am put in the position of passing judgment on myself as an object, for it is as an object that I appear to the Other. Yet this object which has appeared is not an empty image in the mind of another (Sartre 1958, p. 222).

Not only does the Other pass judgment on me as an object but s/he makes me aware that as I am a subject to myself, I am also an object for the Other. As a result, the manner in which I view myself changes slightly. I see myself as the

Other does – an object – and make value judgments. It is this thinking process that partly influences the choice of clothes I wear to work. This rationale also guided my choice of a generic avatar with specific features when I first signed up for a Second Life account and later influenced how I created my 'front' inworld. I am aware of how I might look like and be judged by the Other. I become aware of the state of my body as a subject-object.

Within the situation of virtual worlds, this tension becomes more complex. Referring back to the meanings of avatar, Ninoo is an object for me but also possesses subjective qualities when she functions as a prosthesis, phantom limb or equal. The subject-object tension present in the I entity within virtual worlds is already complex and intricate, which complicates my being in relation to the Other. The Other never sees me sitting at my laptop, and hence is unable to pass judgment on my physical person. Instead, within Second Life, the Other sees my avatar. Hence, my choice to have my avatar wear a specific dress might instead of being guided by my personal tastes, be influenced by the knowledge of I as an object for the Other, or the avatar as an object which mediates my self for the Other to judge.

Inworld, the user has control over the features which inform his/her nominal identity. Yet, the user might not allocate much importance to certain behaviour or actions which are valued by Others and influence how the latter view the user's identity differently from what s/he conceived it to be. From the start, the user unconsciously allows his/her own identity to inform the created identity within the avatar. But the avatar also offers the user the safe distance, removed from the Other's judging physical look, to take risks and try out new personas latent within their physical world identity, whether playing with gender, appearance, tastes, behavioural patterns among several other identity traits.

Furthermore, "it is only so far as each man is opposed to the Other that he is absolutely for himself. Opposite the Other and confronting the Other, each one asserts his right of being individual" (Sartre 1958, p. 236). Identity has two aspects to it: on one hand, complying with the norms and identity of a group and on the other, differentiating oneself from the rest of the group. The latter allows us to create an I against which all the Others can be positioned, an I that is unique, which is crucial to the very existence of the Other. During my first few sessions in Second Life, my shyness stemmed from the fact that I was not different enough from a whole group of generic avatars. This awareness and shame came into being only when I was in a place with other avatars. On my own, I was not ashamed of owning an avatar which was not very sophisticated appearance-wise. Having an awareness of the Other at the back of my mind, I was disappointed that I was unable to modify the avatar as much as I had expected but it was only when located with the Other and judging myself as the object the Other might see that I felt ashamed and as a result became shy. The other avatars did not need to say anything for their possible judgment to affect me. My embarrassment was embarrassment of myself before the Other, without whom this would not have happened (Sartre 1958, p. 222). I probably would have had a very different experience at the start of my inworld adventure had I found new clothes, hair and skin before searching for and finding other avatars.

There is another interesting thing that happens when faced with the Other: "As I appear to the Other, so I am" (Sartre 1958, p. 237). In other words, I am what the Other makes out of me. Hence, within a classroom environment, I become a teacher because this is how the other people, students, in the room perceive me. In other words, the Other constructs an identity for me. In the physical world, this identity might change depending on the context and people I am with. However, this becomes a bit more complicated in the context of virtual worlds. As I have showed previously, during the different stages of the relation with the avatar, a situation whereby 'The user has become the avatar, and the avatar is now the user' is never really reached. The closest I get to achieving this is through my encounter with the Other: I become what my avatar is for Others. Ninoo will never be the sum of Maeva. In fact, in some aspects, she is altogether different from Maeva. Yet, according to the idea that "as I appear to the Other, so I am" (Sartre 1958, p. 237), Maeva becomes, during the inworld experience, Ninoo as she appears to Others. Consequently a fractured sense of identity is created when the avatar temporarily modifies the user's established pre-virtual world identity, usually during a state of deep immersion.

Also, when interactions with other avatars are the main activity taking place, they become the reality of the user during the inworld experience. As a result, the person created by those Others also becomes a temporary reality. During such inworld sessions, as I am thinking of what to type, my thinking process is altered from how Maeva might respond to something and instead comes in line with the created image of Ninoo. I have become what the Other sees. When all the Other sees is an avatar, which can never become the sum of its user, the latter is altered and 'becomes' during the period of interaction with the Other his/her avatar, thereby temporarily modifying the user's pre-virtual world experience identity during the inworld experience. This rationale explains the processes that resulted in my becoming shy during my first few inworld sessions.

5.8 Conclusion

Virtual worlds are a new phenomenon, which has resulted in a change in the way humans are and become. The impact can be strongly felt on several aspects of human life, with identity being one of them. This chapter has examined how modified forms of embodiment within virtual worlds might create the context within which identity exist in virtual worlds. The pivotal aspect lies in relations: the user-avatar relation, the user via avatar relation to the other avatars, the perceived relation other users have with oneself via the two avatars. Processes of identity formation within the new situated experience created by virtual worlds are very similar to those in the physical world, with added layers of complexities and heightened awareness from the users. The nature of the virtual world embodiment, through the user-avatar relation, informs how the user constructs his/her inworld identity. The structure of the encounter with Others defines this identity. This chapter has provided an in-depth analysis of the structures of embodiment created inworld which might influence the process of identity formation in virtual worlds.

References

Boellstorff, T.: Coming of Age in Second Life: An Anthropologist Explores the Virtually Human. Princeton University Press, Oxford (2008)

Boon, S., Sinclair, C.: A world i don't inhabit: disquiet and identity in second life and facebook. Educ. Media Int. **46**(2), 99–110 (2009)

Cooper, R., et al.: Alter Ego: Avatars and Their Creators. Chris Boot, London (2007)

Doyle, D., Kim, T.: Embodied narrative: the virtual nomad and the meta dreamer. Int. J. Perform. Arts Digit. Media. **3**(2), 209–222 (2007)

Gibson, W.: Neuromancer. Ace Books, New York (1984)

Goffman, E.: Performances: belief in the part one is playing. In: Bial, H. (ed.) The Performance Studies Reader, pp. 59–63. Routledge, London (2004)

Jones, S.: Virtual Culture: Identity and Communication in Cybersociety. Sage, London (1998)

Jones, S.E.: The Meaning of Video Games: Gaming and Textual Strategies. Routledge, New York (2008)

Landau, J. (Producer), Cameron, J. (Director): Avatar [videorecording]. U.S.A.: Twentieth Century Fox Home Entertainment South Pacific (2010)

Levinas, E.: Ethics and the face. In: A. Lingis (Trans.), Totality and Infinity: An Essay on Exteriority, pp. 194–219. Duquesne University Press, Pittsburgh (Original work published in 1961) (1969)

Merleau-Ponty, M.: The Phenomenology of Perception. C. Smith (trans.). Routledge: London, (Original work published in 1945) (1958)

Sartre, J.P.: Being and Nothingness: An Essay on Phenomenological Ontology. H. E. Barnes (Trans.). Routledge, London (Original work published in 1943) (1958)

Schroeder, R.: The Social Life of Avatars: Presence and Interaction in Shared Virtual Environments. Springer, London (2002)

Spence, J.: Demographics of virtual worlds. J. Virtual Worlds Res. **1**(2), 1–45 (2008)

Taylor, T.L.: Play Between Worlds: Exploring Online Game Culture. MIT Press, Cambridge (2006)

Turkle, S.: Life on the Screen: Identity in the Age of the Internet. Simon & Schuster, New York (1997)

Veerapen, M.: Leading a symbembodied life: a phenomenological investigation of second life. Int. J. Humanit. **8**(5), 105–114 (2010)

Winder, D.: Being Virtual: Who You Really Are Online. Wiley, Chichester (2008)

Chapter 6
Virtual Fashion Play as Embodied Identity Re/Assembling: Second Life Fashion Bloggers and Their Avatar Bodies

Christine Liao

Abstract Second Life™ fashion bloggers use the virtual environment as a place to re/construct different assemblages of self, thereby creating new potential for and experiences of subjectivity. Drawing on theories of embodiment and Deleuze and Guattari's (A thousand plateaus: Capitalism and schizophrenia. (B. Massumi, Tran.). University of Minnesota Press, Minneapolis, 1987) theories of the Body without Organs, assemblage, and becoming, I propose virtual fashion play as a process through which people continually construct and deconstruct identity. The inquiry centres on two questions: What is the relationship between bloggers and their avatars? How do bloggers construct identities through fashion? The fashion bloggers referenced do not see themselves as constructing identities that are separate from the identities of their physical lives. However, their avatars do have an impact on their physical selves. Their physical and virtual bodies are integrated as they re/assemble identities, and virtual fashion offers a technology of self that expresses practices of identity.

6.1 Introduction

Avatar representations in cyberspace have changed as technology has changed, from text representation to 2D pixel images, and now, 3D graphics. Virtual worlds, especially 3D computer-graphic-rendering environments, are making realistic 3D avatar images possible. The basic setting of many virtual worlds, e.g., Second Life (SL), simulates the physical world,[1] and virtual fashion systems generally replicate

---

[1] Although users can create different world settings and play according to their imagination, most choose to play in worlds that simulate the conventional physical world.

C. Liao (✉)
School of Visual Arts, Pennsylvania State University, University Park, PA, USA
e-mail: cll212@psu.edu

A. Peachey and M. Childs (eds.), *Reinventing Ourselves: Contemporary Concepts of Identity in Virtual Worlds*, Springer Series in Immersive Environments, DOI 10.1007/978-0-85729-361-9_6, © Springer-Verlag London Limited 2011

the fashion mores and conventions of the physical world. In Western society, at least, clothing is strongly connected to self-expression and identity construction. In this regard, designer clothing expresses social status. However, the purchase and wearing of any clothing have socio-cultural meanings that inhere in complicated relationships among price, quality, design, and aspirations—relationships that hold for both those who dress in mainstream styles and those who dress in alternative styles, punk, for example. If avatars are our virtual bodies, then virtual fashion must play an important role in constructing online identities. What the multitude of images/appearances possible in the virtual world means for our online social lives, therefore, is a question of great interest—especially as many people are now spending considerable time online and are creating relationships there.

Yet, so much more than clothing goes into an identity represented by an avatar. Every body part and attribute can be customised in SL: eyes, skin, hair, body shape, and even gender constitute fashion accessories. Changing one's body shape or skin colour is much easier in a virtual world than in physical life. However, although an avatar can be anything in SL, many people choose an idealised human form. Therefore, in the hyper-real culture of 3D virtual environments, the body representations of avatars have taken on a new importance. That is, identities are re/assembled online through the process of donning and frequently changing clothes and accessories, including body parts. People do not engage in this process free of charge: in SL, at least, virtual fashion has become a million-dollar industry.[2] What, then, are the implications of the identity re/assembling that this technology affords? Understanding people's experiences of re/constructing fashionable avatars might be the first step to answering this and related questions.

In order to understand experiences of embodiment through virtual fashion, I conducted a qualitative study in which I interviewed SL fashion bloggers, each of whom constantly changes her avatar's appearance and posts pictures of the resulting images. My inquiry centres on two questions: What is the relationship between bloggers and their avatars? How do bloggers construct identities through fashion? These questions are based on two constructs. First, the computer and the Internet have changed the boundary between machine and human, physical and virtual (Turkle 1995), such that people do not make a clear distinction between physical and virtual bodies. Instead of being seen as merely a virtual object, the virtual body is thought of and even experienced as an extension of the physical body. Second, avatars are our virtual bodies in cyberspace, and thus, our identities on the Internet. How identities are constructed, then, becomes a central question in understanding avatar representations.

---

[2] The Second Life official blog reports that the Second Life economy (user-to-user transactions) totalled 567 million US dollars in 2009. *The New York Times* reported that clothing and accessories account for about 20 percent of the Second Life economy. Therefore, as of 2009, the Second Life fashion industry was worth about 113.4 million US dollars.
Second Life blog article: http://blogs.secondlife.com/community/features/blog/2010/01/19/2009-end-of-year-second-life-economy-wrap-up-including-q4-economy-in-detail
New York Times article: http://www.nytimes.com/2009/10/22/fashion/22Avatar.html?pagewanted=1&_r=1

This study's framework draws on several theories in order to understand bloggers' identity play through their virtual bodies. Fashion plays an important role in embodying identities, because fashion is undeniably about expressing the body (Davis 1992; Entwistle 2000; Svendsen 2006). I begin by considering the virtual body as a technological body (Balsamo 1996) that creates an embodied experience (Ajana 2005; Weiss 1999). Further, I perceive the virtual body and identity through Deleuze and Guattari's (1987) theories of the Body without Organs (BwO), assemblage, and becoming. A brief discussion of these theories follows, and they are also referenced in relation to the bloggers' stories.

6.2   Virtual Body Assemblage as a Technology of Identity

The word "virtual," in this study, involves the concept of the immaterial; that is, the virtual body does not comprise any tangible material. Virtual bodies, simulations of bodies, exist in computer-generated environments. Therefore, the virtual body is a technological body. People rely on technology to restore, escape from, perfect, and revise the physical body (Cruikshank 2001). Yet, fundamentally, a virtual body cannot be created without a physical body (Ajana 2005; Balsamo 1996; Hayles 1999). Through the phenomenological account of embodiment (Ajana 2005), virtual bodies, avatars, become part of the physical body. Therefore, avatars as extensions of the self constitute ways to communicate in virtual worlds. The virtual body is closely connected to the physical body, and both are sites in which identity forms.

A major reason for which a person creates an avatar is to communicate and socialise with other people in a virtual world. An avatar can also be used as an artistic medium and as an actor in the creation of digital images and machinimas.[3] However, can an avatar actually affect/transform identity? To understand the virtual body as having an effect on identity, we cannot "simply contextualiz[e] the body as a culture object" (Buchanan 1997, p. 75). In this regard, Deleuze and Guattari's (1987) idea of the Body without Organs (BwO) provides some conceptual tools.

Deleuze and Guattari (1987) describe the BwO as a living body that is in opposition to organism and organisation. In their terminology, an "organism" is a socially organised category of identities, whereas the BwO is "a body freed from the codes of phallogocentric functions of identity" (Braidotti 1994, p. 124). Deleuze and Guattari consider "the full body without organs" to be "a body populated by multiplicities" (p. 30). "It is the body as pure potential, pure virtuality" (Massumi 1992, p. 71). Therefore, if the virtual body or avatar becomes a BwO, it is freed from identity categories. The virtual body is, then, a space in which multiplicities happen, a space

---

[3] Machinima is a film genre that uses 3D virtual worlds and/or video game technologies to create animation. For more information, go to http://www.machinima.org/machinima-faq.html.

for the production of desire (Grosz 1994; Jordan 1995). By choosing an avatar, we make some aspects of our desires visible. In this way, the avatar functions as a place where transformations can take place, and the virtual body remains closely connected to the physical body, which is the basis for the virtual body's identity.

6.2.1 Avatar Re/Assembling as Assemblage and Becoming

Assemblage is a genre of art that uses found objects to create an artwork. It is strongly connected to collage, an artform in which objects, such as newspaper clippings and pieces of cloth, are attached to a surface in order to create references to life through sensory and representative fragments. In using the term "avatar re/assembling," therefore, I refer to creating avatars through an art-making process. As numerous body parts and items of clothing are available for assembling an avatar in SL, the process of constructing an avatar, for most people, is a process of choosing different items for their avatar. There is no determinate identity in avatar re/assembling, nor is any specific body indicated. To explain the pedagogy of assemblage, Garoian and Gaudelius (2008) referenced Nam June Paik's assemblage *TV Buddha*,[4] an installation that consists of a Buddha statue facing a TV screen and a closed-circuit video camera, which projects the statue of the Buddha onto the TV screen: "Paik challenged the concept of the body as the 'screen' on which the prevailing codes of culture are continually projected and through which identity is determined" (p. 97). We can see the process of avatar re/assembling as similar to Nam June Paik's artwork; that is, in both constructions, we sit in front of a screen that ostensibly projects our self-images. However, the difference between avatar creation and the *TV Buddha* is that the self-image inhering in the former is not an exact projection but an indefinite body image that is always in the making. The process of avatar re/assembling is already an assemblage that includes the virtual body, the actual body, the screen, and everything in-between.

The concept of assemblage proposed by Deleuze and Guattari (1987) is one that addresses "the play of contingency and structure, organisation and change" (Wise 2005, p. 77). As with artwork, assemblages combine components in a particular way. Thus, they inhere in multiplicity. They have no shape, and "their 'law' is rather the imperative of endless experimentation, metamorphosis, or transmutation, alignment and realignment" (Grosz 1994, p. 167).

In order to consider the processing quality of avatar re/assembling, I extend the concept of assemblage to the process of avatar creation in order to think of the process of avatar/reassembling as assemblage. In this way, we can understand how it functions to create changes. That is, avatar creation has its own affect/function, such that it cannot be reduced to a technique or skill that serves the construction of identities. And, the avatar, whether as another assemblage or a BwO, cannot be seen as an object of desire or as a subject with a fixed identity; rather, it is becoming.

---

[4] The image and related information are available here: http://www.paikstudios.com/gallery/1.html

6.2.2 Clothing, Body, and Identity

The relationship between fashion and identity is complex. Using Merleau-Ponty's phenomenology, Entwistle (2000) explained that "the experience of dress is a subjective act of attending *to* one's body and making the body an object of consciousness and [it] is also an act of attention *with* the body" (p. 30). In the physical world, it is through clothing that the body is made an object in public space. Further, clothes provide the body with experiences. Calefato (2004) stated that "the clothed body expresses the way in which a subject is in and of the world through his/her aesthetic and physical appearance, his/her relation with other bodies and lived bodily experiences" (p. 2). In the virtual world, clothing also provides avatar body experience, and this is one influence on how identity forms.

Clothing is an extension of the body (Cixous 1994; Svendsen 2006) in that it creates meanings and fashions a status for the body. Clothing constitutes, rewrites, and transfers the shape and expression of the body (Svendsen 2006). As Entwistle (2000) argued, "human bodies are dressed bodies" (p. 6), and "dress or adornment is one of the means by which bodies are made social and given meaning and identity" (p. 7). In most situations, the virtual body needs clothes, just as the physical body does. As clothing is important in constructing culture and identity in the physical world, virtual clothes are equally important for the same reasons in cyberspace.

Clothing communicates many things about a person: social class, status, gender, profession, taste, and socio-cultural background. This is most dramatically expressed by representatives of subcultures. For example, in a study of the United Kingdom's punk subculture of the 1970s, Hebdige (1979) presented a semiotic reading in which style features as a way of constructing group identity. In subcultures, clothing is coded, intentionally communicating, "giv[ing] itself to be read" (p. 101) as transgressing the main culture. Hence, it establishes a distinctly differentiated identity of its own. Davis (1992) also viewed clothing as a visual metaphor for communicating subtle things about a wearer, such as his/her "reflexive awareness of what is being 'said'" (p. 25). Thus, clothing becomes a technology for managing identity.

6.3 Second Life Virtual Fashion and Fashion Blogs

In order to discuss fashion and identity in the virtual world, I draw on definitions of fashion as set out by Lipovetsky (1994), Svendsen (2006), Hollander (1993), and Entwistle (2000), all of whom perceive fashion as a systematic operation. The fashion system in SL largely mimics physical-life fashion practices, in terms of presenting collections, notions of commerce, and, of course, a focus on producing designs that customers will buy. However, SL fashion diverges from physical-life fashion in terms of advertising, sales, and events. A crucial difference is that it is much easier to create a fashion business in SL than in the physical world, as the costs involved in producing and advertising SL fashion are minimal. In fact, some people start businesses without spending any money at all, so that anyone with some computer graphic design and/or 3D-modelling skills can become a fashion designer. Supply and demand, therefore, work differently in the SL context. For example, unlike physical world fashion houses that follow a strict schedule of showings that includes spring, resort, and fall collections, SL designers can market anything at any time. This is partly because buyers of SL fashion live all over the world and because of the fantasy aspect that means a Londoner in the winter may still want to buy summer fashion for her/his avatar. Yet, it is interesting to note that the majority of SL designers follow fashion seasons in the physical world, but with a very important difference: they are less likely to discard styles than are physical world designers as the traditional fashion seasons change. Nor do SL styles sell out, unless the designer has decided to create a limited edition. Overall, though, there can be no doubt that SL fashion, just like physical fashion, operates according to rules of business and according to the aesthetic creativity of its designers.

Most people in SL use avatars that have a human form. But even avatars with the appearance of fantasy creatures can still wear clothes, as designers of SL fashion also offer clothes for such forms. The fashion industry is an important activity in SL and a significant contributor to its economy. In fact, *The New York Times* reported that clothing and accessories account for about 40% of SL's marketplace (La Ferla 2009 October 22). Because the SL platform itself provides only limited opportunities for advertising and for disseminating information,[5] SL residents look to other sites on the Internet for their news and information needs.

Although, overall, I refer to the blogs about SL fashion as *fashion blogs,* they have different purposes: some are dedicated entirely to posting information about freebies and/or good deals for bargain hunters, some serve as a news source for new releases from designers, and others focus on displaying personal lookbooks[6] or personal experience with SL fashion. The bloggers I interviewed all primarily use their blogs to showcase their own style and to reflect on their fashion experiences in SL. Their blogs are not specifically created for advertising. Yet, their avatars do wear designer clothing, and the bloggers sometimes offer reviews of the designers' products. Predictably, if the presentation of the avatars is anything to go by, there are more female than male SL fashion bloggers. In addition, some female bloggers have created male avatars in order to present looks designed for men. Since many people who are interested in SL fashion read several blogs, there are also several blog feed sites that gather hundreds of SL fashion blogs for the convenience of viewing them on one site. In addition, some individuals and groups post their SL fashion looks in arenas such as Flickr.[7]

---

[5] There is no effective means for advertising using the SL program itself. This is because SL is not like a Web site in that it cannot be viewed in a linear way. Shops are scattered in SL; therefore, it is not easy to find a shop or find out what items it has for sale. Although some vendors do send out information about their merchandise, this is not very efficient as not everyone checks their messages and some messages get lost during transmission.

[6] In real-life fashion, a lookbook is a book that shows the fashions a designer is currently marketing and from which a customer can order. Some people use their blogs as a way to document their different outfits—a sort of historical lookbook.

[7] http://www.flickr.com/

Some SL fashion bloggers have both friendships with designers and a large general readership. Such bloggers often receive free review clothes and accessories from designers, who hope the freebies will bring them some publicity. Blogger groups engage in a related practice, whereby designers join a group in order to distribute their products gratis to bloggers, and bloggers join in order to receive free items that they then review. It seems that for some people the privilege of receiving free products is their key reason for writing a fashion blog. For others, though, especially those whose blogs are established, a relationship with a designer is an important reason for blogging about a new product. However, most bloggers' central reason for creating a fashion blog inheres in a wish to share their SL experience and fashion style; therefore, most bloggers only blog about the fashion that they genuinely appreciate. Regardless, every fashion blogger must be highly enthusiastic and well-informed about SL fashion and clothing in order to establish a following.

In summary, fashion in SL is a systematic operation, just like it is in physical life. Although the virtual fashion system does not directly relate to the bloggers' avatars, it is in this context that many bloggers re/assemble their avatars. Furthermore, it appears that to a great extent the bloggers' avatars reflect new releases in the virtual fashion arena. Therefore, no matter the reason for assembling an avatar, be it for self-expression or business purposes, the influence of the virtual fashion system is evident.

6.4   Fashion Bloggers' Identity Re/Assembling

SL fashion bloggers are users of SL who blog about their fashion practices and consistently change their avatars/looks. They create avatar body images that circulate on the Internet and embody the visual culture of virtual worlds. In this qualitative research, I interviewed three fashion bloggers in order to understand their experiences re/assembling their avatars. The interviews were semi-structured. I asked questions regarding their experiences and thoughts about avatar re/assembling and their fashion-blogging practices. However, the interviews also had an open-ended element, as I asked follow-up questions as necessary. Most interviews with the individual bloggers took place in SL via text chat, but in one interview, I actually talked with the blogger. I found the bloggers through reading a fashion feed, and I selected them because they represent different ways to assemble avatars through fashion and their blogs express their personal experiences in SL. These bloggers are part of the SL fashion system because despite sharing their personal looks, they show designers' new releases and sometimes review products on their blogs. Though each blogger is different in regard to style and experience, they also have some important common ground in that they all embrace and practise "assembling" to a greater extent than do those who merely offer themselves and their blogs as advertising boards. In referring to assembling, I mean they creatively mix and match clothes from different designers and wear them in ways that are different from the designer's original intentions. As well as interviewing the bloggers, I collected data from their blogs and observed the SL fashion system as a whole in order to provide context for the study. These stories are meant to show the different relationships between the physical and the virtual body and to describe how these bloggers construct identities through fashion. My analysis focuses on exploring how three bloggers construct and relate to their avatars through the theories briefly set out in the previous sections.

6.4.1 Embodied Becoming

> I generally don't differentiate between "me" and my avatar. "Me" in my offline, real-world sense. My avatar and I share the same experience of being inhabited by my personality, so I truly consider this an extension of myself into another avenue of expression. (Margarita, personal communication, October 12, 2009)

As many researchers have pointed out (e.g. Ballengee-Morris 2009; Schultze and Leahy 2009), there is no fixed relationship between an avatar and the self; rather, the relationship is multi-dimensional and subject to change (Schultze and Leahy 2009). Margarita's feeling that her avatar constitutes an extension of herself shows how the boundary of machine and human, physical and virtual, is blurred in the culture of simulation, as Turkle (1995) suggested. Her virtual body is her body, and the body is "no longer conceived as an object of the world, but as our means of communications with it" (Merleau-Ponty 2005, p. 54). Margarita's avatar is a means through which she communicates, and it is "never isolated in its activity but always already engaged with the world" (Weiss 1999, p. 1). And, for Margarita, the way her avatar connects with others is through different fashion styles.

Identity politics creates dress codes (Calefato 2004), and the dress and style of those codes establish and communicate identity. Margarita uses more styles than do most of the other SL fashion bloggers. I do not know if in physical life she would wear the same things as she wears in SL. Corsets, high boots, horns, and tattoos are among the items she has worn. Her style vocabulary extends to Goth, Lolita, and steampunk (Figs. 6.1–6.6). Sometimes, I wonder if she creates her styles with the intention of disrupting the mono-standard of beauty presented in many of the other blogs. I would never even consider dressing my avatar in such a way, even though it is the virtual world, so I admire her bravery in combining these different styles. My view of my own identity is defined by the clothing my avatar wears, but her different styles make it difficult to define her identity.

She tells me that SL fashion gives her "a means to express [her] self artistically through fashion that [she] can't afford or wear IRL [in the real world]" (personal communication, October 12, 2009). This seems to be one of the best aspects of SL fashion play. As clothing embodies different social identities (Calefato 2004; Entwistle 2000), there are always some kinds of clothes that one appreciates but does not wear, because of the price, associated social roles, and/or the shape and size of one's body. SL fashion, for Margarita, provides a medium through which she can explore herself beyond the constraints of the physical world. These fashion items are important to the virtual body because they give rise to embodied feelings. The feelings not only involve a sense of satisfaction at owning things that are hard

Fig. 6.1 An example of the styles created by Margarita

or even impossible to acquire in physical life, but, in Margarita's words, there is also a sense of "avatar envy." For example, she envies her avatar because it has a tattoo that she would like to have. The tattoo, therefore, is no longer just an image in the virtual world; instead, it is a connection between her physical and her virtual body. Her virtual body embodies her desires.

I only knew Margarita through reading her blog. However, I visited her skybox[8] after she agreed to be interviewed. This was the first time I had seen her in her avatar form in SL instead of in her avatar images on her blog. If I were to pick a colour to describe her, I would choose orange. It is an October colour. As Halloween was drawing near, many related products were being created and sold, and Margarita's avatar was living in an orange Halloween-themed skybox at the time I visited her. She told me that the skybox was a 30Linden gacha.[9] However, I felt a sense of her

---

[8] A skybox is a living space or house that floats in the sky in SL. Many SL residents build their homes in the sky to gain more privacy and escape from the ugly and unorganised ground space.

[9] *Gacha* is a term that comes from the Japanese word *gachapon* (ガチャポン), which refers to toys sold randomly via a machine vendor. Buyers do not know in advance which item they will receive after paying the machine. Gacha machines have become a popular way to sell things in SL.

Fig. 6.2 An example of the styles created by Margarita

as orange not only because she was surrounded by orange decorations, but also because she wore a pair of orange-rose heels with a matching orange-rose choker, a hat with a pumpkin decoration, and an orange-brown vest and trousers. Her makeup was orange too, orange eye shadow and orange lip colour. Throughout the interview, we lay on a giant orange-striped cat-shaped couch. It was a setting that would be hard to achieve in physical life. This setting and my feeling of her as orange gave me a way to understand how she chooses what to wear in constructing her avatar. That is, somehow, she constructs her avatar based on physical-life seasons and feelings. The physical-life influence is strongly embodied in the virtual world. Because of her charming living space, I wanted to live like her in SL. My desire to become her avatar identity was aroused by the material objects she owns, which I realised indicates the role that material objects play in constituting identity. Yet, she told me that her existence in SL is a lonely one. She wrote, "I am mostly up here in my sky box putting on inventory or photographing =)" (personal communication, October 12, 2009). This is not the first time I have heard that people spend considerable time in SL just playing dress-up. I wondered, why, when there are so many things a person can do in SL, people emphasise this activity. What is special about it?

Fig. 6.3 An example of the styles created by Margarita

I am sure that I recognised Margarita's avatar immediately when I saw her, because I noticed her shape, which was like that shown in her blog pictures. The shape of the virtual body is important to constructing identity; as she said, "I am 'me' in this shape—I've used it for over a year now. I don't feel or look like 'me' in any other shape, unless it's my male shape" (personal communication, October 12, 2009). The shape she chose supports her sense of self. It is a base that creates a territory of identity in the virtual world. It is also the "body" of the virtual body. Without a definite shape, which happens occasionally when logging in is slow, an avatar looks like a cloud floating in virtual space.

Although her avatar images present many different styles, she does not think they are different identities. She said, "When I create different outfits, I don't consider my avatar different. I generally stick to a unified shape, the 'me' shape. Then I put on different skins, hair, outfits, etc. etc., but it's all simply dressing up one main avatar" (Margarita, personal communication, October 12, 2009). Thus, although style and clothing construct identity groups in physical life (Davis 1992; Hebdige 1979), different fashion styles do not necessarily assign different identities in SL, at least not for Margarita. Her avatar re/assembling embodies a single subjectivity, but this subjectivity does not need to have a fixed way to represent itself except for the

Fig. 6.4 An example of the styles created by Margarita

shape of the avatar. All physical-life identity markers, such as skin and clothes, collapse into a single plane in her avatar re/assembling experience.

As Margarita noted, as well as the variety of styles she creates, she also has a male avatar/shape that she uses from time to time. Male is not her identity; as she said, "I make sure people know that I am an old mom even in [a] boy avatar" (personal communication, October 12, 2009). The male shape, then, is a medium that she uses to present men's clothes. Thus, the male avatar can become a BwO, because it is a body without organised gender categories and because through it the gender the body represented is rejected. The BwO consists of multiplicities and "the events of incorporeal transformations" (Markula 2006, p. 38). Margarita has created an assemblage that functions as an in-between space, and her male avatar is that space.

This in-between is also the abstract line that Deleuze (2006) described in explaining his concept of assemblage. That is, an assemblage is constituted by many different lines, and

> an abstract line is a line with no outlines, a line that passes between things, a line in mutation.... It is very much alive, living and creative.... An assemblage is carried along by its abstract lines, when it is able to have or trace abstract lines. (p. 178)

Fig. 6.5 An example of the styles created by Margarita

In other words, the abstract line or the in-between is where creative new possibilities can be fulfilled and the assemblage is the process through which they are produced.

She does not transform into a male because of her male avatar, but her avatar-assembling assemblage transforms and flattens the concept of being male into an abstract line or in-between space, in which identity representation does not function. Deleuze and Guattari explained that "the only way to get outside the dualisms is to be-between, to pass between … never ceasing to become" (p. 277). Therefore, we can use this concept to elucidate the ways in which Margarita transforms the representations of her identity.

The concept of becoming is Deleuze and Guattari's (1987) challenge to the notion of a steady identity (Braidotti 2002). Through their theory of becoming, they address questions about being. And, in doing so, they propose a series of becomings, the first of which is that of "becoming-woman." And, this first becoming "involves a series of processes and movements beyond the fixity of subjectivity and the structure of stable unities" (Grosz 1994, p. 177). The theory offers a way to disrupt the dualistic account of subject and object. Margarita's fashion style is not easy to define, and it is in this indefinability

Fig. 6.6 An example of the styles created by Margarita

that she presents aspects of her identity. Although her avatar re/assembling embodies a single subjectivity, that subjectivity is in the becoming because of her ever-changing styles. The becoming allows her to form new connections with other identities.

6.4.2 Self-Invention

My avatar is very much an extension of my RL self, so I try to behave in SL as I would in RL. However, when it comes to fashion, obviously some things I wear aren't very realistic, and I do love dressing up. So in a way, my avatar is sort of a doll, but mostly just me. (Stella, personal communication, March 22, 2010)

Fig. 6.7 An example of the styles created by Stella

Whether as an extension of herself or as a doll, Stella's avatar identity is deliberately constructed. She gives the impression of being an independent and successful woman. She always creates and arranges her avatar images carefully, and she thinks she tends to overanalyse her work (Figs. 6.7–6.10). The clothes she buys are all high quality and well designed, which in terms of virtual fashion means that they must have good image quality and be expertly crafted (with matching seams, etc.). Her styles are not necessarily high fashion; instead, they are everyday urban styles. The image I have of Stella is of a person continually inventing herself through avatar re/assembling.

In considering her experience, I asked myself if an avatar that is so close to physical-life norms of beauty could transform a physical-life identity. I did not see any evidence that she engages in a critical examination of the clothes her avatar wears. That is, her fashion and avatar representation appropriate physical-life concepts of beauty, and she does not try to challenge these representations. She noted that, "It's funny how we tend to look more and more alike, but I think that's just a product of the fashion community tending to shift toward particular designers" (personal communication, March 22, 2010).

Fig. 6.8 An example of the styles created by Stella

This statement implies that the assembling of an avatar is strongly influenced by popular clothing styles. According to Entwistle (2000), dress is a "situated bodily practice" (p. 39). That is, dress, body, and embodiment provide a valid account of fashion and identity inasmuch as they emphasise the wearing of clothes as an embodied activity within a social environment. Avatar identity re/assembling is unavoidably bounded by the fashion industry.

Her practice appears to centre on transferring her physical-life identity to the virtual world, although I do not know what she looks like in physical life. Stella talked about her style and what this process means to her:

> I don't tend to blog too many things that are extravagant. I tend to stick to casual looks, every day outfits, which are generally very ME. And I sort of use my blog as a way for people to get a better sense of who I am. (Stella, personal communication, March 22, 2010)

Stella's perception that her dressing style is representative of herself shows that clothing is not only an object. Instead, "the body as a socially constituted and situated

Fig. 6.9 An example of the styles created by Stella

object" (Entwistle 2000, p. 12) is managed and disciplined under the operation of power, and dress is an expression of that lived and embodied experience. Stella's avatar re/assembling situates her avatar body within her physical body's experience, and her fashion play is an expression of these experiences.

Physical-life identity is important to Stella, and one of the ways in which she embodies her physical-life identity is through her clothing styles in SL. Stella, then, moves seamlessly between physical and virtual; there is no inconsistent transition. Her physical-life identity determines how she constructs her virtual identity. However, her virtual fashion experience affects her physical life as well:

> I've found that I have a better sense of fashion now than I did before. And I tend to be a bit more adventurous in my RL clothing choices. I was very conservative before, but I've found that my SL fashion choices have pushed me to make more creative RL clothing choices. (Stella, personal communication, March 22, 2010)

She does not see her practice in the virtual world as transforming her identity. She views it, instead, as extending her identity into SL. Yet, her avatar re/assembling experience does change her physical self. Thus, there is no visible boundary between the physical and virtual self for her. Her physical and virtual bodies are like a *Möbius strip*, which "through a kind of twisting or inversion, one side becomes another" (Grosz 1994, p. xii). Her body is extended through her avatar

Fig. 6.10 An example of the styles created by Stella

re/assembling, and it is through her avatar that her body and identity become fluid but not fragmented.

This change is the effect of her avatar assemblage. Stella does not escape from her physical-life identity; instead, she unproblematically brings her physical-life identity into the virtual world and opens up more potential for her physical self through the virtual world self—a process that she considers to be very "therapeutic and personal."

Deleuze and Guattari (1987) suggested that assemblage creates territory but also unmakes territory (their term for the latter is "deterritorialisation"). In this way, the assemblage Stella creates functions to deterritorialise her physical self. At the same time, because of the virtuality of the assemblage, she also deterritorialises her physical self. This is where change happens; in her words, it is a "freedom [that] allows me to really be creative and look in a way that I could never look in RL" (Stella, personal communication, March 22, 2010). The change is in both directions. Her physical-life identity invents her avatar, but her avatar also re-invents her physical body and identity.

6.4.3 Avatar Doll as Prosthesis

It's not how I look like in real life, and I kind of think of my avatar like something I can experiment with. Something like the blank canvas that I can try on different clothes. You know, it's kind of like a doll that I like to put on different colors and patterns and shirts. It's a canvas for me. It's more like a doll of sorts. (Leah, personal communication, April 6, 2010)

The complex relationship between avatar and self can be seen in Leah's statement. Although she thinks of her avatar as her doll, she also thinks of her avatar as herself: "I am just my self. I don't role play or anything like that. I'm just myself. I am always myself in terms of what I wear" (Leah, personal communication, April 6, 2010). In my opinion, Leah is one of the most talented bloggers in terms of her ability to create fashion looks. Her avatar images are usually presented in ways that are similar to fashion photographs in physical-life magazines (Figs. 6.11–6.14). Her avatar's shape, however, is unique, and although very thin, like much-criticised

Fig. 6.11 An example of the styles created by Leah

Fig. 6.12 An example of the styles created by Leah

physical-life models, her avatar does not have a conventionally beautiful face. She told me that she took her inspiration for her avatar's shape from physical-life Asian models. She confirmed that she is Asian and that her avatar had been part of an SL model agency for a short time. In talking about her experiences with the model agency, she expressed concerns that some model agencies have created a standardised shape (referred to as a "mode") for their models. She said, "I don't think it's right. I think you are stripping identity from somebody when you send them to a mode" (Leah, personal communication, April 6, 2010). For many, as for Leah, an avatar's shape is not just an identity marker; it is the basis of the avatar's identity. This is so even though the shape can be changed. What Leah expresses here too, is that it is a question of the avatar reflecting free choices rather than being pushed toward a particular appearance. This free choice is an important aspect of avatar identity that is related to the concept of self-expression.

Fig. 6.13 An example of the styles created by Leah

I actually never met Leah in her avatar form. However, as our interview was through Skype,[10] I did get to hear her voice. I had not formed any ideas about what her voice would sound like, but I did think that her sophisticated voice matched her avatar. Leah told me that she has always been interested in fashion:

> … in real life I've always wanted to go into styling as a professional job. And I think this is, at this point in my life, this is kind of the closest that I can get to it. So, you know, I love styling, like I said, in fashion and in real life, and this is kind of a version of that. Like sort of practice for me. So I like to stretch my brain and I like to challenge myself in what I can put together and what I can create, because I love to do this in real life. I love to have a model there or a mannequin so I can style in the store.(Leah, personal communication, April 6, 2010)

---

[10] http://www.skype.com

Fig. 6.14 An example of the styles created by Leah

   This statement definitely explains why she prefers fashion-magazine looks. On the surface, her SL identity appears to differ from her physical-life identity; yet, this is not the case. Instead, it can be seen as a prosthesis through which she can achieve things that are outside the limits of her physical life. Her avatar doll is part of her that is inseparable from her desire.

   Fashion is a way for her to challenge herself and establish her identity in the virtual world. As she said, "it's all about pushing yourself and about creating new challenges to yourself and to your styling. It's about stepping outside of your comfort zone" (Leah, personal communication, April 6, 2010). Although she affirmed that she has never had an identity crisis in physical life, she recognised that "the hardest part is finding yourself and really being comfortable with it" (personal communication, April 6, 2010); that is, she tries not to be influenced by others in the currents of SL fashion. Her focus is on establishing and enjoying her own style. Fashion styling is her means of enacting identity in SL. Leah stated that in her opinion fashion can also conceal one's identity. In her view, this is especially true in SL; as when people wear the same clothes or mimic others, for her, the similarities mean that people lose their identities. I consider her challenge to herself the beginning of becoming because "becoming explodes the ideas about what we are and what we can be beyond the categories that seem to contain us" (Sotirin 2005, p. 99). Her explorations of avatar re/assembling challenge her to move from familiar territory to unfamiliar that can induce change. Thus, she started a process of becoming that has the potential of identity transformation. As becoming is always in-between (Deleuze and Guattari 1987), her challenge to herself to become will never end as long as she continues her avatar re/assembling process.

Although she observed that her avatar is like her doll, her avatar is also the embodiment of the process of finding her identity. This process is mediated through her avatar doll/virtual body. As Weiss (1999) suggested that embodiment is inter-corporeality, her experience of finding identity through avatar re/assembling consists in a series of interactions between her physical self, her avatar body, and the cultural forces she encounters. This is clearly reflected by Leah's avatar re/assembling—her finding of identity through changing her fashion style. The (virtual) body is a process for understanding embodied identity (Budgeon 2003). Leah's avatar embodies identity not as a fixed object, but as a fluid and ever-changing process. She proudly stated the point as follows:

> finding your own style and being used to it and being comfortable and proud of it. And getting to that place has been a very pleasant journey for me ... kind of where I am now with blogging and my style and my identity. (Leah, personal communication, April 6, 2010)

6.4.4 Summary

Identity transformation for these bloggers does not consist in transforming their physical-life identities into one or more different virtual identities. It consists in how this process allows them to reinvent themselves based on their physical bodies and identities and so connect to other (physical and virtual) bodies thereby forming new assemblages. To understand what it means to conceive of avatar re/assembling as assemblage, we can consider avatar creation as a virtual body image–computer interface–screen–body assemblage.[11] This assemblage not only comprises the avatar's individual body parts and its clothing, it also includes the computer device on which the avatar is rendered and displayed and the physical body that clicks the keyboard, moves the mouse, and sees the avatar image. It also includes how each body part and piece of clothing on the avatar is perceived in the cultural context and the communication experience that the avatar is integral to creating. The adjustments and changes made to an avatar (re)create (another) territory, but they also deterritorialise the avatar. The in-between in this assemblage comprises decisions that are always shifting and so always becoming, giving way to or at least with the potential of yielding to decisions to come. These new assemblages can, in fact, turn

---

[11]See Wise's (2005) example of a mobile phone as a "thumb-key-software-transmission assemblage" (p. 84).

back to affect the physical world identity. Margarita does not differentiate between her avatar and herself. Her difficult-to-define fashion style has made her avatar a BwO, always becoming. Stella's avatar is also herself. There is no boundary between the virtual and the physical for her in re/assembling her avatar. Her fashion is about self-expression. Leah's avatar is more like her doll, which she uses to realise her own ideas. Through her fashion, she challenges herself to find and construct her identity.

More research is needed; yet, I think it reasonable, especially given the similarities of the bloggers' stories, to assume that the viewpoints and experiences of the bloggers in this study are shared by many other SL fashion bloggers. Furthermore, even though their stories are by no means uniform, there are some striking similarities: They all see their avatar's shape(s) as an important identity marker. They also think of the process of re/assembling their avatars as creating art and of designer clothes as art that they can wear. All reject the idea that they are living in a fantasy identity in SL; instead, they consider their lives in SL as an aspect of their physical-life identities. Their avatar body images do not stop functioning after being published. These images are new assemblages that they use to constantly reflect their own processes, serving as connection points for others to interact with them and thereby create new assemblages.

An avatar's shape is an important starting point for identity construction in SL. Because it is inevitable that different avatars will wear the same clothes or even the same skin, shape becomes one thing that makes an avatar unique. Thus, shape embodies a blogger's identity. However, this identity is not unchangeable. For example, Margarita recognises both her female and male shapes. Yet, shape is a bound identity. It creates a territory and a possible limit for people who recognise their shapes and do not change their shapes (or at least do not change often). Even when a blogger changes shape, a particular aspect of personality and desire is expressed and that shape for that time offers the basis for identity and a boundary between the blogger's identity and the arena in which it is functioning.

These bloggers consider that by creating avatar body images, they are, in fact, creating art. As Stella described it,

> I feel like I'm painting a picture. Especially with my photography. I love to showcase as much as I can of this beautiful virtual world, and until I decide to start creating things of my own, my photos and individual style are my art here. (personal communication, March 22, 2010)

The process of avatar assembling creates art. Though it doesn't directly expose an identity, it does position the avatar as a medium. Working with this medium provides the potentiality for creating new possibilities and challenging current identity representations.

Designers' new creations are usually a source from which the bloggers draw in assembling their avatars. They see the designers' work as art; as Stella said, "I love to see designers that put so much work into creating designs to share with us. It's like wearing their art" (personal communication, March 22, 2010). Leah also said that "I can see they [designers] have a vision when they make something. And I can see they took inspiration or they took something that they consider art themselves.

It is art" (personal communication, April 6, 2010). Margarita even considers avatar re/assembling to be a collaborative art. She said, "I think what I do is a complement to what designers do, so it's maybe collaborative art" (personal communication, October 12, 2009). Their collaborative art forms another assemblage that functions on many different levels, including commercialism—they help designers sell their creations, their own consumption—they enjoy owning and wearing designer clothes, and artistic expression—they express their creativity with this medium.

However, their assemblage does not end at the published images. Instead, they connect to other bodies and create new meanings. As Leah said,

> if you look at my pictures you can maybe create a story for yourself and I think that's what I enjoy. Like some people like to take how they want it and they get creative with their own imagination. You know. Why my avatar in that particular sim is wearing that outfit? It's a guessing game. So I kind of more leave it to the reader than myself. (personal communication, April 6, 2010)

Their individual avatar body images cannot be read as separate identities. These are components of their identity assemblages.

Despite the differences and similarities of identity construction through avatar re/assembling, these bloggers' avatar body images all, in some way, represent contemporary ideas of beauty, like those found in physical-life fashion magazines. Does this mean that their ideas about self and identity are unavoidably shaped by the socio-cultural environment they live in? Virtual fashion seemingly provides a window to look into this aspect of identity, that is, to look at the very socio-cultural forces that define subjectivity and identity. Nevertheless, as my analysis of some of the bloggers' experiences shows, the bloggers are negotiating between this force and their desires. The first step to understanding the dynamics of their negotiation is to think of these body images as part of the process of creating their assemblages. In this way, the content and expression of the image are articulated and how the image forms its territory of identity and also deterritorialises the social institution's account of identity are presented.

6.5   Conclusion

Participating in virtual fashion to these bloggers may or may not be the same as recreating their identities online—some see their avatars as dolls, but others think of their avatars as themselves. Nevertheless, the projection of the self through an avatar body is unavoidable. Clothing for these bloggers is a way to creatively express the self and to embody their identities, which is very similar to physical life. However, the body constructed in the virtual world through avatar re/assembling cannot be seen as representing a specific identity. Instead, a virtual body image is only a slice of the continuum of ongoing identity reassembling. Given that a fashion blogger's online identity is mediated through an ever-changing avatar body and clothing, virtual fashion creates an embodied identity experience online. Although it can be argued that the use of these different body images constitutes "identity tourism"

(Nakamura 1999), these fashion bloggers do not think that by creating their avatars they are constructing or trying out another identity. Rather, their physical and virtual bodies are integrated such that they form an assemblage. And, it is this assemblage that continually constructs and deconstructs identity.

It is also important to understand that commercialism, consumption, and artistic expression all have roles in virtual fashion play. Sometimes, a blogger's avatar will wear a certain outfit because it is the blogger's "job" to display and advertise for designers. Although these avatar body images apparently do not directly address identity construction, the wearing of designer clothes in this environment may turn out to connect in meaningful ways to other aspects of physical-world and SL existence. However, it is beyond the scope of this research to consider this point. For some, the privilege of wearing designer clothing fulfills their desires, while others enjoy creating hundreds of looks that cannot easily be achieved in their physical lives. Others enjoy wearing pieces of art or creating their own artwork. Finally, some bloggers are not only consumers of virtual fashion, but they are also creators of fashion. Does the experience of being a creator of fashion mean that they think about identity construction differently from how other bloggers think of it?

Bloggers do not necessarily think critically about the clothes, accessories, or body parts they use to assemble their avatars. Therefore, the body images they produce can be read as simply reproducing physical-world fashion and beauty stereotypes. Nevertheless, we need to remember that a virtual body cannot be separate from a physical body. These body images are slices from identities that cannot be easily defined. Thus, it is important to understand the different processes and experiences that individuals bring to creating their avatars. Though formed by the very social and political forces that they express, these bloggers' avatar body images are capable of creating a new assemblage of the self, one in which the self is always becoming.

References

Ajana, B.: Disembodiment and cyberspace: A phenomenological approach. Electron. J. Sociol. (2005). Retrieved from http://www.sociology.org/content/2005/tier1/ajana.html

Ballengee-Morris, C.: A raining afternoon growing younger and wiser. Vis. Cult. Gend. **4**, 21–34 (2009)

Balsamo, A.: Technologies of the Gendered Body: Reading Cyborg Women. Duck University Press, Durham (1996)

Braidotti, R.: Nomadic Subjects: Embodiment and Sexual Difference in Contemporary Feminist theory. Columbia University Press, New York (1994)

Braidotti, R.: Metamorphoses: Towards a Materialist Theory of Becoming. Polity Press, Cambridge (2002)

Buchanan, I.: The problem of the body in Deleuze and Guattari, or what can a body do? Body Soc. **3**(3), 73–91 (1997)

Budgeon, S.: Identity as an embodied event. Body Soc. **9**(1), 35–55 (2003)

Calefato, P.: The clothed body. (L. Adams, Tran.).Berg, New York (2004)

Cixous, H.: Sonia Rykiel in Translation. In: Benstock, S., Ferriss, S. (eds.) On Fashion, pp. 95–99. Rutgers University Press, New Brunswick (1994)

Cruikshank, L.R.: Avatar dreams: An ethnography of desire for the virtual body. Master's thesis. Queen's University, Kingston (2001)

Davis, F.: Fashion, Culture, and Identity. The University of Chicago Press, Chicago (1992)

Deleuze, G.: Two regimes of madness. In: Lapoujade, D. (ed.) (Hodges, A., Taormina, M. Trans.). Semiotext(e), New York (2006)

Deleuze, G., Guattari, F.: A thousand plateaus: Capitalism and schizophrenia. (B. Massumi, Tran.). University of Minnesota Press, Minneapolis (1987)

Entwistle, J.: The Fashioned Body: Fashion, Dress and Modern Social Theory. Polity Press, Cambridge (2000)

Garoian, C.R., Gaudelius, Y.M.: Specatacle Pedagogy: Art, Politics, and Visual Culture. State University of New York Press, Albany (2008)

Grosz, E.: Volatile Bodies: Toward a Corporeal Feminism. Indiana University Press, Bloomington (1994)

Hayles, N.K.: How We Became Posthuman: Virtual Bodies in Cybernetics, Literature, and Informatics. The University of Chicago Press, Chicago (1999)

Hebdige, D.: Subculture: The Meaning of Style. Routledge, London (1979)

Hollander, A.: Seeing Through Clothes. University of California Press, Los Angeles (1993)

Jordan, T.: Collective bodies: Raving and the politics of Gilles Deleuze and Felix Guattari. Body Soc. **1**(1), 125–144 (1995)

La Ferla, R.: No budget, no boundaries: It's the real you. New York Times, p. E1 (2009, October 22)

Lipovetsky, G.: The Empire of Fashion: Dressing Modern Democracy. Princeton University Press, Princeton (1994)

Markula, P.: Deleuze and the body without organs: Disreading the fit feminine identity. J Sport Soc. Issues **30**(1), 29–44 (2006)

Massumi, B.: A User's Guide to Capitalism and Schizophrenia: Deviations from Deleuze and Guattari. MIT Press, Cambridge (1992)

Merleau-Ponty, M.: The experience of the body and classical psychology. In: Fraser, M., Greco, M. (eds.) The Body: A Reader, pp. 52–54. Routledge, New York (2005)

Nakamura, L.: Race in/for cyberspace: Identity tourism and racial passing on the Internet. In: Vitanaz, V. (ed.) CyberReader, 2nd edn. Allyn & Bacon, New York (1999)

Schultze, U., Leahy, M.M.: The avatar-self relationship: Enacting presence in second life. In: ICIS 2009 Proceedings. Presented at the International Conference on Information Systems, Phoenix (2009). Retrieved from. http://aisel.aisnet.org/icis2009/12

Sotirin, P.: Becoming-woman. In: Stivale, C.J. (ed.) Gilles Deleuze: Key Concepts, pp. 98–109. McGill-Queen's University Press, Montreal (2005)

Svendsen, L.: Fashion: A Philosophy. Reaktion Books, London (2006)

Turkle, S.: Life on the Screen: Identity in the Age of the Internet. Simon & Schuster, New York (1995)

Weiss, G.: Body Images: Embodiment as Intercorporeality. Routledge, New York (1999)

Wise, J.M.: Assemblage. In: Stivale, C.J. (ed.) Gilles Deleuze: Key Concepts. McGill-Queen's University Press, Montreal (2005)

Chapter 7
Embodying Self in Virtual Worlds

**Ali Mazalek, Sanjay Chandrasekharan, Michael Nitsche,
Tim Welsh, and Paul Clifton**

Abstract Players project their intentions, expressions and movements into virtual
worlds. A dominant reference point for this projection is their avatar. We explore the
transfer of a player's own body movements onto their virtual self, drawing on cognitive
science's common coding theory as a model for understanding their self-recognition.
This chapter presents the results of two sets of self-recognition experiments that investigated the connections between player and virtual avatar. In the first set of experiments,
we investigated self-recognition of movement in different levels of abstraction between
players and their avatars. The second set of experiments made use of an embodied interface for virtual character control that was designed based on common coding principles.
The results demonstrate that this interface is effective in personalising a player's avatar
and could be used to unlock higher cognitive effects compared to other interfaces.

7.1 Introduction

Virtual worlds have become personal and social spaces into which players project their
intentions, expressions and movements. Players customise their avatars in terms of
appearance, clothes and accessories, and then control their movements in real time

A. Mazalek (✉) • M. Nitsche
School of Literature, Communication and Culture, Georgia Institute of Technology,
St. Atlanta, GA, USA
e-mail: mazalek@gatech.edu

S. Chandrasekharan
School of Interactive Computing, Georgia Institute of Technology,
St. Atlanta, GA, USA

T. Welsh
University of Calgary, Calgary, AB T2N 1N4, Canada

P. Clifton
Georgia Institute of Technology, St. Atlanta, GA, USA

A. Peachey and M. Childs (eds.), *Reinventing Ourselves: Contemporary Concepts
of Identity in Virtual Worlds*, Springer Series in Immersive Environments,
DOI 10.1007/978-0-85729-361-9_7, © Springer-Verlag London Limited 2011

through the use of a control interface, such as a keyboard, joystick or gamepad. Although widely used, these conventional interfaces provide a limited degree of engagement, because the finite number of response options on the interfaces force the use of a set of standardised mappings between the player's response and resulting movements of their avatar. As a result, these interfaces restrict the player's ability to generate a range of different and, importantly, personalised movements and expressions in the virtual space. Since all movements by characters in the virtual space are the same regardless of who is controlling them, virtual identity is based primarily on appearance, naming conventions, and patterns of communication, not on movement patterns or animations. In the physical world however, identity is a combination of all of these things, because movement profiles are unique to each person. Our work explores the way players identify with the avatar, specifically in relation to movement.

Despite the standardised nature of character movements in virtual worlds, players develop close connections with their avatars, often treating them as extensions of their own selves. Virtual worlds have thus increasingly become part of our socialisation and personal growth, through playful learning, social interactions, even physical exercise and rehabilitation. Our work seeks to strengthen the connection between player and avatar, by giving personalised movements to virtual avatars through tangible and embodied interfaces. The work is driven by recent experimental evidence from neuroscience and psychology showing that execution, perception and imagination of movements share a common coding in the brain. One implication of this common coding system is that it would allow people to recognise their own movements when they are presented as abstract representations, and also to coordinate with these movements better, compared to standardised movements. This theoretical model can help us to better understand the role played by the motor system in our interactions with computational media, specifically with virtual characters that embody our own movements. It can thus enable us to bring the virtual self closer to the physical world self, and perhaps also allow changes in the virtual self to be more quickly transferred back to the physical world self.

In this chapter, we present the results of two sets of experiments that investigated the connections between player and virtual avatar. In the first set of experiments, we hypothesised that players would identify and coordinate better with characters that encode their own movements. This was tested by tracking movement perception in different levels of abstraction between players and their avatars. The results show that participants can recognise their own movements even in abstracted presentations, and even when they do not see their own movements, but just the movements of a puppet they controlled. The second set of experiments made use of a custom full-body puppet interface for virtual character control that was designed based on common coding principles. The results show that this interface is effective in personalising an avatar. We believe this embodied control could be used to unlock higher cognitive effects compared to other interfaces. In the following sections, we examine the differing ways in which we identify ourselves in the physical vs. virtual worlds, and the way in which existing interfaces support character control in the virtual space.

7.2 Identifying Self in the Virtual and Physical Worlds

In the physical world, a large amount of information is conveyed through our movements. Studies in social psychology have shown that after watching 'thin slices' of video (up to 50 s) of two people interacting, participants can predict the relations between the two people (friend/lover, like/dislike), their sexual orientation, and even the state of a marriage. Participants cannot do this if the videos are presented as a sequence of static pictures (Ambady et al. 2000). This indicates that the judgements are based on movement information. Ideomotor or common coding theory explains this effect, as it suggests that when we perceive and imagine actions, our motor system is activated implicitly (Prinz 1992, 2005; Hommel et al. 2001). In other words, seeing someone walk will activate some of the same parts of our brain that are activated when we walk ourselves. This simulation of the actions of others may be the basis of our ability to project ourselves into different character roles, empathise with others, and make judgments about internal states of other people. Whether the actions are performed by another human being or by an avatar in a virtual world, we understand the actions of others through our own body memory reservoir, which is leveraged to predict actions and movements in the world. This understanding of the way we identify ourselves, and with other people, is not incorporated into current designs of virtual characters. In the virtual world, identity is primarily based on the appearance of the avatar, from body type and hair, to clothes and accessories.

7.2.1 Identifying Self in the Virtual World

Early on, academic analyses acknowledged the effect of "presence" as a key design constraint for the emerging virtual environment (Minsky 1980). Definitions of presence, how it might be measured, its causes and effects vary, as the research addressing this question is based on a range of perspectives (e.g., Slater 1999; Witmer and Singer 1998). Defining presence is further complicated with the field of virtual environments spreading from virtual reality to collaborative virtual worlds to video games and augmented reality. Each of these fields has its own technical and perceptual conditions to create and test levels of presence. The quality of the visualisation, individual player's physical condition, responsiveness of the system, and many other elements can affect presence. In the area of video games, the feeling of "being there" is based on a "perceptual illusion of non-mediation" (Lombard and Ditton 1997) and can be divided into two main categories: a physical category (i.e. the sense of being physically located somewhere) and a social category (i.e. the sense of being together with someone) (IJsselsteijn et al. 2000). Both are relevant for self-projection into a virtual world.

In video games, the illusion of a "physical" personal presence is connected to the notion of a "transformation" of the player through the game (Murray 1997). Transformation is caused by interaction with a usually goal-driven virtual environment.

Video games engage players by letting them take on a role with a given purpose inside these virtual worlds (Laurel 1991). The games stage players into a conflict and let them act out parts of this conflict as embedded in the game's universe. The role is enacted by the player through the activity of play (Huizinga 1950). The player's involvement usually operates on multiple levels: engagement with a task, identification with a character, comprehension of a narrative, projection and performance of activity are among the many parallel tasks and activities undertaken by a player involved in a game. A heightened level of involvement can evoke a state of "flow" in the player (Csikszentmihalyi 1991) wherein s/he is so immersed in the virtual activity that s/he loses track of the physical space and time. The immersion can become so dominant that it not only relates to, but sometimes overpowers and replaces, awareness of one's surroundings and conditions. One of the activities in a virtual world that supports high engagement is the connection between a player and the projected self in the game world. This was initially discussed by Turkle (1984, 1997) for characters in text-driven environments. In more advanced 3D worlds, the range of expression is less descriptive and more representational as it includes more details on appearance, movement, and animation from subtle facial reactions to full body moves. These can allow for more effective projections of players into characters (Bailenson et al. 2008). The resulting player-avatar connection has been extensively discussed as a dynamic relationship that shapes narrative construction (Ryan 2004) and serves as a measure of enjoyment of virtual worlds (Hefner et al. 2007). Finding oneself in a virtual world, and the acceptance of the virtual world as such, are thus interconnected. As Wertheim (200) states: "Despite its lack of physicality, cyberspace is a real place. *I am there*—whatever this statement may ultimately turn out to mean" (p. 229). "Being there" ("*I am there*") and the reality of the virtual universe ("cyberspace is a real space") are interdependent. There is a strong correlation between players' acceptance of a virtual game world, their role within it, and the level of self-projection into the game. As we accept a virtual there, we inherit a virtual "I" and vice versa. The virtual world that Wertheim still approaches as a novelty has increasingly become accepted as cultural fact. It is not uncommon to find images of virtual avatars such as Nintendo's Miis or one's Second Life™ avatar as visual representatives for people on Facebook or other social media. Gamer tags serve as connecting links online, and customisation of characters becomes more and more intricate, as video games become part of the cultural realities we live in. As the gap between physical and virtual is shrinking, the step into a virtual self is becoming easier.

Social presence and its role for self-recognition in an avatar is particularly relevant for multi-player games, but also shapes our behaviour in single-player environments. Blascovich (2002) asked how perception of human representations influence social behaviour in virtual environments, and concluded that it hinges on a model of "interpersonal self-relevance" which itself depends on a sense of self in these environments. They highlight the realism of the virtual character as essential to evoke this sense of self. Parts of this realism are the expressive means of that avatar, the texturing, level of detail, and behaviour. In later work, they tested this sense of self in virtual representations of customised avatars whose features resembled those of test participants, and this evoked more personal interactions (Bailenson et al. 2008).

This behaviour change, in what is termed "parasocial" behaviour, highlight the relevance of a sense of self in our interaction in virtual worlds at large. Communication patterns in digital environments are directly connected to an identification of oneself as situated in these worlds. As we play a game, we accept the virtual roles it offers, which may appeal to usually suppressed parts of our identity. This is why these virtual representations can often be used to unlock hidden and suppressed aspects of our inner self. They allow us to question gender (Stone 1998) or race (Kolko et al. 2000) in a safe and playful – virtual – setting.

Virtual environments offer important access points for understanding how the self emerges in the physical world and how we identify selves. But how the mediated virtual environment and the physical player's body interaction affect the perception of one's self continues to produce new research problems. Among them is the question of whether the self-representation should be optimised to suit an ideal image or to realistically reflect the physical features of the player. While players seem to be attracted to more interaction with characters reflecting their own features (Bailenson et al. 2008), others have shown that an ideal self image is more appealing to players (Jin 2010). Another question is whether seeing one's avatar body when interacting with the game system affects self-projection and what qualities in that avatar body's visualisation are important to enhance self-projection (Mohler et al. 2010). This chapter focuses more specifically on the recognition of one's self through movement, which is an important aspect of our sense of self in the physical world.

7.3 Identifying Self in the Physical World: The Role of Movements

One of the key sources of information that we use to identify selves in the physical world is the relative and absolute motion of bodies and body parts during the execution of goal-directed movements. Some initial evidence for the important role of biological motion in identification of the self comes from a long series of psychophysical studies showing that subtle changes in the motions of the most abstract representations of people, such as point-light displays, can be used to identify characteristics of individuals (e.g., gender or weight) and even their emotional states (e.g., happy/sad or nervous/relaxed) (see Troje 2008). Much of the research on the perception of motion has been driven by a developing approach to cognition that is broadly termed "embodied cognition". Proponents of the embodied cognition approach hold that there is an intricate relationship between the body and cognitive operations, such that cognitive processes are influenced by the body's current and future action state, and action planning and control are modulated by cognitive processes. In this way, the mental state of the individual (e.g., their mood) shapes the actions of the individual and, likewise, the actions of the individual (e.g., pulling their hands towards them vs. pushing their hands away) can bias or alter the mental states and perceptions of the individual.

One of the key mechanisms thought to underlie our ability to perceive and recognise actions (and associated mental states) is a neural coding system in which the representations of actions and the perceptual consequences of those actions are tightly bound in a common code (Hommel et al. 2001; Prinz 1997). The main implication of this common coding system for behaviour is that the common codes allow for a bidirectional pathway between responses and their after-effects such that the activation of an after-effect code evokes the response code that would bring about the effect and vice versa. For example, the desire to slow a car down (the after-effect) activates the neural codes for the action that will cause the foot to press the brake pedal (the action) and, likewise, the activation of the plan to press the brake pedal will allow one to predict that the car will slow down. This is the ideomotor effect, where the intention/planning of a movement automatically activates its associated motor action, and executing an action will allow making predictions about future states, and thereby help perceive them. In a more computer-based interaction, the need to generate the letter "F" on the computer screen activates the neural codes that would cause the typist to flex the left index finger and, in the opposite direction, activating the motor plan to press the "F" key can evoke the image of the letter on the screen. In both physical and virtual world interactions, these action/after-effect bindings are developed through extensive practice during which the actor learns to associate a specific action with a specific after-effect. Not surprisingly, the greater the practice, the tighter the association or bind between action and the sensory consequences of the action.

Although the common coding model was developed to provide a reasonable account of action selection and the prediction of the consequences, it is now thought these common codes can also be the foundation for action perception and recognition. Specifically, it is thought that one is able to perceive and recognise action patterns because the perception of biological motion and/or the perceptual consequences of an action in the environment automatically activates the representation of the response via the common action/after-effect code. One important source of evidence supporting the role of common codes in action perceptions is derived from study by Casile and Giese (2006) who observed that the participants' ability to recognise an unusual walking pattern improved after they had learned to perform that unusual walking pattern. Consistent with the results of the study by Casile and Giese, a series of studies has revealed that people are generally better able to identify their own walking patterns than those of their friends (e.g. Beardsworth and Buckner 1981; Jokisch et al. 2006) – though this own-action recognition advantage is not universally observed (see Cutting and Kozlowski 1977). More recent work from Knoblich and colleagues (2006) has expanded this general self-identification finding to a wider array of tasks such as patterned clapping and writing. Presumably this enhanced ability to recognise our own actions is the result of the massive amounts of experience we have had generating our own actions and experiencing the perceptual consequences of those actions. In the framework of the common coding/ideomotor theory, this ability to efficiently identify our own movement patterns, even in extremely abstract and information poor representations such as point-light displays, is based on highly developed action/after-effect codes and/or more intricate coupling between specific and detailed action and effect codes. That is, because we have such extensive experience with our movements and their effects on the environment (i.e., in contrast to the relatively little experience we have watching other people's movements and their after-effects), we have highly developed and accurate common codes. These highly accurate common codes then enable us to identify our own movement patterns/after-effect better than the movement patterns/after-effects of other people.

Of particular relevance to the purpose of the present chapter, these common action/after-effect representations are thought to support a series of other cognitive processes. Specifically, it has been suggested that the activated common codes may be accessed by a variety of other cognitive systems for a number of other purposes, including agency, intention understanding, and empathy. In support of the broader use of common codes, Sato and Yasuda (2005) have shown that there was more agency confusion (i.e. participants were less accurate in determining whether they or another person was responsible for generating a specific after-effect) when the time between response and effect generation increased. In addition, Sato and Yasuda observed a decrease in the sense of self-agency when the after-effect that was presented following the response was different from the one that has previously been established through learning. These decreases in the sense of self-agency were thought to occur because of the discordance between the timing and characteristics of the predicted (learned) after-effect associated with the response and the actual characteristics of the after-effect generated on that specific instance. That is, because there was a difference between the timing and characteristics of the learned after-effect and the actual generated after-effect, the participant was less certain as to whether they or someone else generated the after-effect. Thus, moving these findings into the context of translating an actor's movements into the virtual world, it is likely that: (1) the actor will only feel true "ownership" (agency) of the avatar's movements with the arbitrary relationship between button presses and actions after a period of training; and, (2) a sense of agency will be tighter and more efficiently established if the actors own actions are more accurately transferred onto the avatar.

In sum, action and after-effect representations are tightly bound in a common coding system. The critical implication of this common coding system for the present purpose is that an actor's ability to identify with and feel a sense of control (agency) over the actions of their characters in the virtual world may be largely dependent on the discordance (or lack thereof) between the actor's own movement patterns and those of the avatar. This suggestion is based on the combined findings that: (1) people are better at identifying themselves than other people from the motion of abstract representations of bodies; and (2) people feel a greater sense of self-agency over after-effects that more closely match the after-effects that they have learned to associate with their own actions. Thus, it follows that, since we have a lifetime of experience with our actions and the perceptual consequences of those actions, an actor's sense of agency and identity with an avatar should be greater when HCI designers can more accurately and efficiently translate the actions of the actor in the physical world to the avatar in the virtual world. This is not to suggest that a sense of self-agency and identity with the avatar cannot be developed when the avatar's movements are enabled via a relatively arbitrary matching of button and joystick presses (for a common coding explanation of this identity, see Chandrasekharan et al. 2010). Certainly, the requisite associations can be established through a period of learning. Our contention here is that this sense of self-agency and identity will be more efficiently and accurately established when the movements of the actor in the physical world are more faithfully translated to those of the avatar. With this end in mind, our group has been developing a novel interface to facilitate the transfer of one's self to an avatar. We outline the stages of development and testing of this identity interface in the following sections.

7.4 Interacting with the Virtual Self: Interfaces for Controlling Avatars

For the most part, interfaces for controlling virtual characters, whether for games or film and television production, have been either extremely simple or extremely complex. In the case of game controllers, gamepads and joysticks have been focused on changing the two-dimensional location of objects, and when they are adapted to controlling movements of characters in expressive ways, especially in 3D space, it leads to overly complicated button combinations and unintuitive mappings. Interfaces like The Character Shop's Waldo® devices[1] designed for animating the movements of 3D characters often require multiple people, do not work in real time, require intense amounts of post production, and are prohibitively expensive for use in the home. We look at conventional and embodied interfaces, which have provided a starting point for our work on designing a simple, low-cost, real-time, full-body puppet interface for mapping a person's own body movements to a virtual character.

7.4.1 Conventional Interfaces

Most games use a gamepad, a joystick, or a keyboard and mouse to control a virtual character. Over the course of the evolution of games and controllers, interactions for controlling game characters have for the most part become standardised. For example, walking forward is often mapped to the "W" key on a keyboard, or to the forward movement of the left joystick on a PlayStation®3 or Xbox® controller. Character control in

---

[1] The Character Shop's Waldo® devices are telemetric input devices used for controlling multiple axes of movement on virtual characters or animatronics. They are designed to meet different criteria depending on the character they control. They use different kinds of sensors to capture movements, and are typically made of plastic and metal joints, and leather and nylon strapping. Specific types include the Facial Waldo®, the Body Waldo®, and the Warrior Waldo®

games most often involves controlling the 2D (or sometimes 3D) position of an avatar. Seldom does a player have the ability to fluidly and precisely control the gestures of their avatar. When games do provide this ability, the mapping of the character movements to the button presses either becomes overly complex, using awkward combinations of buttons to achieve a particular arm position or facial expression, or assigns a large array of buttons or commands to access pre-rendered animations of the movement.

The result of these unintuitive mappings is that game players usually control a character's position and not his particular body movement. This limitation in character control is also a legacy of game design. Simple controllers and limited processing power led early games to involve moving 2D shapes around on the screen. The progression from *Ms. Pac-Man*[2] to *Donkey Kong*[3] to *Super Mario Bros.*[4] to the most recent adventure games like *Uncharted: Drake's Fortune*[5] illustrates the carry over of this design feature, in which the primary form of gameplay is to figure out where a character needs to go and how to get them there. These types of games require no more than the ability to trigger certain sets of actions, like walk, run, jump, climb and combinations thereof, in order to be playable. This means that game designers can map animations for these movements to different buttons, define specific behaviours that can be triggered in different contexts, and focus on making levels that are fun given these constraints. Another reason for limiting the control of character movement in games is the relative simplicity of conventional interfaces compared with the range of motions encompassed by the body. This is a problem of a discrepancy between the manipulator and the manipulation task (Jacob and Sibert 1992). Jacob and Sibert have shown that a device that controls the same number of values as required by a manipulation task works better than one that controls fewer. However, when the tasks become sufficiently complex as to be expressive, the number of values that need to be controlled becomes unmanageable with a conventional controller. For example, in the PlayStation®3 video game, *Little Big Planet*[6], various combinations of left and right joysticks, shoulder buttons and the d-pad control either the

---

[2] *Ms. Pac-Man* was originally published by Midway in 1981. The player moves a circle with a mouth around a 2D maze, visible on screen all at once, in order to eat dots while avoiding ghosts.

[3] *Donkey Kong* was published by Nintendo in 1981. The player controls jump man, who must avoid barrels thrown by a giant ape named Donkey Kong, as well as other obstacles, and climb to the top of a structure to save a girl from the ape.

[4] *Super Mario Bros.* was released by Nintendo in 1983. The player controls Mario, who must avoid obstacles as he moves through a series of side-scrolling levels on an adventure to rescue a princess from Bowser, an evil lizard-like king.

[5] *Uncharted: Drake's Fortune*, from Sony Computer Entertainment 2007, follows treasure hunter Nathan Drake, as he jumps, climbs, dodges and shoots his way through the jungle in search of the lost treasure of El Dorado.

[6] *Little Big Planet*, published by Sony Computer Entertainment Europe, allows the player to control Sackboy, a doll-like character, through a series of worlds collecting stickers and other objects that can then be used to build new, custom levels, which can be shared over the PlayStation® Network with other players around the world. Many levels can only be solved collaboratively, either through collocated or remote multiplayer gameplay. The game provides players with different ways to interact with each other during multiplayer scenarios.

arms and hips, or facial expressions, and while the expressiveness of the character is much better than in most games, the complicated control scheme makes it hard for players to use the expressivity for communication.

7.4.2   Embodied Interfaces

Whether designed to move past limitations of standard controllers, or simply created as a novelty to increase sales, different types of controllers have been developed for both gameplay and expressive control of virtual characters. The recent surge of interest in embodied interaction brought about by the Nintendo Wii™ overshadows a long history of embodied controllers for both games and film and television production.

The Wii™ remote (or Wiimote) is the first in the most recent iteration of embodied game controllers, and while it does encourage players to physically perform the same actions that they want their avatars to perform, the mapping between controller and character is still heavily abstracted and oversimplified. For example, in the tennis game that is packaged with the system, swinging the Wiimote like a tennis racket triggers a set of actions for the game character, which includes running to the place where the ball will be hit and swinging either forehand or backhand depending on which makes the most sense in the game world. Furthermore, the system does not require the motion to be very much like the swing of an authentic tennis racket at all. Players can sit on their sofa and play Wii™ Tennis with a very minimal flick of the wrist, which can often lead to better results in the game. The Wii™ is also not the first time Nintendo has experimented with embodied interfaces. The Power Glove, developed by Mattel in the 1990s, mapped standard game interactions onto rotations of the wrist and grasping actions. The Power Glove was the least accurate but also the lowest cost of many glove-based interfaces developed in the 1980s and 1990s (see Sturman and Zeltzer 1994). Another notable example that was used for virtual character control is the DataGlove, which was developed by VPL Research for controlling virtual reality environments. In the early 1990s, Dave Sturman used the VPL DataGlove to explore a "whole-hand" method for controlling a digital character as part of his doctoral research at the Massachusetts Institute of Technology (Sturman and Zeltzer 1993). He defined "whole-hand input" as the full and direct use of the hand's capabilities for the control of computer-mediated tasks, and used the term independent of any specific application or interface device.

Embodied interfaces for expressive character control are often used in television and film production. One example of these is The Character Shop's Waldo® devices, which are telemetric input devices worn by puppeteers and used to control puppets and animatronics. In the late 1980s, a Waldo®-controlled digital puppet, Waldo C. Graphic, appeared in The Jim Henson Hour (Walters 1989). Puppeteers used Waldos® to control the digital puppet's position, orientation, and jaw movements. A simplified representation of the character showed in real time on a screen along with physical puppets. The data was later cleaned and used to add a more complex version of the character into the video. The Sesame Street segment, "Elmo's World" uses a similar approach to perform virtual and physical characters together in real time. The Henson Company's most recent digital puppetry system, implemented in the production of Sid the Science Kid, requires two puppeteers, one for body movements and one for facial expressions. In this case, the performance of the puppeteers is credited with making the actions of the characters "organic and fun – it never drops into math" (Henson 2009). Another technique for animating digital puppets is the Dinosaur Input Device (DID) created by Stan Winston Studio and Industrial Light and Magic for Jurassic Park. The DID is a miniature dinosaur which the animators use to set the keyframes used by the film's animation system (Shay and Duncan 1993). Digital Image Design Inc. implemented a similar system with its Monkey Input Device, an 18" tall monkey skeleton equipped with 38 separate sensors to determine location, orientation, and body position (Esposito et al. 1995). For transferring human motion onto virtual human characters, producers often opt for motion capture systems, which require the performers to wear suits covered in balls or spots of paint that are tracked by a computer-vision system. Motion capture requires the use of multiple cameras and large spaces. These systems are expensive and require a significant amount of work in post production, which makes them impractical for use in games and virtual worlds and unattainable for most other home based applications like online role-playing or machinima production.

Recently, interfaces that can make the expressiveness and control offered by professional puppetry and motion capture systems more widely accessible are beginning to appear, especially in academic research environments. These fall under growing areas of research such as tangible and embodied interaction, which seek to provide more seamless ways of bridging the physical and digital worlds than is possible with conventional interfaces (Ishii and Ullmer 1997; Dourish 2001). Notable examples of research that focus on the control of character in 3D virtual space include the work of Johnson and colleagues on sympathetic interfaces (1999). Their system called Swamped! made use of a plush chicken to control a chicken character in a story that took place in a 3D virtual world. In a similar vein, the ActiMates Barney plush doll had sensors in its hands, feet, and eyes and could act as a playmate for children either standalone or when connected to a television or computer (Strommen 1998). Our own past research has involved hand puppets tracked by computer vision (Hunt et al. 2006) and a tangible marionette that controls characters in the Unreal game engine in real time (Mazalek and Nitsche 2007). These projects served as early tests for our current work which uses common coding principles as a basis for designing interfaces that can map a user's own body movements to a 3D virtual character in real-time.

7.5 Identifying with Self in Virtual Worlds: A Common Coding Approach

As new interfaces such as those described above provide more embodied forms of interaction with the virtual space, it becomes increasingly important for human computer interaction designers to consider fundamental aspects of the interaction between perceptual, cognitive and motor processes. The common coding model discussed above links perception, action and imagination of movement, and can help us better understand the cognitive connection we make with our virtual selves. Moreover, this model can help us determine, as interface and game designers, what level of movement abstraction between our physical and virtual self can still maintain self-recognition, and thus support (movement-based) identification with our virtual avatars. For example, can we still recognise our own movement if it is presented in a visually abstracted or proportionately standardised form, such as a point-light walker or generic virtual avatar? And does self-recognition also hold if the movements of this point-light walker or generic avatar are made using a control interface, such as a puppet?

The answers to these questions require careful experimentation, which can provide a starting point for the design of control interfaces that translate a player's own body movements to their avatar. It is also worth noting that in order to support effective movement translation to a virtual avatar, the control interface needs to provide the ability to map a high level of granularity in action in the physical world onto a high level of granularity in action in the virtual world. The use of canned animations in the game engine triggered by button presses, joystick movements or the flick of a Wiimote is thus not an option for common-coding based interaction design.

In order to understand what level of movement abstraction can still support movement-based self-identification with our virtual selves, we conducted an experiment that tracked different levels of movement perception abstraction between players and their avatars (Mazalek et al. 2009). Based on the results from this experiment, we designed a full-body puppet controller for translating a player's own movement to a virtual avatar.

7.5.1   Self-Recognition of Abstracted Movements

The self-recognition study consisted of two types of experiments to assess the hypothesis that a person can identify their own movement even when the movement is visually abstracted, and even when the movement is made using a controller like a puppet. The first type looked at whether a person can recognise his or her own body movement, and the second type looked at whether a person can recognise his or her movement of a puppet. The first type built on previous work that has shown that when a person sees an abstract representation of their movements, they are able to recognise those movements as their own (Beardsworth and Buckner 1981; Cutting and Kozlowski 1977; Knoblich and Flach 2001; Knoblich and Prinz 2001). The second type allowed us to determine whether people are able to recognise their movements in abstract representations of the movements of objects that they control. The results suggest that we can recognise movements of characters whose movements derive in second order from our own body memories, and this recognition is based on us projecting our own movements into the movement of the character. This indicates that people could potentially recognise themselves in a virtual character that is controlled by a tangible user interface, which encodes their own movements and also translates these movements to the character.

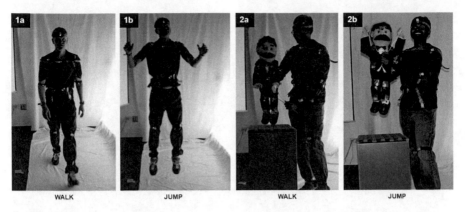

Fig. 7.1 Walk and jump movement tracking with LED straps attached to: participant body (1a & 1b) and both puppet and participant bodies (2a & 2b)

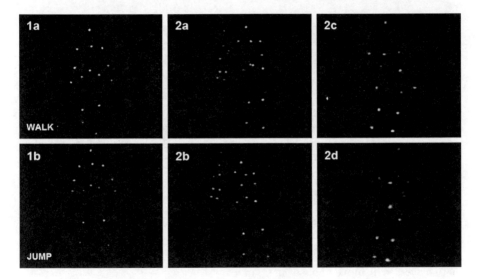

Fig. 7.2 Video stills of visually abstracted walk and jump movements for: participant body (1a & 1b), participant body with puppet (2a & 2b), and puppet only (2c & 2d)

In the first set of experiments, we tested whether people can identify their own body movement (walking and jumping) when it is represented abstractly with either normal proportions or standardised proportions. The second set of experiments looked at whether people can recognise their movements of a puppet (making it walk or jump) when: (1) they can see abstractions of themselves moving the puppet, and (2) when they can only see abstractions of the puppet's movement. In each case, we placed LEDs on the participant, or on the participant and the puppet, as shown in Fig. 7.1, and recorded five videos of each movement. In postproduction, we altered the contrast and saturation of the videos to get point-light images as shown in Fig. 7.2.

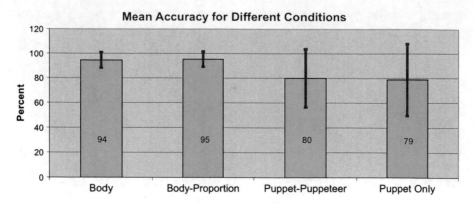

Fig. 7.3 The average percentage of correct results for all tests across all four study trials. The recognition of body movements is higher than the recognition of puppet movements, but both are significantly better than chance

Participants returned after ten or more days to take a set of recognition tests. We tested a total of 20 participants with five males and five females for each type of experiment. In the first type (body movement), participants were shown 70 pairs of videos for each case, normal and standardised proportions, and asked to choose which video showed their own movements. The videos appeared side-by-side and participants pressed 'Q' to select the video on the left and 'P' to select the video on the right. The trials were counterbalanced by showing half of the participants videos with normal proportions first, and the other half videos with standardised proportions first. In the second type of experiment (puppet movement), participants saw 60 pairs of videos for each case, puppeteer with puppet and puppet only. The subjects were again counterbalanced, half of them seeing the puppeteer with puppet videos first, and the other half seeing the puppet only videos first. Participants were asked to select, by pressing 'P' or 'Q', the video that showed their movements of the puppet.

The results showed that participants were able to recognise their movements at a high level in all cases. Fig. 7.3 shows the mean and standard deviations of positive identifications for the four test cases. Since previous studies have shown that people are able to identify the gender of point-light walkers (Cutting and Kozlowski 1977), we compared the results for same-gendered video pairs and different-gendered video pairs and observed no significant difference in the results. This indicates that the self-identification effect is based on a simulation of movements and not on a logic-based elimination process. While the results are better for body movement cases than puppet cases, the puppet results are still significantly better than chance (50% correct) which indicates that people do translate themselves to the puppet and project themselves into characters whose movements derive from their own.

7.5.2 Full-Body Puppet Controller Design

The results of our self-recognition study using abstracted body and puppet movements indicate that it should be possible to design a control interface that can effectively translate a person's own body movements to a virtual avatar in a way that supports (movement-based) self-identification. Our goal was to design an interface that could map the physical body movements of the puppeteer, and thus broaden the expressiveness offered as compared to existing embodied game controllers, while remaining simple to use as compared to conventional interfaces. We also required the interface to be self-contained and in a price range that would make it accessible to everyday game players, which is not the case for existing motion capture or puppetry approaches that are used in professional film and television production.

With these goals in mind, we began with a review of existing approaches to puppetry as inspiration for our own design. In order to support a player's identification with the puppet, our design required a balance of direct contact and level of expression in the puppet. However, the puppet also needed to be accessible to non-professional puppeteers. Fig. 7.4 shows the trade-offs between the ease-of-use and the level of expressiveness and articulation of a puppet. Our interface design combines construction techniques of both full-body puppets and stick puppets, to achieve a good mix between ease-of-use and expressiveness. We focused on full-body puppets, since they conform to our body's configuration and allow expressions that are similar to body movements. At the same time, stick puppets enable direct control of the limbs and are easy to use for even novice puppeteers. Combining these approaches to create a hybrid puppet allowed us to achieve the appropriate balance between ease-of-use and expressiveness that can support a faithful transfer of the player's body movements to the virtual avatar, while retaining the abstraction of a control device in between the player and their virtual self.

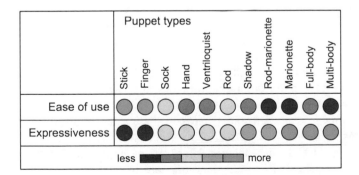

Fig. 7.4 Our review of different puppetry approaches found an inverse correlation between the ease of use and the expressiveness and articulation of the puppet

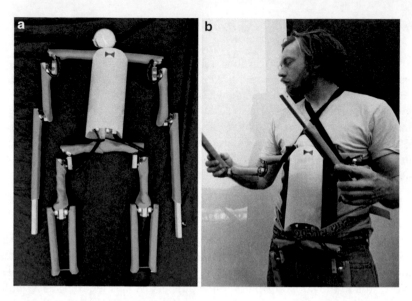

Fig. 7.5 Embodied puppet interface with 10 joints for the knees, hips, waist, shoulders, elbows and neck (left) and player interacting with the puppet (right)

Our puppetry system consists of two main components: the physical puppet and the 3D engine. The physical interface shown in Fig. 7.5 consists of 10 joints with a total of 16 degrees of freedom. The puppet's feet attach to the player's legs just above the knees, and the puppet's body hangs chest high from the player's shoulders. The player grasps the puppet's forearms. This configuration allows the player and puppet to move as one and provides enough information back to the 3D interface to allow for expressive movements. The puppet's bones are made of pieces of wood that are connected at the joints with potentiometers. Joints that rotate in two directions consist of two potentiometers oriented perpendicularly to one another, and each rotates independently. The potentiometers connect to a microcontroller through a multiplexer, which allows us to send 16 analogue signals to a single analogue input on the microcontroller. The microcontroller constructs a serial message out of the numeric data it receives from the potentiometers and sends the message to a computer via a Bluetooth connection. On the computer, an application receives the serial messages and converts them into OSC (Open Sound Control) messages, which are sent to and interpreted by our 3D engine.

The 3D engine is an open-source, OpenGL-based, machinima tool called Movies and box (MSB) developed by Friedrich Kirschner. It stores information about scenes and characters in XML files and translates OSC messages into joint rotations using forward kinematics. Our entire system functions in real-time. There is no need for postproduction. Anyone can use it, and with a relatively new laptop, the system can be implemented for a few hundred dollars.

7.6 Giving Your Self to Your Avatar: Puppet Controller Study

To assess whether our full-body puppet controller supports effective translation of the player's own movements to a virtual avatar, we conducted an experiment similar to our earlier point-light walker self-recognition study, but this time using the puppet and virtual avatar (Mazalek et al. 2010). There were two sets of experiments. The first set looked at whether people can recognise their own walking movements: normal walk, walking with their hands on their hips, and walking with their arms out to the side. The second set of experiments studied whether people can recognise themselves performing standing actions: drinking, tossing a ball from hand to hand, and doing the twist. In each set of experiments, participants wore our puppet interface and performed each action five times. Fig. 7.6 shows the virtual avatar performing each of the movements. We recorded the movements in the 3D engine, and had the participants return 1 week later to take recognition tests. During the recognition tests, participants saw pairs of videos and were asked to choose which video showed their movements. In both sets of experiments, walking actions and standing actions,

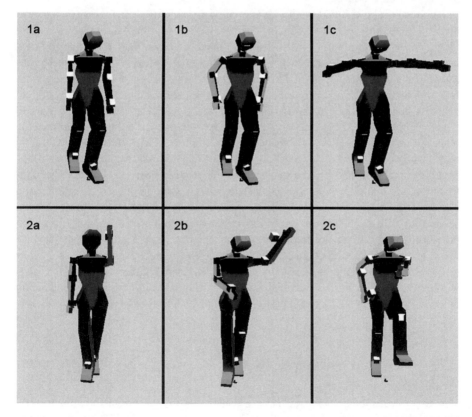

Fig. 7.6 Stills of the 3D avatar in the walking movements (walk (1a), hip-walk (1b), arm-out-walk (1c)) and in the standing movements (drink (2a), toss (2b), twist (2c))

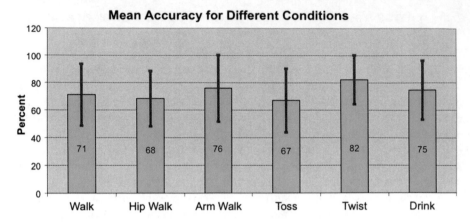

Fig. 7.7 The average percentage of correct results across all six study trials

participants saw 99 pairs of videos divided evenly between the three types of actions, 33 pairs for each action.

The results showed that in all cases people were able to identify their own movements significantly better than chance. Figure 7.7 shows the percentage of correct identifications for each movement. The high standard deviations indicate significant individual differences, an effect that we observed in our previous study and that has shown up in other studies in the literature. Again, since people can recognise gender from movements, we compared the results between same-gendered video pairs and different-gendered video pairs. If participants used gender-based cues and logic to recognise their video (e.g., I am male, one of the videos is of a female, therefore the other video is of me), the performance on different-gendered video pairs would be better when compared to the same-gendered video pairs. Since no pattern or significant difference appears in the results between the two sets, we conclude that the identification is based on a simulation of the movements seen on the screen, and is not a cue-and-logic-based recognition. These experiments show that people project themselves into abstract representations of movements that are based on their own and that providing interfaces that accomplish this representation is an effective way to increase identification with virtual characters. Future experiments will examine the extensions of this effect, which might include enhancing players' body memories through augmenting the movements of a character to which they identify strongly or enhancing mental abilities that are linked to body movement such as mental rotation.

7.7 Discussion and Implications

The two experiments show that people can recognise their own movements in a virtual character, when these actions are translated using embodied interfaces. Combined with experiments in common coding showing the higher coordination with own actions (Knoblich and Sebanz 2006), and the thin slice experiments showing judgement accuracy of others from social psychology (Ambady et al. 2000), this transfer of one's own movements to a character suggests that our puppet interface would enable virtual interactions very similar to those possible in the actual world. Particularly, people interacting in games would be able to judge others' internal states. Also, reflecting on the movements of their virtual characters in relation to others' would give players more insight into their own biases and preferences.

Further, the transfer of one's own movements to a character would enable better immersion in the virtual world, and better coordination with movements of the character. This better coordination could be leveraged for applications such as motor recovery therapy. As an illustrative instance, a stroke survivor with significant gaming experience recently used the puppet interface to play a game in our lab. In the post-game interview, she commented: "I just felt like we were one and the same person. Cause I felt like that was me." Contrasting the puppet with the Wii™ remote, she said: "I'm just handling a piece of machinery, but with the puppet. … It would be like it was my friend." This qualitative difference in her experience suggests that transferring her own movements brought the character's movements closer to her actual experience, thus bringing the character closer to her self. Given the tight feedback loop between execution and perception of movements suggested by common coding, we believe it would be possible to generate movements in the character that would help her recover her lost movements.

More generally, we think the connection between self and virtual avatar enabled by the puppet interface creates a channel that could eventually be used to transfer novel movements executed by the character on screen back to the player, via the common coding between perception of movements and imagination/execution of movements. This could in turn be used to create opportunities for players to shape and grow their own identities in virtual worlds, as well as their notion of self in the physical world. This has a range of potential applications, particularly in the development of social skills through role-playing and increased empathy, as well as in areas such as medical rehabilitation for patients with movement disorders, and also possibly disorders of volition such as schizophrenia, where the common coding system is considered to be damaged (Firth 2006). It has been shown that an increased self-presence can positively affect the educational impact of digital environments (Annetta et al. 2010), improve exercise behaviour (Fox and Bailenson 2009) as support neurocognitive rehabilitation (Panic 2010), among other effects.

From a research perspective, we have found that combining game design with cognitive theory and experiments is very effective and fruitful, and a very promising avenue for systematically exploring the physical and virtual self and their interactions. Others have recognised this synergy, and there are some recent studies that combine the two approaches. For instance, there is some recent work examining the social conditions of both cognitive experiments and game systems (see Jin and Park 2009) and (Blascovich 2002). However, the two disciplines – game design and cognitive science – cannot simply be forced onto each other as the narratives and methodologies of the two disciplines differ considerably. For example, the game industry regularly uses an overload of sensory input to keep a player stimulated, whereas cognitive scientists are usually more interested in single actions and conditions and isolating their effects. Similarly, game engines are often tweaked to ever-increasing levels of complexity, making them unsuitable for therapeutic purposes. Both sides have to reach a middle ground and develop truly shared approaches (Grau et al. 2010). For this, closer collaborations between game designers and cognitive scientists are clearly required, and we hope our work contributes to the coming together of these two research traditions.

7.8 Conclusion

The research presented in this chapter illustrates ongoing work at the interface between basic science and technology development – applying common coding theory to virtual character control through tangible interfaces. It is part of our larger and ongoing project investigating how tangible user interfaces and virtual characters can augment a user's body memory gradually, by exploiting the common coding and self-recognition effect. We presented our implementation of a tangible puppet interface and 3D virtual environment, which are tailored to optimise the mapping between player and virtual avatar. Using this interface, players were able to recognise their own movements when presented alongside others' movements, even though they did not observe their movements being transferred to the avatar, and the recognition occurred after a week of the transfer. We have, thus, demonstrated that our puppet interface design supports players' recognition of themselves in a 3D virtual character. Based on these results, we are conducting a new set of experiments to examine whether controlling the avatar using our puppet interface leads to better cognitive performance of the player, in comparison to other interfaces (such as game controllers and keyboards). Building on that research trajectory, future experiments will examine whether perceiving a "personalised" video game character executing novel body movements can change how a player uses his body to make artistic expressions and unlock new creative potential that will further the evolution of one's self.

Acknowledgements We thank the Synaesthetic Media Lab, the Digital World & Image Group and the Cognitive & Motor Neuroscience Lab for helping shape our ideas. In particular, we thank Andrew Quitmeyer, Firaz Peer, Geoffrey Thomas, Tandav Sanka and Friedrich Kirschner for their work on the project. This work is supported by NSF-IIS grant #0757370, NSF-REESE grant #0909971 (awarded to Nancy Nersessian and Wendy Newstetter), and the Alberta Ingenuity Fund.

References

Ambady, N., Bernieri, F., Richeson, J.A.: Towards a histology of social behavior: Judgmental accuracy from thin slices of the behavioral stream. Adv. Exp. Soc. Psychol. **32**, 201–271 (2000)
Annetta, L.A., Folta, E., Klesath, M.: V-Learning: Distance Education in the 21st Century Through 3D Virtual Learning Environments. Springer, Dordrecht/Heidelberg/London/New York (2010)

Bailenson, J.N., Blascovich, J., Guadagno, R.E.: Self representations in immersive virtual environments. J. Appl. Soc. Psychol. **38**(11), 2673–2690 (2008)

Beardsworth, T., Buckner, T.: The ability to recognize oneself from a video recording of one's movements without seeing one's body. Bull. Psychon. Soc. **18**(1), 19–22 (1981)

Blascovich, J.: Social influence within immersive virtual environments. In: Schroeder, R. (ed.) The Social Life of Avatars: Presence and Interaction in Shared Virtual Environments, pp. 127–145. Springer, London (2002)

Casile, A., Giese, M.A.: Non-visual motor learning influences the recognition of biological motion. Curr. Biol. **16**(1), 69–74 (2006)

Chandrasekharan, S., Mazalek, A., Nitsche, M., Chen, Y., Ranjan, A.: Ideomotor design: Using common coding theory to derive novel video game interactions. Pragmat. Cogn. **18**(2), 313–339 (2010)

Csikszentmihalyi, M.: Flow: The Psychology of Optimal Experience. HarperPerennial, New York (1991)

Cutting, J.E., Kozlowski, L.T.: Recognizing friends by their walk: Gait perception without familiarity cues. Bull. Psychon. Soc. **9**(5), 353–356 (1977)

Dourish, P.: Where the Action Is: The Foundations of Embodied Interaction. MIT Press, Cambridge (2001)

Esposito, C., Paley, W.B., Ong, J.: Of mice and monkeys: a specialized input device for virtual body animation. In: Proceedings of the 1995 Symposium on Interactive 3D Graphics, Monterey, pp. 109-ff. ACM, New York (1995)

Fox, J., Bailenson, J.N.: Virtual self-modeling: The effects of vicarious reinforcement and identification on exercise behaviors. Media Psychol. **12**(1), 1–25 (2009)

Frith, C.: Interpersonal factors in the disorders of volition associated with schizophrenia. In: Sebanz, N., Prinz, W. (eds.) Disorders of Volition, pp. 233–248. MIT Press, Cambridge (2006)

Grau, S., Tost, D., Campeny, R., Moya, S., Ruiz, M.: Design of 3D virtual neuropsychological rehabilitation activities. In: Second International Conference on Games and Virtual Worlds for Serious Applications (VS-GAMES), pp. 109–116. IEEE, Braga, 25–26 March 2010

Hefner, D., Klimmt, C., Vorderer, P.: Identification with the Player Character as Determinant of Video Game Enjoyment. In: Ma, L., Rauterberg, M., Nakatsu, R. (eds.) Entertainment Computing – ICEC 2007. Lecture Notes in Computer Science, vol. 4740, pp. 39–48. Springer, Berlin/Heidelberg (2007)

Henson, B.: Keeping it real. Am. Theatre **26**(7), 56–60 (2009)

Hommel, B., Müsseler, J., Aschersleben, G., Prinz, W.: The theory of event coding (TEC): A framework for perception and action planning. Behav. Brain Sci. **24**, 849–878 (2001)

Huizinga, J.: Homo Ludens. A Study of the Play-Element in Culture. The Beacon Press, Boston (1950)

Hunt, D., Moore, J., West, A., Nitsche, M.: Puppet show: intuitive puppet interfaces for expressive character control. In: Medi@terra 2006, Gaming Realities: A Challenge for Digital Culture, Athens, pp. 159–167. October 4–8, 2006

IJsselsteijn, W.A., de Ridder, H., Freeman, J., Avons, S.E.: Presence: concept, determinants and measurement. In: Proceedings of the SPIE, San Jose, pp. 520–529 (2000)

Ishii, H., Ullmer, B.: Tangible bits: towards seamless interfaces between people, bits and atoms. In: Proceedings of the SIGCHI Conference on Human Factors in Computing Systems (CHI '97), Atlanta, pp. 234–241. ACM, New York (1997)

Jacob, R.J.K., Sibert, L.E.: The perceptual structure of multidimensional input device selection. In: Proceedings of the SIGCHI Conference on Human Factors in Computing Systems (CHI '92), Monterey, pp. 211–218. ACM, New York (1992)

Jin, S.-A.A.: "I feel more connected to the physically ideal mini me than the mirror-image mini me": Theoretical implications of the "malleable self" for speculations on the effects of avatar creation on avatar-self connection in wii. Cyberpsychol. Behav. Soc. Netw. **13**(5), 567–570 (2010)

Jin, S.-A.A., Park, N.: Parasocial interaction with my avatar: Effects of interdependent self-construal and the mediating role of self-presence in an avatar-based console game, Wii. Cyberpsychol. Behav. **12**(6), 723–727 (2009)

Johnson, M.P., Wilson, A., Blumberg, B., Kline, C., Bobick, A.: Sympathetic interfaces: using a plush toy to direct synthetic characters. In: Proceedings of the SIGCHI Conference on Human Factors in Computing Systems: The CHI Is the Limit (CHI '99), Pittsburgh, pp. 152–158. ACM, New York (1999)

Jokisch, D., Daum, I., Troje, N.F.: Self recognition versus recognition of others by biological motion: Viewpoint-dependent effects. Perception **35**, 911–920 (2006)

Knoblich, G., Flach, R.: Predicting the effects of actions: interactions of perception and action. Psychol. Sci. **12**(6), 467–472 (2001)

Knoblich, G., Prinz, W.: Recognition of self-generated actions from kinematic displays of drawing. J. Exp. Psychol. Hum. Percept. Perform. **27**(2), 456–465 (2001)

Knoblich, G., Sebanz, N.: The social nature of perception and action. Curr. Dir. Psychol. Sci. **15**, 99–104 (2006)

Kolko, B., Nakamura, L., Rodman, G. (eds.): Race in Cyberspace. Routledge, New York/London (2000)

Laurel, B.: Computers as Theatre. Addison-Wesley, Reading (1991)

Lombard, M., Ditton, T.: At the heart of it all: The concept of telepresence. J. Comput.-Mediated Commun. **3**(2), 1–39 (1997)

Mazalek, A., Chandrasekharan, S., Nitsche, M., Welsh, T., Thomas, G., Sanka, T., et al.: Giving your self to the game: transferring a player's own movements to avatars using tangible interfaces. In: Proceedings of the 2009 ACM SIGGRAPH Symposium on Video Games, New Orleans, pp. 161–168. ACM, New York (2009)

Mazalek, A., Nitsche, M.: Tangible interfaces for real-time 3D virtual environments. In: Proceedings of the International Conference on Advances in Computer Entertainment Technology (ACE '07), Salzburg, pp. 155–162. ACM, New York (2007)

Mazalek, A., Nitsche, M., Chandrasekharan, S., Welsh, T., Clifton, P., Quitmeyer, A., et al.: Recognizing self in puppet controlled virtual avatars. In: Proceedings of the 3rd International Conference on Fun and Games, Leuven, pp. 66–73. ACM, New York (2010)

Minsky, M.: Telepresence. Omni **4**, 45–51 (1980)

Mohler, B.J., Creem-Regehr, S.H., Thompson, W.B., Buelthoff, H.H.: The effect of viewing a self-avatar on distance judgments in an hmd-based virtual environment. Presence-Teleop. Virt. **19**(3), 230–242 (2010)

Murray, J.H.: Hamlet on the Holodeck. The Future of Narrative in Cyberspace. MIT Press, Cambridge (1997)

Panic, A.S.: Addressing patient motivation in virtual reality based neurocognitive rehabilitation. B.A. Thesis, Hogere Technische School Arnheim, Arnheim (2010)

Prinz, W.: Why don't we perceive our brain states? Eur. J. Cogn. Psychol. **4**, 1–20 (1992)

Prinz, W.: Perception and action planning. Eur. J. Cogn. Psychol. **9**, 129–154 (1997)

Prinz, W.: A common coding approach to imitation. In: Hurley, S.L., Chater, N. (eds.) Perspectives on Imitation: From Neuroscience to Social Science, vol. 1, pp. 141–156. MIT Press, Cambridge (2005)

Ryan, M.-L.: Will new media produce new narratives? In: Ryan, M.-L. (ed.) Narrative Across Media. The Languages of Storytelling, pp. 337–361. University of Nebraska Press, Lincoln/London (2004)

Sato, A., Yasuda, A.: Illusion of sense of self-agency: discrepancy between the predicted and actual sensory consequences of actions modulates the sense of self agency, but not the sense of self-ownership. Cognition **94**, 241–255 (2005)

Shay, D., Duncan, J.: The Making of Jurassic Park. Boxtree, London (1993)

Slater, M.: Measuring presence: A response to the Witmer and Singer questionnaire. Presence-Teleop. Virt. **8**(5), 560–566 (1999)

Stone, A.R.: The War of Desire and Technology at the Close of the Mechanical Age. MIT Press, Cambridge (1998)

Strommen, E.: When the interface is a talking dinosaur: learning across media with ActiMates Barney. In: Proceedings of the SIGCHI Conference on Human Factors in Computing Systems (CHI '98), Los Angeles, pp. 288–295. ACM/Addison-Wesley, New York (1998)

Sturman, D.J., Zeltzer, D.: A design method for "whole-hand" human-computer interaction. ACM Transact. Inf. Syst. 11(3), 219–238 (1993)

Sturman, D.J., Zeltzer, D.: A survey of glove-based input. IEEE Comput. Graph. Appl. 14(1), 30–39 (1994)

Troje, N.F.: Retrieving information from human movement patterns. In: Shipley, T.F., Zacks, J.M. (eds.) Understanding Events: How Humans See, Represent, and Act on Events, pp. 308–334. Oxford University Press, Oxford (2008)

Turkle, S.: The Second Self: Computers and the Human Spirit. Simon & Schuster, New York (1984)

Turkle, S.: Life on the Screen: Identity in the Age of the Internet. Phoenix, London (1997)

Walters, G.: The story of Waldo C. Graphic. In: ACM SIGGRAPH '89, Boston, July 1989 (Course Notes: 3D Character Animation by Computer, pp. 65–79). ACM, New York (1989)

Wertheim, M.: The Pearly Gates of Cyberspace: A History of Space from Dante to the Internet. Virago Press, London (2000)

Witmer, B.G., Singer, M.J.: Measuring presence in virtual environments: A presence questionnaire. Presence-Teleop. Virt. 7(3), 225–240 (1998)

Chapter 8
"Is That Your Boyfriend?" An Experiential and Theoretical Approach to Understanding Gender-Bending in Virtual Worlds

Ferdinand Francino and Jane Guiller

Abstract This chapter aims to provide analyses of real-life player interactions in multiplayer online games/virtual worlds, using traditional theories of identity from sociological and psychological perspectives. The chapter focuses on actual player experiences and social interactions in several online environments. Central to these player experiences are the related theoretical and psychological concepts of gendered selves, status and power differentials and the relationship between online and real-life identities.

Several short narratives are presented throughout this chapter, based on the actual personal and professional experiences of one of the authors, an early user of online games and virtual environments.

These narratives are used to discuss related theoretical perspectives on identity construction and management and highlight key psychological concepts relating to the presentation of self, including how the offline self impacts on the online self/selves and vice versa, and gendered interactions, deception and ethics in virtual worlds.

8.1 Introduction

The aim of this chapter is to provide analyses of player interactions in multiplayer online games/virtual worlds, with a particular focus on the concept of gender. Several short narratives will be presented, based on the actual personal and professional experiences of the first author, an early user of online games and virtual worlds. Even though this author is physically male, his online persona Gwynn has always been a girl. He has composed these scenarios based on his recollections of significant events in his experiences as a player/user. Interpretations of these gender-bending experiences, set in the context of relevant theoretical and empirical work, have been

F. Francino (✉) • J. Guiller
Glasgow Caledonian University, Glasgow, Scotland, UK
e-mail: gwynn.gunawan@gmail.com

A. Peachey and M. Childs (eds.), *Reinventing Ourselves: Contemporary Concepts of Identity in Virtual Worlds*, Springer Series in Immersive Environments,
DOI 10.1007/978-0-85729-361-9_8, © Springer-Verlag London Limited 2011

provided by the second author, a female cyberpsychologist. The chapter will focus on game-based interactions in Diablo, Diablo II, World of Warcraft and Second Life™.

Central to these experiences are the related theoretical and psychological concepts of gender identity, gender stereotyping, gendered power differentials and the relationship between online and offline selves. All of the scenarios have a significant gender-based element and shed light for the player on perceived gender roles. They highlight gender-related issues in virtual worlds such as online deception, chivalry, harassment and the glass ceiling.

8.2 Background

There is a large body of literature on gender and gaming, traditionally concerned with questions about gender differences in gaming and the promotion of gender stereotypes by the games industry (e.g., see Cassell and Jenkins 1998; Yee 2007). However, as Kafai et al. (2008) noted, there has been a move to a more complex approach to the study of gender as situated and constructed with the rise in online gaming and the creation of gendered avatars in virtual worlds.

Online gender-bending or gender-swapping is not as popular as was once suggested by the famous quote from the cartoon by Steiner (1993) "on the Internet, nobody knows you're a dog" and the legendary tales of individuals experimenting with gender-opposite online personas (e.g., see Stone 1991). Indeed, Kafai et al. (2008) note that this topic is highly overrated and suggests that most gamers who do swap gender move back to their actual gender. Nonetheless, there are still individuals who continue to gender-swap and previous investigations may not have included those for which the experience of gender-bending online has had a profound effect and changed their perceptions of who they are. Empirical work in this area has explored the reasons why some players choose to gender-swap (e.g., Bruckman 1993; Hussain and Griffiths 2008; Yee 2001). This chapter takes an alternative approach to understanding the gender-swapping phenomenon by focusing on an in-depth exploration of one long-term gender-bender's online experiences, the construction of a gendered identity through their avatar and social interactions and the consequences for their online and offline selves.

8.3 Methodology

This work follows a phenomenological, single case-study approach. Both authors contributed their relative parts separately – the first author providing the written narratives and the second author providing the interpretive analyses of the texts. However, subsequent discussion took place between the authors in order to facilitate shared reflection, representing a cooperative inquiry approach. Subsequent revisions were then made to both the narratives and the analyses by the respective authors. The limitations of this approach will be discussed at the end of the chapter.

8.4 Player Scenario 1

Preface: Diablo (I and II) are action-adventure games that can be played on the internet over Blizzard's Battle.Net servers. Characters gain experience and level up by defeating monsters. These monsters drop loot that can enhance the character's statistics or be sold to a vendor. In Diablo the gender of a character is determined by the class; a Rogue (Diablo) or Amazon (Diablo II) (ranged attack) was female; Warrior (melee attack) and Mage (magic attack) were male (Fig. 8.1).

The year is 1997; the Game is Blizzard's Diablo. Gwynn is a Rogue, equipped with a bow, good at ranged attack but lacking strength for metal armour; she can't take damage. She has to run around a lot, avoiding direct melee attacks. If she's smart, she learns a bit of magic so she can heal herself. It's an interesting, challenging and very dynamic class to play.

After some solitary adventures Gwynn enters battle.net. She befriends a warrior by the name of Xantar. They crawl through many dungeons together, facing challenges together neither of them could handle alone. Gwynn and Xantar start seeking each other out for adventuring. They learn to play well together and are having fun exchanges in chat. They become friends. They exchange email addresses to be able to arrange days and times to play but soon they talk about all sorts of things.

The friendship slowly intensifies as is evident in chat and email. Xantar treats Gwynn like a girl, never questions her gender. This surprises Gwynn a bit but she plays along.

Xantar falls in love and presents Gwynn with an exquisite ring; the Obsidian Ring of the Zodiac, the best ring in the game and incredibly hard to find.

When a character dies in Diablo I all of the equipment that you are wearing will drop on the ground and can be looted by other players. You will start again in town, dressed in nothing but your small clothes. If you are lucky, skilled, and/or have assistance you can return to your corpse and retrieve your items. One day, in an open game on battle.net, Gwynn gets killed by an evil mage, a player who cast a fire wall on the spot where she was entering the dungeon. The magic damage kills her almost instantly. She rushes back but her gear is gone, and the mage is laughing. Powerless in her underwear, Gwynn calls for help. Xantar arrives. His wrath is terrible. The mage gets slaughtered, and slaughtered again, until he surrenders Gwynn's equipment in return for some of his mage specific gear that Xantar looted. Xantar, the hero who

Fig. 8.1 Gender based on character class

came to the rescue and saved the damsel in distress returns the ring to Gwynn, glowing with pride and satisfaction.

Soon after, Gwynn informs Xantar that she is moving unexpectedly. Her father got another job and there is no internet where they are going to live. Before she moves they are going on a holiday and won't have internet either. Gwynn offers the ring back but Xantar will have nothing of it. They have some days left, crawl some dungeons, and say their goodbyes, never to meet again.

Gwynn is a girl, but I am not. I am male and was at that time 33 years old. This is however an Action Role Playing Game and I take my gaming seriously, not just the action element of it. Xantar is a boy, and thinks Gwynn is a girl. I do nothing to correct this. I'm enjoying the pretending game and admittedly, the attention.

Since I'm administrator of several top level domains it's easy for me to create gwynn@somewhere.nl and maintain anonymity.

Xantar sends pictures. He's a 17 year old boy from Canada. I send some pictures as well, found online. A pretty girl in a bikini, lounging in a garden. Gwynn is now (and from then on ever after) a slender pale redhead. The pictures allow me to pretend to be 17 as well. His emails get more personal.

I'm starting to feel a bit uncomfortable with this ruse, which started out as an innocent bit of role-playing but is now slowly but surely entering the realm of possibly quite dangerous deceit. Xantar could find out what I really am. Gwynn plays on battle.net and many people who know me in the physical world play there as well. This could hurt Xantar's feelings; he'll think he's been played for a fool, not a nice experience, especially not in a romantic realm. And I realise my motivations for this ruse can be seen as very questionable.

When his emails get an increasing level of intimacy I decide this has gone too far. I need to stop this but without shattering his illusions. So, I come up with the idea of moving and, in 1997, you could get away with pretending that you didn't have internet where you were going. I inserted a holiday to speed things up. And Gwynn leaves battle.net. Game over.

Now, I believe this has been a good experience, for the both of us. Xantar thought, and will probably still think, he once had a sexy Dutch online girlfriend. He was respected and trusted and did well. He was there, and victorious, in her moment of need. This can't be bad for your self esteem. And me? I felt looked after and protected. Admired and desired.

I was Gwynn.

8.5   Scenario 1: Analysis and Discussion

8.5.1   Motivation for Gender-Swapping

The motivation behind gender-swapping here is to be a particular type of character known as a Rogue, who is always female. The designation of Rogues in Diablo as female-only is interesting, in that it differs from other games such as World of

Warcraft where one can choose to be warrior or hunter of both genders and gender has no bearing on ability. Morales and Patton (2005) note that this is also the case in Everquest, the first ever Massively Multiplayer Online Role Playing Game (MMORPG); however gender can influence the perceived abilities of the player behind the character.

The link between gender and ability in Diablo is an example of gender stereotyping in games. Rogues are the weakest class in Diablo, lacking in strength compared to other character types. Rogues cannot withstand damage well, but are high in dexterity. This reflects a common perception in our society that females are more dextrous than males, often used to explain why females are found to be doing the more 'fiddly jobs', such as threading a needle. Yet, it is males who are usually considered to have better visuospatial skills and outperform females in tasks such as shooting at a target. Of course, the nature of any observed gender differences in such abilities is debatable.

The player's decision to play a Rogue represents a type of achievement motivation in that this choice is driven by the desire to succeed in the challenge of playing a certain type of character, with specific capabilities and equipment (e.g. the bow). Rogues are the best archers in Diablo. Therefore, the male player's motivation to play a girl called Gwynn is not about aesthetic reasons and the look of the avatar, but rather her unique abilities. The initial motivation is also more about role-play than self-exploration; however as we shall see the latter becomes an inevitable consequence of the former.

Schaap (2002) makes a distinction in relation to motivation for playing MUDs arguing that for some players at least; the game revolves around succeeding at the game and the enjoyment of playing a different role. However, for others it can end up being more about the social relations that develop between characters. This distinction may be important to understanding the events that unfold between the characters Gwynn and Xantar and the importance of their relationship formation inworld to their offline selves in the 'real'[1] world. That is, for 'Gwynn' their relationship did not transcend the boundary into the physical world, despite exchanging email communication outside of Diablo, whereas Xantar wished to continue the romantic relationship offline. The romantic nature of his inworld relationship with Gwynn may have been more meaningful to him that any relationship he had offline. Xantar never questioned Gwynn's physical gender. However, the communications that took place by email outside of Diablo would have only served to reinforce the player represented by Xantar's desire to believe that the player controlling Gwynn was a girl in the physical world who he met online and had an intimate and romantic relationship with. Of course, the player behind Xantar may also have been deceptive in that this character may have been also been played by a boy or a man.

---

[1] Schaap (2004, p. 2) argues that 'the conceptualization of the Internet as 'virtual' and opposed to 'real' reality, sets it up as a radically different space and obscures the importance of the everyday social and cultural practices in which online interaction and presentation of self is embedded'.

Furthermore, as discussed in the introductory chapter, Bailey (2007, p. 20) noted that 'there are people who create an avatar that is completely unlike them... They basically create a whole new person, so role-playing is a natural part of their Second Life'. The player behind Gwynn falls into this category. On the other hand, Bailey draws a contrast with players 'who are staying true to themselves as much as possible, who are maybe even more honest than in First Life'. It is likely that the player behind the character of Xantar falls into this category as perhaps he was able to express himself and his desires and feelings, especially towards members of the opposite sex, more fully and authentically inworld. Xantar may have been an extension of his physical self and a way to overcome social inhibitions and show aspects of his self not usually explored or shared in the physical world. Turkle (1995) discusses this tendency for players to explore hidden and potential selves in her postmodernist take on multiple selves in MUDs and the fluidity of identity.

Yee (2001) investigated reasons for 'gender-bending' in Everquest. Just over a quarter of the players who were surveyed swapped gender for role-play reasons, while another quarter did so because of the visual appearance of the opposite gender. Quite simply, in a third-person perspective, it is claimed that some males would rather look at a female body than a male one. Of course, some feminists would argue this as a postmodern way for men to dominate and control female bodies. However, Flanagan (2002) makes reference to Lara Croft and the multiple ways in which players position themselves in relation to this popular and hyper sexualised female computer game character. She notes that players can act through Lara as they identify themselves as her. This 'first person view' goes beyond simply controlling her.

The following most popular reasons for gender-swapping in Everquest were coded as other (16.8%), in-game advantages (11.8%) and gender exploration (7.1%). Males were found to gender-bend more than females and for different reasons, which supports previous findings of Bruckman (1993) and Stone (1995). Males were more likely to play an opposite-gender character because of the in-game advantages, such as being more likely to be offered help and receiving more attention, whereas females were more likely to do so for gender exploration. However, Hussain and Griffiths (2008) reported that 57% of a much smaller self-selecting sample of players of various games had gender-swapped and significantly more of the gender-benders were female. Consistent with previous studies, females gender-swapped in order to avoid male attention and males did it as female were treated better and afforded certain in-game advantages.

8.5.2   Gender Deception and Ethics

The gender deception in Scenario 1 goes beyond ingame role-play when the player behind Gwynn takes the deception to another level with 'Xantar', extending beyond the game. As the player himself suggests with his increasing level of discomfort, this is unethical, both on a personal and professional level in terms of adopting a girl's photographic identity and taking advantage of his administrator status to create a fictional email address in a bid to maintain the pretence and extricate himself from the now deeply uncomfortable situation with Xantar.

Another interesting ethical issue emerging here concerns the decision of the first author to publish this account of his experiences in online games and virtual worlds as part of his move from an internet designer/consultant to teacher/academic. Anthropological and ethnographical accounts of virtual culture through participant observation in virtual worlds, such as that of Boellstorff (2008) also provide detailed accounts of online experiences. Schaap (2002) collected most of his material through lurking in MUDs; ensuring appropriate steps were taken to protect third-parties. However, there is one major difference in that the intention of the first author at the time of his gender-bending experiences was not to research virtual culture or the gender-swapping phenomenon. This raises an interesting point regarding both ethics and authenticity of the evidence presented here, as although accounts may be tainted through the reliance on the first author's memory of past events; they are not affected by bias and intentions as a researcher at the time of the events.

8.5.3 Gender Performance and Inworld Relationship Development

This scenario charts the formation of an inworld relationship and friendship between Gwynn and Xantar. It is based on compatibilities between their respective skills and a desire to advance in the game. This resulted in successful inworld missions, which served to reinforce and strengthen their friendship, along with the communications out with the game. The importance of the relationship to the male character Xantar is manifest in his presentation of a valuable object to Gwynn, in the form of a rare and precious ring – 'the best in the game'. This gendered aspect of game-based interaction is reminiscent of physical world, heterosexual relationships where traditionally a man presents a woman with a ring, typically in the form of an engagement or commitment ring to signify a bond and a future together. This is perhaps the first external marker of the importance of the relationship with Gwynn to Xanthar and its romantic nature, at least from Xantar's perspective. Rcid (1994) suggested that players offering such items often want more than friendship in return.

When Gwynn is under attack from another character in the game, the mage, Xantar comes to his rescue – 'the hero who came to rescue the damsel in distress'. This chivalrous gesture reflects the gender stereotyping frequently observed in video games – Xantar the powerful male hero takes action to rescue the weaker female in need of assistance. Dietz (1998) found that female characters were portrayed as 'damsels in distress' in 21% of the games she content analysed that had female characters (33% of the 33 games had no female characters at all).

As a female and a Rogue, Gwynn lacks strength and does not take damage well. Xantar's actions could be interpreted as an example of the performance of gender in a virtual world, discussed by Schaap (2002). Butler (1990) proposed that gendered behaviour was not the outcome of an identity, but rather the source of identity.

Gender is what we 'do' in our interactions with others. The act of gender makes us who we are. As Butler puts it "[g]ender is in no way a stable identity or locus of agency from which various acts proceed; rather, it is an identity tenuously constituted in time – an identity instituted through a stylized repetition of acts" (p. 270).

As 'Gwynn' tells us, she also played out the gendered role and conformed to stereotypical notions of what was expected of her as a female and displayed behaviours that are judged to be feminine, she accepted the ring and enjoyed feeling desired and protected by a stronger male.

8.6 Player Scenario 2

Preface: Diablo II had a significant additional option; Hardcore mode. In this mode the death of a character is final. All experience and items are lost (Fig. 8.2).

Another new feature were 'waypoints'; teleportation stones that, once discovered, could be used to travel to areas previously explored. The difficulty of monsters, and the quality of loot they drop, increases with the number of players in the complete game while the game consisted of 5 acts. So, if you were alone in Act I and some others were playing in Act III, you had the increased difficulty but also superior loot.

It is Spring 2002 and the game is Diablo II: Lord of Destruction. Gwynn is an Amazon; a female character using ranged weapons. She is dressed in shining mail armour, an elaborate bow in her hands. Gwynn is Hardcore. So is her friend Gaelath, who is a Paladin, and thus a male character. As with the original Diablo, the class of a character determines the gender (Fig. 8.3). It's good to team up with a variety of classes, especially when increasing the difficulty to Nightmare or even Hell, where the loot is better, and the opposition is harder. Gwynn and Gaelath have been playing

Fig. 8.2 Hardcore confirmation dialogue box

Fig. 8.3 More characters, gender still based on class

together for quite some time. The Paladin thinks Gwynn is a girl a since she didn't want to disclose her gender or age when they just met. He's been treating her like one ever since, flirting a bit, teasing. But Gwynn keeps a little distance, not willing to surrender her character again after too much role play.

This is a Nightmare game and Gaelath was hacking his way through Act III alone while some other players were active in Act V. Gaelath was defeating the 'trash mobs'[2] that stand between him and the Act Boss, who drops good loot. But after slashing through most of the minions, all of a sudden the other three players in the game declared hostility and can now attack him. He did all the work, and they want an easy route to the spoils. This happened moments ago and Gaelath vented his frustration to Gwynn who was running around in another game altogether.

Gwynn dropped everything, entered the game Gaelath is in and now runs toward the waypoint to teleport closest to where she knows the opposition must be. They are after all homing in on the prize while Gaelath is hiding in another Act.

As she reaches the waypoint Gwynn declares hostility on everybody in the game. Gwynn as an Amazon has a skill called Guided Arrow. It never misses. You don't even have to see the opposition. She starts firing as soon as she arrives, constantly moving. Two players die, a third manages to log out of the game in time. Just Gwynn and Gaelath are left.

"You can come out now," she says and so he does. Infuriated. Positively and absolutely infuriated. He tells her he didn't ask for her to come and rescue him.

---

[2] Mobs short for 'Mobile' – Monsters to kill and loot.

She asks if he'd rather have his work, his prize stolen by a bunch of kids who gang up on him. It's all no longer relevant. It's not the point. He maintains he didn't ask for her help. She tells him he did. He sent her that message. Strangely enough, Gaelath seems to believe that informing a friend you are going to be robbed is not a request for that friend to help with preventing the robbery. Gaelath said he also mentioned that all three of them were of much higher level than she is. She shouldn't have come.

They part. Gwynn is bitter. She's not playing with Gaelath anymore. Ungrateful, rude boy. This is Battle.Net. There are more Paladins.

I never took the friendship with Gaelath beyond the game, no email, no role playing in the physical world. It took me some time to realise that Gaelath's pride was hurt. He was hiding and this chick comes running in, takes the fight to three characters with a higher level and wins in half a minute. He would rather indeed have been robbed and moan about it than be saved by a girl and compliment her about it, admitting she outclasses him there. Saving is a man's job. Being saved is a girl's job. Women have protective tendencies toward children and toddlers. He's branded a child. It doesn't matter that an Amazon is an imba[3] character and much better at Player versus Player than a Paladin. He's taken it to a personal level. I wonder if he'd have behaved differently if I had been male or if he just can't stand being outclassed by anybody.

I'm reminded of Gaelath several years later. By now Gwynn is a hunter in World of Warcraft. She is level 70 (at that time the maximum) and has a Gryphon to fly on. Being a hunter she can also track humanoids. A male friend by the name of Severin who is level 60 is trying to complete a quest but is being harassed by two members of the opposite faction. This is a friend she goes to the beach with, to have a swim in their underwear. In her inventory she has got a bouquet of expensive red roses he bought her. She holds those when they walk (not run) through town in their finest. Severin never asked if Gwynn is a girl. By now role playing a female is so like second nature the question hardly gets asked at all.

Gwynn flies to the indicated area, tracks the two players she's been told about: a mage and a priest. Gwynn swoops down, lands and attacks the priest. He's dead before he knows what hit him. The mage tries to run and dies tired. Gwynn camps their corpses, killing them immediately after they resurrect until they give up.

Severin cheers, hugs, applauds, salutes in respect and does a little dance (all this with emotes[4]). He's grateful and happy he can continue on his quest. But he doesn't need her help with that. Gwynn flies up and hovers over the treetops, out of sight, just in case the mage and priest return.

---

[3] Imbalanced, relatively more powerful (in some aspects of the game) than other characters.

[4] Emotes; way to express emotions (beyond ascii textual means like a smiley:P). Typing the pre-configured emote like/dance or/cheer or/laugh in chat provides a text remark feedback in combination with a sound and animation. Typing /me<message>will result in the output of playername<message>in a different colour than a normal text message and is called an emote. /me points at you and smirks gives the output Gwynn points at you and smirks.

8.7 Scenario 2: Analysis and Discussion

8.7.1 Gender Deception, Identity and Expectations

In this scenario the player is continuing to role-play as a female, this time as an Amazon in Diablo II. Still no one has raised suspicions regarding the player's gender in the physical world. Perhaps no one cared about his physical gender. However, Yee (2001) found that female players were more troubled by gender-bending than male players were in Everquest and that males were more bothered by male-to-female gender-bending than female-to-male. Similarly, McKeon and Wyche (2005) discuss cases of participants who report being troubled by gender deception in Second Life. Perhaps no one suspected that Gwynn was not female in the physical world. Lewis notes that research suggests that gender deception is often blatantly obvious to others in online spaces (e.g. Berman and Bruckman 2001) and suspicions are often outwardly expressed.

The player behind Gwynn seems to interpret the lack of questioning as a sign of his success at convincingly presenting a female persona. However this may not have been the case and other players could have suspected that Gwynn was played by a man but went along with the ruse. However, it is interesting that the scenarios and the relationships focus on male avatars who are being assumed to be played by males. Perhaps if he had been interacting primarily with male avatars controlled by female players, or transsexual or transgendered individuals if we stop thinking about gender as a binary category, then his gender would have been doubted, or again, maybe nobody was bothered about physical gender. It is just role-play after all, or is it is a breach of inworld ethics? O'Brien (1999) claimed that online gender-bending is viewed as acceptable when it is understood as just play/performance; however there can be a fine line between role-play and deception as highlighted in the first scenario, especially when the deception is moved out of the game and is therefore perhaps no longer considered play.

The male player behind Gwynn presented as an embodied female in all of the virtual worlds he inhabited. He tells me that he was not consciously aware of altering his behaviour initially to present as female, the other avatars treated Gwynn as female, and he would respond in his performance as a girl called Gwynn. He appeared to find this quite easy unlike the experiences of the female author Lewis (2004) who pretended to be male as described in the following excerpt:

> I found it extraordinarily difficult to maintain the deception, and despite the fact that I was in a virtual environment, I felt that 'everybody' could see that I was indeed a female. I then asked a male friend to repeat the exercise but present as a woman. He also reported feeling uncomfortable and inept in how to portray 'being a woman', as well as saying that he felt others could identify his fraudulent behaviour. (Lewis 2004, p. 95).

So what does this say about the male player behind Gwynn? In terms of sexuality the player behind Gwynn is a heterosexual man, who identifies as male gender devoid of gender dysphoria. However, it is possible that the user's gender deception is an expression of a conscious or unconscious need to express a stereotyped feminine identity and a desire for attention for this hidden self.

By this time, Gwynn feels that he is getting very good at being female. His choices regarding his avatar have been and continue to be as we will see in the subsequent scenarios, particularly those in Second Life, somewhat subtle, not the overt characteristics that are usually considered giveaways to a male playing a female, like being scantily-clad and big-breasted, for example. However, the player is not free of biases himself and is also subject to gender stereotyping. He is acting towards his own preconceptions of what it means to be feminine and expectations of how he should act as a female when male characters give him attention, e.g. he flirts back.

It has been suggested that we are more likely to conform to stereotypes and expectations when social identities such as gender are more salient in anonymous interactions than personal identities. Tajfel and Turner (1979) argued that identity operates at varying levels and can be viewed as a continuum, from personal to social, so that in a particular context combined with self-categorisation processes, a particular identity can be activated. In this context, where the physical world personal identity behind Gwynn is not known, and a gendered identity is salient in terms of the feminine persona, stereotyped norms associated with being a female are activated at a cognitive level. Moreover, in social contexts where females are the minority, gender can become particularly salient and stereotypes are even more likely to be activated.

The Social Identity Explanation of Deindividuation Effects (SIDE) model (Postmes et al. 2000, 2002; Reicher et al. 1995) suggests that the interaction between anonymity and gendered identity salience can evoke behavioural norms and stereotypes of how a female should behave. Self-stereotyping and self-fulfilling prophecies occur online whereby users act towards the stereotyped expectations regarding gender appropriate behaviour. In support of this theory, experimental findings have demonstrated that anonymous computer-mediated communication does not reduce gender-stereotypic behaviour (e.g. Postmes and Spears 2002). This, combined with the historical tendency for computer games to convey gender biases, can create spaces in which gender stereotyping is prevalent and exaggerated. Morales and Patton (2005) have discussed gender bias behaviours in Everquest. They also note that the gender bias in game play in Everquest is reflective of physical world stereotypes and expectations.

Expectations regarding gender roles and gender-appropriate behaviour are very important in understanding Gaeleth's reaction to being saved by Gwynn in the above scenario. Here, Gwynn has not conformed to social norms based on gender. Without hesitation Gwynn has come to his friend's assistance following a message from Gaeleth informing her that he is under attack from three other players of a much higher level, which Gwynn has read to imply that he needed her help. However, instead of showing his gratitude to Gwynn, Gaeleth is outraged that she saved him by using her Amazon skills to defeat the enemies, with only one managing to escape by logging out of the game. She has shown him up, his pride is dented and much to Gwynn's disgust, he cannot bring himself to thank her. This act of rejection could be interpreted in a number of ways. Perhaps the player behind Gaeleth believed that the player was a female and simply was embarrassed that she showed her skill to be greater than his, as games such as these are usually considered a male domain.

Perhaps he was annoyed at himself for having to ask a girl for help. It is possible that Gaeleth did intend to request Gwynn's assistance by sending him the message (otherwise one would tend to think that he would have not wasted any time sending such a message when under such a threatening attack). It could also be the case that Gaeleth suspected the player behind Gwynn was a male, and suspicions may have been raised due to Gwynn's apparent superior game-playing ability, but believed that he should be conforming to the gender role that he had taken in the game and stuck to being saved as opposed to being the one who does the saving. Therefore this could be an example of perceived gender roles and so-called glass ceilings crossing into virtual worlds.

The player behind Gwynn notes that it is hard to know for sure why Gaeleth reacted in the way that he did, and that perhaps his self-concept was damaged irrespective of Gwynn's gender. Being a hardcore player Gaeleth may have seen himself as a highly-skilled and his self-esteem was dented due to him being outclassed. In the afterword, the player behind Gwynn reflects on a much later gaming scenario in World of Warcraft, which reminded him of the incident with Gaeleth in Diablo II. Again, Gwynn saves a male character by the name of Severin, who he has developed a romantic relationship with inworld as symbolised by the bouquet of red roses, which Gwynn carries around when they are together. Severin has a completely different reaction when Gwynn kills two members of an opposing faction that have been harassing him. He is delighted and openly shows his gratitude of Gwynn's actions. Unlike Gaeleth, it seems that Severin would rather be saved by a girl than be killed and it is likely that his reaction is one of relief that he is no longer under threat from the enemies, especially as Severin rejects any further help from Gwynn in his continued quest. Like Gaeleth, it seems that Severin does not want to accept help if he doesn't really need it. Despite this he is unaware that Gwynn is keeping an eye out for him in case his enemies return and instigate a counter-attack. This scenario seems to represent a change in our character Gwynn. With the exception of accepting the red roses as a gift from Severin, Gwynn does not appear to be conforming to gendered norms quite as much and has gone from the one being protected to the protector. To an extent Gwynn is playing the role of an empowered female inworld.

8.8   Player Scenario 3

Preface: The Virtual World is Linden Lab's Second Life.

Gwynn tries to steer clear from all the people learning to navigate their avatar and walks down the ramp to a big floating 'freebie shop' sign, happily ignoring all the friend requests from strangers who haven't even got the common decency to talk to her first. The year is 2006 and the virtual world is Second Life. It's my third go at Linden Lab's invention. The first time lasted long enough to realise I couldn't choose my own surname. The second time delivered such a poor experience that it didn't last long. Now I'm in it again, to see what all the fuss is about. So are many people in the peak of the publicity hype, hence the crowd at the spawn point.

Browsing the goods in the freebie shop a bloke bumps into Gwynn and apologises. That's refreshing. They start talking, decide to explore a bit. Gwynn uses the search function and teleports Ronaldo to popular locations, clubs where there are more freebies to be found. The lag is atrocious. Gwynn steps from the spawn point as soon as she can and waits for the world to render while Ronaldo tries to walk around, bumping into objects that aren't even there yet. I feel for him. He's obviously not just new in Second Life, like so many of the visitors now, but new in these environments in general. He has trouble walking, navigating between the boxes and billboards strewn around. Gwynn teaches him many tricks and even a bit of netiquette. She smiles a lot (/me smiles) and eventually explains emotes to him. She finally accepts his friend request. He is so lost so often I allow him to find Gwynn on the map. Ronaldo is curious how Gwynn, which he assumed to be a girl because she looks like a girl, knows so much about technology in general and stuff like this in particular. I explain Gwynn works in the lunch room of a university and has access to the machines there during the quiet times and has befriended some of the students who taught her. It sounds perfectly reasonable and very low key. If you lie about yourself you don't make up you work in a canteen, do you? This also allows Gwynn to say 'customers' and have an IM conversation with somebody else if Ronaldo is in during the week.

I have realised that even though this virtual world is not supposed to be a game, in a way it is. Nice clothes, nice hair, nice shoes, nice skin, in short, your appearance, costs money. And that's not the end of it. So, the game is; get money. I start to think about ways to get her hands at some, at that time determined not to spend (RL) money but to do it inworld. If people can sell stuff, so can I. The question is what.

In the following weeks Gwynn explores the world full time, almost every waking hour, tries to get a grip on the mechanics, social, technical, commercial. She is experimenting with building and scripts, slowly creating a replica of the coffee shop across the street. In the evening Ronaldo and Gwynn explore the social environment together. They go to clubs and half jokingly Gwynn says she is tempted to have a go at pole dancing or hostess playing at one of the many clubs to make some money. Ronaldo is furiously against it. He's getting moral about it. What is she, a slut? A whore? Gwynn smiles and reminds him it's in the end a bunch of pixels but he insists she is selling her time and attention to strangers, which is the same thing. And in a way, it is. He's getting pushy. He starts requesting physical world information, which is politely declined. He sends her uploaded pictures of him in a little sports car. He starts to invite her over for a weekend trip, all expenses paid. He's getting possessive; when she is slow to respond he starts whining she's having other conversations. Gwynn admits she has, with builders and scripters she's befriended. Ronaldo then sulks. One Saturday she teleports him to her sandbox where they usually don't meet during the day; Ronaldo is camping some place to get money, and Gwynn is 'playing in a sandbox' while they chat using IM. The sandbox is a messy, cluttered place and Ronaldo doesn't understand what the point is. Gwynn takes him to a corner, explains you can build and rezz items here and places the coffee shop she has been building. She is quite proud of her achievement. Ronaldo rezzes the motorbike she found him and drives around, still not very proficient. It takes him a while to realise that it was not the bike but the building that was the reason to be here.

Gwynn admits she has lied to him, a little. She doesn't work in a lunch room, she owns the lunch room. Six of them, actually, and she is here to see if this is an area to do some marketing in. That is why she has been learning how to build, and script. She also hopes to dishearten his 'let's go shopping for shoes, 1,000 Euro is not a problem' boasting by indicating she is quite self sufficient and not easily impressed. She's also aiming to use it as an argument to spend less time together since she has to work. She doesn't just want to chuck him, hurt his feelings. But it doesn't really make an impact. It's all obviously beyond Ronaldo who never dived beneath the social surface of this toolbox we walk around in.

Soon after Gwynn is once again in her sandbox when Ronaldo is boasting about the money he made camping. This camping annoys me to no extent; it's the lamest, laziest way to get some cash. Gwynn explains she doesn't have time to talk now; she needs her hands for building. When she is typing, she cannot build. To her surprise Ronaldo pays her 200 Linden Dollars. So now she has time for him. Gwynn is infuriated and reminds him about the conversation they had in the club, about prostitution in the virtual world. She can almost see him shrugging. She contemplated it, didn't she? He tells her that at least he's not a stranger. Gwynn tries to return the money but Ronaldo declines it. How dare he? How dare the little insignificant camping n00b, still wearing texture hair[5] after all this time, insult her in that way? If she'd been for rent, he wouldn't be able to afford her. L$ 200 is not even a real dollar. Positively fuming, she logs out, deciding to ignore Ronaldo in the future.

Some time later Gwynn is on a deserted beach. Lacking her own place she needs to change her appearance in public and tries to find some privacy to do so. She is with her friend Gonzo, who is surfing on his hooverboard way up in the air, his purple mohawk waving in the wind. She needs to find a sexy (but not too sexy) outfit for the party they are going to later. Then Gonzo drops a snapshot on her. It's called 'pwn3d'.[6] He asks if I know this guy. It's Ronaldo, floating at 200 m, looking down at the beach where Gwynn is changing (Fig. 8.4). I forgot he could see me on the map. Gwynn is being stalked. Ronaldo is peeking on her while she changes. This is just plain creepy. Gwynn calls to her friend Gonzo for help and a minute later he shows up in his magnificent flying car. Gwynn jumps in and they fly away, literally off into the sunset. Ronaldo is subsequently unfriended and muted.

---

[5] Texture hair: In Second Life hair can be a texture applied to a morphed (deformed) skull and comes for free out of the box or made from prims and in a price range from free to very expensive. Currently newly registered avatars come with a range of clothes, skins, shoes and flexi-prim hair 'out of the box' . Previously these outfits and objects had to be gathered for free (freebie) or bought using Linden Dollars. In those days having texture hair indicated being very new, very unskilled or very indifferent.

[6] Pwn3d: l33tsp33ch for owned ☺ L33tsp33ch is adolescent internet lingo. Owned is when you get defeated to the point of humiliation. Leetspeech is frowned upon but pwn3d is one of those irresistible ones.

Fig. 8.4 Pwned. Floating voyeur caught in the act

8.9 Scenario 3: Analysis and Discussion

The initial meeting of Gwynn and Ronaldo is based on positive impression formation, a good start for a future, successful relationship. Ronaldo makes a good first impression on Gwynn, not through his physical appearance, but rather through his manners. Ronaldo's politeness does not go unnoticed by Gwynn and is an example of perceived norms regarding acceptable standards for behaviour in virtual worlds reflecting physical world social norms. Gwynn appears to feel sorry for Ronaldo as a newbie in Second Life, and in a somewhat condescending manner ('bless his cotton socks'), considers him somewhat naïve for believing he is a girl and as such seems to forgive him for his blatantly gender-biased query regarding his advanced technological know-how and skill. Again, the user reinforces beliefs that he truly is a girl behind the avatar by telling a convincing and subtle lie regarding his physical working role.

The user behind Gwynn's view of Ronaldo as naïve, and as a result, potentially harmless, changes following the incident at the club in which Ronaldo makes moral judgments and gets possessive of Gwynn, telling her what she should and should not do. The gender biases and prejudices are clearly parallel to those in the physical world as Ronaldo implies that Gwynn is prostituting herself and is branded a whore and a slut for considering working as a pole dancer or hostess inworld. Interestingly, the subject of gender-benders working in these roles inworld is a subject of discussion on some Second Life blogs. Perhaps surprisingly, this form of online deception is not viewed as acceptable in this inworld context as Cindy Claveau, a Second Life blogger and club manager inworld explains in the following extract:

> This individual worked at a club with me right after I joined SL. I was a manager at the time and they were one of the dancers. The club had "VIP" rooms where girls could take clients for escort work if they so chose, with the club getting a small percentage of the fee. In a moment of candor, this girl confessed to me that she was really a he (for the record, she wasn't the only one – and we added screening questions to the hiring process to try to prevent a recurrence, hoping they would be honest). I had to encourage him/her to resign or be fired in view of the damage to the club's reputation if it slipped to a client that we employed gender benders as escorts. (Claveau 2007, para. 6)

Following the antagonistic exchange between Ronaldo and Gwynn in the club, the boundary between the online and offline, inworld and physical, is blurred when Ronaldo starts to demand information about 'Gwynn's' physical identity and appears to want to pursue an offline relationship. Little does he know, but the male player behind Gwynn is making a mockery of Ronaldo and his attempts to impress, as well as his lack of knowledge concerning Second Life. He continues to annoy the player, but the final straw comes when Ronaldo tries to buy Gwynn's time inworld. This comes as a huge insult to Gwynn, the implication that he can be bought by someone like Ronaldo for such little money, and especially following Ronaldo's earlier moral judgements and arguments regarding prostitution inworld. It is at this point that Gwynn decides she has had enough of Ronaldo, although does not unfriend him quite yet.

Some time later, and again reflecting social and personal norms in the physical world, Gwynn tries to find a private spot in which to get changed in a public place. Alerted by her friend Gonzo, Gwynn is horrified to discover that Ronaldo is spying on him from above, watching him getting changed. Gwynn is being stalked. This experience is crucial in giving the player an understanding of what it is like to be a victim of unwanted attention and harassment, and an experience of what it can be like to be female in a male-dominated environment in which sexual harassment of female characters is not an unusual occurrence. The propensity for female characters to experience such harassment and violence has been noted in text-based MUDs (e.g. Dibbell 1993; Reid 1994) even before graphical virtual worlds such as Second Life were created.

8.10 Player Scenario 4

Gwynn greets visitors, many of them fresh from Help Island and explains some of the basics over and over again while introducing people to the place they have just arrived in. It's a showroom and office with a meeting space merging into a patio overlooking a bay with a pier. It's a very decent place, considering the prim limit. Some of the furniture is bought but Gwynn built the rest for a Brazilian company. Today is the opening. The year is 2007 and the virtual world is still Second Life.

A man bumps into Gwynn. He's wearing decent stuff, no freebies in sight. But his hair doesn't fit, showing his skull and his watch has a bling. Several IMs from people she's been working with the past few weeks inform Gwynn that this is the managing director, visiting the project he commissioned for the first time. They start talking, introducing each other, very polite and civil, pleasantly enough.

Since this is the opening of the virtual office of a Brazilian marketing agency Gwynn smells more opportunity than just this single build. So she has agreed to help receive visitors and dressed the part instead of the torn jeans, big boots, loud t-shirt and gloves which is her usual attire while at work. She even did her hair. The director, let's call him Manuel, compliments Gwynn on her appearance. He ignores the build he is standing in. She is tempted to frown (/me frowns) but holds her horses. Manuel then asks her if she is the expert. She knows he had to sign the expenses for her freelance; it had taken the marketing manager some time to convince him quality doesn't come for free. Gwynn informs him she is indeed Registered Solution Provider and all that jazz. Manuel then asks her if she can fix his hair. Gwynn explains how to do it. It is not an easy thing for this gentleman. And when it is done he goes to mingle but not before befriending Gwynn.

During the next few days Gwynn and the marketing manager show Manuel around, making sure he realises the quality of his build while explaining the potential. Manuel has been active on the internet since the early days, like he knows Gwynn has been as well, and they discuss the similarities. He's interested in talking business.

So when the invite for a teleport arrives a couple of days later Gwynn takes a moment to change into something appropriate and accepts the invitation. To land in a bubble bath where Manuel is smoking a cigar, wearing nothing but skimpy swimming trunks. She jumps out, astonished and asks what this is all about. Manuel explains that he finds it relaxing, seemingly unaware that inviting a lady into a bubble bath without previous notification is not your standard professional behaviour. Gwynn informs him of this very politely and patiently even though she is infuriated. He appears to understand and Gwynn leaves. Opportunity or not, there are limits.

The next day a big bouquet of roses leans against the door of Gwynn's own (squatted) office. Inspection shows Manuel bought it and left it there. To position it that way shows Manuel has put time and effort in it. Gwynn is charmed, very charmed indeed. What a nice apology. She sends him a gracious IM even though he's not online, knowing it will arrive in his email. Some time passes. They don't meet inworld but are exchanging emails and IMs about potential professional collaboration. At first Manuel thinks Gwynn could be his personal assistant and be a hostess during meetings. Gwynn keeps informing him, as polite as possible while her patience is wearing thin, her skills are on a whole different level but isn't sure the message sinks in. After some time another teleport invitation arrives. Gwynn hesitates, and then accepts. Surely he wouldn't make the same mistake twice. She arrives in a small villa on an island. Manuel greets her butt naked. He apparently bought this place in the past weeks and took the time and effort to obtain genitalia and attach them properly. He wants to give her a hug but Gwynn is already on her way home (control-shift-h), typing an infuriated IM as soon as she arrives. Manuel protests.

He thought she wanted to work for him. Gwynn is flabbergasted. Wants to know if this is how he treats all his female employees. Manuel thinks this is different. Gwynn begs to differ. She sets herself to busy.

I alt-tab out to write an email, including a picture of myself. Long hair, angry frown, beard of a week or two. Then I jump back into Second Life and tell Manuel he has got new mail. "Is that your boyfriend?" he asks. I tell him it's me. Manuel needs to sit down. Manuel needs a drink. He didn't have a clue. He then starts wondering why. I tell him about his attitude toward me, the role he envisioned for me. Since I am a girl I need to be a hostess and hairdresser, he is blind for the obvious skills I show. I tell him how sexist it is and how common, how men don't even realise it is what they are doing, that I have experienced it countless times in the past decade or so. I tell him how horrible that actually is and how acutely exposed it is when men believe you to be female, like he did. By then I'm realising I'm lecturing this very Latin, very traditional macho man, that I have made him look like a gullible fool and that I won't be working for him, even if I wanted. I advise him he should try being a girl for a while. And when he asks why I tell him I believe that being a girl online made me a better man.

8.11   Scenario 4: Analysis and Discussion

8.11.1   First Impressions, Gender and Ethics in Virtual Worlds

The importance of first impressions and physical appearance in the virtual world is again highlighted above, as well as the re-enactment of social and behavioural norms online. For example, Gwynn dresses up for a business meeting with the director of a marketing firm, Manuel, and 'she even did her hair'. However, gender-stereotypical norms transcend the medium and Gwynn is disappointed when the male manager compliments her on her appearance, at the expense of praise regarding her advanced inworld building skills, which he doesn't even comment on. This is hugely reflective of physical world discrimination and gender biases in which greater importance can be placed on stereotypically feminine attributes such as the physical appearance of women, over their abilities and achievements. For example, Kanter (1977) found that coworkers and clients were more attentive to female employees' dress and appearance than performance-related behaviour in a male-dominated company.

Manuel later requests Gwynn to meet with him. In the scenario Gwynn tells us that she accepts the invitation but first takes a moment to change into something more appropriate for a business meeting. Gwynn is completely shocked when she is then teleported into a bubble bath with Manuel dressed in scanty men's swimwear and leaves immediately, outraged by the all-too often blurring of boundaries commonly experienced in the physical world, and by women in professional contexts characterised by power differentials.

Manuel later apologises, again reminiscent of earlier scenarios, whereby Gwynn is the grateful, and somewhat flattered, recipient of a bunch of red roses by way of an apology. Perhaps Gwynn should not have accepted these in the context of a professional inworld relationship. Nonetheless, Gwynn soon reverts to her earlier disappointment when Manuel once again overlooks her skills and decides she could be his personal assistant. History repeats itself when Manuel teleports her in to his private island, stark naked and with his newly-acquired genitals on display. Gwynn wonders if this is how he treats all of his female employees, but to give Manuel the benefit of the doubt, perhaps this is restricted to his Second Life and the popular, yet clearly skewed perception that in Second Life 'anything goes'.

8.11.2   Relationship Between Online and Offline Selves

The player behind Gwynn began his gender-bending journey purely as a role-play experience, motivated by a desire to play a particular type of character in Diablo, as opposed to a desire to experiment with gender. However, after years of presenting as the female persona Gwynn, the gendered interactions that he experienced inworld have had a significant impact on his physical identity and understanding of gender roles. This is encapsulated profoundly in the player's final quote "I believe that being a girl online made me a better man". He clearly values this experience in enabling him to view the world from a female perspective and in understanding what it is like to be treated as a female and the associated gender-related power differentials. Presenting himself as a female influenced how he was treated by other characters and avatars inworld, and subsequently limited his opportunities. He encountered the proverbial glass ceiling inworld and has effectively demonstrated how the same gender biases in society transcend the boundary between offline and online worlds. It is a long time since the early optimism of a gender-free utopia online but the scenarios depicted in this chapter show, disappointingly, just how little progress has been made in terms of gender equality. Stereotyping, prejudice and discrimination are just as much features of the virtual world as the physical world.

Playing an opposite-gender avatar in virtual worlds has been a voyage of self-discovery and it has in some ways transformed his sense of self.[7] One is reminded of the writings of the psychoanalyst Carl Jung and his concepts of the 'anima' and the 'animus'; the former being the female element of the male unconscious. Jung noted that in the Middle Ages it was said that 'every man carries a woman inside himself' (1964, p. 17). Gender-swapping in virtual worlds has inadvertently led the player to release a part of his himself, his anima, usually hidden and unexplored.

---

[7] As the second author, I find it fascinating to note that Gwynn has evolved over time in various incarnations and now appears to have become intertwined with the author's physical identity to the extent that his Facebook and LinkedIn profile is in Gwynn's name, the profile picture is of Gwynn, yet the profile conveys details of his real-life adventures, not Gwynn's or his virtual ones. This blurring of boundaries delineating identities is evident throughout this chapter.

However, unlike some of the female sides of Jung's male patients, who he describes as 'not nice', the anima within the male player seems to be an ethical, thoughtful and empowered female. This is compatible with the notion that positive aspects of self can be learned through virtual play and transferred into the physical world (Whitty et al. 2010).

However, for other players the impact of online interactions in virtual worlds can have an even more powerful impact on offline selves and physical lives. Whitty et al. (2010) gave an example of a MMORPG player whose online interactions had a significant impact on her offline self in that she learned that she was bisexual through engaging in sexual activities in the game Sociolotron. This is an example that fits in particular well with the exploration of hidden and stigmatised aspects of self and the facilitation of aspects of this true self through online identities and interactions discussed by Turkle (1995). Similarly, Boellstorff (2008, 2010) gives examples of individuals who opt for an opposite-gender avatar in Second Life and decide that they are transgender or try out an opposite-sex virtual body before opting to change their physical body.

Finally, this case study has served as an interesting example of how the development of an online persona through various virtual worlds and personal and professional contexts, has become intertwined with the player's corporeal self to the extent that he uses this identity in the offline world. This represents, as Steinkuehler (2005) discusses, a move away from Turkle's postmodernist take on multiple identities to a convergence of online and offline selves and fuzzy boundaries between virtual worlds, online spaces and life off-screen.

8.12 Conclusions

This has been a single case study of one man's gender-bending experiences online but it demonstrates the potential for further research into the impact of gender-swapping experiences on identity and the offline self. It also questions previous conclusions in this area that gender-swapping does not impact significantly on the offline self and that such experiences do not lead us to learn anything about gender (see e.g., Lewis 2004). However, this investigation is limited in its approach and it is impossible to generalise on the basis of this single-case study of one man's gender-bending experiences, which may or may not be accurately recollected (and it was not possible, nor ethical, to provide logs of the chat interactions), and one woman's subjective interpretations of those experiences. Nonetheless, we hope that it will serve as a useful starting point for the generation of new hypotheses and theories regarding gender-bending online, which although may be relatively rare, still exists as a phenomenon of the internet-age.

We hope to investigate this issue further with an empirical investigation involving more long-term gender-swapping participants through online interviews using an Interpretative Phenomenological Analysis approach to explore how gender-benders in virtual worlds are making sense of their experiences. Future work in this area could more closely investigate the potential for gender-swapping activities in virtual worlds as a vehicle about learning about the self and broader issues such as gender inequality, stereotyping and bias in the offline world. Yee (cited in CNN.com 2007) noted that it may be harder for men to experience different gender roles in the physical world. Boellstorff (2010) discusses the eye-opening experiences of men who decide to use a female avatar for a day in Second Life and learn that sexism exists even in a virtual world and also what it is like to be someone different than who they really are. An alternative way to give a man an experience of what it is like to be a woman, albeit temporary, may be through virtual reality technology, where men's minds can be mediated through a virtual woman's body, a technique described by Slater et al. (2010).

References

Bailey, T.: Roleplaying: the third life within Second Life. The Konstrukt 10, 20–24 (2007)

Berman, J., Bruckman, A.: The Turing game: Exploring identity in an online environment. Convergence 7, 83–102 (2001)

Boellstorff, T.: Coming of Age in Second Life: An Anthropologist Explores the Virtually Human. Princeton University Press, Princeton (2008)

Boellstorff, T.: Placing the Virtual Body: Avatar, Chora, Cypherg. Interview for 'Focus' (2010). http://will.illinois.edu/focus/interview/focus101104a/. Accessed 29 Nov 2010

Bruckman, A.: Gender-swapping on the Internet. Proceedings of INET '93. The Internet Society, Reston (1993)

Butler, J.: Performative acts and gender constitution: an essay in phenomenology and feminist theory. In: Case, S.E. (ed.) Performing Feminisms: Feminist Critical Theory and Theatre, pp. 270–292. Johns Hopkins University Press, Baltimore (1990)

Cassell, J., Jenkins, H. (eds.): From Barbie to Mortal Kombat: Gender and Computer Games. The MIT Press, Cambridge (1998)

Claveau, C.: Second Life, Second Gender (2007). http://cindyclaveau.wordpress.com/2007/09/20/second-life-second-gender/. Accessed 22 Nov 2009

CNN: Identity in a virtual world (2007). http://edition.cnn.com/2007/TECH/06/07/virtual_identity/index.html. Accessed 14 Oct 2009

Dibbell, J.: A Rape in Cyberspace. The Village Voice, 21st Dec 1993. http://www.juliandibbell.com/texts/bungle_vv.html

Dietz, T.L.: An examination of violence and gender role portrayals in video games: implications for gender socialization and aggressive behavior. Sex Roles 38, 425–442 (1998)

Flanagan, M.: Hyperbodies, hyperknowledge: women in games, women in cyberpunk, and strategies of resistance. In: Flanagan, M., Booth, A. (eds.) Reload: Rethinking Women and Cyberculture, pp. 425–468. The MIT Press, Cambridge (2002)

Hussain, Z., Griffiths, M.D.: Gender-swapping and socializing in Cyberspace: An Exploratory Study. Cyberpsychol. Behav. 11, 47–53 (2008)

Jung, C.: Man and His Symbols. Aldus Books Ltd., London (1964)

Kafai, Y.B., Heeter, C., Denner, J., Sun, J.Y. (eds.): Beyond Barbie and Mortal Kombat: New Perspectives on Gender and Gaming. The MIT Press, Cambridge (2008)

Kanter, R.M.: Men and Women of the Corporation. Basic Books, New York (1977)

Lewis, A.: Gender swapping on the Internet: do boys really want to be girls and girls be boys. Couns. Aust. 4, 1–5 (2004)

McKeon, M., Wyche, S. Life across boundaries: design, identity, and gender in SL, retrieved from (2005). http://www.mattmckeon.com/portfolio/second-life.pdf. Accessed 10 Dec 2008

Morales, E.D., Patton, J.Q.: Gender bias in a virtual world. WSU McNair J. **3**, 81–89 (2005)

O'Brien, J.: Writing in the body: gender (re)production in online interaction. In: Smith, M.A., Kollock, P. (eds.) Communities in Cyberspace, pp. 76–104. Routledge, London (1999)

Postmes, T., Spears, R., Lea, M.: The formation of group norms in computer-mediated communication. Hum. Commun. Res. **26**, 341–371 (2000)

Postmes, T., Spears, R.: Behavior online: Does anonymous computer communication reduce gender inequality? Personality and Social Psychology Bulletin, **28**, 1073–1083 (2002)

Postmes, T., Spears, R., Lea, M.: Intergroup differentiation in computer-mediated communication: effects of depersonalization. Group Dyn.: Theory Res. Pract. **6**, 3–16 (2002)

Reicher, S.D., Spears, R., Postmes, T.: A social identity model of deindividuation phenomena. Eur. Rev. Soc. Psychol. **6**, 161–198 (1995)

Reid, E.: Cultural formations in text-based virtual realities. Unpublished Master's thesis, University of Melbourne, Melbourne (1994)

Schaap, F.: The Words That Took Us There: Ethnography In a Virtual Reality. Aksant Academic Publishers, Amsterdam (2002)

Schaap, F.: Links, lives, logs: presentation in the Dutch blogosphere (2004). http://blog.lib.umn.edu/blogosphere/links_lives_logs.html. Accessed 15 Sept 2007

Slater, M., Spanlang, B., Sanchez-Vives, M.V., Blanke, O.: First person experience of body transfer in virtual reality. PLoS ONE, **5** (2010). http://www.plosone.org/article/info:doi/10.1371/journal.pone.0010564. Accessed 12 May 2010

Steiner, P.: On the Internet, nobody knows you're a dog. The New Yorker **69**, 61 (1993)

Steinkuehler, C.: Cognition and learning in massively multiplayer online games: a critical approach. Doctoral dissertation (2005). http://website.education.wisc.edu/steinkuehler/thesis.html. Accessed 29 Nov 2010

Stone, A.R.: Will the real body please stand up?: Boundary stories about virtual culture. In: Benedikt, M. (ed.) Cyberspace: First Steps, pp. 81–118. MIT Press, Cambridge (1991)

Stone, A.R.: The War of Desire and Technology at the Close of the Mechanical Age. The MIT Press, Cambridge (1995)

Tajfel, H., Turner, J.C.: An integrative theory of intergroup conflict. In: Austin, W.G., Worchel, S. (eds.) The Social Psychology of Intergroup Relations. Brooks-Cole, Monterey (1979)

Turkle, S.: Life on the Screen: Identity in the Age of the Internet. Simon & Schuster, New York (1995)

Whitty, M., Young, G., Goodings, L.: What I won't do in pixels: examining the limits of taboo violation in MMORPGs. Comput. Hum. Behav. **27**(1), 268–275 (2010). Accessed 22 Sep 2010

Yee, N.: The Norrathian scrolls: a study of EverQuest (2001). http://www.nickyee.com/eqt/home.html. Accessed 12 April 2005

Yee, N.: Motivations of play in online games. Cyberpsychol. Behav. **9**, 772–775 (2007)

Chapter 9
Constructing Disability in Online Worlds; Conceptualising Disability in Online Research

Diane Carr

Abstract In this chapter the online construction of disability is investigated, and the implications for educators working in virtual worlds are considered. Based on the analysis of data collected through interviews with deaf residents of Second Life™, it is argued that research into online identity, disability and education needs to allow room for self-description, and that educators need to recognise the power relations that can lurk within practices of provision or accessibility support. Working through these issues involves reconciling Disability Studies with e-learning and accessibility perspectives. It is proposed that strategies that would support this reconciliation might be found in recent literature on disability and technology.

9.1 Introduction

Educators are increasingly interested in the teaching and learning potentials of virtual worlds such as Second Life (Kirriemuir 2008). However, participation in virtual worlds may not be straightforward for disabled people. For example, during 2007 an integrated voice feature was introduced into Second Life by its developers, Linden Lab. Prior to the introduction of this voice feature most users (or 'residents') communicated by typed text-chat. With the arrival of the voice feature, some deaf residents found themselves suddenly excluded from relationships, groups and events. Of course, it was not the voice feature as tool that disabled these users, so much as the various practices and conventions that emerged in its wake.

To explore these matters interviews were conducted with deaf Second Life residents. The impact of the voice feature was investigated, and the construction of deafness as a disability in Second Life was examined. A major theme that emerged during analysis of the data was that of 'loss', which encompassed references to

D. Carr (✉)
Media and Cultural Studies, Institute of Education, University of London, London, UK
e-mail: D.Carr@ioe.ac.uk

A. Peachey and M. Childs (eds.), *Reinventing Ourselves: Contemporary Concepts of Identity in Virtual Worlds*, Springer Series in Immersive Environments,
DOI 10.1007/978-0-85729-361-9_9, © Springer-Verlag London Limited 2011

learning, adjustment and identity. The interviewees offered clarifications and revisions when discussing these issues. They were forthright and articulate about the impact of voice, yet wary of and resistant to being positioned as bereft or passive. These matters are explored using a Cultural Studies framework, while reference is made to literature from Disability Studies, Deaf Studies, and education in Second Life research. These different literatures offer insights relevant to the topic, yet these approaches are not especially compatible, particularly in terms of the conceptualising of disability itself. This chapter begins with a consideration of these differences.

9.2 Disability and Second Life

Residents of Second Life (or SL) who identify as disabled have been active in establishing facilities and social networks to welcome and support participation by disabled people (see http://virtualability.org). In addition to creating and contributing to these services, it is reasonable to assume that residents who experience physical life disability are spread across the general SL population, enjoying various aspects of this virtual world, creating content and contributing to its communities.

As yet, little has emerged within the Second Life and education literature on the topic of disability. This study draws on relevant research into disability, deafness and new media (Goggin and Newell 2003), and deaf people's use of the Internet (Guo et al. 2005; Valentine and Skelton 2008). Research on social aspects of Internet use by disabled people also informs this research (Bowker and Tuffin 2003, 2004; Seymour and Lupton 2004). When disability is mentioned in relation to SL there is a tendency to list the various modes of communication, socialising and mobility on offer in this virtual world, and to 'match' these offers to a corresponding set of physical life impairments (see, for example, Boellstorff 2008, p 137, 147). The ways in which SL might be rendered accessible to blind and visually impaired users has been researched (White et al. 2008), and educators interested in the inclusive potentials of Second Life have noted its capacity to support a range of learners due to its varied modalities (Ball and Pearce 2008; Sheehy 2008). It is important to recognise that the new voice feature may have made SL more accessible to some users, but it is also necessary to acknowledge that navigation and the interface may still present considerable difficulties.

While academic papers on SL, education and disability are still rare, disability is certainly discussed at blogs, on mailing lists, at educator's seminars in SL, and at physical life SL and education events. In these contexts, disability tends to be discussed in terms of exemplar projects, special facilities or perhaps compensation ("Will using SL improve the life of disabled users?"); in terms of the development of tools to support participation, or in relation to compliance (educators' recognition of their legal responsibility to comply with legislation as regards disability and equal opportunities). This framing of the issues reflects e-learning and accessibility perspectives. For reviews of the literature in this area, see Kinash et al. (2004), Seale (2004) and Seale (2006).

A focus on accessibility is legitimate. Yet if the education and Second Life community adopts this perspective without deliberation, there is a risk that the central concepts (relating to identity and disability in online contexts, for example) will remain under theorised. One such risk, for instance, involves the inadvertent propagation of an 'impairment as problem/technology as solution' dynamic. Such patterns implicitly define disability as a property of potentially marginalised individuals who are in need of special support. Research that frames disability in terms of individualised impairment (as a medical condition or tragic deficit, for example) has been soundly and exhaustively critiqued within Disability Studies (Oliver 1990). By contrast, a *social model* of disability (see Barnes 2000) attends to the disabling aspects of an environment - as when cultural practices, assumptions, expectations or material phenomena assume a standardised or 'normal' body, and exclude or penalise those who deviate from this pattern (Davis 2006). Simi Linton describes Disability Studies as a distinct field involving humanities or interpretive social science research that conceptualises disability as cultural construct. Linton thus distinguishes between the 'socio-political-cultural examination of disability [and] the interventionist approaches that characterise the traditional study of disability' (Linton 1998, p 525). According to Linton, a common feature of the latter approach is a lack of reflection on the ways in which the disabled subject is conceptualised.

Various authors (Gronvik 2007; Shakespeare 2006) have critiqued the social model of disability for ignoring personal or practical aspects of disability - including researchers engaged with the development of tools to support accessibility and inclusion (Dewsbury et al. 2004). Educators active in SL may need to find a way to work between these perspectives: to address practical aspects of accessibility, without ignoring the social, political and cultural aspects of disability and online identity. Goggin and Newell have warned that research on disability and ICT is 'replicating charity, medical and other oppressive discourses of disability' as a result of a failure to engage with Disability Studies (2006, p 310). Evidently this is a trap that educators and researchers working in *Second Life* should strive to avoid.

9.3   Deaf in Second Life

As the above suggests, disability can be variously conceptualised. So can deafness. It is possible, for example, to self-describe as upper-case 'Deaf' or lower-case 'deaf'. Being Deaf involves laying claim to a socio-linguistic and cultural affiliation and fluency in a sign language (Davis 1995, 2007). A Deaf person living and working in a sign literate community would not be disabled (Ladd 2003). On the other hand, the term 'deaf' might be used simply to refer to a hearing loss. It does not express a specific degree or severity of hearing loss, so it arguably encompasses terms like 'hard of hearing' and 'hearing impaired'. All of these definitions are emotive and contested (Grushkin 2003; Lane 2006). In this chapter the term 'deaf' will be used in a general, inclusive sense, except where the words Deaf or D/deaf appear in cited work or quotations. This is for the sake of simplicity and in recognition of the fact that some Deaf people whose first and preferred language is sign, and who have limited fluency in a second language such as English, may face problems when attempting to access SL or the Internet generally (Correll and Maruyama 2005).

The introduction of voice to SL was controversial (Carr and Oliver 2010) and the potential impact on deaf residents was noted. For example, in an short article published in *Second Opinion* (July 2007) a Linden Lab newsletter, titled 'Voice: Another Valuable Choice' SL's developers acknowledged the social ramifications of voice for deaf residents, while suggesting that the technology (and hence, presumably, the developers) are not accountable: 'While a deaf Resident may find him or herself excluded in some social contexts, their ability to communicate in SL has not been diminished from a technical viewpoint.' Later in the article it is stated that: 'Most educators would agree that learning is better facilitated between individuals with voice' – a statement that 'normalises' the experience of hearing educators and students.

Considering the above in relation to literature on the cultural construction of difference, disability and deafness, such as Lennard Davis's (1995) *Enforcing Normalcy: Disability, Deafness and the Body*, makes it possible to articulate some key points. Firstly, Davis argues that 'disabilities appear or are highlighted in environments that produce disability' (p 165). It is arguable that the voice feature within SL (or, at least, the take-up of this voice feature by residents) changed the manner in which deafness was produced in that particular environment. If this is the case, then another point by Davis becomes relevant. He argues that 'In the task of rethinking and theorising disability, one of the first steps is to understand the relationship between a physical impairment and the political, social, even spatial environment that places that impairment in a matrix of meanings and significations' (1995, p 3). What is interesting is that the introduction of voice to SL involves a situation where the political and social environment changed due to a technological alteration, in a manner that had specific implications for those with a particular impairment. There were indications that, in some circles at least, voice would become the 'norm' and, as Davis argues, (Davis 1995, p 29) when a norm is constructed, so is deviation. Difference, in such a case, encounters a 'hegemony of normalcy' (Davis 1995, p 44) that renders 'deviant' (or at least marginalises) particular identities.

Thinking about disability and education in online worlds solely in terms of tools that support participation is insufficient. It is also necessary to look at the conventions that emerge in the wake of these tools, and the implications for online identity. Investigating these issues also involves thinking about how the disabled or deaf subject is constructed in and through research itself.

9.4   Research Strategy and Methods

As the above indicates, engaging with literature relevant to virtual worlds and deaf residents, disability and technology, while thinking about the implications for education, involves traversing several fields that are themselves multi-disciplinary. This multiplicity increases once issues of methodology are raised. Anthropological and ethnographic studies of online worlds and online communities (Boellstorff 2008; Taylor 2006) are relevant, as is earlier work on online identity (Turkle 1995) and 'virtual ethnography' as methodology (Hine 2000). A positive side-effect of field traversal is that it potentially destabilises the role of researcher-as-expert. Rather than approaching the job of research as an authority, he or she is compelled to grope beyond his/her 'comfort zone'. A second (less speculative) point to make about research that shifts between and across different fields, involves the need to clearly identify the conceptual framework on which the research is founded (Lesham and Trafford 2007). In this instance, the conceptual framework employed is that of Cultural Studies.

Cultural Studies as 'a field of enquiry' (Gray 2003, p 12) is compatible with Disability and Deaf Studies. These fields share an interest in the construction of difference, discourse, and issues of subjectivity, identity, power and reflexivity. Given the topic under investigation, the dynamic between researcher and informant is particularly sensitive. There are issues of responsibility in terms of ensuring a non-exploitive relationship to an online community (Ess and the AoIR ethics working committee, 2002). Additionally, there is a need to recognise the long history of exploitative relations between disabled people and scientific research, medical research and education (Branson and Miller 2002). Cultural Studies often involves exploring people's investments in texts and practices, rather than the pursuit of large scale research, representative samples or generalisability. There is a focus on the relationships between text, practices and identity (Gray 2003, pp 15–16). Identity is often discussed in terms of subjectivity, which is 'made up of our positions in and encounters with particular discourses' (Gray 2003, p 75). Cultural Studies research tends to be modestly scaled (Gray 2003, p 74). There were also practical limitations as regards the scale of this study. Voice rolled-out in August 2007 and these interviews were conducted in March 2009. Locating the resources to support a larger study would have resulted in further delay. The delay between the introduction of voice, and the interviews, was advantageous, however, in that it allowed for longitudinal perspective and reflection on the part of the interviewees.

To investigate the impact of the new voice feature on deaf residents, semi-structured interviews with residents who identify as deaf in their first or physical lives were conducted. Interviewees were recruited from mailing lists and from within SL itself, through contacts, and through deaf groups. Within SL I used instant messenger (IM) and the search function to make contact with the leaders and founders of various deaf groups. These individuals acted as 'gate-keepers' (Wittel 2000) who volunteered to be interviewed, offered to circulate my request, or introduced me to potential interviewees. There was an element of 'snowballing', as the following quote from an interviewee suggests:

> Treasure: A resident of mine emailed me this morning all excited hearing about you from someone she wants to be interviewed too, lol, but could not be here at this time. [...] Max is the one who told Zarya about you. She contacted me.

The recruitment was performed in English, which had an impact on the sample. Five interviews were conducted, each lasting approximately an hour. The questions asked during the interviews involved experience and preferences in SL, the introduction of voice, the resident's recollections of the roll-out, and the subsequent impact of voice on their experiences in SL.

My avatar met interviewees at a time and location of their choosing. To allow for informed consent, interviewees were handed a note-card within SL prior to the interview starting. The note-cards were prepared using the ethics guidelines produced by Ess and the AoIR Committee (2002). On the card, various definitions were offered (of 'deaf' for example) and a commitment to the interviewee's privacy was affirmed. It was noted that pseudonyms would be used for all avatars, and that the interviews would be chat-logged. Interviewees were advised that minor changes (to spelling, for instance) might be made for the sake of clarity. As the researcher, I was identified in terms of relevant aspects of my physical-life identity, including my deafness and my university affiliation. A link to my research blog was supplied. It was noted that the research is unfunded, and that the goal of the research was 'to contribute to and extend the debate on 'disability' and identity within virtual worlds and in online communities'. Interviewees were asked to confirm in chat-text […] 'that you have read this note-card, and that you are happy for the interview to proceed.' Interviewees were advised that they were welcome to ask questions before, during or after the interview. All of the interviewees indicated their agreement, although one contributor, Treasure Ballinger, chose to be identified by her SL avatar. As she explained:

> Treasure: :) Thanks. I've read the notecard and agree, however I don't need to be anonymous. I advocate for deaf/Deaf/hard of hearing in rl [real life], and am on the rl board of Virtual Ability [in SL]. Not very anonymous anyway. No need to start now :)

The material collected through the chat-logged interviews totaled 30 pages of text. Analysis involved fragmenting the text and identifying clusters of meaning or themes that formed links and continuities across the data (Gray 2003 pp 148–168). To do this, the data was considered statement by statement. Initial codes were derived from these statements. The codes were then reviewed in order to identify any organising or structuring themes. By these means, a set of categories was developed. For example, 'loss', as an umbrella category, encompassed references to adjustment and change, identity, risk, privacy, learning and role. The level of attention directed by the interviewees themselves to particular issues (where attention was marked by qualifying statements, repetition, or emphasis by emote, for example) was regarded as significant. Later in the process, respondent validation was sought: the interviewees were invited to read through an early version of this chapter (Gray 2003, p 72). Two of the interviewees offered additional clarifications at that point.

This focus on the statements generated at the interviews did mean that other aspects of the interviews (as event or experience) were not considered. For example, each of the interviewees expressed aspects of their identity or tastes through the look (shape, species, gender, skin, hair, etc.) of their avatar. Additionally, each of the interviewees chose to meet me in a space of their own (a garden, a room, a gallery, for example). This account does not incorporate these phenomena. One reason for this is that I suspect it would be difficult to connect an analysis of an avatar's hair or wardrobe, to the issues at the centre of this study. Additionally, describing a participant's SL home in any detail would be likely to undermine their anonymity. The representation or overview of the material from the interviews that follows reflects the aforementioned focus on the emergent category of 'loss', with references to adjustment, learning, change, role and identity.

9.5   The Interviews

The five interviewees quoted in this section are Treasure, Max, Anna, Zarya and Grace. These are pseudonyms, apart from Treasure who (as explained) preferred to be identified by her SL avatar. Anna had been resident in SL the longest, at 4½ years. The interviewees were experienced, land-owning SL residents. Depending on their interests, they worked in SL (providing a service, developing tools or teaching classes, for example), built facilities, founded organisations, maintained friendships and/or engaged in various forms of play.

All of the interviewees had an opinion about the introduction of the voice feature, but the intensity of feelings as regards these changes definitely varied. Most reported that voice had a negative impact on their SL social lives. As Max explained, it can be "an issue when I'm in areas where people are socialising, using voice" in which case, the "biggest problem of course is feeling left out". Max moved away from certain areas, and "drifted away from that circle of friends" – and continued to enjoy SL. Grace was much more emphatic about the negative impact of voice ("oh hell I was angry"), while Zarya made reference to people, groups, activities and areas that are no longer accessible. She described these changes in terms of loss, as well as adjustment and learning.

> Zarya: I think I've gotten to the point where I can safely avoid the Voice issue. Become more SL savvy, I don't know! LOL [...] I've had to adjust and work around [voice]. I enjoy SL, but I've had to enjoy it differently [...] I've given up trying to belong to poetry groups. And I don't go to the clubs anymore.

Treasure admitted to losing at least one friend to voice, and was clear that the impact of voice on some deaf residents should not be underestimated: "Standing around, socially isolated while people chat around you in voice is at the very least uncomfortable". Treasure was initially 'militantly' or even 'rabidly' anti-voice, but reports that her experiences as a disabilities advocate in SL have brought on a change in perspective: "If I had to type with my feet, I'd want to be able to use voice also."

In addition to having different perspectives on voice in SL, the interviewees had different experiences of deafness. All were fluent in written English. Treasure, Max and Grace are also fluent in ASL (American Sign Language). All were accustomed to explaining themselves in particular ways in different contexts while contending with various assumptions, as when Treasure notes that "nothing is more annoying to me than to have a hearing person say, 'treasure you are deaf? but you speak so well!' lol – it's actually insulting!" Remarks about self-definition incorporated references to shyness, different aspects of deaf identity, connections with a Deaf community, and negotiations with the hearing world:

> Zarya: Hmmm.....it's pretty obvious I have a hearing loss in RL. I speak and lipread though, so sometimes I can get away without having to (like paying for groceries, pumping gas, etc.). I describe myself as deaf (lower case d) [because] I never learned sign language, so I don't consider myself part of the Deaf culture. And, if I say "hearing impaired" people assume I can use the phone (which I can't.) It's easier and more accurate for me to say I'm deaf.

Explaining deafness within SL is also complicated, and as Treasure explained, some "people [in SL] are mean about deaf using type chat and not liking voice". At times this hostility is rooted in hearing residents' disbelief, and their assumption that continued text use involves a wish to conceal a RL gender. Zarya referred to an incident where she had been pressed to explain her use of text to another resident. He had then coaxed information from Zarya about her experience of deafness, while acting "fascinated and enraptured". She discovered later that he had logged and shared this conversation with others ("I was really upset...I don't talk about [that] in detail to anyone...and I haven't since"). However, after relating the incident Zarya smiled (by emote), and described it as "all part of the SL learning experience". (See Bowker and Tuffin 2003; Seymour and Lupton 2004, for research on risk, disability and online identity).

Treasure is involved in education and advocacy, and Anna's job involves developing tools and sites for educators. Anna has experienced instances where students, enrolled in her classes in SL, left after discovering her use of text-chat, despite her having explained her preference for text in terms of her deafness.

At the same time, Anna wanted to make it clear that she has "presented at a few conferences in SL [using] text chat, and the organisers have always been supportive of that". I contacted Anna again after the interview to ask if it would fair to say "that at least some of the people who leave your classes because of voice preference, are educators in (SL and RL)?" which she confirmed. Anna's experience suggests that educators might not be any more sensitive as regards issues of inclusion or disability than the general SL population. When interviewees were asked if the wider SL community had been supportive or understanding of the impact of voice on deaf residents, Zarya remarked that "Quite honestly, I don't think the general SL community had ANY idea", while Treasure responded "Supportive of us? Not at all. still aren't really, much. A little better but not much."

9.6 Analysis

The arrival of the voice feature had ramifications for these interviewees in terms of their online identity. Analysis of the interview data led to the identification of 'loss' as a significant theme. What is clear, however, is that 'loss' does not simply involve a deficit. Rather, loss was discussed in terms of an (admittedly unwelcome) change; a negotiation, and strategies of adjustment. The negative aspects of loss involved being 'outed' as deaf in a new context, the explanations (and exposure) that this entailed, and sudden exclusion from friendships, conversations and events. Yet there were repeated instances where reference to such losses was followed by a qualifying or clarifying comment. For example, Anna talks about students leaving her class but saw it as important to balance this by acknowledging the supportive attitudes shown by some conveners of SL and education events. Max referred to being left out, and changing his SL companions, but when I asked if "voice could be said to have cost you friends", he responded "well, I wouldn't put it that way. Not so strongly. But it's caused me to shift a little, yeah". The point is not that some responses to the introduction of voice are laudable or positive, and others are less so. What is important is that the interviewees acted to 'make a space' when discussing these issues; to shift and reframe their references to loss and the management of loss, while articulating it or qualifying it in various ways.

During the interview participants made use of a wide range of elements when defining their deafness. These include sign language fluency, pride, and their relationship to Deaf Culture – as well as references to medical history, work life, family, preferences within SL and personality traits (such as shyness). This ability to fluently define this aspect of their identity (deafness) from a range of perspectives, using a variety of indicators, suggests that these subjects are accustomed to explaining themselves. As noted, the introduction of voice made it necessary to 'come out' as deaf in SL. Max, Anna and Treasure did not consider this an issue in relation to their online identities, but Grace and Zarya certainly did. Grace commented: "Isn't it awful? You have to carry a big sign and slap a label on yourself and people see you differently…over and over".

Grace was the most emphatic about the impact of voice and the personal loss it entailed: "Why bother staying in SL when I have to deal with barriers in RL [real life] as a deaf person?" Despite being fluent in ASL Grace does not feel strongly affiliated with a Deaf community and her physical life experience of isolation was one reason why her disappointment following the introduction of the voice feature to SL was so acute. Her collaborators within SL gradually shifted to voice use and as a consequence her leadership role within a particular organisation was diminished. She expressed vivid frustration and sadness in relation to these changes. She was contemplating leaving SL and voice was a contributing factor. Despite her colleagues' well-intentioned efforts to include Grace (they apologised and tried to transcribe or "to type as fast as they could" while conversing), the voice feature and associated practices had proved disabling.

Grace linked the voice feature to the disintegration of her leadership role. Role was an issue for several of the interviewees, who mentioned it in relation to the destabilisation that followed the introduction of voice. Treasure's experience suggests that role can be used to construct a viable oppositional identity; a position from which to actively resist the 'hegemony of normalcy' (Davis, p 44). Treasure's role within the SL community as advocate and activist provides her with a position to speak from. Perhaps the role of researcher functions similarly for the author. For another interviewee, Max, 'role' has particular implications because he is a keen Role-Player. These sociable and creative forms of play are popular in SL. Generally such games have a rule-set that is derived from *Dungeons & Dragons* style social games, although settings vary a great deal. Role-Players develop a fictional identity and act in character, while collectively undertaking missions and intrigues. Role-Players in virtual worlds often deliberately avoid using voice. It is too revealing of physical life identity – and limited acting skills. Educators using role-play to teach in SL have also noted the limitations of voice (Addison and O'Hare 2008).

For some deaf residents, depending on their SL roles and preferences, voice might have had a relatively limited impact. For others, such as Grace, the impact has been more marked. Most of the interviewees made reference to the attempts of their hearing SL friends and colleagues to accommodate their use of text – but they also noted the limited success of these attempts (Max: "a few will try to type for me what's being said […] but obviously it's too hard to keep up"). Of course it is important to appreciate attempts to be inclusive, but no matter how well intentioned such attempts are, they tend to position those involved as either provider or petitioner.

9.7   Discussion

The interviewees' careful articulation of loss as involving a process of adjustment and learning suggests the importance of the scope for self-description in this context. It suggests sensitivity to being positioned in particular ways (as passive, dependent or tragic, for example), and resistance to a reductive focus on impairment. This raises two points relevant to questions of online identity, disability and education: the evident importance of self-definition and self-description; and the need to be conscious of the power relationships embedded in attempts at provision.

In relation to this second point, consider the apparently determining nature of some technologies, institutional policies and services. Goggin and Newell write that there is a danger that 'People with disabilities are expected to cut their cloth to fit the temporarily able-bodied world, and its new media technologies.' They identify a paradox when they argue that 'in its desire for the same, inclusion always requires the "other" to stay in its niche' (2003, p 149). Harlan Lane (citing R.A Scott's work in *The Making of Blind Men*) makes a related point when he argues that the 'unco-operative' client of support services, is the one who believes that 'he is basically fine' (Lane 2006, p 82). Together these points suggest a scenario in which staff and students are compelled to experience disability in a manner that conforms to the 'accessibility support' that is provided.

Such scenarios indicate the benefit of greater levels of exchange between Disability Studies (with its focus on subjectivity), and research on accessibility and design (with its focus on tools and technology). What Disability Studies would bring to Second Life, e-learning and accessibility debates is an insistence that researchers consider the ways in which disability is conceptualised in their work. It would also involve educators working in virtual worlds having to consider the ways in which their practices 'normalise' certain identities. These practices include teaching, as well as peer/professional activities such as virtual events, conferences and seminars.

The interviewees' interest in self-description, clarification, resistance and 'talking back' (Hooks 1989) is significant. Without such capacity, subjects who are disabled in online contexts risk being positioned in particular ways. Disabled colleagues may face the unenviable choice of either participating in events in a partial, limited and conditional manner, or leaving. Both options are self-defeating. Each involves performing a marginalised identity; and this marginalisation in turn confirms the centrality and power of the 'normal'. This is why educators working in virtual worlds such as Second Life need strategies that make it possible to acknowledge the importance of developing tools to support inclusion (as per e-learning and accessibility research) without ceding the political and critical agenda of Disability Studies.

There are precedents within Disability Studies that suggest how such strategies might be developed. For example, Ingunn Moser (2006) has used Actor Network Theory – or ANT (Latour 2005; Law 1994) to explore the relationships between subjects, disability, contexts and technologies. Likewise, Valentine and Skelton have used ANT to study deaf people's use of the Internet, arguing that adopting this approach entails acknowledging that 'society is produced in and through patterned networks of heterogeneous materials in which neither the properties of humans or non-humans are self-evident, rather they emerge in practice' (Valentine and Skelton 2008, p 471). An ANT approach is reconcilable with a Cultural Studies agenda and, interestingly, it is increasingly being applied by academics studying computer games and identity in educational contexts (Jenson and de Castell 2008). While there would be various limitations to be considered (as with any research strategy), this approach may offer us a way to reconcile the need to produce and evaluate tools, with the need to think about the ways in which social and cultural factors (including tools and practices) construct and perpetuate disability. Perhaps such an approach will enable us to work towards a more expanded, better contextualised, more responsive conceptualisation of disability in education and virtual world research.

9.8   Conclusion

Here, again, are Linden Lab's comments on deaf people, the introduction of the voice feature and education: 'While a deaf Resident may find him or herself excluded in some social contexts, their ability to communicate in SL, has not been diminished from a technical viewpoint.' At the crux of this statement is recognition that exclusion is socially determined in online worlds – although various degrees of accessibility will be supported or undermined by different technological features. It might well be the case that 'Most educators would agree that learning is better facilitated between individuals with voice', as Linden Lab have claimed. It may be that new technical features will become available, equipping us to counter-act the potentially excluding practices found in various social, educational and professional contexts within SL. It is certainly the case that virtual worlds present us with an opportunity to rethink educational practices, including those that relate to inclusion (Sheehy 2008). We do not have to replicate the conventions and limitations of the physical world.

The research described in this chapter has shown that deafness as disability is reproduced in virtual worlds, through discourse and practice. This suggests that identity within online worlds should be regarded as collaboratively constructed, and that the dynamics and resources that underpin and impact on these constructions are carried into virtual worlds from our everyday lives. There is nothing new about the exclusionary practices experienced by disabled residents in SL. However, online worlds and their various communities do demonstrate in new, clear ways, just how pervasive inequitable practices and discourses can be, and how difficult it can be to articulate and hence resist the power relations that are embedded within, and disseminated by, these same practices. Educators with an interest in equality, online learning, inclusion and technology cannot afford to overlook the implications.

Acknowledgements This chapter was first published as Carr, D. (2010) 'Constructing disability in online worlds: conceptualising disability in online research' in *London Review of Education Special Issue 'Being Online: A Critical View of Identity and Subjectivity in New Virtual Learning Spaces* 8: 1, pp 51–61. © Institute of Education, University of London and is republished with minor edits by permission of Taylor & Francis Ltd on behalf of Institute of Education, University of London.

References

Addison, A., O'Hare, L.: How can massive multi-user virtual environments and virtual role play enhance and embed with traditional teaching practice? Paper presented at ReLive08 Conference, November 2008. Open University (2008)

Ball, S., Pearce, R.: Learning scenarios and workplaces with virtual worlds: inclusion benefits and barriers of 'once-removed' participation. Paper presented at ReLive08 conference, 20–21 Nov 2009. Milton Keynes (2008)

Barnes, C.: The social model of disability: A sociological phenomenon ignored by sociologists? In: Shakespeare, T. (ed.) The Disability Reader: Social Science Perspectives, pp. 65–78. Continuum, London (2000)

Boellstorff, T.: Coming of Age in SL: An Anthropologist Explores the Virtually Human. Princeton University Press, Princeton (2008)

Bowker, N., Tuffin, K.: Dicing with deception: people with disabilities' strategies for managing safety and identity online. J. Comput. Mediat. Commun. 8(2) (Jan 2003)

Bowker, N., Tuffin, K.: Using the online medium for discursive research about people with disabilities. Soc. Sci. Comput. Rev. 22(2), 228–241 (2004). Summer 2004

Branson, J., Miller, D.: Damned for Their Difference: The Cultural Construction of Deaf People as Disabled. Gallaudet University Press, Washington, DC (2002)

Carr, D., Oliver, M.: SL, immersion and learning. In: Zaphiris, P., Ang, C.S. (eds.) Social Computing and Virtual Communities, pp. 205–222. Taylor & Francis, London (2010). 2009/10

Correll, J., Maruyama, T.: 'Deaf people: Fact sheet no. 3' project output. Deaf people and the internet: Has the internet changed deaf people's lives? University of Leeds, Loughborough University, University of Sheffield (2005). Project Website: http://www.geog.leeds.ac.uk/projects/deafweb/. Accessed Apr 2009

Davis, L.J.: Enforcing Normalcy: Disability, Deafness and the Body. Verso, London (1995)

Davis, L.J.: Constructing normalcy: the bell curve, the novel, and the invention of the disabled body in the nineteenth century. In: Davis, L.J. (ed.) The Disability Studies Reader, pp. 3–16. Routledge, New York (2006)

Davis, L.J.: 'Deafness and the riddle of identity' The chronicle of higher education, 12 Jan 2007. Online at http://seattlecentral.edu/faculty/nwilso/ASL202/Define_deafness.pdf. Accessed Sept 2009

Dewsbury, G., Clarke, K., Randall, D., Rouncefield, M., Sommerville, I.: The anti-social model of disability. Disabil. Soc. **10**(2), 145–158 (2004)

Ess, C.: The AoIR ethics working committee: 'Ethical decision-making and internet research. Recommendations from the aoir ethics working committee' (2002). Online at www.aoir.org/reports/ethics.pdf. Accessed Apr 2009

Goggin, G., Newell, C.: Digital Disability: The Social Construction of Disability in New Media. Rowman & Littlefield, Lanham (2003)

Goggin, G., Newell, C.: Editorial comment: disability, identity and interdependence: ICTs and new social forms. Inf. Commun. Soc. **9**(3), 309–311 (2006). June 2006

Gray, A.: Research Practice for Cultural Studies. Sage, London (2003)

Gronvik, L.: The fuzzy buzz word: Conceptualizations of disability in disability research classics. Sociol. Health Illn. **29**(5), 750–766 (2007)

Grushkin, D.A.: The dilemma of the hard of hearing within the U.S. Deaf Community. In: Monaghan, L., Schmaling, C., Nakamura, K., Turner, G.H. (eds.) Many Ways to Be Deaf. Gallaudet University Press, Washington, DC (2003)

Guo, B., Bricout, J.C., Huang, J.: 'A common open space or a digital divide? A social model perspective on the online disability community in China'. Disabil. Soc. **20**(1), 49–66 (2005)

Hine, C.: Virtual Ethnography. Sage, London (2000)

Hooks, B.: Talking Back. South End, Boston (1989)

Jenson, J., de Castell, S.: Theorizing gender and digital gameplay: oversights, accidents and surprises' Eludamos. J. Comput. Game Cult. **2**(1), 15–25 (2008)

Kinash, S., Crichton, S., Kim-Rupnow, W.S.: A review of the 2000–2003 literature at the intersection of online learning and disability. Am. J. Distance Educ. **15**(19), 5–19 (2004)

Kirriemuir, J.: A Spring 2008 snapshot of UK higher and further education developments in Second Life (2008). Online at http://www.eduserv.org.uk/foundation/sl/uksnapshot052008. Accessed May 2009

Ladd, P.: Understanding Deaf Culture. Multilingual Matters Ltd., Clevedon (2003)

Lane, H.: Construction of deafness. In: Davis, L.J. (ed.) The Disability Studies Reader, pp. 79–92. Routledge, New York (2006)

Latour, B.: Reassembling the Social: An Introduction to Actor-Network-Theory. Oxford University Press, Oxford (2005)

Law, J.: Organising Modernity. Blackwell, Oxford (1994)

Lesham, S., Trafford, V.: Overlooking the conceptual framework. Innov. Educ. Teach. Int. **44**(1), 93–105 (2007). February 2007

Linden Lab: 'Voice: Another valuable choice' (2007). In second opinion URL: http://secondlife.com/newsletter/2007_07/awsi.html No longer online

Linton, S.: Disability studies/not disability studies. Disabil. Soc. **13**(4), 525–540 (1998). 1998

Moser, I.: Disability and the promises of technology. Inf. Commun. Soc. **9**(3), 373–395 (2006). June 2006

Oliver, M.: The Politics of Disablement. Palgrave Macmillan, Basingstoke (1990)

Seale, J.: The development of accessibility practices in e-learning: an exploration of communities of practice. ALT J Res. Learn. Technol. **12**(1), 51–63 (2004)

Seale, J.: E-learning and Disability in Higher Education: Accessibility Theory and Practice. Routledge, New York (2006)

Seymour, W., Lupton, D.: Holding the line online: exploring wired relationships for people with disabilities. Disabil. Soc. **19**(4), 291–305 (2004)

Shakespeare, T.: The social model of disability. In: Davis, L.J. (ed.) The Disability Studies Reader, pp. 197–204. Routledge, New York (2006)

Sheehy, K.: 'Virtual environments: issues and opportunities for developing inclusive educational practices'. Paper presented at ReLive08 Conference, Nov 2008. Open University

Taylor, T.L.: Play Between Worlds. MIT Press, Cambridge (2006)

Turkle, S.: Life on Screen: Identity in the Age of the Internet. Weidenfeld & Nicolson, London (1995)

Valentine, G., Skelton, T.: Changing spaces: the role of the internet in shaping deaf geographies. Soc. Cult. Geogr. **9**(5), 469–485 (2008)

White, G.R., Fitzpatrick, G., McAllister, G.: Towards accessible 3D environments for the blind and visually impaired. In: Proceedings of the 3rd International Conference on Digital Interactive Media and Arts. Athens, 10–12 Sept 2008. DIMEA '08, vol. 349. ACM, New York (2008)

Wittel, A.: Ethnography on the move: from field to net to internet. Forum: Qual. Soc. Res. **1**(1), Article 21 (Jan 2000)

Chapter 10
As Long as They Don't Know Where I Live: Information Disclosure Strategies for Managing Identity in Second Life™

Poppy Lauretta McLeod and Gilly Leshed

Abstract Thirty Second Life™ residents were interviewed about their perceptions of the boundary between their virtual world and material world identities and the practices they used to share or to conceal identity information across that boundary. A range of stances toward the boundary – from completely open to completely closed – was found, although even the people who were the most open kept some kind of boundary. Stances toward the boundary and choices about sharing information were related to two broad motivations – relationship formation and reputation maintenance. The interview data is discussed in terms of social penetration theory, social identity theory, theories of stigma, theories of the self and theories of anonymity. Ethical issues in virtual world research are also addressed. Suggestions for future research on identity in virtual environments, for the design of virtual environments, and implications for modern conceptualizations of the self are discussed.

10.1 Introduction

Anonymity is a central explanation for some of the major effects and characteristics of communication and relationship formation over the Internet (Anonymous 1998; Bargh et al. 2002; Jessup et al. 1990; Postmes et al. 2001; Rains 2007). Disinhibition can result from anonymity under some circumstances because people feel protected from sanctions against expressing ideas and behaviours that violate social norms (Bargh et al. 2002). Examples of negative effects of anonymity include flaming

P.L. McLeod (✉) • G. Leshed
Department of Communication, Cornell University, Ithaca, NY, USA
e-mail: plm29@cornell.edu

A. Peachey and M. Childs (eds.), *Reinventing Ourselves: Contemporary Concepts of Identity in Virtual Worlds*, Springer Series in Immersive Environments, DOI 10.1007/978-0-85729-361-9_10, © Springer-Verlag London Limited 2011

(e.g., Vrooman 2002), social loafing (e.g., Jessup et al. 1990) and deception (e.g., Caspi and Gorsky 2006; Hancock 2007). The disinhibition that arises from anonymous Internet communication also can lead to greater intimacy and the formation of close personal relationships (e.g., McKenna et al. 2002). The question of what exactly is meant by anonymity has been of interest for some time within the computer mediated communication literature (e.g., Anonymous 1998; McLeod 2000; Rains 2007; Tanis and Postmes 2007; Valacich et al. 1992), and as argued more recently by Kennedy (2006), developments in both technology and scholarship on technology call for reconceptualisation of the meanings of identity and anonymity.

The advent of the virtual environment through which users navigate with a constructed identity – the avatar – presents unique glimpses into the formation, communication and management of identity, and of the protection of knowledge about that identity from other people. This is our central interest in the current chapter. Drawing from interviews conducted with Second Life users, we examine how people conceive of anonymity and identity in this environment, how they perceive the boundary between their virtual and "real" world identities and their boundary management strategies.

We use here the term material rather than "real" world and "real" life to reflect a key learning from our data (and from others such as Turkle 1995) that the virtual world is indeed a part of reality for many users.[1] The material is the world or the life in which the individual's physical body resides; where hands manipulate computer keyboard and mouse to participate in the virtual environment through the virtual world avatar. At the same time, we do not take the position that the virtual environment is "equal to" or "just as important" as the material environment. Rather, we examine how our respondents approach the equivalency between these two environments, and we seek explanations that may account for differences among their approaches.

10.2   Anonymity

We define anonymity as the separation of pieces of information about one's identity across social domains such that others are unable to recognize that the pieces connect within a single, specific individual. This definition applies both in face-to-face settings and on the Internet. That friendly clerk we chat with at the grocery store, though we may know her name is Olga, is relatively anonymous until we gradually learn that she is a student, and maybe we see that she lives in the apartment building near our home, and then one of our friends mentions an "Olga" who is in his chamber orchestra, etc. Eventually we come to know who Olga is and we feel she is no longer anonymous, though we may not know anything very intimate about her. Our interactions with Olga are still only in the grocery store, but we now have expectations of other

---

[1]The terms "real", "real life", "rl" will nevertheless appear in the direct quotations from respondents.

specific domains where interactions with her might occur, and we could even bring about some of those interactions if we chose. The discoveries we made about her identity were largely outside of Olga's control, though it is less likely that we would have made them if she had never talked to us in the first place.

In Second Life we meet an avatar named Graham Pennyweather, and eventually learn that he is an artist, is a divorced father of three, and lives in Melbourne, Australia. Within a very short time of meeting Graham (days or perhaps even hours), we may also learn intimate details of what went wrong in his marriage. All of this information is under his control to share or not share with us. At the same time, we may not know that in his material world Graham is quite a famous artist who is the winner of that year's Archibald Prize. Though we may feel close to Graham and think that we know him well, he nevertheless is anonymous because of the separation between parts of his identity.

In the two examples above, anonymity and identifiability are interwoven, and there is no absolute anonymity or absolute identifiability. Keeping pieces of information undisclosed in different settings, intentionally or unintentionally, exemplifies the boundaries people may have between the different aspects of their identities that they present in different settings. Our focus on maintaining boundaries between Second Life and the material world boundaries fits with the perspective on privacy presented by Derlega and Chaikin (1977, p 102), in which privacy is seen as the "process of boundary regulation" wherein a person controls "how much (or how little) contact" he or she maintains with others. We argue that privacy serves the purpose of controlling anonymity in that people control the information that others have as well as the amount of contact.

Our definition is also guided by assumptions drawn from social identity theory (Brewer 1991; Tajfel 1982; Tajfel and Turner 1979; Postmes et al. 2001), that people derive their identities in part from the social groups to which they belong. These groups contribute both to the construction of self-identity and to perceptions of identity from the perspective of external observers. The unique relationship among an individual's various group memberships – their relative salience and importance for example – provides important cues to identity. The level of someone's anonymity is reduced the more other people learn the connections among that individual's social group memberships (e.g., "You know who I mean – Olga who works at the Stop-n-Go"). Of interest in this chapter is how the virtual world context affects the relationship between social group membership cues and anonymity.

10.3   Second Life Interviews

To understand how people perceive their anonymity in virtual worlds, what strategies they use to maintain or eliminate boundaries between the material and the virtual worlds, and their motivations for using these strategies, we conducted in-depth interviews in Second Life. Because we wanted participants to be open about the kinds of Second Life identities they construct and how they manage their Second

Fig. 10.1 The interview setting

Life material world boundaries, we held the interviews in Second Life, where the researcher's avatar met with the participant's avatar and carried out the interview via text. In this section we describe our participants, the procedures we followed to recruit and interview them, and some ethical issues we encountered and how we addressed them.

Participants – In the spring of 2008 we interviewed 30 Second Life residents. Interview participants were recruited via a third-party Second Life market research company that specialises in Internet sampling and research.[2] This company made contact with potential participants, scheduled the interviews, gave us a conference room in Second Life to carry out the interviews in private, and paid participants in Linden Dollars (Second Life's currency) following the interview. The material life gender of half of the participants was female, the range of their Second Life age was 93 days (3 months) to 1,410 days (3 years and 10 months) (median=434 days, or 1 year and 2 months), and the range of their material life age was 21–68 years (median=35). Based on demographic information provided by quantcast.com, the age distribution of the sample is representative of the demographics of Second Life users, except users under the age of 18. The gender distribution in the general Second Life population is slightly more than 50% male at the time of the study, but because we wanted an even split we slightly oversampled for women. All participants were US-based.

Interview protocol and procedure – The researcher's avatar met the participant's avatar at the set time at the entrance to the conference room allocated for us by the recruiting company. We invited each participant to come in and sit at the conference table (See Fig. 10.1), handed him or her a notecard[3] with the consent form, and after the participant returned it to us signed electronically, we switched from communicating via public chat, which can be seen by anyone nearby, to private instant messaging between the researcher and the participant.

---

[2] www.markettruths.com.

[3] A notecard in Second Life is an item containing text or other objects. Notecards are stored in one's inventory list.

The semi-structured interview included open-ended questions about how the participant sees the boundaries between their Second Life and real life identities (we used the terms "real life" and "RL" in the interview questions rather than "material life"), whether they have alternative avatars and how they are similar or different from the current avatar, how and why they protect or eliminate their real life identity by sharing or not sharing different kinds of information, and whether and how they share real life information in order to develop relationships with others in Second Life (and vice versa). To deepen our understanding of how their perceptions and behaviours regarding their identity information sharing are related to their daily lives and activities, we asked them to describe how much time they spend in Second Life, and how that time is spent. Each question was followed with more probing questions to ensure we received a full depiction of the participant's point of view. Interviews lasted approximately 90 min.

The data included the text of the interview conversation, in addition to information we gathered about participants from their Second Life profiles. Information in these profiles is voluntarily added by Second Life residents and could include images, descriptions of themselves in Second Life and real life, Second Life groups they belong to, Internet links, and so on. In the analysis presented below we disguised avatar names and other identifying information, but kept gender identification. Given a relaxed norm in Second Life about typos in chat, we edited interview quotations to remove typos and other errors only enough to clarify meaning.

Ethics – Our choice to carry out interviews in Second Life, with the researcher's avatar interviewing the participant's avatar with no material world contact, raised ethical issues we had to address (Nosek et al. 2002). For example, whereas during in–person interviews the interviewer can verify the participant's physical characteristics such as gender, we had to rely on what the participant's avatar told us about their material life during the interview (Taylor 1999). We had to believe Justine saying she is a female working as an administrative assistant in a hospital and Connor saying he is a retired male. This had consequences for our university's Institutional Review Board, a unit that ensures the compliance with ethical guidelines for protecting human participants in social, behavioural, and medical research, because for example special consideration should be given to participants who fall into certain categories such as children and people with disabilities. We could not verify directly whether these categories applied and thus had to rely on the information participants gave the recruiting company before volunteering to participate. It turns out that some of our participants, for example, did report having some kind of disability, but we were not able to determine whether our interview procedures should have been altered for those participants. We believe that the data we collected through inworld-only interviews nevertheless provide a valid representation of our sample's information management strategies and identity management. As we will discuss near the end of the paper, however, we do not try to argue that ours is a representative sample on the whole.

Another issue was conducting the interview in a medium controlled by a third party, Linden Lab, which owns Second Life. Although the interviews were carried out via private instant messaging, and we changed the respondents' Second Life names into codes, a record of the interview transcript remains on the servers of Linden Lab. This was outside of our control and we made sure to notify participants about this prior to carrying out the interview.

Time spent in Second Life – One of our interview questions asked how much time participants spent in Second Life. Responses varied from spending a few hours each week inworld, logging in occasionally in the evenings for an hour or two, to spending many hours every day, sometimes all day long or after work hours into the late night hours. We also asked participants how they spend their time in Second Life. More than 50% (17 participants) described that time as mostly fun, social, and recreational: hanging out with friends, exploring the world, clubbing, partying and dancing, shopping, and role-playing. Five participants said they spend their time in Second Life mostly working, managing an estate or working at a Second Life company. The rest combined work and recreation, and many of them reported that they also considered the work aspects of their Second Life time to be fun, such as building and selling objects, working as DJs or hosts in clubs, and teaching classes.

10.4 Primary Information Management Motivations

Our preliminary review of the transcripts suggested two broad themes describing primary considerations in the management of information across the virtual and material world boundary. The first theme was represented by words of one of our respondents, "the reason i play MMO games is mainly for communicating and meeting new people." We examined what participants told us about how they form personal relationships within Second Life, and how they make decisions about what kind of identity information to share through that process. Second, we found a theme related to self-expression and the management of reputation. Although considerations of reputation are important for relationship development, we found that our participants discussed a distinct set of issues related to this theme. Our analysis will be organised around these two themes, and we will end the chapter with recommendations for future inquiry.

10.5 Self-Disclosure and Relationship Development

Self-disclosure reciprocity has been recognised since the pre-Internet era as the chief mechanism in the development of close personal relationships (Altman and Taylor 1973; Derlega and Chaikin 1977; Collins and Miller 1994; Derlega et al. 1976; Rubin 1975; Parks and Floyd 1996; Thibaut and Kelley 1959; Worthy et al. 1969). People reciprocate offers of personal information when they feel interpersonal trust and because of social norms (Rubin 1975). Early research in face-to-face settings showed that people would readily follow reciprocity norms in matching the level of intimacy in disclosures with interaction partners (e.g., Worthy et al. 1969), and that the level of trust moderated the extent of reciprocity (e.g., Johnson and Noonan 1972; Wheeless and Grotz 1977).

Important for current research on the development of personal relationships over the Internet were early findings that intimacy and self-disclosure could develop more rapidly and reach deeper levels among strangers than among close acquaintances. Derlega et al. (1976), for example, found that following reciprocity norms in a one-time encounter was more likely to occur between strangers than between friends. Rubin (1975) examined the "passing stranger" effect in which previously unacquainted individuals with no expectation of future encounters quickly reach deep levels of intimate and mutual self-disclosure. He suggested that people feel invulnerable in such encounters because they are unaccountable to a stranger. That is, they are free from concerns over maintaining this relationship in the future. But another reason for lower inhibition in disclosing personal information to strangers is that such disclosures also lack consequences for one's everyday and normal life. Because a passing stranger cannot easily find you again (and usually does not care to), your reputation, position within your social circles and your pre-existing friendships are not likely to be affected by the intimate information you have divulged.

Internet interactions share some features of the passing stranger phenomenon, while they also differ in important respects. The face-to-face encounter with a passing stranger is characterised by a certain level of anonymity, wherein the stranger is unable to connect together vital pieces of one's identity. This factor makes the encounter inconsequential in any material way. Anonymity in Internet communication is similar. A great deal of theoretical work and empirical evidence have shown anonymity to be a key factor in the formation and maintenance of close personal relationships over the Internet (e.g. Bargh et al. 2002; Ben-Ze'ev 2003; Christopherson 2007; McKenna and Bargh 2000; McKenna et al. 2002; and see Bargh and McKenna 2004 for a review), and Bargh et al. have argued that Internet anonymity reduces the possible costs of revealing "negative or taboo aspects of oneself" (p 35) in one's life outside of the virtual Internet world.

Self-disclosure over the Internet departs from the passing stranger phenomenon in the important respect that on the Internet people often want the strangers to linger. Forming and maintaining personal relationships is the top reason for which people use communication affordances of the Internet (Bargh and McKenna 2004), and virtual communities have been thriving since the advent of the Internet infrastructure through discussion groups, chat rooms, role-playing games, and more (Preece 2000; Rheingold 1993; Smith and Kollock 1999).

The Internet provides people with the unique capability to separate aspects of their identities and to choose which aspects to present to whom (Turkle 1995). Of course, people present themselves differently in different contexts in their material life and not only online, engaging in what Goffman calls "face work" to form and maintain impressions others make of them (1959). There are aspects of the material self, however, that are bound to the observable body and are constant across material life contexts: sex, height, weight, skin colour, eye colour, voice, body posture, and much more. On the other hand, the affordances of mediated communication enable individuals to be strategic about what they choose to present about themselves, as compared to offline interactions in which many self-presentation processes are more unintentional and unconscious (Walther 1996).

At the same time, the ever increasing power and sophistication of Internet search engines provides the capability to re-connect the separate aspects of a person's identity, given the key bits of information (Frye and Dornisch 2010). The challenge then is figuring out and then managing the desirable balance between self-disclosure and a certain degree of anonymity (Ben-Ze'ev 2003; Christopherson 2007; Joinson et al. 2010; Omarzu 2000).

Self-disclosure and boundary management – This challenge was the central focus of our interviews. We asked the respondents to tell us how they conceived of and managed the boundary between their activities, identities and lives in Second Life and their material world. Their responses to this central question could be thought of as falling along a continuum that ranged from keeping a strict separation, through a blended approach, to having no boundary at all. Despite the fact that people described their approaches in these terms, we nevertheless observed that everyone maintained some kind of boundary by imposing limits on what information about their material world they would reveal within the virtual world. The limits were characterised by choice of information to divulge, choice of to whom to divulge the information and the timing.

Harry, perhaps having the most permeable boundary of the people we interviewed, told us, "I can say at the outset that I am not trying to keep my first life private…SL is an extension of my RL work", but he also described a certain degree of caution in how quickly he discloses information to visitors to his Second Life business location:

> One of the first questions I or one of my greeters asks a visitor is why they have come to EnviroCo… It becomes very clear if they are giving us an honest answer and we can respond to that… I don't wear a tag with my home phone number on it…If someone wants to learn about me they have to jump through a few hoops…

In a similar vein, Radclyffe is a musician whose Second Life profile displays a photograph of his material self with the caption, "That's the real me!" He explains, "I want to be real to people…I am a musician …and I mingle SL and RL…I'm Radclyffe in rl…I don't have much to hide." Radclyffe nevertheless "pays yahoo extra to protect my rl address… phone #, etc." Radclyffe and Harry represent examples of people whose business interests are furthered by having fairly permeable boundaries between their material world and Second Life identities. Harry uses Second Life as a laboratory to test potential customers' reactions to ideas for material world products. Radclyffe, due to the reputation he has made in Second Life, is "making rl money" and has "a growing fan base" for his music in the material world.

Reciprocity – Unlike Radclyffe and Harry, for most of our respondents with these permeable boundaries, the primary reason for divulging material world identity information was to nurture Second Life relationships. Sharing bits of material life information signalled trustworthiness and invited reciprocation ("they will know i'm a real person and not some poseur…and also they might tell me the truth" (Cycyll): which in turn laid the groundwork for developing meaningful relationships: (Greg: "it is much easier to … form strong bonds with people when you're willing to open up a bit").

Despite the attitude of openness described by these individuals, the process of disclosing material world information was nevertheless described as a gradual one unfolding over time. Permeable as their boundaries may be, they still wanted to get to know people before letting them into their material world. "…i wont give any info that could be used to contact me directly like email address, phone number… unless i get to know you first," says Kevyn. It was also common for people with open boundaries to describe their approach as the same as in their material environments, as described by Robin: "as in real life…when you get to know some one… you choose to share information…it is the same here, on a case by case basis." Further, Harry's comment that he is willing to share his material life identification information with people "if they are being real with me", and Kira's statement that "I share what other people are willing to share," reflect expectations of reciprocity.

These attitudes are consistent with some of the fundamental predictions derived from theories of self-disclosure literature. Reciprocity – both as signal of trust and as normative practice – was a main driving mechanism in bringing people closer together across both their virtual and material worlds (Altman and Taylor 1973; Dietz-Uhler et al. 2005; Rubin 1975; Worthy et al. 1969). In fact, although we asked participants about what information they *gave*, their responses frequently described an *exchange* of information.

Metaphors of self-disclosure – A prominent theory on relationship development – social penetration theory (Altman and Taylor 1973) characterises the self-disclosure process as gradual, orderly and linear. The process moves from the disclosure of relatively trivial surface information through deeper layers until the core information of a person's self-hood – vulnerabilities, fears, hopes – is reached. Altman and Taylor use the metaphor of a pin passing through the layers of an onion to describe this process. But because Internet relationships quickly move to mutual disclosure at the innermost level and frequently bypass altogether the traditional surface levels, we believe a different metaphor is needed to characterise self-disclosure in the development of these relationships. We find more useful the metaphor suggested by one of our respondents who explains that she does not give her last name because it "makes it easier for someone to pin point me and put the pieces of the puzzle together."

The metaphor of a jigsaw puzzle captures the ability on the Internet to separate segments of one's identity from each other – the material from the virtual, the core from the periphery, and even one virtual from another. This metaphor is compatible with observations that the Internet fosters, or perhaps reflects, the existence of multiple selves that are simultaneously present across various domains (Bargh and McKenna 2004; Markus and Nurius 1986; Turkle 1995). The process of getting to know another person is very like piecing together bits of information in ways that yield a coherent picture, but where multiple solutions may be possible Even with full disclosure the picture is not static and can never be complete. The jigsaw puzzle metaphor also is consistent with the social identity theory perspective discussed earlier (Brewer 1991). Social group membership information can play a pivotal role because of the identity cue information the memberships may carry.

The knowledge that people have of their acquaintances within Second Life can be compared to coherent and recognizable sections of a puzzle. Less clear may be the knowledge that it indeed is only a section of the person's whole identity, how big a section it is, or how it fits into the whole. Some of our respondents' strategies for managing their boundaries reflected this ambiguity. Walt told us for example that although he was truthful about being male and "an adult in the United States," very little else about his Second Life persona or the registration information he provided to Linden Labs was "accurate" about his material world self. At the same time Walt says he is not "trying to hide" and that he has "no incongruity" between his Second Life and his material world identity.

The analogy of coherent parts of a whole applies to the phenomenon of how rapidly people can reach levels of deep intimacy in their Internet relationships. We can think of a holographic type of jigsaw puzzle wherein separate coherent segments contain the essential whole of a person's identity including emotions, passions, dreams and fears. People are able to connect to each other through aspects of the essential core contained within the coherent segments of identity that they have agreed to share with each other. ("In Sl, even though I do not disclose my real identity, I do freely disclose my real feelings.") How the segments fit into the whole does not have to have a bearing on the virtual world relationship. Connor, who takes the stance that "its best to keep it separate", nevertheless reported that he shares "lots of information about who i am", which for him includes "passions, likes and dislikes." He describes further the emotional closeness of his relationship with his Second Life "fiancée." Although this relationship is contained only in Second Life, these two individuals seem to have a clear sense of coherence of their shared virtual world identities as well as the edges of those segments:

> [she] has made me very happy in RL...i actually smile the whole time we are together...and it give me a reason to get up in the morning...lol...it is very close to a RL relationship as you can get here...we share everything...but alas she is married too...so...it never will progress further...which is fine

Distinguishing between inner puzzle pieces that are at the core, including information about one's emotions, passions, and life experiences, and boundary pieces at the periphery, including factual information about one's name, age, location, and occupation, creates an interesting distinction between the ways in which the puzzle is revealed and constructed in Second Life versus the material life. When we interact with someone in the material life, we see their sex, estimate their age, greet each other by name, and meet at a certain location, thus enabling the construction of the puzzle starting from the boundaries. On the other hand, when meeting in Second Life, our interviews reveal that people tend to first "get to know each other" at the deeper level, i.e., disclosing inner pieces of the puzzle, and over time reveal more boundary information pieces such as material life name, location, and so forth.

Some information is more equal than other – To push the jigsaw metaphor further, there often is the one key piece that helps a lot of other pieces fall into place.

This notion is reflected in the respondent's earlier reported statement about not revealing her last name. What that piece is may vary depending on what other pieces are already known, but the key piece often is something quite close to the centre of the image. In the process of uncovering identity, some information may be the key through which many other pieces of information about a person's identity can be known or easily obtained. Leon described a kind of calculation of what weights to assign to certain information: "I try to consider things from the extreme view. If a person really wanted to "track me down" what clues would they use to do that. Where I go to school? Very unique experiences? Things I've done recently that gained public attention?" Even in the absence of a key piece, the sheer accumulation of information and the work it takes to see how it fits together will also aid in revealing the picture, as illustrated by Anna who describes her Second Life identity as "an extension of my RL identity", but is nevertheless quite strategic in her decisions about divulging information about her material world persona:

> My RL name is fairly unique and can be Googled... so I don't give it out...of course not things like location other than generic city and state...and I am even careful who I tell about my job as again the work I do it can be looked up online... I have to know and trust the person enough to believe that A) our relationship will benefit from the sharing of the information through increased closeness, trust etc. and B) that they won't misuse it.

Physical location was one such key piece of information for many participants. This was information they said they explicitly would not provide, or were careful that any other information they shared did not allow someone in Second Life to discover their physical location: "no address nope...where i live... give them my home address... no way," says Irene even though she says she does not keep her "rl and sl separate." For some respondents real names almost seemed secondary in themselves and were important only insofar as they could provide a way for undesired material world contact, as suggested by the following comment from Gerome: "It depends on how much information they find out. If they know my name, I see no consequences... A name alone I don't think is enough."

Boundaries and safety – People who kept strict boundaries had very different attitudes about the role of material life information in their Second Life relationships. Some of them approached Second Life as a game, as described by Justine: "I see no reason to purposely interject my real self into a game." These respondents perceived that who they were in the virtual world was enough, and that "tidbits" of material life information were unimportant and even trivial. For the majority of them, however, their attitudes were dominated by concerns over physical safety and security, and they tended to see disclosure of material world identity as dangerous. The importance they placed on safety was reflected in part by their use of strong, vivid, and value-laden language and a focus on worst-case scenarios to describe their concerns. The importance of safety for these respondents is represented in the grave concerns expressed by Angel:

> ... some people... would love to know where I live... I fear that they will try to ruin my personal real life. I am afraid of people coming to hurt me sometimes... For example this one person I was friends with that I became an enemy of he/she ... went to this extreme of threatening to hurt me in RL... I don't know 100% what these people want to do. But I do know that they could be a harm to me...

Even when said in jest, these respondents used extreme language when referring to possible safety risks: "Hopefully any who discover [RL identity] aren't crazy axe-murderers. :),"or, "just in case I meet a psychopath that is looking for his next 3 months of human to eat or something," and "oooo...murder...lol..." In contrast, respondents who reported that they had basically no boundary did express safety concerns but with language indicating a cautious but not overly concerned attitude, such as: "Mostly I worry about unstable individuals, small chance that it may be;" or "My only fear is that of a possible stalker... or a love interest that won't take no for an answer in rl", and "I guess there is always that chance of someone griefing[4] me in rl, spam email, etc."

In keeping with their concerns over safety, some of the respondents with strict boundaries described elaborate precautions to ensure that the boundary would not be breached. Alyson explained that she has set up an email account in her avatar name, different even from the email address she gave to Linden Lab for the initial registration in Second Life. Note also her concerns over security even within Second Life in the following description:

> it [the email account] is from a large ISP so that it is not associated with the domain names I own in RL...And can't be tracked back unless you really are a good hacker...I even use it in scripts so that if someone in SL steals an object and gets into the script, that is the email found and not my real email.

Josh similarly employs multiple safeguards to keep the boundaries separate:

> My web-site...is private... if people try to look at who owns the domain name they won't see any of my rl info... In real life I have a thing called Earthclass Mail...where people send mail to another address...so they don't get my real address... I have a lot of privacy features enabled on my facebook page... So people can not see my REAL INFO unless I approve it... I have a "Virtual Assistant" ...where I can block phone numbers from calling me ... and does not leave a trail to my home address or mailing address.

Shari has "created an internet persona, not just for Second Life but for all internet related activity," and she told us:

> I subscribe to SL through my internet persona. I have a paypal subsidiary account in my persona's name. I have a skype and cell phone in my persona's name...my persona is the interface between my RL identity and my SL identity.

Our respondents with more permeable boundaries rarely described such involved, multi-faceted strategies. Rather they were more likely to report simply that "i do not go out of my way to reveal anything in my real life, besides the state and country i live in," or "I don't mind revealing any information that isn't integral on preventing identity theft." Not that they were unconcerned about personal safety – but rather their responses indicated a belief that it was largely under their control what information would be revealed, and that to keep their material world private within Second Life was merely a matter of not sharing what they didn't think was appropriate.

---

[4]Boellstorff (2008) defines griefing as "participation in a virtual world with the intent of disrupting the experience of others" (p. 185). Examples are using abusive or offensive language, filling up an area with useless objects, or sending flame messages to a group's chat space.

For these individuals, exercising "reasonable precautions" was sufficient protection from undesirable and undesired incursions by Second Life acquaintances into their material world.

Calculating the intimacy-privacy tradeoff – The emphasis these respondents placed on physical safety and security is one manifestation of the more general issue faced by all Second Life residents of getting what they want from their inworld relationships while also controlling the effects of those relationships on their material world. In her analysis of Internet anonymity Christopherson (2007) describes intimacy and control as "commodities" arranged in a balance such that increasing one depletes the other. The exchange of personal information facilitates the development of intimate personal relationships, but at the same time personal information gives one's relationship partners more control over the how, when and where of contact. The precautions described by our respondents to maintain the boundary between the two worlds kept the control in their hands of whether other people would contact them.

Our respondents who described themselves at the extremes of the boundary established between the material and virtual worlds resolved the issue by essentially making it a non-issue. They either opened their material world such that there was not a separation between their Second Life and material world circles ("I am open about my RL identity") or they allowed no possibility of cross-over and kept all Second Life relationships contained strictly within that environment ("Best to keep it separate"). The majority of our respondents in fact placed themselves somewhere between these two extremes, and their responses show a dynamic sizing up of each social situation leading to decisions about what to disclose, when and to whom. Jerome's response is illustrative:

> It really just depends on what feels right at the time. I have some rules on what I reveal, such as no addresses, phone numbers, etc. Things less sensitive, such as what college I go to really depends on the situation and the person; whether or not i feel I trust them

10.6   Self-Expression and Reputation

Social relationships form an important part of the context for the expression of identity (Banaji and Prentice 1994). Alongside relationship development, our respondents also considered how the management of the between-worlds boundary expressed who they were. We saw fairly sharp departures in views of the virtual selves vis-à-vis the material world self between respondents with stances at the extremes of the boundary continuum. Participants who reported no or very permeable boundaries overwhelmingly told us variations on statements such as, "I am my avatar... I don't pretend to be someone I'm not" and "I actually live my second life as I live my first life." These participants tended to characterise themselves as "open", and sometimes this norm of openness could be expressed more intensely as an aversion to being a different "self" in Second Life than in the material world, as suggested by Anna: "I personally find it difficult to role play a persona completely separate from my real life. When I tried (very briefly), I found that my real life identity slipped in anyway and it was less confusing to everyone for me to just be myself." Further, some responses reflected an assumption that engaging in some kind of taboo activities would be the main or only reason to keep identities separate, e.g., "Nothing in my life is overtly criminal or shameful, so why hide it?"

Permeable boundaries, or permeable identities? – The people who reported keeping firm boundaries were more likely than those with loose boundaries to report that their virtual and materials world selves were different from each other, but the differences tended not to be associated with any taboos. Rather, these individuals' responses tended to suggest that their avatars allowed them to express of parts of themselves that were difficult to express in their material worlds.

We saw many variations of this idea expressed by the participants in our interviews, as exemplified by Josh, who told us that he sees "a big difference as me in sl versus RL... I am more open in second life than in RL, I have more friends here than in RL...It is more easy for me to be myself in second life then in real life." But what we found striking in our data was that this sense of personal transformation was expressed by nearly all of the people who kept strict boundaries, whereas only rarely by those who kept looser boundaries. Eight individuals in our sample reported unequivocally that they preferred a strict boundary, and all except two of them gave examples such as, "I have learned new ways of communicating, have learned to be less shy and retiring, in general I enjoy RL a bit more since discovering SL," and, "now, my anti-oppression background is strong and I can break down sexism, classism and racism...SL has...challenged my stereotypes." Only seven of the remaining 22 people told such stories. Instead, these respondents were more likely to talk about peripheral, even trivial effects of Second Life on their material life such as "my house is dirtier and I don't watch as much tv."

Finding the true self – The work by Bargh et al. (2002) and McKenna et al. (2002) on self-expression in Internet communication and relationship formation may offer insights into what may account for this pattern. They point to anonymity as a specific feature of Internet communication that facilitates the expression of the "true self", which they define as "those identity-important and phenomenally real aspects of self not often or easily expressed to others" (Bargh et al. 2002 p 34). At the same time, they argue, the true-self is what a person most needs to express. The more difficult it may be for a person to express the true self in "one's usual social sphere" (ibid. p 35), the more that person may be drawn to anonymity in a virtual environment. The pattern in our data is consistent with this reasoning, and suggests a relationship between anonymity and the expression of the true self. Our participants who sought greater anonymity between their virtual and material identities were the ones who most often reported not only that their Second Life selves possessed more positive characteristics than their material selves, but also that in Second Life they were more the self they always believed themselves to be: ("i know i am a great person...i have learned to be more open here").

McKenna et al. (2002) suggested that people who may have trouble forming social relationships in their material worlds, such as those who are socially anxious, may be better able to express the true self through the Internet. In our interviews we did not collect any direct data about social anxiety or other problems in forming social bonds, but the structure of the personal transformation stories fit a pattern that Second Life facilitates a way of being that had not been available to them previously. This role of Second Life in facilitating the expression of the true self resonates with Turkle's (1995, p 263) description of virtuality as "the raft, the ladder, the transitional space...that is discarded after reaching greater freedom."

The metaphor of a connector between the virtual and material selves suggested by Turkle (1995) is compatible with the stories we heard from our respondents. The connections are overt, explicit and intentional for those with open boundaries. As boundaries became less open, the connections were more internal to the individual controlling the avatar, but not necessarily any less intentional. Kennedy (2006) has argued that the connection of virtual selves back to the off-line self is a much stronger one than seems to be assumed by much of the current literature on Internet identity. We saw Kennedy's argument reflected in our data in the frequent statements about the importance of remembering, "that there is a person behind the pixels... SL is just a whole bunch of RL people. Same attitudes, same issues, same everything."

Reputation maintenance – Protecting their reputation or image – within both the virtual and material worlds – was also a reason participants gave for maintaining firm boundaries. One man told us that his friends in Second Life "would be shocked to know that I am a 65 year-old grandfather", and that among his inworld friends, "I... don't talk about grandchildren." Another man said he kept his material world identity separate because "I felt it destroyed the illusion...My RL identity is considerably different than my SL persona."

Concerns over people learning about discrepancies between the identities in the two worlds centre on two issues – deception and stigma (Caspi and Gorsky 2006; Goffman 1963; Hancock 2007). These are distinct, but not unrelated issues. Some respondents kept secret their material world identity, or aspects of it, because of the potential stigma attached to those aspects. The stigma was more serious in some cases than in others. For the 65-year old grandfather, the mild stigma associated with old-age in Western culture led him to live his Second Life as a youthful "man about town", and to be strategic when talking in Second Life about his material world situation such that the illusion would be maintained. Several respondents faced stigmas in their material worlds associated with physical disabilities, and their maintenance of the separation between an able-bodied avatar and the material self gave them a place where the stigma did not colour their relationships and they could, as one woman put it, "live the fantasy that i am young and beautiful again."

The boundary was seen as a way of protecting material world reputation as well. Shari told us that she is a visible public figure in her material world who must consider the widespread effects of her words and actions: "even posting an opinion on a blog in my real name can result in people drawing conclusions about my organization." For her, keeping the strict separation between the two worlds not only is necessary for the welfare of her material world organization, but it also frees her "from the responsibility to always consider my words and their impact."

Second Life activities or roles that would carry stigma within the material world were another reason to keep those activities behind a firm boundary, as reflected in one man's expectation that people in his material world "would freak out to find I am a slave owner...one who uses pleasure slaves."

Keeping up inworld appearances – Reputation solely within Second Life was a reason for maintaining a special kind of anonymity associated with using multiple avatars. Participants who routinely used alternative avatars (known as "alts") reported varying approaches to the anonymity of those alts and the boundary between the alts' identity and the material world identity. For the most part, people described their approach to the boundary for their alts as similar to that for their principal avatar. Anonymity of the alts *within* Second Life was important, for reasons that also were largely associated with stigma. For example, Irving told us "I hate to admit this, but Alt 2 does a lot of camping. That is why I don't let people know who he is; it is a little embarrassing." Camping in Second Life is a popular way to earn money, and involves leaving one's avatar parked in certain locations for a specified time. Second Life residents who own inworld land use the practice as a way to increase the traffic in their region, which has the effect of raising its inworld visibility (Boellstorff 2008). But it is generally considered an activity for "newbies" and others who lack skills to earn money in more sophisticated ways. It is seen by many as somewhat "low-class" and "cheap." With Alt 2 to do the dirty work of making him money, Irving can maintain his worldly image and lifestyle.

Alyson also uses an alt to do the chore of cleaning the objects that other avatars leave behind on her land. Such "littering" poses a problem because there is a finite number of objects that every parcel of land can support, and it can ruin the atmosphere or aesthetic appeal the owner wants to create. The reason Alyson gives for keeping the identity of her alt a secret illustrates the different senses of identity she perceives between herself and her avatars: "You should see the hate mail she gets! If I broadcast that she is me then I would get the hate mail in this avatar. It is strange, but I can take the abuse in that avatar but not this one."

"Please do not disturb" – Privacy from Second Life friends and acquaintances was a further reason for using alts. People needing undisturbed time for building, for example, may simply enter Second Life as an alt unknown to any of their acquaintances. Less prosaic reasons for keeping separate inworld identities, however, often were related to sanctioned activities– primarily associated with sexual behaviour. Role-playing that involved BDSM (bondage, discipline, sado-masochism) is an example. These alts might be kept anonymous to the main avatar's social circle because of stigma attached to such behaviour, or alternatively in order to allow that character to immerse fully into the world of the role-play. Robin explains this latter approach:

> I exist...primarily in a mature roleplaying environment...the activities there can involve sexual activities, intimacy and a fair amount of revealing behavior. I have an "alt"...he is used for roleplay in which my primary identity needs to be concealed.

Robin keeps anonymity between his alts within Second Life, yet he was one of the respondents who reported having an open boundary between the identity of his main avatar and his material world identity. Anonymity between alts also concealed sexual liaisons with multiple partners. Kira for example participated in the interview as her main avatar, and told us she has three avatars in total. She said of her relationship with her Second Life partner, "everyone knows that we are a couple... but he is not the one that i spend time with as the third avatar...hehe...lifts her finger to her lips and whispers, 'Ssshh'."

10.7   The Right Identity for the Right Situation

The management of identity across multiple inworld personae illustrates not only the enactment of multiple identities but also the fluidity with which people move in and out of these different shades of self. Turkle (1995) relied on Lifton (1993)'s conception of the self as protean to analyse the way that the Internet fosters easy movement between these multiple enactments. Similar to the shape-shifting Greek god Proteus our respondents crafted identities in response to the internal demands of their motivations and the external demands of social context. We saw in their strategies for managing the boundaries among the virtual and material selves efforts at finding the "right self for the right situation" (Gergen 2000). At the same time, we got a sense from all of our interviews of the presence of an essential core through which the multiple personae were connected, as illustrated by the following quote from Leon:

> my RL perspective will guide my behavior in Second Life.. I don't believe that I am a completely different person in second life just because I have new opportunities here. I believe RL experiences will influence my choices in second life. I believe that my opinions of things in real life will influence things I try, places I visit, and the people I interact with...

Even when Alyson who says, "SL...has no relationship to RL other then fantasies that I have had and try to do in SL, such as owning a club, being a real estate mogul, etc." is nevertheless expressing fantasies that obviously were born from her own psyche.

We do not think this means that it all boils down to the "person behind the avatar." The material world avatar, as some like to like to call it, can be significantly transformed by the virtual world avatar (e.g., Yee et al. 2009), which can then of course be recursive in revealing further nuances in virtual personae, and so on. At the same time, we believe it is important to take heed of Lifton's (1993) and Turkle's (1995) caution that the ease of shifting between different lives –as distinct as they may be – does not imply the absence of an identifiable core self. The jigsaw puzzle does yield a picture.

10.8   Future Research (or Questions We Wish We'd Asked)

The anthropologist Clifford Geertz (1983, cited in Boelstorff 2008) has been widely cited for his critique that Western notions of self-hood as being "bounded, unique and more or less integrated" motivationally and cognitively. There is much evidence that the self is not this way. Perhaps it never has been. The mutable, constructed, deconstructed and reconstructed self is as much a reflection of as a product of the Internet Age (Boellstorff 2008; Gergen 2000; Teske 2002; Turkle 1995). In her recent critique Kennedy (2006) suggests that the focus in Internet identity research on the multiplicity of the self may have gone too far and that the strong focus on anonymity may yield limited new insights. The stories told by our respondents are consistent with Kennedy's argument that a fair amount of continuity exists between virtual and material world identities. Although our participants described the barriers they used to keep knowledge about specific pieces of data about their lives from passing between the two worlds, we saw that there was nevertheless a great deal of data that passed through those boundaries, for all our participants, and the direction of travel was two-way.

Our interview protocol asked participants whether they had multiple accounts in Second Life, and now we wished we had thought to ask them whether they ever had occasion to use other people's existing accounts, as also observed by Boellstorff (2008). Sometimes, for example, people may have permission to use the avatar of a close acquaintance in order to fill in when that person has obligations within Second Life, such as teaching a class, but is unable to log in themselves. The questions of how they felt taking over a persona not of their own making (or knowing someone else inhabited their persona), how they communicated with other people who know the other person's persona, and what identity information they disclose while inhabiting this other persona would yield interesting insights into identity management in virtual environments, and into the limits of the mutability of the self.

We also wish we had asked our participants about their experiences in other virtual environments, though some did volunteer information about this in the course of answering our planned interview questions. It would be useful to examine how information management strategies are carried over between different environments. To what extent do those strategies reflect characteristics of the individual? To what extent do the strategies reflect the nature of the environment? Responses to these questions would yield information of potential importance to understanding the role of design features of virtual environments in identity construction processes.

The question of sampling is important to take into consideration in the interpretation of our data, and of implications for future research. Was our sample representative, and representative of what? It was not clear to us at the outset (and still is not) what population characteristics we wanted to represent in the sample. We made some choices that seemed to be reasonable starting points. Our choice to limit the sample to U.S.-based residents was centred on limiting the variation within a population whose parameters were already difficult to ascertain. An important direction for future research would be to examine cultural and national differences in the approach to anonymity and identity (Markus and Kitayama 1991). Equal numbers of men and women with a median age close to the published Linden Lab demographics seemed about as far as we should go. We made no attempt to sample or to eliminate participants from specialised populations or subcultures such as elves or furries,[5] though we did ask whether people were involved in such groups.

---

[5]People who "identify with animals or who are animal like" (Boellstorff 2008: p. 184) and whose main avatar is usually an animal or has prominent animal features.

Our sample consisted of people who were largely happy with their Second Life experience, and who spent a reasonably large amount of time there, and who get a lot of personal enjoyment for their time in Second Life. They might also represent people who are more likely than are other populations to find the Internet an easier place to express the true self (McKenna et al. 2002). It may be reasonable to assume that people who are less satisfied with their experience will not stick around Second Life for very long, and thus our sample might indeed be representative, but we cannot be certain. We are just as uncertain of the extent to which people who are interested and willing to participate in research studies are representative of Second Life users.

10.9   Conclusions

At the outset of this study, we hypothesised a linear process of anonymity elimination and identity disclosure. In this simplistic process, comparable to the onion metaphor (Altman and Taylor 1973), as relationships between individuals interacting in Second Life unfold, they disclose more and more pieces of information to the point where anonymity can no longer be assumed, and one's "true" identity is revealed to another. Our interviews reveal a much more convoluted, recursive, ever changing and never ending process. Being anonymous or identified in a virtual world is not a dichotomy, but consists of many facets. Even if we take into consideration the material world only, self identity is ever evolving, spanning multiple social environments in which individuals identify themselves in different ways given social situations they find themselves in. Adding to this interaction in a virtual world, where one can add additional layers of identity, multiplies the complexity of the relationship between anonymity and identifiability. Each of our participants represents a whole universe where the complexities of the different parts of one's identity can cohere in one situation and collide in another. There may not be layers of onion to get through to reveal one's true identity. Even the puzzle metaphor is an oversimplification because the full picture, as well as the pieces, is ever changing.

Acknowledgments The authors thank O. Candelario, Mary Ellen Gordon, Peggy Daniels Lee, and Harriet J. McLeod for helpful comments on this chapter.

References

Altman, I., Taylor, D.: Social Penetration: The Development of Interpersonal Relationships. Holt, Rinehart and Winston, New York (1973)
Anonymous: To reveal or not to reveal: a theoretical model of anonymous communication. Commun. Theor. **8**, 381–407 (1998)
Banaji, M.R., Prentice, D.A.: The self in social contexts. Annu. Rev. Psychol. **45**, 297–332 (1994)
Bargh, J., McKenna, K.: The internet and social life. Annu. Rev. Psychol. **55**, 573–590 (2004)

Bargh, J., McKenna, K., Fitzsimons, G.: Can you see the real me? Activation and expression of the "true self" on the internet. J. Soc. Issues **58**, 33–48 (2002)

Ben-Ze'ev, A.: Privacy, emotional closeness, and openness in cyberspace. Comput. Hum. Behav. **19**, 451–467 (2003)

Boellstorff, T.: Coming of Age in Second Life. Princeton University Press, Princeton (2008)

Brewer, M.B.: The social self: on being the same and different at the same time. Pers. Soc. Psychol. Bull. **17**, 475–482 (1991)

Caspi, A., Gorsky, P.: Online deception: prevalence, motivation, and emotion. Cyberpsychol. Behav. **9**, 54–59 (2006)

Christopherson, K.M.: The positive and negative implications of anonymity in internet social interactions: "On the internet, nobody knows you're a dog". Comput. Hum. Behav. **23**, 3038–3056 (2007)

Collins, N., Miller, L.: Self-disclosure and liking: a meta-analytic review. Psychol. Bull. **116**, 457–475 (1994)

Derlega, V.J., Chaikin, A.L.: Privacy and self-disclosure in social relationships. J. Soc. Issues **33**, 102–115 (1977)

Derlega, V.J., Wilson, M., Chaikin, A.L.: Friendship and disclosure reciprocity. J. Pers. Soc. Psychol. **34**, 578–582 (1976)

Dietz-Uhler, B., Bishop-Clark, C., Howard, E.: Formation of and adherence to a self-disclosure norm in an online chat. Cyberpsychol. Behav. **8**, 114–120 (2005)

Frye, N.E., Dornisch, M.M.: When is trust not enough? The role of perceived privacy of communication tools in comfort with self-disclosure. Comput. Hum. Behav. **26**, 1120–1127 (2010)

Geertz, C.: Local Knowledge: Further Essays on Interpretive Anthropology. Basic Books, New York (1983)

Gergen, K.J.: The Saturated Self. Basic Books, New York (2000)

Goffman, E.: The Presentation of Self in Everyday Life. Anchor Books, New York (1959)

Goffman, E.: Stigma: Notes on the Management of Spoiled Identity. Simon & Schuster, New York (1963)

Hancock, J.T.: Digital deception: when, where and how people lie online. In: McKenna, K., Postmes, T., Reips, U., Joinson, A.N. (eds.) Oxford Handbook of Internet Psychology, pp. 287–301. Oxford University Press, Oxford (2007)

Jessup, L.M., Connolly, T., Tansik, D.A.: Toward a theory of automated group work: the deindividuating effects of anonymity. Small Gr. Res. **21**, 333–348 (1990)

Johnson, D.W., Noonan, M.P.: Effects of acceptance and reciprocation of self-disclosures on the development of trust. Journal of Counseling Psychology. **19**, 411–416 (1972)

Joinson, A.N., Reips, U., Buchanan, T., Schofield, C.B.P.: Privacy, trust, and self-disclosure online. Hum-Comput. Interact. **25**, 1–24 (2010)

Kennedy, H.: Beyond anonymity, or future directions for internet identity research. New Media Soc. **8**, 859–876 (2006)

Lifton, R.J.: The Protean Self: Human Resilience in an Age of Fragmentation. Basic Books, New York (1993)

Markus, H.R., Kitayama, K.: Culture and the self: implications for cognition, emotion, and motivation. Psychol. Rev. **98**, 224–253 (1991)

Markus, H., Nurius, P.: Possible selves. Am. Psychol. **41**, 954–969 (1986)

McKenna, K.Y.A., Green, A.S., Gleason, M.E.J.: Relationship formation on the internet: what's the big attraction? J. Soc. Issues **58**, 9–31 (2002)

McLeod, P.L.: Anonymity and consensus in computer-supported group decision making. In: Griffith, T.L. (ed.) Research on Managing Groups and Teams: Technology, pp. 175–204. JAI Press, Stamford (2000)

Nosek, B.A., Banaji, M.R., Greenwald, A.G.: E-research: ethics, security, design, and control in psychological research on the internet. J. Soc. Issues **58**, 161–176 (2002)

Omarzu, J.: A disclosure decision model: determining how and when individuals will self-disclose. Pers. Soc. Psychol. Rev. **4**, 174–185 (2000)

Parks, M., Floyd, K.: Making friends in cyberspace. J. Commun. **46**, 80–97 (1996)

Postmes, T., Spears, R., Sakhel, K., de Groot, D.: Social influence in computer-mediated communication: the effects of anonymity on group behavior. Pers. Soc. Psychol. Bull. **27**, 1243–1254 (2001)

Preece, J.: Online Communities: Designing Usability, Supporting Sociability. Wiley, New York (2000)

Rains, S.A.: The impact of anonymity on perceptions of source credibility and influence in computer-mediated group communication: a test of two competing hypotheses. Commun. Res. **34**, 100–125 (2007)

Rheingold, H.: The Virtual Community: Homesteading on the Electronic Frontier. Addison-Wesley, Reading (1993)

Rubin, Z.: Disclosing oneself to a stranger: reciprocity and its limits. J. Exp. Soc. Psychol. **11**, 233–260 (1975)

Smith, M.A., Kollock, P.: Communities in Cyberspace. Routledge, New York (1999)

Tajfel, H.: The social psychology of intergroup relations. Annu. Rev. Psychol. **33**, 1–39 (1982)

Tajfel, H., Turner, J.C.: An integrative theory of intergroup conflict. In: Austin, W., Worchel, S. (eds.) Social Psychology of Intergroup Relations. Brooks/Cole, Monterrey (1979)

Tanis, M., Postmes, T.: Two faces of anonymity: paradoxical effects of cues to identity in CMC. Comput. Hum. Behav. **23**, 955–970 (2007)

Taylor, T.L.: Life in virtual worlds: plural existence, multimodalities, and other online research challenges. Am. Behav. Sci. **43**(3), 436–449 (1999)

Teske, J.A.: Cyberpsychology, human relationship, and our virtual interiors. Zygon **37**, 677–700 (2002)

Thibaut, J.W., Kelley, H.H.: The Social Psychology of Groups. Wiley, New York (1959)

Turkle, S.: Life on the Screen: Identity in the Age of the Internet. Simon & Schuster, New York (1995)

Valacich, J.S., Jessup, L.M., Dennis, A.R., Nunamaker Jr., J.F.: A conceptual framework of anonymity in group support systems. Group Decis. Negot. **1**, 219–241 (1992)

Vrooman, S.S.: The art of invective: performing identity in cyberspace. New Media Soc. **4**(1), 51–70 (2002)

Walther, J.B.: Computer-mediated communication: impersonal, interpersonal, and hyperpersonal interaction. Commun. Res. **23**(1), 3–43 (1996)

Wheeless, L.R., Grotz, J.: The measurement of trust and its relationship to self-disclosure. Hum. Commun. Res. **3**, 250–257 (1977)

Worthy, M., Gary, A.L., Kahn, G.M.: Self-disclosure as an exchange process. J. Pers. Soc. Psychol. **13**(1), 59–63 (1969)

Yee, N., Bailenson, J.N., Ducheneaut, N.: The proteus effect: implications of transformed digital self-representation on online and offline behavior. Commun. Res. **36**, 285–312 (2009)

Chapter 11
Multiple Personality Order: Physical and Personality Characteristics of the Self, Primary Avatar and Alt

Richard L. Gilbert, Jessica A. Foss, and Nora A. Murphy

Abstract One hundred and four participants, all of whom had multiple avatars in the 3D virtual world of Second Life™, completed a set of measures to assess how physical characteristics, activity preferences, personality features, and social-emotional processes are similar or different across various combinations of the physical self, the primary avatar, and the sole or most frequently used alt. Data was also obtained on the frequency of alt use, motivations for constructing alts, and the main forms of identity experimentation engaged in with alts. The combined results were then used to construct a model of how personality systems composed of multiple offline and online identities operate and form a "multiple personality order." As 3D virtual worlds and the global population of avatars continue to grow, creating and coordinating a system of multiple offline and online identities will increasingly become a normative feature of human development and, like a choreographer managing a company of dancers or a conductor leading an orchestra, the operation of personality will take on a quality of performance art.

11.1 Introduction

Throughout history, human beings have demonstrated an interest in modifying aspects of their identity and experimenting with alternative personas. Early expressions of this tendency generally involved brief alterations of identity including: participating in

R.L. Gilbert (✉) • J.A. Foss
The P.R.O.S.E. Project, Loyola Marymount University, 1 LMU Drive, Suite 4700, Los Angeles, CA 90045, USA
e-mail: richard.gilbert@lmu.edu; jnunnally2@gmail.com

N.A. Murphy
Department of Psychology, Loyola Marymount University, Los Angeles, CA 90293, USA
e-mail: nora.murphy@lmu.edu

A. Peachey and M. Childs (eds.), *Reinventing Ourselves: Contemporary Concepts of Identity in Virtual Worlds*, Springer Series in Immersive Environments, DOI 10.1007/978-0-85729-361-9_11, © Springer-Verlag London Limited 2011

ceremonial rituals in which participants concealed their true selves behind elaborate masks and costumes; performing roles that were discrepant with one's daily persona following the advent of formal theatre, and attending masquerade balls that were popularised during the Renaissance. The contemporary practice of wearing costumes on Halloween, and other similar holidays around the world, also involves the short-term adoption of an alternative persona or identity.

Examples of lengthier and more elaborate efforts to experiment with core aspects of personal identity, such as gender, race, and age, can also be found. Some of these identity modifications were undertaken for practical aims such as those involving women who pretended to be male in order to serve as soldiers in wars such as the American War of Independence (De Pauw 1981) and World War I (Royster 2006). However, others were initiated for more psychological purposes – an effort to experience the world from the perspective of individuals from an alternative identity group and to convey this experience to others. In the arena of race, the classic work, Black Like Me, chronicled the experiences of Caucasian journalist John Howard Griffin who darkened his skin and lived in the Deep South as a black man for 6 weeks during the pre-Civil Rights era of the late 1950s (Griffin 1961). Similarly, a number of individuals have experimented with identity by living as a member of another social class for an extended period of time (Camigliano 1983; Ehrenreich 2001; Spurlock 2005).

With the coming of the digital age, the capacity to experiment with alternative personas and different components of identity has become far easier and more commonplace. The anonymity of the online world disinhibits its users (Goleman 2006), offering them an expanded sense of freedom and opportunities to experiment with minimal threat of physical life repercussions or social rejection (Suler 2004). At times this capacity has been used for exploitative or abusive purposes, such as when individuals have assumed the identity of celebrities on various social networking sites in order to promote their own businesses or products (Stone and Richtel 2007) or the tragic example of Lori Drew who posed as a teenage boy on MySpace as a means of bullying her adolescent daughter's peer, who subsequently took her own life (Steinhauer 2008). Despite these notable abuses, research has found that the inclination to create alternative digital personas is usually grounded in motivations such as reducing loneliness and a desire to connect with others (Marcus et al. 2006), impression management (Ellison et al. 2006; Gosling et al. 2007), seeking an outlet for creativity and self-expression (Papacharissi 2002), a desire for emotional and sexual outlets (Ranon 2006), and the wish to express hidden aspects of the self and experiment with different sides of one's personality (McKenna and Bargh 1998; McKenna and Bargh 2000).

The recent emergence of the Immersive Internet (Driver and Driver 2008) has expanded the capacity for individuals to vary aspects of the self and engage in identity experimentation even further (Amdahl 2006; Peachey 2010). In this latest phase of cyberspace, individuals go beyond accessing information via two-dimensional web pages (The Informational Internet and Web 1.0) or interacting via chat rooms, wikis, and social networking sites (The Interactive Internet and Web 2.0) and construct avatars (i.e., 3-Dimensional digital representations of self) that operate within intricate, increasingly vivid, 3D online environments. Within these immersive settings, users have the ability to customise their avatar into almost any form of imagined self by varying characteristics such as age, sex, race/ethnicity, and health and personality traits that are central components of their physical identity. Moreover, in a subset of cases, participants design and operate one or more additional avatars called "alts" in addition to using a primary avatar (Second Life Herald 2005), with one study finding that on average Second Life users have a total of three different avatars per account (Ducheneaut et al. 2009). In 98% of cases, users could identify one of these accounts as the main or primary avatar, the other accounts were alternative avatars or "alts." Thus, a single human driver may control one or more avatars possessing a wide array of physical and psychological attributes and create a personality system composed of multiple constituent identities in the physical and virtual realms (i.e., a "multiple personality order").

While the subjects of identity experimentation and identity coordination in 3D virtual environments are often considered in discussion forums and blogs, empirical research on the topic is more limited. Some studies have looked at the extent to which individuals construct avatars whose characteristics are similar or different than those of their physical selves. Au (2007) found that approximately 94% of virtual world users create anthropomorphic (male or female) avatars vs. non-humanoid (i.e., animal or object) avatars. Au also cites a 2007 survey conducted by Global Market Insight (GMI) of 479 residents of Second Life in which 45% of the participants indicated that, relative to their physical self, their avatar had a better body or physical appearance (45%); was younger (37%), was a different gender (23%) or had a different skin colour (22%). A later study by Wallace and Marryott (2009) also found low rates of choosing a Second Life avatar whose ethnic appearance differed from the participant's physical self. In addition, Ducheneaut et al. (2009) studied 137 participants across three immersive environments (World of Warcraft, Second Life, and Maple Story) and supported the GMI findings regarding the tendency to create avatars with idealised physical characteristics (especially among physically female participants) and the less frequent use of gender-discrepant avatars (especially physically male participants functioning as females in the virtual world.) Overall, these data indicate that while avatars almost always reflect an allegiance to the human form, and a majority of participants do not vary core characteristics of the physical self in the creation of their avatar, a meaningful segment of virtual world users do. This is especially true in the area of body image and age, and less so in the area of gender, race, or ethnicity.

Several previous studies have also investigated the relationship between the personality characteristics of the physical self and those of the primary avatar. Bessiere et al. (2007) used the Big Five Personality Inventory (described below in Sect. 11.2.1) to compare the physical life and avatar personality characteristics of 51 predominantly young male participants in World of Warcraft. The data indicated that players tended to ascribe more positive or idealised personality traits to their avatars (i.e., higher extroversion and conscientiousness and lower neuroticism) and similar findings were also found in Ducheneaut et al.'s (2009) study across several virtual environments.

The current investigation builds on these initial empirical studies on the relationship between characteristics of the physical self and avatars. Specifically, working with residents of Second Life, it compared the physical, personality, and social-emotional characteristics of the human driver and primary avatar. In addition, for the first time, it extended the empirical comparison of physical life and 3D virtual identities to include alts. Specifically, it explored (a) the physical and personality characteristics of alts relative to the physical self and the primary avatar, (b) the preferred activities of avatars and alts, and (c) the frequency of alt usage, motivations for constructing alts, and the main forms of identity experimentation engaged in with alts. By building upon prior work on the physical and personality features of the physical self and the primary avatar, adding comparisons of social-emotional data between the physical self and primary avatar, and collecting initial data on the relationship of the alt to the primary avatar and physical self, the current study sought to increase our understanding of personality systems composed of multiple, constituent, online and offline identities.

11.2   Methods

One hundred and four participants, all of whom had multiple avatars in Second Life, were recruited via posted announcements in the Second Life Events Calendar, notices sent out by heads of large groups representing major constituencies in Second Life (e.g. social, business, educational, and artist networks), a CNN IReport (www. ireport.com, a website where citizen journalists can post stories), and word-of-mouth communication. Each method of recruitment offered potential participants the opportunity to come to a virtual research lab located within Second Life and earn 1,000 Lindens (virtual currency equivalent to slightly less than 4 U.S. dollars) for completing approximately 40 min of psychological questionnaires. The recruitment notices also specified that the participant's primary avatar must have had at least 6 months residency in Second Life. This "minimal residency requirement" ensured that all data were derived from at least moderately experienced users as opposed to newcomers with unstable patterns of behaviour and use of the virtual environment. This reasoning parallels that of Young (1998), who advised that measures of Internet behaviour should be used cautiously with novice users in their first 6 months of exposure to the medium. Essentially, the 6-month minimum duration requirement used in the current study extends Young's methodological guideline from Internet research conducted within Web 1.0 to the emerging 3-dimensional Internet. Participants were also required to be at 18 years of age or older to qualify for the study.

The multi-method, incentivised approach to recruiting participants yielded a sample with the following characteristics: Of the 104 participants, 57 were female, 46 were male, and 1 was transgendered. A majority of participants (n = 51) were between the ages of 18 and 29, and a wide array of education levels (ranging from no high school diploma to doctoral degrees) were represented by the sample, with a high school diploma or equivalent being the most frequently reported education level (n = 39). The vast majority of participants came from North America (n=82) and Europe (n=15), although, Asia (n=3), South America (n=3), and Australia (n=1) were also represented. Participants had been using Second Life from 6 months to over 3 years, with 1–2 years (n=43) being the most frequently reported length of time in Second Life. Additionally, the most frequently reported rate of Second Life usage, ranging from daily to less than once a month, was daily or almost every day (n=89). It is important to note that while the current sample is subject to selection biases that affect all online studies, the gender and age characteristics of the sample are similar to those found in larger demographic surveys of Second Life users (Linden 2008; Market Truths 2009) which provides some support for its representativeness with respect to the wider population of inworld residents.

11.2.1   Procedures and Measures

Upon arriving at the virtual lab, participants were screened to ensure that they met the 6-month residency criterion and had not previously taken the Second Life identity survey. Participants who satisfied these screening criteria and electronically agreed to provisions of an informed consent were then linked to an online survey where they provided physical life demographic information and basic Second Life utilization data. Subsequently, participants completed four measures assessing the physical, personality, and social-emotional characteristics of the physical self.

Survey of physical characteristics: Participants were asked to provide information regarding five physical characteristics: age, sex, hair colour, eye colour, and body type (i.e. small/lean, medium, and larger/somewhat overweight).

The Big Five Personality Inventory (BFI; John et al. 1991): The BFI is a 44-item measure in which each item assesses one of the Big Five personality traits: extraversion, conscientiousness, agreeableness, neuroticism, and openness. Participants rate themselves on each item using a 5-point scale ranging from strongly disagree (1) to strongly agree (5).

The Social Connectedness Scale (SCS; Lee and Robbins 2001): The SCS is a 20-item questionnaire indicating the degree of social connectedness felt by the subject in their social relationships. The measure conceptualises social connectedness as a personal attribute reflecting enduring closeness with the social world in general. Participants respond to positive and negative statements about their social relationships (e.g., "I find myself actively involved in people's lives;" "I have little sense of togetherness with my peers") using a 6-point scale ranging from strongly disagree (1) to strongly agree (6).

The Satisfaction with Life Scale (SWLS; Diener et al. 1985): The SWLS is a five-item questionnaire indicating the extent to which subjects are satisfied with their current life. The SWLS is designed to assess global life satisfaction, which is a component of subjective well-being. Participants rate statements regarding their view of their life (e.g., "In most ways my life is close to ideal;" "So far I have gotten the important things I want in life") using a 7-point scale ranging from strongly disagree (1) to strongly agree (7).

After completing this set of measures with regard to the physical self, participants were asked to fill out each of the measures again with respect to the characteristics of their primary avatar. The instructions and wording of the items were modified so that participants' responses should represent the characteristics or perspectives of their primary avatar instead of their physical self. For example, with respect to questions regarding physical characteristics, participants were prompted with questions such as, "What age is depicted by your avatar's appearance?" and "What is your avatar's typical eye colour?" Similarly, items on the BFI completed with respect to the physical self such as, "I see myself as someone who likes to cooperate with others" were changed to read, "My avatar is someone who likes to cooperate with others." The same process of instructional and item-wording revision was applied to the SCS and SWLS questionnaires so that all items on these measures clearly referenced perceptions of the primary avatar. Participants were also asked to fill out a fifth measure with respect to their primary avatar, one that assessed their *Second Life Activity Preferences.* Using a 5-point scale (1=not important at all to 5=extremely important), participants rated the perceived importance of 11 Second Life activities: building virtual objects, buying/selling, exploring the virtual world, finding/enhancing a relationship, learning/education, role playing/fantasy, scripting (i.e., writing computer code to animate objects), sex/sexual experiences, shopping, socialising, and working/employment.

After responding to the five primary avatar measures, participants completed several measures related to their third identity: their alt or most frequently used alt (if the participant had multiple alts). Specifically they completed the Survey of Physical Characteristics, Second Life Activity Preferences questionnaire, and the BFI with respect to the physical, behavioural, and personality attributes of their alt. However, due to time constraints and the length of the questionnaire administration, social-emotional data was not collected for participant's alts. As with the primary avatar version of these measures, items on the questionnaires were modified to reflect the constituent identity for whom the participant was responding (i.e. the alt). Participants also completed the *Alt Usage Questionnaire* (Foss and Gilbert 2009), a 13-item measure assessing the number of alts used by a participant, the motivations for creating an alt, and the activities engaged in when using alts for the purpose of identity experimentation, including what elements of identity were varied when using alts (e.g., age, gender, race, etc.).

11.3   Results

The presentation of results is organised into three sections: physical and activity characteristics; personality and social-emotional characteristics; and alt usage characteristics. In the first section examining physical and activity characteristics, all physical comparisons are conducted using participant's three identities: the physical

Table 11.1 Measures administered to participants according to identity status

| | Identity | | |
Measures	Physical self	Primary avatar	Alt
Physical characteristics	✓	✓	✓
Second life activity preferences	NA	✓	✓
Personality characteristics (BFI)	✓	✓	✓
Socio-emotional characteristics (SCS, SWLS)	✓	✓	–
Alt usage characteristics	NA	NA	✓

Note: BFI = Big Five Inventory (John et al. 1991), SCS = Social Connectedness Scale (Lee and Robbins 2001), SWLS = Satisfaction with Life Scale (Diener et al. 1985). "NA" = not applicable to that identity status. "–" = not administered

self, primary avatar, and alt. However, with respect to activity data, activity comparisons are conducted between primary avatars and alts only. This is due to the fact that several of the measured Second Life behaviours did not have physical life activity equivalents (e.g. scripting, building virtual objects, etc.) and thus, no physical life behavioural data were collected for comparison. In the second section, which explores personality and social-emotional characteristics, personality data was collected for the physical self, primary avatar, and alt. However, as previously noted in Sect. 11.2.1, social-emotional data were not collected for participants' alts. Table 11.1 summarises the measures used for each identity status.

For each of the categories of characteristics mentioned above, descriptive data are provided with respect to each identity type followed by statistical comparisons across participants' three identities. Thus, with regard to physical characteristics, descriptive information about the age, gender, hair colour, eye colour, and body type of participants' physical self, primary avatar, and alt are presented. Subsequently, for each of these characteristics, statistical comparisons between participants' physical selves and primary avatars, physical selves and alts, and primary avatars and alts, are then provided. This same approach is followed with the activity, personality, and social-emotional characteristics and their respective data. Finally, the third section examines participants' use of alts, including descriptive data, motivations for alt creation, and types of identity experimentation.

11.3.1 Physical and Activity Characteristics

Age: Participants ranged in age from 18 to above 60. The majority of participants (n = 51) reported that they were between the ages of 18 and 29 in physical life. With respect to their virtual identities, a variety of ages, ranging from under 18 to 60 or older, were represented, with 18–29 also being the most frequently depicted age category for both primary avatars and alts. See Fig. 11.1.

Effects of identity type on age: Age was measured using the following categories: under 18, 18–29, 30–39, 40–49, 50–59, and 60 or above. Each of these categories

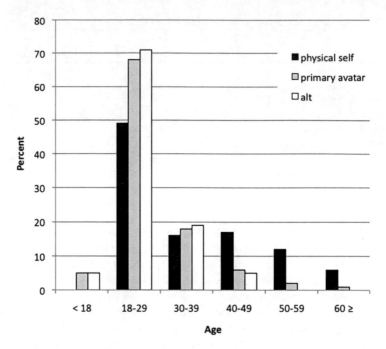

Fig. 11.1 Age by identity status

was then coded as 0, 1, 2, 3, 4, and 5, sequentially, from youngest to oldest. Thus, in the analyses below, a larger mean reflects an older age on average.

A repeated measures ANOVA was used to compare participants' age across their three identities (physical self, primary avatar, and alt). A significant effect of identity was found $F(2,206)=45.94$, $p < .01$, $\eta p\ 2 = .31$. Comparisons across pairs revealed that participants' actual age ($M=2.09$, $SD=1.29$) was significantly older than that depicted by their primary avatars ($M=1.35$, $SD=0.82$), $t(103)=6.62$, $p < .01$, $d=0.68$ or alts ($M=1.24$, $SD=0.62$), $t(103)=7.88$, $p < .01$, $d=0.84$. Thus, participants' virtual identities tended to be younger than participants' actual age. However, no significant difference was found between the ages depicted by primary avatars and alts, $t(103)=1.73$, $p = .09$, $d=0.15$.

Gender: Of the 104 participants (57 females, 46 males, 1 transgendered), 62 (60%) used a female as their primary avatar, 36 (35%) used males, and 6 (6%) used an animal, mythical creature, or non-human as their primary avatar. Additionally, with respect to alts, 64 (62%) used females, 34 (33%) used males, and 6 (6%) used mythical, animal, or non-human alts.

Due to small cell size, one transgendered participant was dropped from the gender analyses. Thus, the following analyses were run using 46 physically male participants and 57 physically female participants.

Effects of identity on gender: Chi-square analyses revealed a significant effect for gender when comparing the physical self and primary avatar, $\chi^2(2, N=103)=81.01$, $p < .01$, Cramer's $V = .89$. Of the 46 male participants, 36 (78%) used male avatars,

Table 11.2 Patterns of gender stability and change across identities

Gender identity	Total n	Maintained gender	Changed gender	Changed to non-gendered form
Physical self to primary avatar				
Male	46	36 (78%)	5 (11%)	5 (11%)
Female	57	56 (98%)	0 (0%)	1 (2%)
Physical self to alt				
Male	46	26 (57%)	16 (35%)	4 (9%)
Female	57	47 (82%)	8 (14%)	2 (4%)
Primary avatar to alt				
Male	36[a]	24 (67%)	11 (31%)	1 (3%)
Female	61[b]	50 (82%)	9 (15%)	2 (3%)

Note: Non-gendered form reflects unidentified gender (i.e., when the participant chooses an animal, mythic figure, or inanimate object as their Second Life identity). Numbers in parentheses reflect percentage of participants within that category row (numbers do not always total 100 because of rounding)
[a] The total number of male avatars ($n=36$) is lower than the total number of male participants ($n=46$) because a number of physically male participants had primary avatars who were female
[b] The total number of female avatars ($n=61$) is higher than the total number of female participants ($n=57$) because total female avatars includes *both* physically female participants with female avatars and physically male participants with female avatars

5 (11%) used female avatars, and 5 (11%) chose a non-gendered form such as an animal, mythic figure, or inanimate object. Thus, there was a tendency for some male participants to use a female avatar or a non-gendered form. Interestingly, females did not demonstrate this same tendency toward gender experimentation; of the 57 female participants, 56 (98%) used females and 1 (2%) used a non-gendered form.

There was also a significant effect for gender when comparing the physical self and alt gender, χ^2 (2, $N=103$)$=24.56$, $p < .01$, Cramer's $V = .49$. Twenty-six (57%) male participants used male alts, 16 (35%) used female alts, and 4 (9%) used a non-gendered form. Forty-seven (82%) female participants used females as their alts, 8 (14%) chose male alts, and 2 (4%) chose a non-gendered form.

Finally, there was a significant effect of gender between primary avatar and alt, χ^2(4, $N=103$)$=50.94$, $p < .01$, Cramer's $V = .50$. Of the 36 male primary avatars, 24 (67%) used male alts, 11 (31%) used female alts, and 1 (3%) chose a non-gendered form. Of the 61 female primary avatars, 50 (82%) used females as their alts, 9 (15%) chose male alts, and 2 (3%) chose a non-gendered form.

Table 11.2 summarises these findings regarding gender characteristics across the various identities.

Hair colour: The majority of participants reported having brown ($n = 52$), black ($n=19$), or blond(e) ($n=16$) hair in physical life, while a few reported red ($n=8$), grey/white ($n=6$), or other (e.g. green, purple, bald) as their hair colour. With respect to their virtual selves, a variety of hair colours were represented by primary avatars and alts in the sample, with black ($n_{av}=47$, $n_{alt}=46$) being the most frequently occurring hair colour, followed by brown ($n_{av}=15$, $n_{alt}=21$), red ($n_{av}=15$, $n_{alt}=16$), other ($n_{av}=12$, $n_{alt}=9$), grey/white ($n_{av}=8$, $n_{alt}=7$), and blond(e) ($n_{av}=7$, $n_{alt}=5$).

Effects of identity on hair colour: Chi-square analyses revealed a significant effect for hair colour when comparing the physical self and primary avatar, χ^2 (25, $N = 104$) = 40.47, $p < .05$, Cramer's $V = .28$; and between the primary avatar and alt, χ^2 (25, $N = 104$) = 109.79, $p < .01$, Cramer's $V = .46$. While no single, consistent pattern of colour shifting was observed (e.g. black to blond/blonde, red to brown, etc.), participants with a variety of hair colours experimented with altering the hue of their hair across virtual identities.

Eye colour: Of the 104 participants, 36 reported having brown eyes in physical life, while 28 had blue, 21 had hazel, and 19 had green eyes. With respect to their virtual selves, a variety of eye colours were represented by primary avatars and alts in the sample, with colours not represented in physical life such as orange or purple, being the most frequently reported eye colour ($n_{av} = 41$, $n_{alt} = 52$), followed by brown ($n_{av} = 28$, $n_{alt} = 24$), blue ($n_{av} = 25$, $n_{alt} = 10$), and green ($n_{av} = 10$, $n_{alt} = 18$). No primary avatars or alts were reported as having hazel eyes.

Effects of identity on eye colour: A significant effect for eye colour was found when comparing the physical self to the primary avatar, $\chi^2(9, N = 104) = 42.02$, $p < .01$, Cramer's $V = .37$; and between the primary avatar to the alt, $\chi^2(9, N = 104) = 46.75$, $p < .01$, Cramer's $V = .39$. Thus, shifts in eye colour across participants' different identities did occur; however, further inspection did not reveal a particular pattern with respect to these colour changes (e.g. brown to green, blue to hazel, etc.).

Body type: Body type was measured using three categories: small/lean build, medium build, and larger build/somewhat overweight. Forty-three (42%) of the 104 participants reported their physical life body type as medium build, 37 (36%) reported having a larger, somewhat overweight build, and 24 (23%) reported having a small, lean build. Of these 104 subjects, 54 (52%) had primary avatars with a small, lean build; 45 (43%) had primary avatars with a medium build, and 5 (5%) had primary avatars with a larger build. Additionally, with respect to alts, 49 (47%) had a small lean build, 49 (47%) had a medium build, and 5 (5%) had a larger build. These results are summarised in Fig. 11.2.

Effects of identity on body type: A one-way repeated-measures ANOVA was calculated to compare participants' body type across their three identities and a significant effect for body type was found, $F(1.73, 178) = 33.07$, $p < .01$, $\eta_p^2 = .24$.[1] Follow-up pairwise comparisons revealed significant differences between participants' actual body type and the reported body type of their primary avatar, $t(103) = 7.54$, $p < .01$, $d = 0.88$, and alt, $t(103) = 5.60$, $p < .01$, $d = 0.73$; on average, participants' actual build was larger than the body type portrayed by their primary avatars or alts. However no significant difference between the body type reported for the primary avatar and alt was found.

Activity preferences: Using a 5 point scale ranging from 1 = *not important at all* to 5 = *extremely important*, participants rated their Second Life activity preferences for

---

[1] Due to a violation of sphericity, a Greenhouse-Geisser correction was used.

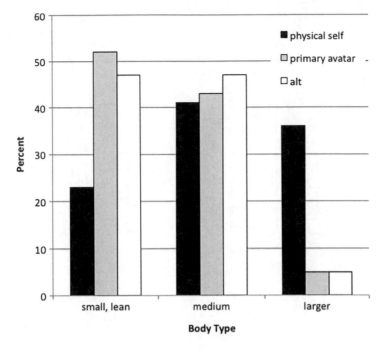

Fig. 11.2 Body type by identity status

their primary avatar and alt. Activities included: building virtual objects, buying/selling, exploring the virtual world, finding/enhancing a relationship, learning/education, role playing/fantasy, scripting (i.e., writing computer code to animate objects), sex/sexual experiences, shopping, socializing, and working/employment.

Effects of identity on activity preferences: Paired samples *t*-tests using a Bonferroni correction were calculated to compare the activity preferences of participants when using their primary avatar versus their alt. Significant differences in preferred activities were found for the following eight activities: building, buying/selling, exploring the virtual world, learning/education, scripting, shopping, socializing, and working/employment. (All $ts > 2.87$, $ps < .01$, $ds > 0.28$.) In each case participants ascribed greater importance to these activities for their primary avatar versus their alt. In contrast, no significant differences were found for the activities of: finding/enhancing relationships, role-playing/fantasy, sex/sexual experiences. Thus, the primary avatars had a greater role in practical and business-related activities (e.g. building, working, etc.) while alts had an equal role in matters of relationships, sexuality, and activities associated with identity experimentation such as role playing/fantasy. These results are summarised in Fig. 11.3.

There were significant differences between the primary avatar and alt on preferences for building, buying/selling, exploring the virtual world, learning/education, scripting, shopping, socializing, and working/employment. Participants ascribed greater importance to these activities for their primary avatar versus their alt. (Error bars represent standard errors.)

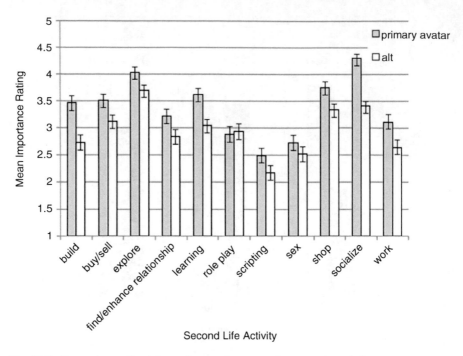

Fig. 11.3 Comparisons of activity preferences between primary avatar and alt

11.3.2 Personality and Social-Emotional Characteristics

The Big Five Personality Inventory: A series of one-way repeated measures ANOVAs were used to compare participants' personality traits across their three identities. A significant effect of identity was found for all five personality characteristics. (All $Fs > 2.55$, $df_{means} = 2$, $df_{error} = 206$, $ps < .01$, $\eta_p^2 > 0.07$).[2] Pairwise comparisons with a Bonferonni adjustment revealed significant differences such that (1) participants' primary avatars were more extroverted, agreeable, conscientious, open, and less neurotic, than their physical life selves, (2) alts were less neurotic and less open than participants' physical selves and (3) primary avatars were more extroverted, agreeable, conscientiousness, and open than their alts. (All $ts > -6.16$, $ps < .05$, $ds > -0.55$) These results are summarised in Fig. 11.4.

Social connectedness and satisfaction with life: A paired samples *t*-test compared participants' physical life social connectedness scores with their primary avatar social

---

[2] Due to the violation of sphericity, a Greenhouse-Geisser correction was used for all tests results in this section, except for agreeableness, which did not violate the assumption.

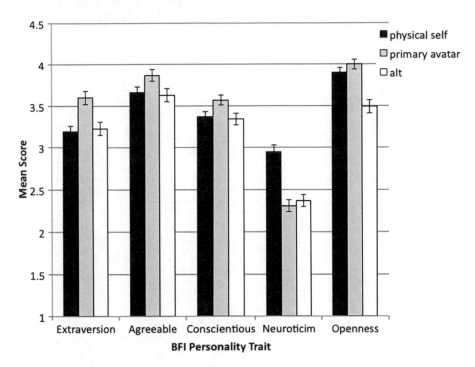

Fig. 11.4 Comparisons of Big Five personality traits across three identities. There were significant differences in which (*1*) participants' primary avatars were more extroverted, agreeable, conscientious, open, and less neurotic, than their physical selves, (*2*) alts were less neurotic and less open than participants' physical selves and (*3*) primary avatars were more extroverted, agreeable, conscientiousness, and open than their alts. (Error bars represent standard errors)

connectedness scores. Results showed that participants feel significantly more socially connected as their primary avatar ($M=89.25$, $SD=18.24$) than they do in their physical lives ($M=79.35$, $SD=17.78$), $t(103) = -6.55$, $p < .01$, $d = -0.55$. Similarly participants' reported higher satisfaction with life scores for their primary avatar ($M=27.04$, $SD=6.06$) than for their physical selves ($M=19.08$, $SD=7.41$), $t(103) = -8.67$, $p < .01$, $d = -1.18$.

11.3.3 Alt Usage Characteristics

Number of alts: Of the 104 participants, 36 (35%) had one alt, 29 (28%) had two alts, 13 (13%) had three alts, 4 (4%) had four alts, and 22 (21%) had five alts.

Motivations for alt usage: Participants were provided with eight questions addressing possible motivations for creating an alt. For each question participants indicated

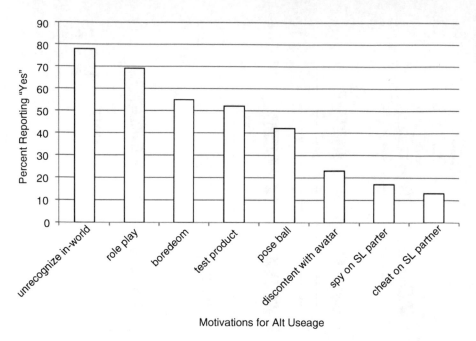

Fig. 11.5 Motivations for alt creation and usage (participants were able to select more than one option)

yes or no depending upon whether or not the particular motivation applied to the creation of their alt. Eighty-two (79%) cited the ability to be inworld without being recognised, 72 (69%) cited role playing/experimenting with a different identity, 57 (55%) cited boredom, 54 (52%) cited testing of a product, 44 (42%) cited testing a pose ball or animation intended for use by two avatars, 24 (23%) cited discontent with the life of their primary avatar, 18 (17%) cited spying on a Second Life romantic partner, and 13 (13%) cited cheating on a Second Life romantic partner as one of their primary reasons for creating an alt. See Fig. 11.5 for a summary of these results.

Types of role playing/experimentation purposes for alts: Of the 72 participants who cited role playing/experimenting with a different identity as one of their motivations for using an alt, 41 (57%) reported experimenting with their style of dress or persona, 33 (46%) reported experimenting with a different gender, 28 (39%) reported experimenting with their body type, 27 (38%) reported role playing a different species or mythical creature, 26 (36%) reported sexual experimentation, 21 (29%) reported experimenting with their sexual orientation, 18 (25%) reported experimenting with their age, and 17 (24%) reported experimenting with a different race. See Fig. 11.6 for a summary of these results.

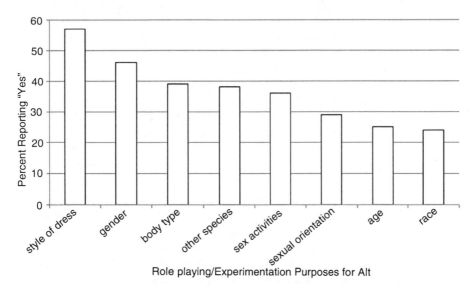

Fig. 11.6 Types of role-playing and/or experimentation purposes for alt identities. Seventy-two participants cited role playing/experimenting with a different identity as one of their motivations for using an alt. (Participants were able to select more than one option)

11.4   Discussion

11.4.1   Major Findings

In the area of physical characteristics, the results supported the findings of Ducheneaut et al. (2009) and the 2007 Global Market Insight survey cited in Au (2007) that individuals tend to construct primary avatars that are younger and have a smaller/leaner body type than their physical selves. Moreover, the same pattern was found in examining the relationship between the physical self and the alt. Thus, overall, participants' virtual representations more closely approximate the lean, youthful body ideal found in many contemporary cultures than their physical selves. Given the consistency of this pattern across multiple studies, the tendency of individuals to express a more idealised physical appearance in the 3D domain can be considered a reliable, established finding.

Also within the area of physical characteristics, the study found a number of interesting differences in gender characteristics across the various identities. As presented in Table 11.2, the study found a gender difference between the physical self and the primary avatar that was due in part to a segment of physically male participants (5 out of 46, 11%) functioning as females in the virtual world. In addition, this tendency for physically male participants to vary their gender characteristics in the virtual world was even more pronounced with regard to alts, with over one-third of male participants

(16 of 46) employing female alts. It is also noteworthy that 11% of male participants changed their gender status in the virtual world by employing a non-gendered (i.e. animal, mythic, or object) primary avatar and 9% used a non-gendered alt.

The tendency toward gender experimentation was far less common among participants who were physically female. Not a single participant who was physically female had a primary avatar that was male, and only one had a non-gendered primary avatar. However, a meaningful number of physically female participants did employ a male alt (8 out of 57, 14%) or a non-gendered alt (4%).

Overall the findings on gender characteristics across the constituent identities indicate that (1) there is a greater level of gender experimentation by physical males in the virtual world compared to physical females and (2) this difference is most pronounced with regard to the gender characteristics of the primary avatar and somewhat less so with regard to the alt. One possible motivation for the subgroup of males to employ female avatars and/or alts is to take advantage of the fact that virtual females receive more assistance, freebies, and handouts than male avatars (Lee and Hoadley 2007). Other motives that might apply to both physical males and females would be to use a gender-discrepant avatar or alt to surreptitiously participate in sex with same sex physical life partner, or to psychologically explore the feelings and experience of being a different gender. Additional research will be needed to precisely identity the underlying motivation or motivations accounting for cross-identity gender experimentation in general, why this tendency is greater among physical males than physical females, and why physical females tend to concentrate their gender experimentation almost exclusively with their alts.

With respect to the data on virtual world activity preferences, an interesting difference was found between the preferred activities of the primary avatar and the alt. Specifically, the primary avatar indicated significantly higher preferences for activities that reflect the practical, functional, or business-related aspects of virtual life (e.g., building, buying/selling, scripting, shopping, working/employment, etc.) However, in areas of relationships, sexuality, and activities related to identity experimentation such as role-playing, the activity preferences of the alt and the primary avatar were equivalent. One way to interpret these data is that the primary avatar plays a dominant role in carrying out activities related to what Mark Childs (see Chapter 2, this volume) referred as the "persistent" identity in the virtual world – those activities that build and maintain stable connections to other avatars and the virtual community (Jackobsson 2002). However, when the human driver wants to go outside of the stable, persistent aspects of his or her virtual identity, the alt assumes a role that is equally important as the primary avatar.

In the domain of personality and social-emotional characteristics, the tendency toward idealization observed in the comparisons of physical characteristics, was found once again. Consistent with previous research by Bessiere et al. (2007) and Ducheneaut et al. (2009), participants ascribed more positive or idealised personality traits to their avatars. On the Big Five Personality Inventory participants rated their primary avatars as more extraverted, agreeable, conscientious, open, and less neurotic than their physical selves. In addition, the current study found that participants also viewed their primary avatar as more socially connected and more satisfied with life than their physical selves. It is interesting to note, however, that the tendency toward personality idealisation in the virtual realm was centred on the primary avatar and did not extend to the alt. As with the physical self, the primary avatar was viewed to have more positive personality characteristics than the alt and there were far fewer differences in the personality ratings for the physical self and the alt. At this point, one can only speculate as to why the primary avatar, and not the alt, is the main focus of psychological idealisation in the virtual realm. Based on the previously discussed findings on the activity preferences of the primary avatar and alt, it may be that alts are viewed in a less positive or idealised manner because they are more frequently employed in activities such as role play, identity experimentation, and forms of sexual expression that the physical self might be uncomfortable with, or able to do, outside of the virtual realm. However, this is an area that needs additional study to more fully understand the relationship between the personality characteristics of the physical self, primary avatar, and alt.

The current study also extended past research by acquiring data on the use of alts, the motivations for alt usage, and the types of role-playing or identity experimentation that involve alts. With respect to the use of alts, the current study is embedded within a wider program of research on the psychology of 3D virtual worlds being conducted by The P.R.O.S.E. (Psychological Research on Synthetic Environments) Project (www.proseproject.info). In the context of this broader research, it has been determined that approximately 50% of Second Life users with 6 months or more inworld have an alt. Consequently, dividing the percentages of participants in the current study of 104 Second Life users (all of whom have alts) by 2, yields the following estimates of alt usage among the overall user base of Second Life: Participants with 1 alt (17.5%), 2 alts (14%), 3 alts (6.5%), 4 alts (2%), 5 alts (10%). Thus, while the current sample focused on participants' use of a single alt and personality systems composed of three identities, about a third of experienced Second Life users are coordinating a multiple personality order consisting of a physical self plus three or more virtual identities.

The findings on motivations for alt use and identity experimentation involving alts will be considered in the following section on the operation and dynamics of multiple personality orders. As we will see, the alt carries out a number of important functions within the multi-realm identity system.

As a final note regarding these major findings, the primary purpose of the current study was to provide detailed descriptive data on the relationship between characteristics of constituent offline and online identities. At the same time, the current data set, and others like it that may be collected in the future, could also be used to investigate a host of more specific and theoretically driven relationships such as: Is there a relationship between personality characteristics like neuroticism and wider discrepancies between the physical and inworld identities? Similarly, is there a relationship between emotional variables such as social connectedness and the separation of identities in which people who feel less connected in their physical lives are more likely to create avatars that diverge from their physical selves? More fine-grained cross-category analyses like these will serve to build upon the detailed descriptive data provided in the current report.

11.4.2   The Operation of Multiple Personality Orders

Thus far we have viewed the data with a close lens, focusing on the ways that physical characteristics, activity preferences, personality features, and social-emotional processes are similar or different across various combinations of the physical self, the primary avatar, and the sole or most frequently used alt. However, it is also possible to step back from these comparisons and consider the different functions of the various components within the overall multiple identity system and how they may relate to each other. As depicted in Fig. 11.7, the current findings suggest that the primary avatar and the alt each have three distinct functions and one common function within the multiple personality order.

The first function of the primary avatar, as previously discussed, is to reflect a stable or "persistent" identity within the virtual world, to build and maintain stable connections to other avatars and the virtual community as a whole. A second function is to extend the physical self into the 3D virtual arena. As the data on virtual world activity preferences indicate, the human driver is more likely to use the primary avatar when engaged in virtual activities such as working/employment and learning/ education that have physical world correlations and may directly relate to activities that he or she is engaged in within the physical world. Another central function of the primary avatar is to enhance the physical self within the virtual arena by embodying a more youthful and attractive physical appearance and by reflecting more positive personality, social, and emotional characteristics. This view is consistent with statements expressed by McKenna et al. (2001) and Taylor (2002), and developed by Childs in this volume, that individuals in virtual worlds are able to express their truer, hidden, more authentic and ideal selves, or, what can be summarily termed, their "aspirational selves." The current data indicate that the tendency to enhance

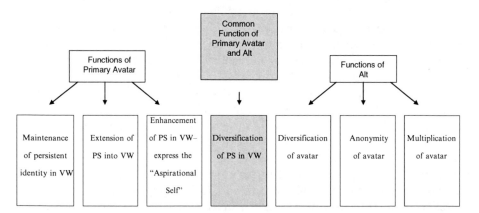

Fig. 11.7 Multiple personality order: The functions of primary avatars and alts relative to the physical self (PS) and to each other. VW = Virtual world

the appearance and psychology of the physical self in the virtual realm is mainly carried out by the primary avatar.

Finally, in a function that overlaps with that of the alt, the primary avatar may be involved in diversifying the human driver's physical world identity within the virtual realm by adopting a different gender, race, or age – a process termed "identity tourism" by Taylor (2002). However, the primary avatar's freedom to engage in identity tourism may be constrained by its concurrent responsibility to maintain a stable, persistent identity in the virtual world, as showing up 1 day as a man and the next day as a woman, or shifting races on a frequent basis, can have a disruptive effect on the avatar's social relationships and business or practical activities. One way to deal with the primary avatar's conflicting functions of identity stability and identity variability is to assign the more dramatic practices of identity experimentation to the alt within the identity system, consistent with this study's findings in the area of gender experimentation. In this way, the alt functions to vary or diversify the identity characteristics beyond *both* the physical self and the primary avatar. Of course, in cases where multiple alts are being employed, each subsequent alt has the same diversification function toward earlier or previously constructed alts as the initial alt has toward the primary avatar.

One of the remaining two functions of alts is to achieve anonymity within the virtual world. The primary avatar, while carrying out the more instrumental and persistent elements of virtual life, has less freedom to move through the virtual world privately. Usually an avatar's virtual friends are notified when the avatar first comes inworld or logs off, and the friends can also check the avatar's on or offline status at any time. They can also send an inworld instant message (IM) or place an inworld call to the avatar at any time. To enhance privacy, avatars have the ability to set their status to "busy" (which will prevent inworld calls from going through and store IMs for later viewing) or periodically change their account preferences so that friends are not notified when they log in or out. However, even taking these steps doesn't ensure complete anonymity as anyone the primary avatar encounters is still able to view their virtual profile and learn identifying details such as their length of residence in Second Life, group affiliations, favourite destinations and residents and, if applicable, the name of their partner. Thus, the only sure way for a virtual world user to be inworld with complete anonymity is to create an alt that his or her friends are unaware of. This practice is reflected in the number of participant's who cited motivations for using an alt related to privacy considerations including: the ability to be inworld without being recognised (72%), spying on a romantic partner (17%), or cheating on a romantic partner (13%).

Finally, alts can function to multiply the human driver's virtual presence for pragmatic purposes. Because the primary avatar and an alt can be inworld simultaneously (if either two computers are used or one computer is enabled to run two Second Life viewers at the same time), the alt can assist the primary avatar in performing tasks that are more easily accomplished by a dyad. For example, approximately half of the sample indicated that they used their alt to help their primary avatar test a product or an animation that that is intended for use by two avatars, such as a dance or sexual animation for a couple. While it was not assessed in the current study, the Second

Life knowledge-base assessable through the company website (www.secondlife. com) also notes that concurrently logging in as one's primary avatar and an alt can simplify the process of sharing inventory (virtual assets such as clothes, objects, snapshots, etc.) across virtual identities.

11.5   Conclusion: Toward a New Phase of Human Identity?

Moving the lens back a final step, we can consider the broadest implications of the self being composed of multiple offline and inworld identities. It is possible that, rather than merely being an interesting process associated with avatars and 3D virtual worlds, it may reflect the beginning of a new phase in the history of human identity.

In the latter half of the twentieth century dramatic advances in transportation and telecommunications turned the world into a global village where individuals were constantly exposed to new perspectives, narratives, styles, and psychological realities. In this context, modernist conceptions of the self, such as the classic models of Freud (1953) and Erikson (1950), came under attack by post-modern theorists who argued that there is no stable, consistent, coherent, individual identity (Gergen 1991; Lifton 1993). Instead they maintained that identity is fragmented, multiple, and constantly shifting (what can be called, "The Multiple Self"). Like a Windows program, to echo a metaphor introduced by Turkle (1995), the post-modern self is conceived as an operating system that can maximise or minimise multiple aspects of identity according to shifting personal desires and the demands of a particular context.

The rise of 3D virtual worlds, and the introduction of avatar-mediated forms of expression and interaction, may once again reshape humanity's conception and experience of the self and usher in new model of identity that we will tentatively label "The Distributed Self." In this conception, consciousness and aspects of the self (while ultimately still embodied within the human driver) will be increasingly externalised and distributed into digital forms reflecting any number or combination of race, gender, age, style, body type, personality, and physical health. Whereas the Windows operating system serves as the technological analogue to the post-modern conception of The Multiple Self, the rise of "cloud computing" (i.e., the storage of resources in the Internet that are available for distribution on demand to multiple platforms or devices) forms the technical basis for a new distributed conception of identity and the self. Within this new model, the source of identity remains internal and embodied (in the "cloud" of consciousness), but the expression or enactment of this consciousness becomes increasingly external, disembodied, and distributed.

As 3D virtual worlds and the global population of avatars continue to grow, creating and coordinating a system of multiple offline and online identities will increasingly become a normative process in human development. Individuals will manage their multiple personality orders in a manner analogous to a choreographer managing a company of dancers, or a conductor leading an orchestra, and the operation of personality will increasingly take on, as Goffman (1959) once suggested, a quality of performance art.

Acknowledgments Portions of this project were funded by the Bellarmine College of Liberal Arts, the College of Science and Engineering, and the Office of Research and Graduate Studies at Loyola Marymount University, as well as a private donation by Edward D. Holly.

Portions of this data were presented at the 2010 Summit of the Immersive Education Initiative, Boston, MA.

References

Amdahl, K.: Secrecy, identity, truth and lies [Web log message]. http://kateamdahl.livejournal. com/7276.html (2006)

Au, W.J.: Surveying Second Life [Web log message] (2007). http://nwn.blogs.com/nwn/2007/04/ second_life_dem.html. Retrieved 30 Apr 2007

Bessiere, K., Seay, A.F., Kiesler, S.: The ideal self: identity exploration in world of WarCraft. Cyberpsychol. Behav. **10**, 530–535 (2007)

Camigliano, A.J.: Günter Wallraff: b(e)aring the facts. Monatshefte **75**, 405–418 (1983)

De Pauw, L.G.: Women in combat: the revolutionary war experience. Armed Forces Soc. **7**, 209–226 (1981)

Diener, E., Emmons, R.A., Larsen, R.J., Griffin, S.: The satisfaction with life scale. J. Pers. Assess. **49**, 71–75 (1985)

Driver, E., Driver, S.: The immersive internet: make tactical moves today for strategic advantage tomorrow. Think Balm. Immersive Internet Analyst Report Series, 1 (2008). http://www.thinkbalm. com/wp-content/uploads/2008/11/thinkbalm-immersive-internet-report-nov-20084.pdf

Ducheneaut, N., Wen, M., Yee, N., Wadley, G.: Body and mind: a study of avatar personalization in three virtual worlds. In: Proceedings of CHI, Boston, 4–9 Apr (2009)

Ehrenreich, B.: Nickel and Dimed: On (Not) Getting by in America. Metropolitan Books, New York (2001)

Ellison, N., Heino, R., Gibbs, J.: Managing impressions online: self-presentation processes in the online dating environment. J. Comput. Mediated Commun. **11**, 415–441 (2006)

Erikson, E.: Childhood and Society. W.W. Norton, New York (1950). Revised paperback edition, 1963

Foss, J., Gilbert, R.: Alt Usage Questionnaire. Unpublished instrument. Available from the Psychological Research on Synthetic Environments (P.R.O.S.E.) Project, c/o Dr. Richard Gilbert, Loyola Marymount University, Los Angeles (2009)

Freud, S.: A General Introduction to Psychoanalysis (J. Riviere, Trans.). Perma Books, New York (1953). Original work published in 1935

Gergen, K.: The Saturated Self: Dilemmas of Identity in Contemporary Life. Basic Books, New York (1991)

Goffman, E.: The Presentation of Self in Everyday Life. Penguin, London (1959)

Goleman, D.: Cyberdisinhibition (2006). http://www.edge.org/q2006/q06_5.html#goleman

Gosling, S.D., Gaddis, S., Vazire, S.: Personality impressions based on Facebook profiles. In: Proceedings of the International Conference on Weblogs and Social Media, March 2006, Boulder (2007)

Griffin, J.H.: Black Like Me. Houghton Mifflin, Boston (1961)

Jackobsson, M.: Rest in peace, Bill the Bot: death and life in virtual worlds. In: Schroeder, R. (ed.) The Social Life of Avatars, pp. 63–76. Springer, London (2002)

John, O.P., Donahue, E.M., Kentle, R.L.: The Big Five Inventory–Versions 4a and 5b. University of California/Institute of Personality and Social Research, Berkeley (1991)

Lee, J.J., Hoadley, C. M.: Leveraging identity to make learning fun: Possible selves and experiential learning in massively multiplayer online games (MMOGs). Innovate, August/September, **3**(6), (2007) [Online]. Available: http://innovateonline.info/index.php?view=article&id=348

Lee, R.M., Robbins, S.B.: Social connectedness, dysfunctional interpersonal behaviours, and psychological distress: testing a mediator model. J. Couns. Psychol. **48**, 310–318 (2001)

Lifton, R.: The Protean Self: Human Resilience in an Age of Fragmentation. Basic Books, New York (1993)

Linden, M.: Key economic metrics through January 2008 [Web log message]. http://blogs. secondlife.com/community/features/blog/authors/Meta.Linden. Retrieved 22 Feb 2008

Marcus, B., Machilek, F., Schütz, A.: Personality in cyberspace: personal websites as media for personality expressions and impressions. J. Pers. Soc. Psychol. **90**, 1014–1031 (2006)

Market, T.: Limited psychographic segments and media consumption (Q1 2009) (2009). http:// sl.markettruths.com/

McKenna, K., Bargh, J.A.: Coming out in the age of the internet: identity "de-marginalization" through virtual group participation. J. Pers. Soc. Psychol. **75**, 681–694 (1998)

McKenna, K., Bargh, J.A.: Causes and consequences of social interaction on the Internet: a conceptual framework. Media Psychol. **1**, 249–269 (2000)

McKenna, K.Y.A., Green, A.S., Smith, P.K.: Demarginalizing the sexual self. J. Sex Res. **38**, 302–311 (2001)

Papacharissi, Z.: The self online: the utility of personal homepages. J. Broadcast. Electron. Media **46**, 346–368 (2002)

Peachey, A.: Living in immaterial worlds: who are we when we learn and teach in virtual worlds? In: Sheehy, K., Ferguson, R., Clough, G. (eds.) Virtual Worlds: Controversies at the Frontier of Education. Nova Science, New York (2010)

Ranon, N.: Young women's use of the internet to explore secret identities. Disser. Abstr. Int. Sci. Eng. **67**, 3498 (2006)

Royster, P.: The life and surprising adventures of Mary Ann Talbot in the name of John Taylor (1809). http://digitalcommons.unl.edu/libraryscience/32/. Retrieved May 2006

Second Life Herald: Wooot! 100K dormant alts. http://alphavilleherald.com/2005/12/wooot_100k_ dorm.html. Retrieved Dec 2005

Spurlock, M.: (Producer) Living on minimum wage [Television series episode]. In: 30 Days. FX Network (2005)

Steinhauer, J.: Woman who posed as boy testifies in case that ended in suicide of 13-year-old. New York Times. http://www.nytimes.com. Retrieved 20 Nov 2008

Stone, B., Richtel, M.: The hand that controls the sock puppet could get slapped. New York Times. http://www.nytimes.com. Retrieved 16 Jul 2007

Suler, J.: The online disinhibition effect. CyberPsychology Behav. **7**, 321–326 (2004)

Taylor, T.L.: Living digitally: embodiment in virtual worlds. In: Schroeder, R. (ed.) The Social Life of Avatars, pp. 40–62. Springer, London (2002)

Turkle, S.: Life on the Screen: Identity in the Age of the Internet. Touchstone Press, New York (1995)

Wallace, P., J. Maryott.: The impact of avatar self-representation on collaboration in virtual worlds. Innovate **5**(5), (2009). http://www.innovateonline.info/index.php?view=article&id=689

Young, K.: Internet addiction: the emergence of a new clinical disorder. CyberPsychology Behav. **1**, 237–244 (1998)

Chapter 12
Comparing Avatar and Video Representations

Ralph Schroeder

Abstract The key to collaboration and enjoyment in virtual worlds is interpersonal interaction, which in turn depends to a large extent on bodily representations of users – or their avatar appearance. Videoconferencing is also becoming more popular, and people also increasingly represent themselves online via photographs on social networking sites. Thus we confront a world in which avatar and photo-realistic (video) identities present a fundamental choice for users in mediated interactions. What difference does it make whether a person is represented by an avatar – as against a video-realistic presentation – of themselves? And what are the implications for how people interact with each other in spaces for collaboration, learning, socialising and play? This chapter examines the range of avatar representations and representations in video-mediated communication and discusses the various findings related to both. It also draws out the implications of video-realistic versus computer-generated user representations for the future of mediated interaction.

12.1 Introduction

In this chapter, I will compare how people interact in virtual environments, where they are represented by computer-generated avatars, as against when they interact via videoconferencing, where they interact as captured by cameras. The more conventional contrast is to compare avatar interaction with face-to-face interaction, and I will also make this comparison here. But the contrast between avatars and video

R. Schroeder (✉)
Oxford Internet Institute, University of Oxford, Oxford, OX1 3JS, UK
e-mail: ralph.schroeder@oii.ox.ac.uk

A. Peachey and M. Childs (eds.), *Reinventing Ourselves: Contemporary Concepts of Identity in Virtual Worlds*, Springer Series in Immersive Environments,
DOI 10.1007/978-0-85729-361-9_12, © Springer-Verlag London Limited 2011

representations, I will argue, is just as instructive. What is more, I shall argue that these two are the major options for the future of mediated communication, so that their possibilities and constraints deserve close analysis.

What difference does it make whether a person is represented by an avatar – as against a video-realistic presentation of themselves? And what are the implications for how people interact with each other in spaces for collaboration, learning, socialising and play? The other contributions to this volume examine virtual worlds, large-scale online spaces for socialising such as Second Life™ that are populated by avatars. In this chapter, I shall take a broader view – analysing avatar and video-realistic representations of people as they might occur in any system or for any uses: on personal computers, mobile devices, or immersive Cave-type virtual reality systems – and for uses such as online games, social networking sites, distributed conferences and distance learning. These distinctions may or may not remain so distinct in the future. Yet my argument is that the two forms of self-representation – avatar and video – can be found in all of these devices (and again, apart from mixes of the two, these are the only two options). Further, different possibilities and constraints apply to each and, despite limited research on how people interact via these self-representations, it is possible to make some fundamental comparisons between them which will apply across the different settings.

Before setting out on the comparison, multi-user virtual environments (MUVEs) can be defined as technologies for 'being there together', or having a sense of being in a place other than the one that you are actually in, interacting with that place, and being there and interacting with another person (Schroeder 2011, p 5). No definition of video representations is needed for our purposes – except to say that the key difference is that users are captured by cameras rather than being computer-generated.

12.2   Two Directions: Virtual Versus Video

Research on virtual environments, avatars and virtual worlds has received a lot of attention in recent years. Yet it is curious that much less research has been devoted to technologies like videoconferencing, even though cheap means to communicate via video – such as Skype – have become widespread. This is possibly to do with the fact that virtual environments have often been developed in an academic context or because they are accessible to researchers. Videoconferencing system on the other hand, especially of the high-end or expensive variety, have not generally been available to researchers. Similarly, more accessible forms of videoconferencing, like Skype, are perhaps too new to have been subject to research. This is true even though videoconferencing prototype systems have been available for several decades.

While there is little research directly comparing the two (Sallnas (2002) is an exception), much can be learned from comparing findings from the two separate research areas. Both these two forms of mediated interaction, with full computer-generated or video-captured body representations, will become much more widely used in the years to come. As this chapter will show, there are also non-obvious implications in making this comparison. To give just two examples (described in Schroeder (2011)); although it has often been suggested that avatar representations allow people to create new identities (Turkle 1995), what in fact often happens – for example in 3D graphical virtual environments that use text-communication – is that people reveal themselves more thoroughly via text to strangers, even if this takes longer than in first encounters with face-to-face appearances (chiming well with Walther's (1996) concept of 'hyperpersonal relationships'). That is to say, in the absence of full life-like self-representations, in MUVEs people can put a lot into representing themselves faithfully or in more depth to others – for example, by describing themselves in words.

On the other hand, while technology developers often argue that videoconferencing has not taken off because of a lack of high-quality images and sound, in fact one study (Kirk et al. 2010) has shown that regular users of Skype are hardly concerned with visual fidelity since they are mainly interested in emotional co-presence with distant others. They studied 17 participants in 12 households who used video-mediated communication regularly (at least three video calls per month) and found a variety of motivations for this mode of communication. Examples include grandparents seeing grandchildren and long-distance couples who live far apart from each other. Interestingly, in the former group, video quality hardly matters, and in the latter group, sometimes the audio is switched off. Instead, it is the sense of visual togetherness that is most important. In other words, video togetherness can take different forms which do not necessarily depend on visual fidelity. Put the other way around, systems with a high degree of visual realism are not necessary for many purposes.

While 3D environments thus allow users to interact in some ways in a more true-to-life way (getting to know each other more 'authentically' via text), users of visually realistic environments (Skype) sometimes ignore realism and value emotional connection more highly than being able to see the other person 'live'.

We therefore have a paradox: what video conferences are best at (realistic user representations) is not important for some users, whereas a sense of copresence is. What avatar mediated communication is poor at – emotional richness – can be technologically and socially enhanced. As technologies like Microsoft's Kinect (http://en.wikipedia.org/wiki/Kinect) are beginning to implement agents that respond in emotionally powerful ways, the picture becomes even more complex, since such agents will be hard to distinguish from real users in some situations.

How is this related to virtual worlds? The key to collaboration and enjoyment in virtual worlds are interpersonal relationships, which in turn depend on bodily–especially facial – representations of users (since voice is the same as in face-to-face interaction, and text interaction relies even more on what the user 'puts into' self-presentation than in face-to-face interaction). People's interactions in virtual worlds will thus be strongly tied to their avatar appearance, and they will often choose an avatar appearance related to a particular type of interaction, even if they also choose a representation that relates to physical appearance (see, for example, Vasalou et al. (2008)). At the same time, apart from the growth of video conferencing, people are also increasingly representing themselves online via photographic still or moving images, for example on social networking sites or video blogs on sites like YouTube.

Thus we confront a world in which avatar and photo-realistic (video) representations present a fundamental choice for users in mediated interactions. In virtual worlds, users' avatar representations need to be persistent (so that people can recognise each other over time), distinctive (so that avatars can tell each other apart in larger groups or meetings), and expressive (to enhance rich interaction and communication). As avatars become more photo-realistic, however, the line between avatar and video representations will become increasingly blurred. Apart from the intrinsic interest in comparing video and virtual self-representations, there are therefore bound to be implications of photo-realistic representations for virtual worlds in the future.

Before we turn to the comparison, however, we can ask: What accounts for the disparity between the extensive research on interaction in Multi-user Virtual Environments (MUVEs), as against the scarcity of research on Video-mediated Communication (VMC)? And along similar lines, we can ask: What accounts for the disparity in the uptake of the two technologies – since MUVEs in the form of virtual worlds have had at least hundreds of thousands of users for some years now (or millions, if we count online games), whereas videoconferencing has only very recently become widely used (though there are, to my knowledge, no systematic statistics on videoconferencing uses)?

These disparities cannot be due to technological maturity, since videophones (or 'picturephones', as they were known) have been around for far longer than virtual environments. Nor can the disparity be attributed to cost, since both are now available in the form of cheap off-the-shelf technologies and require only an internet connection. What about 'uses and gratifications' (McQuail 1987, pp 233–237), or how useful these two modalities are to people? This theory might go some way towards an explanation, since it could be argued that people often prefer a communications medium with fewer social cues. Perhaps people prefer for voice-only or text-only or avatar-only communication over voice plus video-representations? Yet both video and avatar representations of people and their environment make these media 'richer', so 'uses and gratifications' only provides a negative explanation: fewer social cues is often preferable.

Hence it is necessary to move beyond technology diffusion as well as media and communications theories in examining the difference between them. The differences in the amount of research devoted to both can partly be explained in relation to research opportunities. Research on high-end videoconferencing systems, as mentioned, has been confined to companies (Hirsh et al. 2005; see also the contributions in Finn et al. (1997)), while research on off-the-shelf (Skype) videoconferencing is too recent for all but initial studies (Kirk et al. 2010). Expense used to be a factor in the uptake of videoconferencing systems (and it still is for high-end systems), while nowadays the lack of a network effect (whereby additional users make the technology more valuable; as with the telephone – the more people have one, the more useful it becomes) accounts for a lack of uptake.

Thus videoconferencing has not been adopted widely even though the technology has been available for decades. On the one hand, people don't feel the need to see each other to communicate, and on the other, there is what can in shorthand terms be called the 'I'm having a bad hair day' problem, which is that we don't like to be seen in certain circumstances. Put in sociological terminology, audio-only or text-only communication means that we do not need our visual 'frontstage' – discussed below – for self-presentation.

For user uptake (or the failure of user uptake) of MUVEs, on the other hand, we can note first the popularity of online gaming as against the weak uptake of virtual worlds such as Second Life and its predecessors and current rivals (Spence 2008). This can be explained by the lack of sustained sociable and exciting activities in online social spaces. Online games, on the other hand, are quite restricted in terms of what people can do with each other compared with online social spaces or worlds (Schroeder 2011 esp. pp 141–175). This is a point we will come back to in the discussion of virtual worlds. In any event, what we see in the case of both media is that users have not yet settled on the most appropriate uses of the technology.

One further point to add in relation to both technologies is that they do not scale easily in terms of the number of participants in interpersonal encounters. Group sizes beyond a handful are hard to cope with, and this is not so much to do with technology limitations (though in videoconferences it is currently difficult to connect more participants), but rather with the medium: it is simply difficult to interact with more than a few avatars or video-represented people at any one time – unlike in a face-to-face (F2F) setting where it is possible to interact with many other people.

Finally, online virtual spaces are useful when there are spatial rather than facial interactions. This will change with technologies for capturing and displaying gaze, but it currently applies both to small group interaction (which allows co-visualisation of space) and persistent online settlements for larger groups. Video interactions lack the spatial component, but niches for when visual closeness is useful for meetings and contact will proliferate, not least driven by the increasing environmental costs of travel and by mobile telephony which includes video images. Therefore it is not so much the communication differences, but facial versus spatial togetherness – quite different in their respective affordances for interaction – that require more research that goes beyond the 'richness' or otherwise of the two media. Research so far has revealed that online spaces and faces fulfil quite different needs, though this has been shown to date only in studies isolating aspects of the two phenomena, and not through systematic comparison. Against this background it will be useful to examine people's representations first, and in the section thereafter compare how people interact in the two modalities.

12.3 Comparing Representations

Even in the absence of research – and especially comparative research – there are many comparisons that can be made, albeit speculatively, about the differences between video and avatar forms of representation in interactions. For example, if we assume that only the person is represented, without the background in which they

Table 12.1 Key characteristics of avatar versus video-mediated interaction

	Video	Avatar
Representation	True to life	Constructed, but can approach realism
Body capabilities	Limited to physical ones	'Super powers'
Environment apart from person representation	Typically limited to context of head and shoulders, i.e. table and room	From room-size spaces to vast interconnected worlds
Interpersonal interaction	Focus on facial expressions	Focus on spatial encounters with bodies
Number of participants	Two - to small groups	Two - to large populations (though still focused on the group)
Advantage	Few concerns about deception	Plasticity of self-presentation
Disadvantage	Concerns about one's appearance (can be avoided with picture-in-picture)	Inability to come across as oneself

are located, and if we assume in the first instance that these person representations are static, then the following differences can be highlighted (see also Table 12.1):

- Faces or head-and-shoulders tend to be used in video, whereas full bodies tend to be the default for avatars.
- Video (or photo-realistic static representations) will force users to be themselves, whereas avatar representations, no matter how realistic, will leave people wondering whether the representations of the other are 'real' or manipulated in some way. This fundamental difference arises simply by virtue of the technology: in videoconferences, people are captured with a camera, while as avatars, they are 'constructed' (even if, say, their expressions are captured by tracking sensors, and if a photorealistic image is constructed that includes inputs from these sensors).

An objection to the second point will be that the two technologies will increasingly overlap. Yet we can also think of the distinction between them from a user point of view: a user will simply react differently to the representation of another person depending on whether their image has been captured by a camera or if it has been generated by a computer. Another factor influencing the difference in interaction between the two settings that can be mentioned in passing is simply the size of the person in a virtual world against a person in a videoconference: both could be small on a desktop screen, or both could be life-size on a larger screen or in a full-size 3D environment.

For this background- or environment-less setting then, we can compare a realistic camera captured person versus an avatar. Now an initial inclination might be to say that an advantage of (especially highly realistic) videoconferencing is that participants feel that no deception is possible. However, it is more complicated than that: anecdotally, when people explain why they need to be at important meetings in person rather than via videoconferencing, they say that they feel that they might be missing important cues of face-to-face interaction and they miss the atmosphere and trust of F2F meetings (Hirsh et al. 2005). Trust is not an issue in the same way in MUVEs or virtual worlds (Schroeder 2011, pp 158–168).

If we now add the environment to the representation of the person, the following differences arise:

- For videoconferences, the environment will typically be irrelevant since the point of these conferences is to talk to people and to have an image of them in order to add expressiveness. Thinking through the exceptions here, these also involve special cases of environments where there is a need to show a remote object or an image of a remote place.
- For MUVEs, environment-less settings will be rare (training in interpersonal encounters that require only head and shoulders, and the like), whereas environments that are navigable and extensive will be useful for spatial tasks. A good way to make this point the other way around is to note that the settings that are video-conference-like in MUVEs – people sitting still concentrating on interpersonal communication tasks – have been highly unsuccessful in MUVEs: why should avatars sit still, on chairs, talking to each other around the table, in a MUVE?

12.4 Comparing Interactions

Against this background, it will be useful give concrete examples that illustrate the difference that appearance makes to interaction. In virtual environments, for example, it is possible for avatars to walk through each other. To illustrate this point, we can can take the case of highly immersive environments such as Immersive Projection Technology or Cave-type systems, virtual reality systems in which the environment is projected onto several walls and the user wears stereoscopic glasses and typically holds a 3D tracked wand to interact with the environment – for example using the wand to 'fly' or pick up objects. Here it has been found that full-size avatars sometimes unselfconsciously walk through each other. At other times, however, this causes embarrassment: people will say 'Ooops, excuse me' and they jump back when they accidentally bump into each other (see Schroeder (2011) for documentation of these examples). This is also a common experience in desktop online virtual worlds: sometimes avatars will pass through other's bodies, whereas on other occasions, touching another person's avatar will be treated as a source of amusement or result in people commenting on this breach of physical world conventions. It is useful to think here of offline differences in cultural conventions around body space: English people, for example, are thought to be unusually protective of intrusions into their 'body space', whereas many other cultures are much more relaxed about such 'invasions' (see also Becker and Mark (2002) for these conventions in virtual worlds; Friedman et al. (2007) and Smith et al. (2002) for studies of interpersonal distance in virtual worlds).

What about videoconferencing bodies? To my knowledge, this has not been studied. It is a safe bet to assume, however, that people will treat their bodies much more like physical ones and thus be much more protective of their body space. There is some indirect evidence from experiments with interpersonal distance in MUVEs (see Blascovich 2002), where higher degrees of realism caused avatars to 'respect' interpersonal distance more. Put the other way around, video representations will be subject to much greater adherence to physical world conventions – even though technically, bodies in both settings can walk through each other or 'invade' each other's body space – unlike in F2F settings.

An observation that goes in the other direction is that people find it difficult to treat each other as anything but physical. For example, in an Immersive Projection Technology setting, people will lean towards the other person in order to hear them (even when there is no spatialised sound!), or (in the case where they only have one tracked joystick!), they will use the untracked arm to point things out to the person they share the environment with – even though neither of these behaviours makes sense (Schroeder 2011). Moreover, this kind of behaviour has been found to continue for hours – which goes against the idea that people might learn and avoid these 'mistakes' over time.

Realistic representations in videoconferencing have not been studied in the same way, though a number of early studies addressed issues such as screen size or how people are best placed in relation to each other in conversations involving more than two persons (Finn et al. 1997; Van der Kleij et al. 2005; Vertegaal 1998). What is more important in video settings is turn-taking, and we can now move to this topic.

As a number of studies have shown (Finn et al. 1997), for both types of video-conferencing, the main obstacle to smooth turn-taking is not so much video quality but rather audio quality. Stops and starts in replying to each other are an important part of conversational turn-taking, and this has long been identified as a key problem in videoconferencing systems. In high-end videoconferencing, the smoothness of the interaction is evident in turn-taking because of the technical improvements that have been made in audio quality and 3D audio. Turn-taking is still difficult in videoconferencing via low-end Skype systems and the like where there is a lag of some milliseconds and the cues for turn-taking are missing. Still, even in poor-quality videoconferencing in two-person mode, people can become habituated to this lag. In a high-end videoconferencing system, however, this problem has become almost unnoticeable and more than two people can take turns fluidly. One indication that a point of technological saturation is approaching in high-end videoconferencing systems is that the high visual fidelity of these systems almost makes participants seem "hyperrealistic" (that is, so realistic that they seem too real).

In avatar-mediated communication, turn-taking is difficult primarily because of gaze or if partners in a joint spatial task don't know which object is being referenced via gaze (Heldal et al. 2005; Hindmarsh et al. 2002). In text-mediated interaction in virtual worlds, on the other hand, it may be difficult to know who is speaking and to follow the thread of conversations. Hence it is interesting to compare text versus voice in virtual worlds (Wadley et al. 2009; Williams et al. 2007), because voice, for example, is best for rapid coordination (but it is difficult for more than a few people to speak simultaneously), whereas text may be better for following threads and orderly turn-taking.

As already mentioned in relation to MUVEs, in videoconferencing there is also a maximum number of people that can participate effectively in 'being there together' for a meeting. In both videoconferencing and MUVE settings this is to do with the fact that it is difficult to pay attention to or keep track of many people simultaneously. A further similarity is that larger meetings are much more difficult to manage, and this true of work meetings via videoconferencing just as it is for classes in desktop virtual worlds like Second Life. Visually and socially, there is an upper limit in the number of people (perhaps between five and ten) who can actively participate (as opposed to being passive audiences) in a meeting, and high-end videoconferencing and MUVE meetings are both limited to this number. It should be noted again that this is not a technical limit – there is no technical reason why dozens or more people should not be displayed in a videoconference or MUVE settings. The limits are rather those of visual and social attention that can be paid to others in a mediated as opposed to face-to-face setting. While it is true that there are also limits to visual and social attention in face-to-face settings, these are prima facie different from the limits of virtual worlds: think of the number of people you can pay attention to in a crowded room or in a stadium filled with people – and now think of the same situations in a virtual world.

MUVEs have advantages here, such as that this limit of attention can be expanded by means of giving them 'artificial' features to allow people to focus attention on them – such as highlighting who is speaking, or arranging avatars so they are easily viewable. One thing that nevertheless happens as the number of participants increases is that these settings become like one-way 'broadcasts' (think here of teaching a large group in Second Life). This, incidentally, is part of the reason why it becomes worth considering in these large settings whether a simple PowerPoint presentation with voice – without embodiments of the lecturer or the student – wouldn't be more useful: what do bodies add in this case?

In any event, in small groups in MUVEs, a common focus of attention needs to be maintained, the flow of the interaction needs to be kept going, and the absence of attention of any one participant is noticed (if we consider that active participants are annoyed and distracted if other participants' attention is noticeably preoccupied elsewhere, as with videoconferences). In larger groups, participants still congregate to face each other – so they form small clusters and these can be treated like small-group conferencing. Yet as we move away from smaller groups to larger ones, the requirements shift from supporting turn-taking and a common focus of attention to the rules and conventions governing social behaviour that apply to the populations of large online spaces.

In videoconferencing, a popular technology that addresses the problem of many simultaneous users are Access Grids, which allow a number of head-and-shoulders video images (or images of several people in a room) to be arranged on a wall (Fielding and McIntyre 2006). Unlike in videoconferencing, there is no attempt to create the space of a conference room where people face each other, but all participants are visible to each other in close-to-life size format. Webcams can be seen as a lesser version of Access Grids where participants are displayed in small windows and not all participants may be visible to each other. Yet Access Grids and webcams, like videoconferencing generally, often entail confusion about what is going on at other sites, and questions are often raised such as "how many sites or faces are supposed to be participating?", "are others supposed to have joined the meeting but cannot due to technical difficulties?" or "what is going on in the background outside the field of view?"

12.5   Uses of Videoconferencing

People do not just use videoconferencing for work meetings, but also use various kinds of video-mediated communication (VMC) for non-work purposes. As Kirk et al. (2010) point out, with inexpensive tools like webcams and Internet-based video telephony (such as Skype), VMC is poised to become routinely used in everyday life. Videoconferences, not MUVEs, which reduce the need for travel and yet approximate face-to-face meetings, are likely to be by far the most widespread *workaday* use technologies for 'being there together' at a distance. Unless MUVEs provide realistic capture of people's facial expressions in a setting in which these expressions can be conveyed adequately, MUVEs will not succeed in replacing face-to-face meetings.

This point can be put the other way around: There are many technologies for 'being there together' where facial expressions are *not* critical and other features – interactions with other bodies and spaces in VEs, interacting with large numbers of people, having a sense of other people's online availability, and cases where non-realistic self-presentations are appropriate. Nevertheless, this point highlights again that spatial and facial interactions are useful in quite different ways.

Videoconferencing is typically used for social interaction that is intensely interpersonal – needing to 'read' the other person's intentions and being able to get them to 'read' yours in meetings are of the utmost importance. This 'mutual reading' is something that co-located people can do easily. Further, it is something that we are used to achieving with other forms of mediated communication like telephones, when no visual channels are involved.

Thus there are two directions in videoconferencing: high-end videoconferencing for formal meetings, and ad hoc videoconferencing for informal purposes in the home. The former are structured and need to get something accomplished, hence the frustration when the meetings are poorly structured after much effort was made to set up, go to, and attend such a videoconference – which does not apply in the same way to face-to-face meetings. The latter are suited for people who know each other well, for flexible encounters, and where the quality may not matter since the point is more a kind of visual togetherness or co-presence.

It is also interesting to note why certain technology combinations do not work, such as video heads on cartoon bodies, for example, even though this is a low-tech solution that is easy to implement. Still, with this combination there is a lack of reciprocity or a disconnect between heads and bodies (it will be hard to interact with a head that does not seem to belong to its body). So although this solution will be implemented where this disconnect does not matter (it is easy to envisage certain scenarios for co-design or co-inspection of a space), this combination will not suit scenarios where heads, bodies, and spaces need to be connected in a natural or seamless way.

A point that goes in the opposite direction is that technologists typically want to make videoconferencing like face-to-face, but this may not the best way forward. For example, people might want to know what they appear like, and having a window with your own appearance in a videoconference ('picture in picture') is highly 'unrealistic' and unlike face-to-face interaction (how often do people talk to others while needing a mirror of their own appearance!) On the other hand, it is understandably an important support for 'being there together' in a videoconference – despite the fact that one could also say that there is a 'disconnect' in this case. A similar feature in MUVEs such as Second Life is that there is a 'bird's eye' or 'third person' view on one's avatar, which is useful not so much for checking on one's appearance, but for locating oneself in the space and in relation to others. Again, this may not be a realistic mode of interacting, but it can very useful

In MUVEs, the major shortcoming is that facial expressions are often static, missing, or unrealistic. This can be put in perspective by noting that social cues (or the absence thereof) are in a sense overrated: After all, we use email and telephones on a daily basis and compensate for the absence of facial expressions. And avatar interactions can in a similar way be seen as (social cue-less) text- or voice conversations (depending on which modality is used). Still, there is a bias in our perception of communications media toward regarding face-to-face communication or interaction as the gold standard, and this prevents us from recognising that we engage without problems in various forms of distributed collaboration or socialising.

It is thus worth stressing that technical improvements are not the main issue for videoconferencing or in MUVEs, even though technologists insist that they are. Instead, making the systems fit for the purpose – which may involve less technology or lower quality or non-naturalistic or non-realistic technologies and environments – is more important from the user's point of view.

12.6 Uses of Virtual Worlds

Before we turn to online virtual spaces, it is worth noticing for the purpose the topic of this chapter that – unless we stretch the definition beyond recognition – there are no 'video *worlds*' or 'video online *spaces* for gaming and socialising'! We can think of counter-examples only if we stretch the definition of interacting in another space very far, so that Facebook or Videoblogging or Webcam uses become 'spaces' for real-time interaction. Apart from these technologies which use video representations, we can therefore focus the discussion on virtual online spaces or worlds with avatar representations. Even these virtual spaces come in many varieties, though it will be useful to restrict the discussion for the moment to persistent online virtual spaces with large populations – for which the label 'virtual worlds' is best suited.

The main distinction among virtual worlds is between online spaces for gaming that require adopting a game-defined character and pursuing game-defined objectives – as against online spaces for socialising that involve open-ended interaction in the manner of a 'third place' (Steinkuehler and Williams 2006). In both, the emphasis is on the interaction between avatar bodies and less on the experience of interaction with other people's facial expressions. The main difference between online socialising as against online gaming is function: Socialising involves 'free' interaction, interacting for a variety of purposes (conversation, building together, exploring places, and the like), whereas gaming entails adopting a particular character and pursuing the game (collecting points, undertaking defined tasks, coordinating with others in the pursuit of quests, and the like) The two are not mutually exclusive; indeed one study has shown that game players engage in more social activity as they become longer-term users (Axelsson and Regan 2006).

Online gaming interaction is constrained by its rules and by being organised around highly structured environments – for example, in socialising according to guilds and quest groups, partitions of the environment into different worlds (player versus player, player versus environment, different regions, and the like), the definition of characters by roles, and the tasks for achieving levels. Interaction in online spaces is typically via text, though some virtual worlds and MUVEs also have voice. And in online spaces, the environments (buildings, landscape) provide a context, whereas in videoconferencing the environment plays little role – and can be a distraction. The 'free' socialising that takes place in (non-gaming) online spaces takes a variety of forms and is governed by the social norms appropriate to these spaces (Becker and Mark 2002; Schroeder 2011, pp 141–175). For the sake of the comparison with videoconferencing, the key point is that these spatial environments provide a context for a host of learning and playful activities that would be out of place in the context of videoconferencing (we can think here of the examples of worlds where learning to build with objects or showing each other around in spaces is central to the task).

12.7 Multimodal Online Relationships

Having argued that MUVEs (including virtual worlds) and videoconferencing are analytically distinct, they may nevertheless come to be blurred in practice, as people maintain a variety of relationships via various online tools. So, for example, Baym (2010) describes how people maintain relationships via social networking sites such as Facebook or music fan sites in order to stay connected with friends and larger groups of like-minded people. Here, the interaction is mostly asynchronous, but with more of these technologies becoming added, it will become difficult to distinguish between virtual worlds and 'always on' (Baron 2008) technologies. Where should one draw the line, for example, between a webcam on a social networking site or a video blog when they are used to interact with other people, as against MUVEs? One's availability or self-presentation can be expressed across several devices (a status update icon on a mobile phone, a webcam on a social networking site, or a still photograph in Internet telephony). Thus, the mechanism for representing oneself – whether by means of an avatar body, a photograph, a geo-location indicator, or simply having the device switched on to signal availability – can be transferred across devices and thus make up a single representation. And voice, text, and video- or computer-generated representations and spaces may travel with the user rather than being fixed to the physical location of the device.

As we increasingly move online, there will be growing engagement with both video-captured persons and with avatars. And as the spaces that include these representations of others become more common, they will provide a familiar and popular context for interacting with others. In this sense, the shift to 'being there together' via a variety of online representations is becoming a preferred 'media-rich' mode of communication. At the same time, in certain circumstances users may prefer a mode of 'communication' (in the broader sense just mentioned) without online representations or via media that are less rich. Here we need to bear in mind, as mentioned earlier, that fewer social cues or less media richness does not necessarily mean that people do not have a rich sense of the other person. As Walther (1996) has argued, in computer-mediated communication where social cues are minimal, such as text-only collaboration, people make more of an effort to represent themselves in words; they put more into constructing or controlling the way they represent and communicate themselves and may in this way, in fact, reveal more about themselves (Walther calls these "hyperpersonal" relationships). This may take longer than in richer media, but it can also mean that people get to know each other better than in face-to-face interaction or in rich-media interaction.

In the context of how we represent ourselves to each other in larger online spaces, it is worth remembering that there may be a requirement for consistent self-representation (where avatars need to recognise each other by appearance, or if one needs to find the same person via a profile on a social networking site). In other situations where one is known offline to others, such as social networking sites or a personal web page, a continual modification of one's self-representation may be the appropriate norm to keep others interested or engaged (Lenhart and Madden 2007).

In the larger online world, consistency may also have a broader significance, not just in terms of a consistent representation of oneself, but also being consistently represented as being available or aware of others in the same space: The online world, like virtual spaces for socialising and gaming, is very large – but unlike online spaces for gaming and socialising, it is not one space or world but many. Thus, it may be important to know which online space the other person is available in, or whether they are available in several? The same applies to availability generally: Where are others available? And again, are they available in multiple online spaces? Online populations must be distributed in a consistent way across different worlds or spaces so that people and groups know where and when they can find each other (and people will, of course, want to be unavailable in some spaces and worlds). On the other hand, despite being vast, our engagement with others or with our networks only consists of a few people in terms of routine interaction and engagement.

12.8 Roles and Stages

These ideas about having a consistent self-representation online bring us to the larger context of how our self-representation is shaped by the context of mediated interactions. There are powerful theories in social science about how micro- social interaction works (Turner 2002) – at least in face-to-face interaction. These theories posit that the self is shaped by the other in interaction. The unit, in other words, is the interaction or the encounter (to use Goffman's terminology) rather than the individual self, and in these encounters people develop roles in relation to each other (as described in the introduction to this volume). Again, in physical life encounters, how the self is shaped by encounters with others is well-known. In VMC and MUVEs, however, interaction and roles are shaped by technology and thus by the mechanisms of mediated (micro-) social interaction, and this is far less well theorised.

In video settings, the assumption is that you present yourself as yourself as in physical life. But this is only partly true. Mediated communication always involves a staging of the self – we can think here of how there are norms for self presentation in telephone or mobile conversations (Fischer 1992; Ling 2008). For videoconferences, similarly, there are constraints: you cannot but be represented as you are, but there also Goffmanian possibilities for staging yourself (see also Hogan (2010) for such online 'performance' in social networking sites). Both are different from physical life – think of how you are presented in a highly artificial way in videoconferencing: not in a natural context, and in 2D, and only via vision and audio – and in terms of the ritualised setting of meetings and other typical situations when videoconferencing is used.

Similarly, the constraints with MUVES are video and text/voice, and the situations too are highly staged and artificial. As we have seen, this involves a 'staging' of the self and the development of roles in a Goffmanian sense in online spaces as well as in fully immersive environments. So in both cases, there is no (full, realistic) embodiment, but nor can we narrate or construct our selves as we like in either case. Rather, these are two quite different forms of mediated selves, each with quite different non-realistic but also not-completely made up forms of interacting and communicating.

In one sense then, it is possible to compare 'roles' in video- and virtual. In another sense, 'roles' in the everyday sense of the word are only played in games where you take on a character (which has not been addressed here except in passing). In yet another – Goffmanian – sense, it is only possible to play or adopt or put forward a role in the virtual since, in video, there is no 'role distance'. It is not possible to engage in self-presentation in video except within very narrow bounds, such as perhaps being able to choose the camera angle, or moving partly out of the frame, or ensuring a well-kempt appearance and the like. Note, however, that even if self-presentation can be powerfully manipulated in virtual environments, there are constraints here too: technical, insofar as avatars have different constraints in different systems (fully-tracked body or not, or restricted to changing certain parts of appearance and not others – and even in this case, there are the constraints of the graphics available) as well as social (not just that, in practice, users choose avatars not too distant from their physical appearance, but also that they must be recognisable as persons and have a degree of consistency in their representation for the sake of ongoing interaction and many other conventions).

On the other hand, it is easy to understand that avatars have much scope for Goffmanian backstages: they can present themselves as one thing, but do something else behind the screen. Note again, however, that there are limits: it is difficult to maintain a persona other than who you are in a consistent way over time. Note also that there are also 'backstages' in videoconferences: people can excuse themselves to leave the videoconferencing room or switch off the webcam, or they can move outside of the frame, so that unlike in a face-to-face setting, their communication partner will not know what the person at the other end is up to. Apart from this, however, videoconferences have no 'backstage', and so also no 'front stage' that can easily be manipulated. Now think of avatar interaction: avatars can remove themselves from the interaction (teleport), or manipulate their appearance. At the same time, they are constrained by being constantly under surveillance since their movements and whereabouts are being tracked and possibly recorded. Still, this difference (being able to stage the self more in avatar condition), apart from the differences in technology and in the different uses of the technology that have been discussed, is perhaps the main difference from the user's point of view between the interaction in the two systems. Further, these differences are not due to the representations of users in the two types of systems per se, but to the *context* of these user representations.

12.9 Conclusions

This chapter has compared video and avatar representations in terms of how these affect people's mediated interactions. Systems using both these types of representations have been developed to a technically high standard, even if there is room for improvement. And both MUVEs and videoconferences are bound to become more widely used because time, money and environmental reasons dictate less travel, and because certain things can be done well in shared and distributed spaces.

Again, the two types of systems will technologically converge and become more powerful. For example, in immersive virtual environments, even with highly realistic computer-generated representations of fully tracked bodies, the key obstacles to rich interaction are realistic facial expressions, and especially eye movement. Gaze and other eye movements are crucial, among other things, for trust, deception, turn-taking and object-focused collaboration. These eye movements, however, are increasingly being implemented in virtual environments so that avatars can interact as well as (for example, in relation to lying and deception; see Steptoe et al. 2010) people do via videoconferencing. Or again, as we have seen, one of the major requirements for fidelity of expression and awareness in small groups is to support turn-taking. Thus for small groups, the expressiveness of avatar faces and bodies (nonverbal communication) has been a major research agenda within videoconferencing and MUVE research (Garau 2006; Vinayagamoorthy 2006).

In any event, regardless of technological improvements, and even if avatars become more 'photo-realistic', the two types of systems and self-representations will continue to be used in divergent ways. I have tried to show that there are fundamental differences in how people interact in the two settings as well as in the possibilities and constraints they face with the two kinds of representations. Apart from converging and improving technologically, these two options also afford people with different choices about what they can do with each other in settings for 'being there together'. When we consider settings such as distributed teaching and learning, socialising, and other applications of these two technologies, the choice between them will remain fundamental, not just technologically, but above all socially.

References

Axelsson, A.-S., Regan, T.: Playing online. In: Vorderer, P., Bryant, J. (eds.) Playing Video Games: Motives, Responses, Consequences, pp. 291–306. Lawrence Erlbaum, Mahwah (2006)

Baron, N.: Always On: Language in an Online and Mobile World. Oxford University Press, New York/Oxford (2008)

Baym, N.: Personal Connections in the Digital Age. Polity Press, Cambridge (2010)

Becker, B., Mark, G.: Social conventions in computer-mediated communication: a comparison of three online shared virtual environments. In: Schroeder, R. (ed.) The Social Life of Avatars: Presence and Interaction in Shared Virtual Environments, pp. 19–39. Springer, London (2002)

Blascovich, J.: Social influence within immersive virtual environments. In: Schroeder, R. (ed.) The Social Life of Avatars: Presence and Interaction in Shared Virtual Environments, pp. 127–145. Springer, London (2002)

Fielding, N., Macintyre, M.: Access grid nodes in field research. Sociol. Res. Online. **11**(2) (2006). www.socresonline.org.uk/11/2/fielding.html

Finn, K., Sellen, A., Wilbur, S. (eds.): Video-Mediated Communication. Lawrence Erlbaum, Mahwah (1997)

Fischer, C.: America Calling: A Social History of the Telephone to 1940. University of California Press, Berkeley (1992)

Friedman, D., Steed, A., Slater, M.: Spatial behaviour in second life. In: Pelachaud, C. (ed.) Intelligent Virtual Agents, pp. 252–263. Springer, New York (2007)

Garau, M.: Selective fidelity: investigating priorities for the creation of expressive avatars. In: Schroeder, R., Axelsson, A.-S. (eds.) Avatars at Work and Play: Collaboration and Interaction in Shared Virtual Environments, pp. 17–38. Springer, London (2006)

Heldal, I., Steed, S., Spante, M., Schroeder, R., Bengtsson, S., Partanen, M.: Successes and failures in co-present situations. Presence J. Teleop. Virt. Environ. **14**(5), 563–579 (2005)

Hindmarsh, J., Fraser, M., Heath, C., Benford, S.: Virtually missing the point: configuring CVEs for object-focused interaction. In: Churchill, E., Snowdon, D., Munro, A. (eds.) Collaborative Virtual Environments: Digital Places and Spaces for Interaction, pp. 115–139. Springer, London (2002)

Hirsh, S., Sellen, A., Brokopp, N.: Why HP people do and don't use videoconferencing systems. Technical Report HPL-2004-140R1, Hewlett-Packard Laboratories, Bristol (2005). http://www.hpl.hp.com/research/mmsl/publications/bristol.html

Hogan, B.: The presentation of self in the age of social media: distinguishing performances and exhibitions online. Bull. Sci. Technol. Soc. **30**(6), 377–386 (2010)

Kirk, D., Sellen, A., Cao, X.: Home video communication: mediating closeness. Forthcoming in Proceedings of CSCW, pp.135–144 (2010)

Lenhart, A., Madden. M.: Social networking and teens: an overview. Pew Internet and American Life Project. http://www.pewinternet.org/PPF/r/198/report_display.asp (2007)

Ling, R.: New Tech, New Ties: How Mobile Technology is Reshaping Social Cohesion. MIT Press, Cambridge (2008)

McQuail, D.: Mass Communication Theory, 2nd edn. Sage, London (1987)

Sallnas, E.-L.: Collaboration in multi-modal virtual worlds: comparing touch and text and voice and video. In: Schroeder, R. (ed.) The Social Life of Avatars: Presence and Interaction in Shared Virtual Environments, pp. 172–187. Springer, London (2002)

Schroeder, R.: Being There Together: Social Interaction in Virtual Environments. Oxford University Press, New York/Oxford (2011)

Smith, M., Farnham, S., Drucker, S.: The social life of small graphical chat spaces. In: Schroeder, R. (ed.) The Social Life of Avatars: Presence and Interaction in Shared Virtual Environments, pp. 205–220. Springer, London (2002)

Spence, J.: Demographics of virtual worlds. J. Virtual Worlds Res. 1(2) (2008). http://www.jvwresearch.org/v1n2.html

Steinkuehler, C., Williams, D.: Where everybody knows your (screen) name: online games as 'Third Places'. J. Comput. Mediat. Commun. 11(4) (2006). http://jcmc.indiana.edu/vol11l/issue4/steinkuehler.html

Steptoe, W., Steed, A., Rovira, A., Rae, J.: Lie tracking: social presence, truth and deception in avatar-mediated telecommunication. In: Proceedings of CHI 2010, Atlanta, Apr (2010)

Turkle, S.: Life on the Screen. Simon & Schuster, New York (1995)

Turner, J.: Face to Face: Toward a Sociological Theory of Interpersonal Behaviour. Stanford University Press, Stanford (2002)

Van der Kleij, R., Paashuis, R.M., Schraagen, J.M.C.: On the passage of time: temporal differences in video-mediated and face-to-face interaction. Int. J. Hum. Comput. Stud. 62, 521–542 (2005)

Vasalou, A., Joinson, A., Bänziger, T., Goldie, P., Pitt, J.: Avatars in social media: balancing accuracy, playfulness and embodied messages. Int. J. Hum. Comput. Stud. 66(11), 801–811 (2008)

Vertegaal, R.: Look who's talking to whom: mediating joint attention in multiparty communication and collaboration. Ph.D. Thesis, Cognitive Ergonomics Department, University of Twente (1998)

Vinayagamoorthy, V.: User responses to virtual humans in immersive virtual environments. PhD. thesis, Department of Computer Science, University College London, London (2006)

Wadley, G., Gibbs, M., Ducheneaut, N.: You can be too rich: mediated communication in a virtual world. In: Proceedings of OzChi 2009 (no page numbers), Melbourne (2009)

Walther, J.: Computer-mediated communication: impersonal, interpersonal, and hypersonal interaction. Commun. Res. 23, 3–43 (1996)

Williams, D., Caplan, S., Xiong, L.: Can you hear me now? The impact of voice in an online gaming community. Hum. Commun. Res. 33, 427–449 (2007)

Chapter 13
What Is My Avatar? Who Is My Avatar? The Avatar as a Device to Achieve a Goal: Perceptions and Implications

Marc Conrad, Alec Charles, and Jo Neale

Abstract This paper examines how senses of online identity may converge with, and diverge from, those of offline identity through a case study of the intentions behind, and interpretations of, avatar use within the virtual environment of Second Life™ among a group of UK university students. In exploring the participants' rationales for their choices of avatar names and avatar appearances, the study witnesses ongoing shifts in notions of selfhood (and the conditions and strategies by which selfhood is determined), which may reflect theoretical projections as to the redefinition of paradigms of subjectivity fostered by the incremental virtualisation of societal experience.

13.1 Introduction

This chapter explores how a group of university students use, shape, respond to and interpret the functions of their avatars within a virtual learning scenario. It explores the extent to which these students view themselves within their avatars, on functional, representational, reflective, symbolic and fantastical levels, and suggests that these different views of the relationship between the original self and its online presence in the form of an avatar may result in different modes of influence by the process of avatar use upon the user's sense of self and integrity of self.

Cyberoptimists, as they are sometimes called, tend to suppose that new media information and communications technologies offer a panacea for all of the ills of

M. Conrad (✉) • A. Charles
Department of Creative Arts, Technology and Science,
University of Bedfordshire, Bedford, UK
e-mail: Marc.Conrad@beds.ac.uk

J. Neale
Institute of Applied Social Research, University of Bedfordshire, Bedford, UK

A. Peachey and M. Childs (eds.), *Reinventing Ourselves: Contemporary Concepts of Identity in Virtual Worlds*, Springer Series in Immersive Environments,
DOI 10.1007/978-0-85729-361-9_13, © Springer-Verlag London Limited 2011

the world and thus usher in an electronic Utopia of democratic, economic and educational freedoms and rights on a global scale – advancing a "link between utopian visions and technological development [that] has been called technotopia" (Storsul and Stuedahl 2007, p 10) or "a New Alexandria" (Koskinen 2007, p 117) – "a new Museion of Alexandria open to the world" (Tiffin and Rajasingham 2003, p 26). Cyberpessimists, by contrast, tend to suppose that George Orwell was right that we are increasingly living in a surveillance society, a hegemonic and homogeneous realm, a media dictatorship of totalising ideologies and corporate hyperpower. The latter have, for example, noted that research into habitual Internet use has suggested that online activities are altering not only the functioning of society and our notions of self but also the very structures of the human brain. Indeed as Gary Small, a researcher into this field at UCLA, told *The Guardian* newspaper on 20 August 2010, "the Internet lures us. Our brains become addicted to it. And we have to be aware of that, and not let it control us."

The news media have been keen repeatedly to stress those cases when this apparent addiction to or dependence upon the World Wide Web has been taken to extremes. On 5 March 2010 *BBC News* reported the case of a South Korean couple who became so "addicted to the Internet" – so immersed specifically in the virtual world of an Internet role-playing game – that they "let their three-month-old baby starve to death while raising a virtual daughter online." This is an isolated incident, but it is not unique: we need look no further than the much-reported case of David Pollard (see, for example, de Bruxelles 2008) – who in 2008 left his physical world wife (whom he had also married in *Second Life*) for a woman he had first met in *Second Life*, and with whom (his wife alleged) he had committed acts of marital infidelity in *Second Life*, in order to marry his new partner both in *Second Life* and in physical life – to see that the ontological prioritisation of the virtual world is already, for some at least, a *fait accompli*.

The virtual realm of *Second Life* falls somewhere between a digital game and a world in itself: it is a simulacrum which some use for play, others for such activities as communication, socialisation, art, education and commerce. Launched by Linden Lab in 2003, it allows its users to escape the confines of the material world and of their corporeal and psychical selves. There is nothing unique in this: whether we subscribe to *World of Warcraft* or socialise on Facebook, it seems that physical reality is often no longer enough for us. Ours is a world in which technologies for the habitual augmentation of reality are now available in such convenient, pocket-sized devices as mobile telephones and handheld digital game systems. As Charlie Brooker pointed out in an article on the arrival of 'augmented reality' in *The Guardian* (18 January 2010), "the Nintendo DSI has a built-in camera with a 'fun mode' that can recognise the shape of a human face, and superimpose pig snouts or googly eyeballs and the like over your friends' visages when you point it at them." In an article for *The New York Times* (30 June 2010) David Colman quoted Bryan O'Neil Hughes, the product manager for Photoshop on the growing trend to augment one's own photographic image: "Everybody is suddenly representing themselves to the world this way, and you see people doing different things, just to make themselves look better or stand out – anything from mild retouching to putting themselves in pictures and making themselves look like paintings, and all that 'Avatar'-y sort of stuff."

New media technologies allow us to enhance our appearances, abilities and identities within the virtual worlds which we so frequently inhabit and which are assuming increasing (or even overwhelming) significance in our existences. As this augmented or virtualised reality takes precedence over the material realm, our online identities may become our primary selves: the selves, after all, through which many expend the greater part of their time in their professional, social and/or emotional lives. The user thus becomes her own avatar. On 12 January 2010 the *Daily Mail* reported what it called 'the Avatar effect' – an unforeseen response to James Cameron's computer-generated 3-D epic: "movie-goers feel depressed and even suicidal at not being able to visit utopian alien planet" – but the impact of this phenomenon is hardly limited to devotees of Cameron's film; it is perhaps a condition increasingly shared by all those (from the email addict to the *Halo* junkie) whose daily experience has been transformed by the proliferation of digital media technologies.

13.2   Societal and Epistemological Context

The attraction of a virtual existence – that is, not only an enhanced but specifically an artificial existence – seems almost irresistible. Jorge Luis Borges (1970, p 42) famously imagined the fantasy world of Tlön, a world conceived as a theoretical model by intellectuals, a virtual world whose structures come to overwhelm the physical world: "How could one do other than to submit to Tlön, to the minute and vast evidence of an orderly planet? It is useless to answer that reality is also orderly. Perhaps it is, but in accordance with divine laws – I translate: inhuman laws – which we never quite grasp. Tlön is surely a labyrinth, but it is a labyrinth devised by men, a labyrinth destined to be deciphered by men." There is clearly something very attractive about such an artificial world, and perhaps, as Borges suggests, the most attractive thing is its artificiality – a condition which allows for the possibility of its rationalisation. The psychical pull of the virtual world is evident, yet it remains unclear whether we can maintain the distinction between the temptingly virtual world and the daily burden of material reality, or whether, like David Pollard, like South Korea's Internet addicts and like those obsessive fans of James Cameron's *Avatar*, we might be losing our senses of proportion, ontological discrimination and critical detachment, and thereby entering into a fundamental existential disconnection between self and presence, a disconnection recognised by Albert Camus (1975, p 13) as definitively absurd insofar as that "divorce between man and his life [...] is properly the feeling of absurdity."

But to what extent might our subjectivity itself be translated into the existential idiom of the virtual world in which we are immersed? Sébastien Genvo (2009, p 135), in an essay on digital play, suggests that the video game player may be "engrossed in his game although he knows that after all it is only a game". King and Krzywinska (2006, p 198) argue that immersion in a virtual world would only result in the assumption of the subjectivity of a character within that world if that virtual reality were to become as convincingly naturalistic as the external lifeworld. One is reminded of Walter Benjamin's distinction between a critical immersion within culture and an uncritical absorption of culture (Benjamin 1992, p 232): that "a man who concentrates before a work of art is absorbed by it [but] the distracted mass absorb the work of art." For Benjamin, the former state of immersion permits the survival of an integral subjectivity – an essential selfhood and worldview (if such a pre-existent essence exists at all); the latter process incubates an ideological identity within the passive subject. This notion of the integrity of identity in the face of cultural or virtual immersion requires, however, the assumption of the existence of an a priori subjectivity – one founded upon the romantic or religious notion of an essence of selfhood (a spirit or soul replete with aesthetic or moral qualities) or upon the prioritisation of material experience as somehow more influential upon the propagation of subjectivity than digitally mediated experience (as though our physical interactions might for some reason mould our identities more forcefully than those hours spent in the virtual space of the electronic media).

Yet there is no essential difference between material and virtual experience: it is just that we tend to use the word 'virtual' in depicting forms of experience mediated by more recently evolved technologies, and that therefore different factors come into play in the mediation and negotiation of existence within those two areas of experience. We are defined by performance and play as much as by 'real life' activity – insofar as there is no difference between these phenomena, except one imposed by economically and ergonomically determined epistemologies. Jean-Paul Sartre (1969, p 59), in *Being and Nothingness*, famously described the way that a waiter in a café plays at being a waiter: "All his behaviour seems to us a game." Sartre's point is that it is such play or pretence which defines identity: existence precedes essence, the parts we play define our subjectivity – they are who we are (we do not exist qualitatively prior to experience and performance).

Slavoj Žižek (2008, p 83) also notes that pretence, performance or play has always generated 'real' subjectivities. When immersed in performative activity (as we always are) our suspension of disbelief creates an identity for which that belief is permanent and absolute:

> This other subject who fully believes need not exist for the belief to be operative [...]. From the so-called 'weepers', women hired to cry at funerals in 'primitive' societies [...] to the adoption of an avatar in cyberspace, the same sort of phenomenon is at work. When I construct a 'false' image of myself which stands for me in a virtual community in which I participate [...] the emotions I feel and 'feign' as part of my onscreen persona are not simply false. Although what I experience as my 'true self' does not feel them, they are none the less in a sense 'true'.

If there is no difference, then, between the ways in which material and digital experience construct subjectivity, should the notion of identity within the virtual realm in any way concern us? What is radically different about contemporary digital culture is its globally homogeneous nature, and (through the speed and seamlessness of its operation) the ease with which it disguises its ideological and economic construction. The virtual environment, like any mode of conventional realism, smoothes out the wrinkles in material reality, offering a realm whose continuity of logic makes more sense (and appears more realistic) than the incoherence of the material world. Like Borges's Tlön, its realism offers an immersion in the ultimate escapist fantasy – the fantasy of ontological logic – the dream that human existence may make rational sense. John Fiske (1987, p 24) has written that conventional realism "reproduces reality in such a form as to make it understandable. It does this primarily by ensuring that all links and relationships between its elements are clear and logical, that the narrative follows the basic laws of cause and effect, and that every element is there for the purpose of helping to make sense." Reality lacks this seamless and cosy continuity, one which makes things so understandable that we do not make the effort to understand them.

The ubiquity, homogeneity, seamlessness and rationality of the virtual environment are precisely the factors which may reduce its users' ability to resist its influences: it makes us feel safe (in as much as it is not real) and it therefore becomes the easiest reality to accept (it therefore becomes real). Its processes of mediation come to seem increasingly natural and incontrovertible. Bolter and Grusin (2000, p 24) have written of digital technology's "need to deny [its own] mediated character" through the promotion of the notion of a transparent or invisible interface. Our immersion in the digital experience allows us to deny or to ignore the fact that the experience is merely digital; and this denial – this sus-pension of our awareness and therefore of our disbelief – remains essential to the processes of immersion.

If the quality of authenticity and naturalness shifts from the province of the mate-rial to that of the digital, then this has an impact not only upon the world in which the self is immersed but also upon the self that is so immersed. Those whose pri-mary worlds are virtual will come to prioritise their virtual selves. Bolter and Grusin (2000, p 253) have thereby argued that "virtual reality will change our notion of self." They have suggested that "the virtual self seems to be defined precisely as a series of such empirical accessories that the individual puts on, just as she takes on characteristics in the game of Dungeons and Dragons" (Bolter and Grusin 2000, pp 247–248). If the virtual self, then, is determined by fundamentally different factors to those which define the offline self, and if the user's virtual self therefore radically diverges from their physical world identity, then is it not possible that the former might come to subsume the latter – inasmuch as the former appears so much more empowered and so much more attractive?

The virtual world sponsors an illusion of empowerment or agency which places the user at the centre of its universe – which thereby for the user becomes *the* uni-verse (or at least the user's universe – that which the user feels central to). This illu-sion is not immediately recognisable as such; from the user's perspective the virtual world's devices remain invisible. This illusion is central not only to the pleasure of the virtual realm but also to its purposes (to its uses, then, as well as to its gratifica-tions): in Louis Althusser's terms, it *interpellates* its users, recruiting them to its (ideological) perspectives through its seductive (and deceptive) promises of empow-erment (Althusser 2006: 117–118). Klimmt and Hartmann (2006, p 138) write:

> Players experience themselves as causal agents within the game environment [...]. Most games allow players to modify the game world substantially through only a few inputs. For example, in a combat game, players often need only a few mouseclicks to fire a powerful

weapon and cause spectacular destruction. The ability to cause such significant change in the game environment supports the perception of effectance, as players regard themselves as the most important (if not the only) causal agent in the environment.

Second Life allows its users precisely this sense of transformation and agency. It promotes itself as "a place to connect, a place to shop, a place to work, a place to love, a place to explore, a place to be." Through its communicational, economic and pseudo-geographic facilities, it offers its users the possibilities of emotional and existential fulfilment: the chance to love and to live. It specifically presents opportunities for its residents to "be different, be yourself, free yourself, free your mind, change your mind, change your look, love your look, love your life." The slogans for many such websites offer similar strategies of interpellation, strategies which recruit users to their perspectives through promises of empowerment. The multi-player first person shooter online game *America's Army* (a public relations and recruitment tool devised by the U.S. military) for example announces that it gives you the opportunity to "empower yourself" – while YouTube famously tells you to "broadcast yourself." But *Second Life*'s promotional copy here goes rather further: it suggests that its transformational process – which takes place at both a mental and a physical level – might allow one to develop a self-identity worthy of both love and life, insofar as one's offline identity might not, by implication, deserve such conditions of being.

Second Life, one might therefore say, promises the same kind of developmental and transformational experiences one might traditionally associate with liberal and progressive educational processes. There appear, however, to be several key differences between *Second Life* and the ideals of liberal education: while the former covertly determines its users' senses of selfhood through the impression of empowerment within an artificial environment, the latter seeks to empower its users' self-identities within (or towards) experiential reality through their independent and critical engagement with overt (and therefore refutable) processes of determination and guidance. The latter purports to move its users away from the limitations and influences of the simulation; the former maintains their dependence upon that simulation.

Despite these differences, *Second Life*'s transformational model and its prioritisation of the virtual (which might be seen to correspond to a focus upon the intellectual or the theoretical) and of technological innovation (and fashion) have clearly appealed to those involved in education: over 300 universities across the world are believed to use *Second Life* for the purposes of teaching, learning and research. Academia's interest in virtual worlds stretches back to well before the invention of *Second Life*. In the mid-1990s Tiffin and Rajasingham (1995, p 7), for example, hypothesised the development of online education systems, virtual classrooms that might one day represent "wrap-around environments for learning where students as telepresences can see, hear, touch and perhaps 1 day even smell and taste." Their enthusiasm for the potential of this mode of education places them firmly in the category of the cyberoptimists. They noted, for example, that "VR offers us the possibility of a class meeting in the Amazon Forest or on top of Mount Everest; it could allow us to expand our viewpoint to see the solar system operating like a game of marbles in front of us, or to shrink it so that we can walk through an atomic structure as though it was a sculpture in a park; we could enter a fictional virtual reality in the persona of a character in a play, or a non-fictional virtual reality to accompany a surgeon in an exploration at the micro-level of the human body" (Tiffin and Rajasingham 1995, p 7).

More recently – and again in the context of the uses of virtual reality in education – Tiffin and Rajasingham (2003, p 28) have imagined not only how such simulations might reflect and enhance perceived realities, but also how they might enhance one's self, or at least one's sense of one's self (that is, one's self-identity):

> One day, when wearable computers linked to transceivers develop to the point where they are part of the weft of the clothes we wear, we can imagine that our avatar in a virtual reality could look and act and even feel like a replica of our physical selves. We could in fact come to feel even better in virtual reality than in physical reality.

Tiffin and Rajasingham appear to see a number of possible functions of the avatar within their projected virtual classrooms in relation to the user's self-identity. The first of these functions are practical and have their own clear and conventional counterparts in the offline world: the facilitation and equalisation of communication and identification. Tiffin and Rajasingham (1995, p 6), for example, explain that "the idea of a virtual class is that everybody can talk and be heard and be identified, and everybody can see the same words, diagrams and pictures, at the same time." In other words, the primary and most necessary function of the virtual learning space is to replicate and indeed enhance the fundamental conditions of the physical classroom. Another key function of this virtual space is also to replicate the qualities of its subject – Tiffin and Rajasingham (2003, p 146) stress that the avatar may represent the physical appearance and reflects the emotional condition of its user: "the avatar could look like the person it represents and reflect their facial expressions." However, as Tiffin and Rajasingham (2003, p 30) also suggest, "for many students being in a university is an opportunity to experiment with their persona and appearance" – and the virtual classroom opens up innumerable possibilities for such experimentation. As such the avatar may also represent its users' desires for, or fantasies of, themselves, in terms both of physical appearance and of emotional symbolism: "it would also be possible to adjust the avatar cosmetically so that it looked more the way a person wanted to be seen or it could be anything at all" (Tiffin and Rajasingham 2003, p 146). Indeed, as Tiffin and Rajasingham (2003, p 30) emphasise, "avatars do not need to be replicas of the person using them. They can be changed to make a person look older or younger, male or female, black or white. It is possible to [...] have telepresence as a tiger or mouse, or as Attila or Cleopatra."

In their account of social interaction within virtual environments, Cheng et al. note that, while most participants in their study used their avatar "to convey something about their true identity" (Cheng et al. 2002, p 98), others deployed their avatars as expressions of their wish-fulfilment, representing themselves with images of "famous or attractive, sexy people" (Cheng et al. 2002, p 99). In their study of the uses and meanings of avatars in social media, Vasalou et al. (2008) also noted that, in choosing or constructing an avatar, users may select options most closely aligned to own perceptions of their own attributes, while often at the same time idealising their avatars by either concealing or emphasizing particular aspects of themselves. As Tiffin and Rajasingham suggested, the avatar can thereby express a user's desire for their appearance or identity. This dual phenomenon is, as we shall see, clearly witnessed within this study.

In his anthropological survey of *Second Life* Boellstorff (2008, p 120) observes the formation of "distinct identities in virtual worlds versus the actual world." He suggests that within the parameters of *Second Life* "one's self is open to greater self-fashioning and can be more assertive" (Boellstorff, 2008, p 121). One might argue however that the senses of safety and of empowerment generated by this virtual environment give the user an impression of autonomy that fails to register – and therefore to resist – the constraints and influences placed upon it, and that therefore the blurring of offline and online identities through what Boellstorff (2008, p 121) describes as a "permeable border between actual-world self and virtual-world self" might foster modes of offline being inconsistent with socio-political existence within the traditional paradigms of the material world. Boellstorff (2008, p 122) comments that a number of the *Second Life* residents within his study "spoke of their virtual-world self as 'closer' to their 'real' self than their actual-world self." If it is the case, as this suggests, that the virtual self becomes the user's primary benchmark of subjectivity, there might appear to be something increasingly problematic in this identity seepage between these two modes of being, and it might seem likely that this phenomenon may have a significant impact upon the prevalent conditions of human experience in both the physical and the virtual worlds.

13.3 Methodology

This chapter is based upon a user-group case study carried out in the context of an assignment for an undergraduate computing class at the University of Bedfordshire that ran from October 2009 to June 2010. Focused upon the principles of Project Management this class required student groups to implement and manage specific dedicated tasks. One of these tasks involved the production of a *Second Life* showcase about a topic related to their subject of study (such as Computer Science or Networking); this showcase comprised the construction of a building or other structure containing and displaying informational materials related to their own academic discipline. The rationale behind this mode of assignment based within *Second Life* is also discussed in Conrad et al. (2009). In addition to the Project Management activity 12 of the 40 students that participated in the study took an introductory class into Linden Scripting Language over the course of 4 weeks during November and December 2009; this also involved the use of *Second Life*. At the end of the assignment students were asked to complete an online questionnaire (see below) that aimed to elaborate their relationships to the avatars they had created.

A similar study was conducted the previous year with postgraduate computing students. The main focus of the earlier study (see Conrad et al. 2010) was upon quantitative data, and it quickly became clear that in order to achieve a sound understanding of the relationship users have to their avatars this quantitative data needed to be complemented with qualitative responses. The survey for this study was therefore specifically designed to address the students' reasons for, and feelings about, their choices and uses of avatars. The following qualitative questions were included in the questionnaire:

- Why did you choose this particular avatar?
- Why did you choose this particular first name?
- Why did you choose the particular last name of your avatar?
- How do you feel this avatar's name reflects you or your group?
- What do you think is the function of your avatar?
- How do you feel this avatar's appearance reflects you or your group?
- How do you feel about the look of your avatar?
- Why, in your opinion, does your avatar have a physical appearance?

For the purpose of future reference the full online questionnaire is available at http://perisic.com/whoismyavatar.

13.4   Demographics: Ethnicity, Age, Gender and Avatar Use

A total of 40 students participated in this study. It should be noted that while the ethnicities of these participants suggest a slightly greater degree of diversity than in the general UK population (see Table 13.1), their ages fall within a narrower range than the general population (see Table 13.2), as would be expected of a student body. As this study addresses the ongoing development of users of avatars within virtual space, the skewing of the age range towards a younger demographic should not necessarily be considered unrepresentative of the current generation of habitués of such environments. It may also be noted (as Table 13.3 demonstrates) that this study's participants were overwhelmingly male. This is perhaps an inevitable consequence of the study's focus specifically upon computing students. The advantage

Table 13.1 Ethnicity of respondents

Ethnicity	No. of responses	Percentage (%)
White	19	47.5
Black – African	7	17.5
Asian – Pakistan	4	10
Black – Caribbean	2	5
Asian – Indian	2	5
Chinese	1	2.5
Other	3	7.5
No response	2	5
Total	40	100

Age band	No. of responses	Percentage (%)
18–24	25	62.5
25–34	10	25
35–44	4	10
45–57	1	2.5
Total	40	100

Table 13.2 Age of respondents

Gender	No. of responses	Percentage (%)
Male	32	80
Female	7	17.5
No answer	1	2.5
Total	40	100

Table 13.3 Gender of respondents

of the focus on computing students is their expected familiarity with, and proximity to, the technologies and cultures addressed in this study (and therefore the possibility or at least the expectation that they might represent a vanguard in developing uses of, and attitudes towards, such technologies); the disadvantage is the gender imbalance thus encountered.

It may also be noted that of the 75 students who created avatars for this project only 40 (53.3%) volunteered to participate in this study. It may therefore be inferred that the participants were those who were more enthusiastic about (or indeed more cognitively involved in) their experiences in the virtual environment. Again, the advantage of this effect is that – although to some extent skewing the results – it focuses the study upon those users more likely to demonstrate progressive trends in the uptake of, and involvement in, these technologies.

13.5 The Avatars

13.5.1 The Human Form

Second Life offers its new users a selection of a dozen template avatars which may then be customised by those users. The mechanics of *Second Life* enable its users to craft their avatars into, or purchase, various forms. They can adopt human forms, or can become fantasy figures (such as fairies or vampires), animals like dogs, cats or tigers, or such mechanistic forms as robots. However, 37 out of 40 participants in this study stated that they chose human characteristics for their avatar. One of those who did not informed us that he had chosen to represent himself as a "giant robot" – apparently in keeping with the electronically mediated environment.

13.5.2   Gender Issues

The majority (89.7%) of the 39 participants who disclosed their gender used an avatar of their own gender. As detailed in Table 13.4, none of the male students reported that they had chosen a female avatar but two of the seven female students chose a male avatar. Within the context of the gender imbalance of this cohort, and within the context of gender-based power imbalances still prevalent in society at large, the fact that nearly a third of female participants chose a male avatar might suggest (though the sample is hardly statistically significant) an adoption of the strategies of fantasy empowerment or self-redefinition explored in Sect. 13.6.

13.5.3   Ethnicity

Tables 13.5 and 13.6 demonstrate that white participants typically selected template avatars with lighter skin tones, ranging from the clearly Caucasian avatars to those of greater racial ambiguity. All participants who registered black ethnicities chose

Table 13.4 Physical gender against avatar gender

	Female in physical life	Male in physical life
Female avatar	4	0
Male avatar	2	31
Not answered	1	1
Total	7	32

Table 13.5 Avatars chosen by male respondents in relation to user ethnicity

	White	Black – African	Black – Caribbean	Black – other	Asian – Indian	Asian – Chinese
[av6.png]	5					
[av5.png]	6				2	1
[av4.png]		5	1	1		
[av9.png]		1				
[av12.png]	3					

Table 13.6 Avatars chosen by female respondents in relation to user ethnicity

	White	Black – African	Asian – Pakistan
[av2.png]			1
[av3.png]	1		1
[av5.png]			1
[av4.png]		1	

the same (clearly black) avatar. Students of Asian ethnic backgrounds were more ambivalent in the ethnicity of their avatars: this may be because none of the avatars was clearly and exclusively Asian in appearance. Overall, participants tended to select ethnicities which, if not directly representing their own ethnic background, would not exclude that background. One might therefore suppose that while the avatar may be seen as extending and evolving the offline self, there may be resistance to the notion that the avatar might overtly negate that self.

It should be noted that *Second Life* regularly changes the selection of template avatars it makes available to new users. Youth is, however, a perennial feature of their selection. It may also be noted that the selection tends to feature a rather higher proportion of Caucasian faces than might reflect the global ethnic mix.

13.6 Interpretation and Contextualisation

13.6.1 The Name of the Avatar

When joining *Second Life* the user is asked at the very outset to create a first name for their avatar and then choose a second name from a pre-selected list of 40 available names. If, however, one's first name is as common as, say, John, one is told that "all the last names have been taken" for that particular given name and is asked to "try a different first name." The user is thereby given a very restricted sense of self-determination, of agency over what is traditionally considered the primary signifier of their identity; and yet within this highly limited – or indeed illusory – mode of agency, our survey revealed a range of very different reactions from its respondents.

As Table 13.7 demonstrates, when asked how they chose the first name of their avatar, 20 of the students surveyed responded that it was related to their own 'real' name – either wholly (in five cases) or partially (in 15). A further 17 participants stated that their choice of first name was not related to their own real names. It seems significant that those who chose a name identical or related to their own names are only slightly greater in number than those who chose unrelated names, and that only 13.5% of respondents used precisely their own names: the majority of users might thus appear to be distancing themselves from their avatars, either partially or wholly, and one might surmise that this is either because they are acknowledging the distance which already exists between the self and its avatar, or because they are aware that this distance is not so great, or is diminishing, or has the potential to diminish, and are therefore (in resisting that convergence) keen to emphasise (or extend or exaggerate) that distance.

Five participants specified in their accompanying comments that their avatar name was identical to the nickname they used online (in social networking and chat sites or online gaming). Two further participants said that their first name was chosen because it was their nickname (or closely related thereto), although it is unclear whether this referred to an online or offline name (although considering the currency of the term in computing parlance to signify an online pseudonym and the

Table 13.7 Choice of avatar name in relation to the real name

	No. of respondents	Percentage of respondents (%)
Avatar's first name is the same as respondent's real name	5	13.5
Avatar's first name is derived or related to my real name	15	40.5
Avatar's first name is unrelated to my real name	17	46

demographics of the test group the latter may be more likely). Only one user speci-fied that it was her nickname "in real life."

This is not insignificant. A nickname in the offline world is, like one's actual name, not, for the most part, something one has chosen for oneself: it is something which is conferred through familial and social relationships within the material world, one which may be (happily or grudgingly) accepted by the recipient and so, one may assume, reinforce, or coincide with, their self-identity. An online nickname is, con-versely, most often a name that the user has chosen for herself: it reflects how one sees oneself, or how one wants to be seen, rather than how one is born or how one is per-ceived (one's familial background or social status). The fact that more members of the group surveyed appeared to have chosen an online nickname than have chosen a nick-name taken from their offline lives suggests not only an increasing prioritisation of online identity, but also a reason for that prioritisation: the opportunity to style one's self (even one's own name) in the online world. Like Borges's Tlön, an invention (an invented name, an invented self, an invented world) is often more comfortable – because it is more comprehensible and more controllable – than the arbitrary condi-tions and contingencies of material reality. Anything is, after all, preferable to the real: as one respondent commented, he chose his avatar name simply because he "didn't want to use [his] real name." This apparent barrier against the blurring of offline and online environments and selves stresses the need for such a barrier and therein implies a resistance to the growing prioritisation of the virtual realm.

When it came to the selection of the avatar's second name two students were evidently affronted by the limitations put on their choices: one said he had not had "a lot of options" and another that he had had "no choice" – although, overall, this show of resistance to the way in which, from the very first, the *Second Life* system attempts to shape its users is perhaps slightly muted. Six students chose their name for positive aesthetic reasons – because it sounded funny or 'funky' or artistic – or just because it sounded good. Two gave what one might describe as a negative aes-thetic rationale for their choice of name: because they were the least 'weird' or 'horrible' possibilities – which again suggests some resistance to the limitations which *Second Life* places upon its users' capacity to determine their own identifica-tion and identity.

One participant said that she could not find "anything else suitable" and another that he chose the most "suitable" name on offer. While the former again implies some level of resistance to the process of name selection (that is, to the fact that this process was based on a structure of in-built pre-selection and therefore limited the possibilities of selection), both sought to discover suitability in their name, although it is ambiguous as to whether the name should prove suitable to their own self-identities or to external, social or situational acceptability. As such, it appears that both were engaged in a compromising and sense-making process, a process which attempted to reconcile their own perspectives with the paradigms of the virtual environment, rather than promoting the possibilities of resistance fostered by the tensions between those points of view. One student made this sense-making activity explicit, explaining that he chose his avatar's last name because it "was the only one that made sense." This desire to make sense of the world (or of any names or signifiers within the world: to find meanings or patterns or correlations within arbitrary signs) is complicit with the fundamental principles of the virtual world: the attraction of the virtual environment is that it offers to make more sense than the world offline. This is why in Borges's story the fantasy realm of Tlön becomes the model for the physical world: the map or simulation of the world may, in its design and artifice, make so much more sense than material reality that it may come, as Baudrillard (1994, p 1) suggests, to create the world in its own image: "the territory no longer precedes the map, nor does it survive it [...]. It is [...] the map that precedes the territory [...] that engenders the territory." The desire to make sense of the significatory practices and parameters of the virtual world implies an acceptance of that environment and its systems – not only because to make sense of something is to accept its existence, but insofar as the sense-making imperative is rooted within the original desire to build virtual worlds as more comprehensible, sensible, suitable places in which to live our lives.

We should note that eight of the students surveyed suggested that their *Second Life* second names were, at least in part, chosen completely randomly. There is perhaps a pragmatic materialism within their reasoning (or lack of reasoning) which resists the artificial nature – or which at least wishes to be seen to resist the artificial nature – of this virtual scenario. Others displayed a greater degree of inworld or task-based pragmatism about their choices: that is, they based their choices upon the requirements of their virtual environment or of their project. Seven chose their first names and four chose their second names because they considered them memorable, although it is unclear whether this memorability was merely a matter of convenience for the users (in order to enable them to recall their name more easily when logging on) or in their view conferred some level of empowerment (through recognisability) in social situations online. Two respondents specifically stated that they chose their name for the latter purpose: so that they would most easily be recognised when online.

Only three respondents – and this perhaps seems surprisingly few – suggested that they had chosen a name which described or represented themselves, metaphorically or metonymically. One suggested the name reflected his eccentricity; another that it reflected her character, sense of fun and sophistication; the third that it alluded to his and his friends' favourite hobby. In two cases the choice of name appeared to project ambition or desire; for one of these it simply recalled the name of a famous person, but for another it appeared to symbolise his own destined empowerment: it was chosen because he was "going to be successful in life" – because he "was born a leader." To Louis Althusser this might have appeared stereotypically symptomatic of the false sense of self-importance generated by what he called 'interpellation': the mode of disempowerment which undermines the possibilities of resistance or independence through an illusion of empowerment.

One respondent stated that he selected his avatar name "because of [his] identity." Another stated that he did not think that it represented "anything other" than himself in *Second Life*. These two perspectives represent diametrical opposites on the scale of acceptance and resistance, and on that of identification and functionality. The former respondent suggests a direct relationship between his avatar's name and his own identity, and appears to acknowledge the inevitability of that correlation or convergence; the latter implies that the only thing which the name represents is its user's functionality within the virtual environment. For the former, the name of the avatar equates with the user's identity in ways suggested by other respondents (those who connected their selection with their aesthetic tastes, personal characteristics, activities, aspirations or offline or online names); for the latter the avatar name is as arbitrary and as functional as for those respondents who specified no reasons for their choice other than the random and the pragmatic. And yet, we can also see in this pragmatism the very inverse of the sceptical materialism it implies: for, if this virtual environment remains a matter of arbitrary signification and of practical functionality, then does its condition not start thereby to converge with that of the physical world? Does not this pragmatism eventually reveal that the virtual and the physical may not be so different after all, suggesting that this act of virtual signification (this arbitrary naming within the logic of an imaginary environment) is not "anything other" because there is not anything other (because there is no more real or meaningful process anywhere)? This virtual environment is imbued with significance by virtue of the fact that we acknowledge it is as arbitrary (and as flawed and irrational) as the physical world while at the same time we understand it to be the product of intelligent design.

Names, like any signifier, hold no a priori or inherent meaning within themselves. Yet they become meaningful (or significant – or simply important) to us because we believe that they already are. It does not matter how a user names their avatar except in as much as the user believes that it does matter – in the same way that we imagine (and therefore synthesise) meaning in those things of which we try to make sense. Although the respondents in this study may have had very different reasons for the names they selected for their avatars, it is perhaps most significant that so many stated they had reasons at all: that they registered the presence of a logic in this activity, and therefore recognised the significance of the relation between this activity (the first stage in the process of self-invention in this virtual environment) and their own senses of self-identity.

13.6.2   The Choice of Avatar

Having chosen one's avatar name, the *Second Life* initiate is then asked to choose a face from a dozen choices: half of which are male and half female. These proto-avatars can then be altered or exchanged by the user once fully engaged in the virtual world.

Of the students surveyed, 16 stated that they had chosen their avatar because it physically resembled themselves, and 4 of these specifically referred to their shared ethnicity or skin colour. Two chose their avatar for what might be considered metonymic or synecdochal reasons: one because it reflected the user's sartorial style, another because it reflected her age. (One might note in passing that this seems an eccentric rationale: all of the avatar choices look about the same age, an idealised early twenties.) One cited the fact that their avatar looked 'realistic' as the reason for their choice. All of these 19 might be seen as reflecting a desire for realism, a connection between the virtual world and the material world, in their choice of avatar.

A further 17 members of the group based the choice on their own aesthetic tastes: because the avatar seemed to them cool, stylish, funny, handsome or attractive. Four of these said the avatar looked 'smart' although it is unclear whether this refers to the appearance of intelligence or sartorial elegance; indeed, in this virtual, depthless world of images, this ambiguity perhaps reveals a convergence of those two meanings within the one word, in that smartness as knowledge or intelligence has come to be represented or replaced by the smartness of appearance. One respondent specifically linked these two attributes when he suggested that his choice of avatar was "stylish and not constrained by conventionality" and therefore represented a "free thinker". In this virtual world of flamboyant fashion and full-body makeovers, it appears that the superficial and the cosmetic have become congruous with (or come to replace) internality and depth.

Three of these seventeen aesthetes specifically linked the attractiveness of their avatar to its resemblance to their own physical appearance: "my avatar looks great and resembles me" – "it reflects me because I am a young handsome black man" – "it's cool like me." This attitude may be seen as reflecting the user's desire as much as their ego (for what else is the bloating of the ego other than its own desperate beseeching?), or their tacit interpretation (or unconscious awareness) of this virtual world as a space for the performance of such transformational desire. Two other respondents were more explicit in their understanding of *Second Life*'s mediation of desire: one suggested that his avatar reflected what he "would like to look like" while another said that her avatar had been chosen to reflect her "positively in real life." The latter's turn of phrase may be revealing: the avatar does not only make its user look better *than* in physical life, it makes its user look better *in physical life*. The implications of the desire for one's virtual experience to improve one's physical-world status are coming to seem increasingly less far-fetched, as the virtual blurs with the material, comes to seem more prevalent and ontologically dominant than the material, and comes to be the new real.

Seven of the group said there was no particular reason for their choice, while two chose their avatar because it looked "simple" or "normal". Three chose theirs because it was fit for purpose: easy to control, manipulate and customise. These 12 may be seen as viewing the avatar as primarily serving a practical function in relation to their inworld experience and specifically to their academic project work in *Second Life*. They do not appear to have reflected upon the existential or aesthetic meanings of their choice. It is not perhaps insignificant that they are substantially outnumbered by those who have done so.

Two other responses stand out. One respondent – a white male of traditional student age – said that he did not like his avatar because it represented a white teenager. His response displays a resistance to the limitations and aesthetic (or ideological) stereotyping imposed by *Second Life*'s pre-selection of avatars, even though he himself fell more or less within its assumptions as to its typical user. Another respondent suggested that he chose his avatar on the grounds that it was the one that came closest to how he would look if he were an avatar. Not how he looks, nor what he would like to look like; not a reflection of some aspect of himself or his aesthetic tastes; not even an arbitrary or pragmatic choice: this is how he would look if he were the virtual resident of a virtual world. Which is, of course, what he is.

The majority of respondents in this study clearly saw a significance in their choice of avatar – as in their choice of avatar name – which suggests an increasing understanding of the importance of their experiences in virtual space, and which might therefore come to imply an awareness of the convergence or the competition between the avatar and the original self.

13.6.3   The Function of the Avatar

When asked as to the function of their avatar, the most common answer among the students surveyed was that its purpose was to allow them to complete their assignment for this particular study project. These ten responses suggested that there was nothing more to their relationship with their chosen avatar than practical necessity. A further four students saw the avatar as allowing them to experience and interact with *Second Life*. Others took a broader view: four suggested that the avatar allowed them to participate, communicate and interact in the more general possibilities of virtual space, and four saw the avatar primarily as a representation of themselves within this space. One saw it not as something through which to see, act and interact but merely (with a particular passivity) something to be seen on screen. Three respondents took a rather more sceptical or resistant line, suggesting that they could not see a purpose in an avatar at all.

These responses are all perhaps obvious enough. Other respondents, however, offered rather more complex answers. Two students – apparently immune to the seamless illusion of *Second Life*'s imagery (an unsurprising response perhaps for a computing student) – saw the avatar in terms of its digital mechanicity: what one described as an "interface with the game code." On the other end of the ontological spectrum, however, two described the avatar not only as a representation of themselves or an instrument of their own agency, but more as an extension or mirror of themselves: "an extension of myself allowing me to exist by proxy in another world." The avatar would "act like me and would do what I would do originally in [the] real world." The first of these sees the avatar functioning – as Marshall McLuhan would suggest all media functions – as an extension of his own human subjectivity, one which specifically allows the user an existence (rather than a representative or tool) in the virtual world: an existence by proxy, as through an alternative (and already extant) subjectivity. The second goes further, assigning not only subjectivity but independent agency to the avatar: the avatar reflects the user's original self, it acts like the user but not as the user's tool. From this perspective the avatar appears to take on a life of its own, it becomes the user's uncanny double, mirroring her actions, or indeed anticipating them. This is the shadow which walks ahead of its subject, the mirror image which seems to develop an autonomy and which might therefore assume a position of control over its original. This is Jean Baudrillard's simulacrum: the image which precedes, determines and engenders its object.

When asked what was the function specifically of the avatar's physical appearance, the students surveyed offered a varied range of responses. Seven of these suggested that the physical appearance allowed for greater ease and naturalness of communication and interaction; four suggested that it made them recognisable within the virtual space. These responses may be seen as envisaging a function which contextualises the subject within the virtual society, and are therefore based upon an expectation of dialogical relationships. These participants understood that the avatar gave them a presence within the virtual realm which encompassed markers equivalent to those necessary for interaction within the material world.

Others in the group also saw the avatar as allowing for parallel systems of interaction and sense-making as those operating in physical space. Three of these suggested that the avatar created a semblance of the physical; another three specified that it was the human appearance of the avatar which accommodated the paralleling of physical-world interactions, one of these arguing that the function of the avatar's appearance was "to simulate a community of people in a virtual world." One respondent simply suggested that the avatar's mimicry of physical reality "made more sense."

For all of these 17 respondents, the appearance of the avatar again functioned as a device to facilitate communication and interaction by simulating a sense of the logic of material reality. Ten respondents, however, saw the function of the avatar's appearance not as a facilitator of social dialogue so much as a monological expression or projection of their own subjectivities, personae or desires. Three of these said that the purpose of the avatar was merely to represent them in the virtual world; three said that it reflected and expressed the user's thoughts and feelings; another three said that the avatar's physical appearance allowed them as users (rather than other users) to relate to it: "having a human appearance [...] makes it more easy for newly registered users [...] a user that is new to online gaming can have that 'human' feeling and feel more comfortable." One suggested that the avatar might not only represent the subjectivity of its user, but might also reflect their desire for the enhancement of their appearance and abilities: "it may reflect the owner of the avatar or his imagination (desired appearance) or something which cannot be done in the real world."

There therefore appeared to be two major fields of opinion emerging in relation to the purpose of the avatar's appearance: the first (which we might describe as extrospective) viewed this device as focused upon social, communicative and interactive functions; the second (which might appear introspective, even egocentric) saw within the avatar the possibility of the expression, extension and transcendence of the user's subjectivity. Only two of the respondents fell significantly outside these two general positions of pragmatic socialisation and imaginative self-expression. One managed to be both pragmatically functional and at the same time focused upon the practical demands of his own subjectivity (rather than upon the conditions for social interaction), suggesting that the avatar had a physical appearance only "because you need to move around in a physical world simulation." Another (who had repeatedly argued for the lack of any rationale for the avatar and his choices for it) continued his resistance to the illusion of physical reality offered by the virtual world: "it is just a 3D mesh placed into a 3D environment."

When asked, however, about the meaning of their avatar to other users – and specifically how its appearance would affect interaction with other participants in *Second Life* – only three respondents suggested that the avatar's humanity was key to that interaction, only three suggested that it might facilitate interaction by reflecting the user's persona, and only two emphasised the importance of the avatar's recognisability. By contrast, a total of 12 respondents argued that the avatar's aesthetic visual appearance might appeal to or attract other users "just like in the real world" – or as one respondent put it, "if you're female, blonde and with a good body then guys tend to want to speak to you." One of these respondents pointed out that "in real life you tend to interact with people who make themselves more appealing to the eye and the same is the case in *Second Life*."

The resident of *Second Life* tends to have a greater ability to make her/himself appealing to the eye than the average inhabitant of the physical world. Two respondents stressed this transformational capacity, while a third added that "if you are male and take a female avatar, people tend to relate to you as a female." The avatar's capacity for self-expression and self-transformation is, however, clearly limited by the number of original choices of avatar and the cosmetic and artificial nature of the enhancements available; yet only one respondent pointed out that the appearance of the avatar was in itself meaningless "because it's generic." The vast majority of respondents fail to acknowledge that beneath the seductive aestheticisation and hegemonic lack of depth offered by the avatar, the appearance of the avatar might be seen as having a homogenizing effect upon both subjectivity and communication. This does not suggest that this process of homogenisation does not take place so much as it may remind us that this process may be so prevalent and all-encompassing only because it is so covert or insidious.

13.7   Conclusion

We stand, we are told, at the dawn of a virtual age. It is not only that emerging technologies have made these new social, educational, commercial and occupational environments possible; it is also that during the first decade of the twenty-first century a transnational state of economic and geopolitical uncertainty and flux has made these virtual environments increasingly attractive. The virtual workplace, trading zone, classroom and social space are cheaper, safer, more flexible and more convenient than the physical locations which have traditionally been associated with these areas of activity.

If then, as it appears, we are adopting a radically different existential paradigm, it would seem prudent to imagine how these emergent conditions of being might affect human interaction and subjectivity. It is clear that, insofar as people are products of their environments, the effects of such a paradigm shift are likely to be profound, and that it might therefore be sensible to consider what we are getting ourselves into. That is not to say that we might be able to (even if we wished to) reverse or even mitigate these effects; it is to suggest that we might simply do well to prepare ourselves.

This study has explored the responses of a new generation of e-citizens to the adoption of a virtual self and immersion in a virtual environment. The participants in this study may be considered, by virtue of their own choice of academic discipline, to be at the forefront of the trend towards the digitalisation of culture and society. Their equivocation or ambivalence towards this trend is perhaps therefore significant.

Some of the participants in this study saw their presence within virtual life – as reflected in the name, image and function of their avatar – as a direct extension of themselves; others suggested that this presence represented a parallel subjectivity, one aligned both to and by their own selfhood, yet distanced therefrom by a detachment we might consider equivalent to an ontological *cordon sanitaire*; others still (self-consciously or otherwise) saw in this presence possibilities for the expression or even the realisation of their fantasies of themselves; others overtly resisted the promises of liberation advanced by the virtual environment and instead observed its limitations and absurdities.

The greatest of these absurdities may perhaps be found in the notion of the avatar itself. The *Oxford English Dictionary* defines an avatar as "the descent of a deity to the earth in an incarnate form [...] manifestation or presentation to the world as a ruling power or object of worship." Yet the virtual avatar gives its user only the illusion of that divine power. It is not the incarnation of a god in human form but the illusory manifestation of a human in the image of, as the *OED* puts it, a "ruling power". As such, the pseudo-utopia of the virtual world may not represent a process of empowerment but one of interpellation; its processes of redefinition may not advance its subjects' liberation so much as their (often unwitting) subjection. The anxieties and uncertainties raised by this situation may not be the exclusive province of cultural philosophers; as this study suggests, such reflections may usefully come to be shared by the very subjects the virtual paradigm looks to absorb.

References

Althusser, L.: Lenin and Philosophy (trans. Brewster, B.). Aakar Books, Delhi (2006)
Baudrillard, J.: Simulacra and Simulation (trans. Glaser, S.). University of Michigan Press, Michigan (1994)

Benjamin, W.: Illuminations (trans. Zohn, H.). Fontana Press, London (1992)

Boellstorff, T.: Coming of Age in Second Life: An Anthropologist Explores the Virtually Human. Princeton University Press, Princeton (2008)

Bolter, J., Grusin, R.: Remediation: Understanding New Media. MIT Press, Cambridge (2000)

Borges, J.: Labyrinths (trans. Yates, D., Irby, J.). Penguin, Harmondsworth (1970)

Camus, A.: The Myth of Sisyphus (trans. O'Brien, J.). Penguin, Harmondsworth (1975)

Cheng, L., Farnham, S., Stone, L.: Lessons learned: Building and deploying shared virtual environments. In: Schroeder, R. (ed.) The Social Life of Avatars: Presence and Interaction in Shared Virtual Environments, pp. 90–111. Springer, London (2002)

Conrad, M., Pike, D., Sant, A., Nwafor, C.: Teaching large student cohorts in second life. In: Proceedings of the First International Conference on Computer Supported Education (CSEDU 2009). Lisboa, Portugal (2009)

Conrad, M., Neale, J., Charles, A.: Of mice or men? – The avatar in the virtualscape. In: International Conference on Information Society 2010, London (2010)

de Bruxelles, S.: Second life affair leads to real-life divorce for David Pollard, aka Dave Barmy. In: The Times, 14 Nov 2008

Fiske, J.: Television Culture. Routledge, London (1987)

Genvo, S.: Understanding digital playability. In: Perron, B., Wolf, M. (eds.) The Video Game Theory Reader 2, pp. 133–149. Routledge, London (2009)

Harris, J.: How the net is altering your mind. In: The Guardian, 20 Aug 2010

King, G., Krzywinska, T.: Tomb Raiders and Space Invaders. I.B. Taurus, London (2006)

Klimmt, C., Hartmann, T.: Effectance, self-efficacy and the motivation to play video games. In: Vorderer, P., Bryant, J. (eds.) Playing Video Games: Motives, Responses and Consequences, pp. 133–45. Lawrence Erlbaum, Mahwah (2006)

Koskinen, I.: The design professions in convergence. In: Storsul, T., Stuedahl, D. (eds.) Ambivalence Towards Convergence, pp. 117–128. Nordicom, Göteborg (2007)

Sartre, J.-P.: Being and Nothingness (trans. Barnes, H.). Methuen, London (1969)

Storsul, T., Stuedahl, D.: Introduction. In: Storsul, T., Stuedahl, D. (eds.) Ambivalence Towards Convergence, pp. 9–16. Nordicom, Göteborg (2007)

Tiffin, J., Rajasingham, L.: In Search of the Virtual Class. Routledge, Abingdon (1995)

Tiffin, J., Rajasingham, L.: The Global Virtual University. RoutledgeFalmer, London (2003)

Vasalou, A., Joinson, A., Bänziger, T., Goldie, P., Pitt, J.: Avatars in social media: Balancing accuracy, playfulness and embodied messages. Int. J. Hum. Comput. Stud. **66**(11), 801–811 (2008)

Žižek, S.: Violence. Profile Books, London (2008)

Chapter 14
Situated Learning in Virtual Worlds and Identity Reformation

Anne Adams, Lluïsa Astruc, Cecilia Garrido, and Breen Sweeney

Abstract Situations shape how we learn and who we are. This chapter reviews two case-studies in order to identify key points of interplay between physical world and virtual world identities and how this impacts on identity reformation. The first study reviews findings of a study that explored the use of simulated language learning scenarios (i.e. a Spanish virtual house) and gaming within a virtual world. The second study presents evidence from a comparison of virtual and gaming world interactions and a comparison of Second Life™ tutorial situations (i.e. environments that are; realistic compared to surreal, enclosed compared to open, formal compared to informal). Identity reformation was enabled and inhibited by conceptual links (i.e. students' physical world identities, memories and concepts of self) between virtual and physical world situations. However, academics' role in identity reformation within these new learning contexts is posed as the current barrier to virtual world learning.

14.1 Introduction

It was the educational philosopher Rousseau (1762) who proposed that education shapes who we are and laid one of the foundations for the notion of learning as a route to reforming our identity. Personal development is a key concept in identity reformation and has great resonance with the concepts of lifelong learning since we can never cease to learn nor develop and reform our identities. However, as Kehily (2009, p 6) notes 'the temporality of identity is commonly overlooked ... identity is never complete and can incorporate aspirational and fantasy elements'. The transient nature of identity and its tendency towards retaining potential inaccuracies

A. Adams (✉)
Institute of Educational Technology, The Open University, Milton Keynes, UK
e-mail: a.adams@open.ac.uk

L. Astruc • C. Garrido • B. Sweeney
The Open University, Milton Keynes, UK

A. Peachey and M. Childs (eds.), *Reinventing Ourselves: Contemporary Concepts of Identity in Virtual Worlds*, Springer Series in Immersive Environments, DOI 10.1007/978-0-85729-361-9_14, © Springer-Verlag London Limited 2011

have been noted as relating to social situations (Goffman 1959; Giddens 1991) However, the physicality of a situation, whether it be our home, an airport, or up a mountain, are factors of situations that are continually overlooked. Yet to learn to climb a mountain or to deal with a situated phobia (e.g. claustrophobia) is tightly interwoven with physical situations and has both an impact on our notions of identity and our ability to change that identity through learning.

A key aspect of elearning, within virtual worlds in particular, are their potential to allow exploration and continual reformation of our identities through the rapid interaction with different situations. Yet societal, institutional and social pressures continually seek to confine, categorise, stabilise and control situations and consequently identities within these worlds. The tensions between virtual world identities, the value of situations and their impact on identities is central to the concepts explored within this chapter.

Initially virtual environments were used for entertainment and training purposes. Virtual simulations have continued to be used for many years as learning environments for various conditions (Smets et al. 1995; Delwiche 2006). However, the objectives of virtual reality have digressed to three main themes (Fluckiger 1995):

1. The user's exploration of the virtual world.
2. The user's actions on the physical world through virtual replications (simulations).
3. The user's interaction with other users participating in the virtual world.

This chapter concentrates primarily on 1, the concept of virtual world exploration, whilst there are elements of 2, the use of virtual replications, in the exploration of language learning simulation. However, even though the main focus of these studies is not directly on the interaction of students with others, a student's concept of social context has a strong impact on all of their interactions. This means that indirectly students' prior interactions have an impact on all their subsequent interactions inworld and are reviewed with this in mind. Psychologically we have built into us the concept of acceptable behaviours for appropriate places, for example, even if we were alone in a traditionally public space (e.g. a supermarket) we would feel uncomfortable completing a private act (e.g. taking off our clothes in this context). This is an example of social norms guiding our behaviours for 'places' irrespective of our current social interactions. Social norms (such as politeness and acceptable behaviour) guide social interactions and determine socially rich responses irrespective of whether a system was designed to cater for them (Laurel 1993; Reeves and Nass 1996). Based on existing knowledge, users construct social representations that allow them to recognise and contextualise social stimuli. These representations originate from social interaction and help us construct an understanding of the social world, enabling interaction between groups sharing social norms within these representations (Augoustinos and Walker 1995). Social situations provide cues that allow people to make assessments of those situations. Harrison and Dourish (1996) argue that it is a *sense of place* that guides social interactions. This is because social norms guide our perceptions of spaces allowing us to interpret them as places and adapt our behaviours accordingly. Virtual worlds have long been understood to allow end-users an increased sense of place for interactions. However, there is still more to be understood about how this impacts on our learning and subsequent identity reformation.

This chapter builds upon the Chap. 2 of this volume and previous published literature (Sweeney and Adams 2009; Adams 2011) focusing on reformation of identity specifically within virtual world situated learning. Therefore, this chapter will help those specifically using virtual worlds for elearning to understand identity reformation within these contexts and to design the learning to support it. Two studies in virtual world language learning and situated elearning will be used to support an understanding of the diversity of scenarios for implementing online identities within virtual world contexts e.g. place for tutorials, simulations of scenarios. This will enable a deeper understanding of the virtual world technologies (e.g. Second Life, Runescape) and practices (e.g. simulation and game interaction, situation design) that support situated elearning for students' identity formation. The study findings provide an insight into the potential benefits and barriers to students' virtual world identity reformation. The findings will be used to support conclusions about how to create plans for situated good practice in virtual world learning identity reformation.

14.2 Background

14.2.1 Virtual Worlds and Education

For centuries we have sought to develop ourselves and our concepts of self through our personal exploration in work and play. Who we are can therefore be tightly interwoven with what we have learnt (Bernstein and Solomon 1999; Lave and Wenger 1991). This learning, however, is not a static individualistic concept as our sense of self and learning as part of that identity is embedded in our social and cultural contexts. As Lave and Wenger (1991) emphasise, learning within any domain is more than a formal acquisition of knowledge, it has a strong social element. Bernstein (Bernstein and Solomon 1999) highlighted this strong interplay between what we learn within a social context and our formation of social identities. This aligns well with the fluid and social nature of social worlds. As noted in Chap. 2 of this book the concepts of situated learning highlight how learning and its development relates to socio-cultural contexts and how this impacts on our identities.

Goffman (1959) highlights that our identities are not fixed. Students are one person inhabiting multiple social worlds. We have complex identities that we adapt and present alternative sides of for different social situations. Bowker and Star (2000) note the importance of space and time in the complexity of a learning process and how this increases the potential for chaos. Latour (1999) emphasises our need to create order in these processes and the increased likelihood of disorder elsewhere. Education, through supporting our development and identity reformation, often involves widening the gap between these worlds before some resolution is made. However, it has been argued, that this gap should never be fully bridged otherwise how can we ensure that students are encouraged to continually develop and transcend their immediate practices and identities (Guile 2006)? Learning will inevitably always involve dissonance and disequilibrium, not only within our own identities but upon others, as identity reconstruction can have a dramatic impact on organisational and socio-cultural objectives (Alvesson and Wilmott 2001).

14.2.2   Identity Reformation and Situated Learning

Collaborative virtual environments have been argued as providing remotely located users with the ability to collaborate via real interactions in a shared artificial environment (Brna and Aspin 1997). The advantages of virtual reality for collaborative learning are frequently argued by constructivists[1] to relate to the importance of authentic context (Vygotsky 1962, 1978). However, the real value of virtual worlds within an elearning context are disputed. Some educationalists are sceptical about using virtual worlds for learning (Foster 2008). Others, however, are enthusiastic and feel it is possible to achieve ambitious educational goals (Oishi 2007). Ultimately these resources provide students with an opportunity to recreate their physical world identity through supported staged exploration and development of their digital identities. This is a difficult process for a student to undergo as they are required to balance and merge multiple digital identities with their physical world identities whilst all are in constant flux through the learning process.

Technology can increase the potential for access to learning within a variety of different contexts. These have been reviewed from different perspectives with regard to situated learning (Lave and Wenger 1991; Tuomi-Gröhn et al. 2003), situated design (Suchman 1987; Star and Griesemer 1989) and boundary objects (Star and Griesemer 1989). This not only has the potential to speed up the transformational potential of education but also distort how the processes occur. Whilst it is important to understand the reformation of virtual world identities, it is also important to understand how this has an impact on ourselves and others in the physical world. Understanding the strong link between identities and virtual worlds would imply a strong link to virtual worlds that can act as a bridge between physical and artificial realities. However, understanding how well this supports transitions or removes us from the physical world into an artificial world with artificial identities needs to be understood to support effective identity reformation.

Key affective concerns for teaching and learning are student focus and motivation. Anything that helps the student remain motivated and will focus their attention will aid in the process of learning, whereas conversely anything that distracts and de-motivates the student will hinder them. It could be argued, therefore, that situated attention through immersion in a virtual world is a key aspect of virtual world learning. Virtual reality (VR) communication environments have been argued to

---

[1] Constructivism is a predominant psychological process theory in collaborative learning. They highlight the importance of learning environment actions, real interactions and translating abstract concepts into those that are concrete. For further information see Vygotsky (1978).

provide a natural, intuitive environment for communication whilst removing some of the social taboos from social interactions (Kaur 1997). However, as virtual worlds increase in their appearance as accurate replications of reality there is an increased likelihood that users will make inaccurate assumptions about the world's capabilities and limitations. This could have an inappropriate impact on end-users' task attention and ultimately immersion in the environment and task. For example, a realistic classroom could produce user assumptions that the environment's walls and doors retain physical world characteristics, thus implicitly making conversations within a VR room appear private when they may actually be public with potential privacy and noise pollution issues.

The issue of 'social identity' in relation to language learning has been a subject of discussion for a long time. Tajfel (1974, 1981) believed that identity is a result of group membership and that individuals may chose to leave it if they don't identify with the elements of social identity prevailing in the group. Giles and Johnson (1987) focused on language as a salient marker of group membership and social identity. Many other interactional sociolinguists have followed the same thread and although in many cases the main discussion is around the importance of ethnicity and other environment related features of social identity, what is interesting for our analysis is whether, in this case, there was a common social identity around language but perhaps more importantly around the environment in which interactions were taking place.

14.2.3   Reformation of Self in Virtual Worlds

Research by Wadley and Gibbs (2010) presents contrasting perspectives over avatar usage by users. On the one hand, do users employ avatars to present a character in a virtual world? Or to represent their true identity? Initially, it could be thought that online environments that allow for role playing would facilitate the use of avatars for character representation whilst more formal contexts would reveal the true identity. However, identity formation and reformation is far more complex than this simple binary distinction. Do we ever really present our 'true identity' as, since Goffman (1959) has highlighted, we have several sides to ourselves that we present in different situations? It would be easier to think of our students as having several sides to their identity that they reveal and present in different ways according to the relevant situations. As virtual worlds can easily present those different situations, they can potentially allow users to explore and present those different sides more effectively. Savin-Baden (2010) revisited these issues with the concept of 'multiplication' which relates several concepts of 'self' back to consistent physical world identities. The question of whether these virtual concepts of self are completely separate identities or parts of the whole self and how these representations relate to real concepts of self is an interesting concept which requires further exploration. Workman (2008) reflects a stronger situated learning perspective with regard to communities with Lave and Wenger's (1991) notion of Communities of Practice. Many of these approaches connect to the concept of social norms and behaviours within a community. This would mean we adapt our presentation of self not only to situation but to the social norms that seem applicable in that situation.

Peachey and Withnail (2011) review the concepts of consistent avatars linked to the stability of social identities. They argue, as does Schroeder and Axelsson (2000), that continuity in an avatar's physicality can be linked to effective community building as social norms of concepts and behaviours are more effectively established. However, strong communities require an acceptance for different levels of engagement and identity formation within that group. Lave and Wenger (1991) highlight the notion of different levels of community engagement through the concepts of legitimate peripheral participation. They argue that communities need to allow participation at different levels and that it is legitimate to have initial peripheral participation within many communities. This would mean that virtual world student participant should allow different levels of engagement and ways to present our identity from those that are inconsistent to those that are consistent. Peachey and Withnail (2011) present a detailed account of an avatar's changing identity as two members became increasingly engaged with the community. This should be a model of a healthy sequence of engagement with a community.

14.3   Case Study 1: Spanish Language Learning House Simulation and Game

Language and how we use it can be a linchpin to how we interact with others and thus how we define ourselves and others within different cultures. The interaction between a country's culture and its language is tightly interwoven. Learning a language must therefore mean understanding its cultural context. The spoken language is also closely linked to social norms and social interaction patterns within that society. Those teaching and learning languages have understood these issues for many years and have often been at the forefront of utilising novel teaching approaches that understand learning within a cultural context. For many years, students learning a language have 'role-played' spoken language interactions to understand language within specific scenarios (e.g. shopping, eating out and booking a hotel room). Language students have also taken part in social learning games (e.g. nursery rhyme and number games) to help gain vocabulary skills. The use of these simulated situations and gaming approaches tie in closely with virtual world interactions. How these technical advances of traditional approaches impacted on language learning was a key focus of this research project. Within this chapter specific findings that were related to identity formation and re-formation are detailed.

14.3.1   Study Method

This study related to language elearning and focused on specific support for this discipline. It also reviewed the use of situated constructions i.e. a Spanish house, a

Spanish family and a Spanish waiter to support investigation of language, norms and identities within these situations.

Two scenarios were investigated:

- Spanish home simulation with artificial avatars representing the members of a Spanish family speaking about their lives in this home.
- Spanish tutorials within a standard virtual world setting with a game playing component incorporated (both virtual world and verbally). An interactive bar with barman avatar was present (see below).

Participants were 24 learners of Spanish at different levels of proficiency, from low-intermediate to high. They were recruited among staff and students at The Open University and The University of Cambridge.

Spanish home The Spanish home simulation was designed and developed by Eygus Ltd (www.eygus.co.uk) from an original idea by the second, third and fourth author. The simulation presented a Spanish house and garden and labelled all the objects within that home. Once a participant clicked with their mouse over the object, the Spanish word popped up and an audio clip was played where the Spanish pronunciation of the word was given. Students were able to wander with their avatar through this simulation exploring and clicking on all the different objects within this environment. The environment also has a selection of family members who are represented with avatars (e.g. Father cooking in the kitchen). These avatars were static and specifically designed to look distinctly different from the virtual world avatars (e.g. they looked like cardboard cut-outs), which was to to reduce confusion about the nature of these avatars. Once the static family avatars are clicked on they gave an account (in Spanish) of who they were and what they were doing in their home (e.g. cooking). The home had interesting cultural and socio-psychological aspects planned into it. A balcony was placed on the front of the house, the food being cooked was Spanish, the daughter's room had a notice on it in Spanish saying 'keep out' and the door was locked (i.e. when clicked upon it wouldn't open).

Spanish tutorial and bar game The students were able to sit in the tutorial circle for a traditional virtual world social interaction. The students either used the audio chat or the text chat to communicate with other students or the tutor. Interactions were all completed in Spanish. As the students entered the language learning site they were asked to take on a Second Life HUD (Heads Up Display–see full description in http://vivacity-games.co.uk/language-learning.html) to participate in the Bar Game, which was designed and developed by Vivacity Games. The HUD would provide them with a 'drink gauge' showing how thirsty they were and would change their avatars appearance, with thirsty animations, when it reached zero (see Fig. 14.1). These visual feedback systems were thus analogous to gaming status bars in that they help to identify and monitor avatar motivated language interactions.

This expression on the avatar would continue until the student went to the bartender for a drink. The bartender would only respond with a drink for the student if they asked for it correctly and if this was completed the avatar would lose the thirsty animation and their drink gauge would increase (see Fig. 14.2).

Display on players screen shows a *drink* gauge

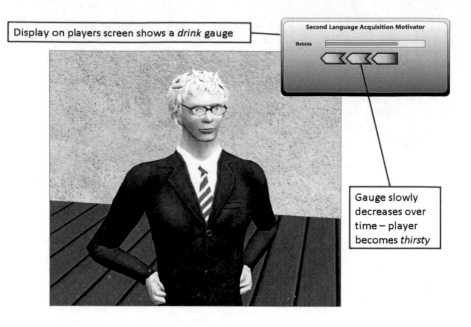

Gauge slowly
decreases over
time – player
becomes *thirsty*

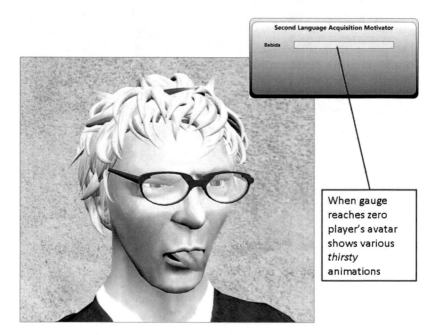

When gauge
reaches zero
player's avatar
shows various
thirsty
animations

Fig. 14.1 Student avatar with thirsty gauge and facial expressions

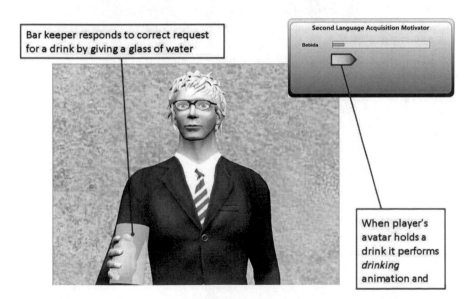

Fig. 14.2 Automated bartended avatar with language usage for drink to increase gauge

14.3.2 Research Procedure

The students arrived for an initial induction session which supported them in developing their avatar and Second Life interaction skills. Six follow-on tutorial sessions were conducted by the second, third and fourth authors inworld, in a traditional tutorial setup (i.e. all students sitting around in a circle). Students were invited to explore the Spanish House which was situated next to the tutorial. To that effect, they would be escorted in and out of the house by the second author. The first author, who was represented by an avatar (see Fig. 14.3), arranged to interview students inworld, through text and audio communication channels. The participants then explored the simulation and were observed by the researcher using remote camera viewing. Key critical incidents and interaction patterns were recorded throughout this exploration. After the students' avatars left the house they completed a further inworld interview with the researcher. The interview data were recorded, transcribed and analysed.

14.3.3 Situated Learning and Identity Findings

The findings identified several accounts of how virtually simulated situations have an impact on language learning. For language learning, the findings highlighted the importance of having a psychologically reasoned situational placement, both within physical and social contexts. With regard to identity reformation three factors are detailed: (i) our identity within physical simulated situations; (ii) our identity within social simulated situations, and; (iii) virtual world concepts of self as a student.

Identity within physical simulated situations The findings from participant interviews identified that the students found the concept of 'setting a cultural scene' within the virtual world simulation very valuable for their learning experience as a whole. For example:

> Whole world experience, setting scene for Spain, was useful – I've been into a Portugal world but [this was] not in Portuguese, so linguistically a write off - but experience-wise good (St 11).

The physical placement of objects within appropriate contexts was designed so that it would help the students to cognitively map associative schemas between objects, their pronunciation and contextual location. The goal was to help students in developing mental models for objects within a house. As noted by several students this made learning the vocabulary easier than through many other more traditional methods (e.g. vocabulary lists): *"SL [second life] is more interactive than books and vocab lists [vocabulary lists]"* (St 3). The placement of these objects within physical contexts of use also supported the students in developing scenarios that would support them in understanding the active use of the language in action.

> maybe as well as a house, there could be the option for other scenarios, such as at the market (St. 12)

Fig. 14.3 Interviewer avatar outside the Spanish house

This then allowed them to personally empathise with these scenarios and consider how they could utilise the settings of these objects in context.

[the house] covers the main objects you'd need to buy or replace when living in Spain (St. 3)

Finally, the audio clips also were noted as helping them understand the pronunciation of objects within the right context of use. The multiple sensory input as well as increasing its realism also increased the complexity of the situation: *"Objects and sounds - more disorientating and more realistic... More naturalistic than Elluminate* (synchronous web conferencing system) *on one hand"* (St. 11). However this realism was noted as harshly breached when systems didn't fulfil expected norms of physical world behaviour: *"sliding downstairs / walking through walls, LESS REALISTIC"* (St. 11)

Identity within social simulated situations Virtual world simulation interactions allowed the students to explore their physical world identities within a simulated environment. Several students noted that the value of these environments is that although everyone co-exists within the same virtual world they enabled comfortable social interactions with people from a wide variety of physical world social, economic and cultural backgrounds. Students often valued the leak between physical and virtual identities, as they could easily learn from experienced people with a multitude of different professional and physical identities. Language students in particular found the international appeal of Second Life beneficial: *"best thing - the number of physically local native speakers"* (St 6). The value of informal learning from native speakers whose identities were routed in a foreign language was especially valued by the students:

It is good if you go to French people for example you pick up local colloquialisms, expressions etc. (St 9).

The social interactions which were both audio and textual provided extra levels of interaction that could enable control over that interaction. Some of the students were positive about the increased communications media: *"Much better than just text chat"* (St 10). Whilst others retreated away from the interactive elements: *"nice house - left quickly, didn't want to speak"* (St 7). However, simply interacting within the simulation allowed the students to uncover social norms for that culture which they could build into the learning development process. Opening a door and turning on the lights within different rooms allowed more realistic interactions within the world. The realistic structure of fireplaces, kitchens and balconies also gave a sense of being provided with a window into that culture.

As Goffman (1959) highlighted we strongly link to socially acceptable behaviour to specific social situations, e.g. we would say and do things with our family that we wouldn't with our friends and visa versa, and these different social situations consequently reveal different sides to our identity. Sometimes this led to embarrassment in social interactions. For example, one person walked in on an avatar sitting on the toilet causing the second avatar to leave quickly with comments of *'errr ohhhh arrrr excuse me'* (St 15). The fact that the avatar using the toilet was a large dragon did not seem to dispel the demonstration of norms within social interactions and the level of embarrassment presented by the avatar having opened the bathroom door on them. Another student inquired from the researcher why they hadn't been able to get into one of the family rooms and was embarrassed that they hadn't realised that they'd been informed by the nonexistent little girl to keep out of her room. Although it is not necessarily an ethical approach to seek to embarrass students there is a grey line identified here since language students are frequently motivated to learn a language to save embarrassing situations when they don't understand what is being said or can't communicate what they mean. Reforming their identity to one that is comfortable using a foreign language can then be a useful motivator in language learning. Student 3 noted this discomfort: *"At moment feel out of depth amongst people who have a lot higher level of Spanish to me"* but also noted how useful this was as a motivator for them *"Useful to urge people on"* (St 3).

One observation from some of those running the pilot was that although the tutorials had defined start and end times, some students were not very eager to leave at the end of the session. It is possible that their shared identity as language learners in Second Life was a contributing factor that motivated their wish to extend the learning experience beyond the set times.

Ultimately, the simulation presented various types of automated and real avatars which investigated some interesting contradictions in identity. Is this a real person's avatar or simply an automated person? Initial pilots with the static avatars in the house simulations identified problems with students confused by the concept of avatars looking and speaking like real people but just being automated programs. The representation of them as obviously false (i.e. cardboard cut outs) helped the students to clearly distinguish between the different real and artificial identities within this representation. It is interesting to note that the game automated avatar for the bartender (Pablo) remained looking like a real avatar which produced more natural interactions with him but again caused some confusion with some students: *"Met Pablo tried to have conversation with him but then realised he wasn't real person"* (St 5).

Virtual worlds concepts of self as a student As with many other virtual world research projects (e.g. Oishi 2007) this study identified positive responses with regard to motivation, confidence building and enjoyment associated with language learning through the simulation and gaming interactions. The students noted that whilst traditional material could be poor motivational experiences this approach was: *"LESS boring"* (St 3). Most of the students highlighted concepts of 'enjoyment' and 'fun' when describing their interactions: *"I think it's a good idea! I enjoyed it!"* (St 12). Of particular interest in identifying why the students found this approach fun were the almost contradictory statements about its complex and confusing nature: *"The more I use SL the more I find new things and get more and more confused but it's fun"* (St 5). Changing concepts of space, place and identity allowed this environment to be flexible but also complex which some people felt was disorientating and disconcerting or *"Odd"* (St 8) whilst others simply found it annoying: *"I've only been here a few minutes and it's very frustrating"* (St 13).

However these qualities were not necessarily considered by everyone as valuable for learning. Whilst some students found this language learning environment empowered the development of their skills and identity, others simply felt a discomfort at the ease with which they could reform their identities; *"It's just not me, but then its not supposed to be me - right?"* (St 4) One apparent conflict in developing situated identities that occurred was through the development of their student identity. Some participants' pre-defined concepts of learning and being a student clashed with the environment's realisation of these concepts. This ultimately led to, apparently, contradictory statements highlighting how some students made clear distinctions between learning and emotive factors supported within these environments: *"haven't really learnt a lot of Spanish yet but talking to other students has been good for my confidence"* (St. 3).

This highlights some preconceptions that students have about the identity of a good student and how this relates to learning. Students' concepts of what makes a 'good' student and its relationship to elearning are poorly researched and key focus for further research. From an analysis of the interview data it could be said that 'good students' were perceived to have the following aspects to their identities: 'serious' about learning, goal orientated and achieving quantifiable results. These concepts led some students to perceptions of these environments as: *"Not so good for learning - fun though"* (St 8). The flexible nature of these environments encouraged some students to feel detached as they simply dipped into their virtual identities as they would 'arrive and then quickly go'. Other students were identified to have found a greater level of student presence through multitasking their physical and virtual identities i.e. they could feel more involved as a student whilst at the same time keep their busy lives in the physical world going doing something else e.g. 'cooking for the family'. What this shows is how some people find it beneficial to adapt to this frequent duplicity of identities whilst for other it makes them almost 'sea-sick'.

14.4 Case Study 2: Virtual World Situated Elearning

Social interaction is known to encompass implicit assumptions that are made to assure the interaction is successful. Concepts of ourselves and thus our identity (e.g. "I've been here before so I'm comfortable with this situation", "I'm not happy with this situation", "I don't understand how to behave in small enclosed parties") within those situations show that it's essential to aid and support our assessment of assumptions of those situations. We must remember though, if those assumptions are incorrect, we are more likely to misjudge a situation and act inappropriately. Equally if those assumptions are correct they can increase a sense of being engaged within that situation thus enhance attention. Within a learning context, however, it is important to understand what the implications of different environmental design decisions are both on our sense of self and student learning. All these factors then impact on how we see ourselves within different situations.

Evidence presented here is based on work in Sweeney and Adams (2009). This study sought to review the concept of 'virtual self attention' when other variables are impacting on end-users learning focused interactions. The argument was proposed that the more immersed a user is, the more they will have an increased attention on their own avatar, rather than look at other areas of the screen. This is because they will be more interested in what their own avatar is doing, and identify with it, rather than looking at other activities or objects in the surrounding area. It was proposed that this increased sense of self was linked to an increased sense of presence in that situation. Hence the link between situation and the perception of ourselves within that situation is related. The following study reviewed concepts of situations, situated learning and their impact on students' identity.

14.4.1   Study Method

The previous study related to language elearning and focused on specific support for this discipline. This study relates to a generic review of learning within virtual worlds but again concentrates on interpretations of altered situations. As such the research into this world focuses on situated elearning and identity reformation within a virtual world situation. Within the virtual world settings three issues are focused on with regard to situated virtual identity formation and reformation:

- Situated Identity: concepts of identity formation within different virtual environments
- Situated Practice: The impact, within virtual worlds, of interactions with objects, environments and their own avatar.
- Impact of Elearning: The relationship of elearning within these environments with developments in identity formation.

The case study under review here is based upon the work in Sweeney and Adams (2009). Within this study an in-depth multi-method investigation from 12 virtual worlds participants was completed in three stages; initially a small scale within-subjects eye-tracking comparison was made between the role playing game 'RuneScape' and the virtual social world 'Second Life', secondly an in-depth evaluation of eye-tracking data for Second Life tasks (i.e. avatar, object and world based) was performed, finally a qualitative evaluation of Second Life elearning tutorials in comparative 3D situations (i.e. environments that are; realistic to surreal, enclosed to open, formal to informal) was completed.

The hardware for eye tracking is a useful tool for determining where a user is gazing at any time through recording eye movements. Previous studies have used this method to test immersiveness to see if the nature of the eye movements are altered as a user becomes more immersed (Cairns et al. 2006). In contrast this study reviewed the concept of participants foci of attention so that the more immersed a user is, the more they will have an increased attention on their own avatar, rather than look at other areas of the screen (Sweeney and Adams 2009). As a user progresses through a virtual world they are presented with a range of stimuli, and will look at various parts of the screen. However, once immersed, it is argued, they will concentrate more on their interaction with that world than the world itself. This would then impact on their increased concept of self and identity within this world rather than their removed interaction with it as a distanced observer of the world.

14.4.2 Research Procedure: Stage 1

Initially an evaluation was completed on the impact of environmental interactions (i.e. social world compared to gaming) upon end-users attention and thus immersion levels. This was completed through a small scale within-subjects eye-tracking assessment made between the role playing game RuneScape and the virtual social world Second Life (see Fig. 14.4). An attempt was made to standardise environment interactions (e.g. position of the camera and viewing see Fig. 14.4) however, some controls are standard to the environments.

Fig. 14.4 RuneScape (*Left*) and Second Life (*right*) interactions with 'in picture' image of participants

Within further detailed in-depth analysis of the Second Life the participants were divided into three types. First of all the 'World' tasks consisted of activities where participants were dealing with the general environment, for example navigating to various places. Within 'Avatar' tasks participants were concerned with their own avatar, such as changing their Second Life appearance. Finally 'Object' tasks were concerned with the activities which had participants doing things with objects inworld, such as, for example, carrying out building tasks.

This first study used six university staff members as participants, all of whom were women that were unfamiliar with either of the worlds, although participant number 5 had played other role playing games.

For the purposes of these experiments a female Second Life avatar was created which complied with RuneScape regulations stating that individual RuneScape avatars were created and brought through the game's orientation tutorial. To ensure that each person had the same starting point in the game, the avatars were placed in the same position in the game world. This was important because in a role playing game, as a player progresses their avatar's characteristics change. Each participant was then asked to log into Second Life and carry out a number of standard tasks, such as navigation, teleportation, changing avatar appearance, and so on. The full duration of the sessions was approximately 30 min with a break in the middle after which the participants then carried out standard tasks in RuneScape, such as navigation, fighting monsters, fishing, starting quests, and so forth.

The experimental design of the tests ensured an increase within the initial task engagement and immersion to allow for standardised comparisons between general world engagement as opposed to initial encounters and interactions with obstacles. However, to counterbalance the rigidity of an experimental approach an attempt was made to ensure a naturalistic yet focused approach to interactions. To increase this relaxed atmosphere instructions were called out and participants were free to ask for help if they didn't understand anything. Participants were informed about their ability to carry out slightly different activities, whilst the verbal instructions ensured a level of standardisation between participants' tasks. It was hoped that taking this approach to tasks increased the likelihood that they were naturalistic while still being standardised.

14.4.3   Findings: Immersion and Sense of Self Within a Virtual Situation

The findings from this study (Sweeney and Adams 2009) identified that there was an increased end-user focus in a gaming environment (RuneScape) compared to social world interactions (Second Life). In Fig. 14.5 we can see the time spent in the central area as a percentage of the game window, which was 44% for Second Life and 56% for RuneScape to the nearest integer. These initial findings, although not statistically significant, do highlight an increased level of end-user focus within the gaming world compared to social world interactions.

Fig. 14.5 Percentage of attention focus for Second Live and RuneScape

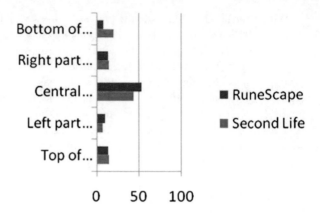

Fig. 14.6 Average percentage by tasks in Second Life

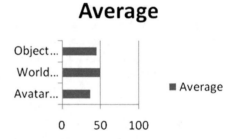

For the researchers to understand how alternative social world designs might impact on attention a set of further eye tracking analysis procedures were conducted on just the Second Life data. Within this analysis the time spent looking at the central part of the screen was analysed for each of the separate tasks (Fig. 14.6). The intention of this analysis was to see if the participants were more or less immersed during the different types of activities.

This analysis found that Second Life interactions specifically for 3D world exchanges increased participants' focus more than with object and avatar tasks. The average percentage time spent in the central region (to the nearest integer) was 37% for avatar tasks, 50% for world tasks, and 45% for object tasks (see Fig. 14.6). This analysis identified that Second Life interactions on 3D world tasks increased participants' focus more than with object and avatar tasks. Ultimately interaction with an environment impact on attention levels and thus could be argued to increase a sense of being there.

14.4.4 Research Procedure: Stage 2

At stage two within the research six participants attended a series of Second Life virtual world tutorials. The student participants were studying a second-level course

Fig. 14.7   Participants attending an orientation meeting in Second Life

in Pure Mathematics. Introductory material for this course, covered linear algebra, group theory and real analysis. This material was circulated beforehand and then discussed during the tutorials. For this experimental procedure inworld voice facilities were utilised, whilst conversations were controlled via turn-taking. However, students were allowed to use text-chat to ask questions or indicate their desire to speak.

At the beginning of this study there were three orientation meetings completed (see Fig. 14.7), which were then followed by seven tutorials. Sessions were initially deemed essential to allow students to overcome technical problems and learn about the environment.

Within these elearning tutorials virtual world settings were altered to identify the impacts of virtual world situations on situated learning. Situations were devised according to three separate factors;

- Realistic to surreal,
- Enclosed to open,
- Formal to informal.

For these studies several situations used were: two different platforms in trees, one which had couch-like seats, a purpose-built classroom and a corridor in the sky (see Fig. 14.8), the same room with the roof removed, a purpose-built chessboard room with wall and chairs, and a bandstand.

It was deemed important to set up a forum on the university's intranet, where agendas and minutes of each session were posted for the students to utilise. Further data was collected in the form of an experiments log of comments made and lessons learned, in particular with relation to the practical and technical aspects of teaching in Second Life.

Fig. 14.8 One of the locations used for tutorials

Finally telephone interviews were completed with five students and the data used for as a comparative analysis. Interview questions focused on four themes: participant perceptions of motivation, task interactions, input / output devices and 3D situations. This qualitative data were transcribed and thematically analysed in a grounded theory type approach.

14.4.5   Findings: Situated Awareness and Identity

The findings identified several useful threads; however, this paper presents only one thread from a sample of the students which highlighted issues of attention. Ultimately the different 3D situation designs presented altered levels of task engagement and distraction through perceptions of comfort, fun and fear.

When the students were asked about the different environments, in general their opinion was that the differences didn't have a great effect. However there were issues of affective memories triggered by environments that had an impact on end-user perceptions.

> I quite liked the tree house. …Silly reason for that is that going back to primary school it's quite nice sitting outside doing various things, and it kind of reminded me of that, and I thought this is kind of fun, it's good. … The one with the roof open was quite interesting. As you said last night at that time as well we went through a complete day, where we had the dawn and then watched the evening and the stars came out. … Yeah, it just reminded me of a sort of bar outside of a hotel you know where you sit in an evening. That was OK actually, but there is something about somebody sort of standing around who you're not quite sure who they are, 'Oh, who are they then? (Student 1)

None of the students were found to like the classroom with the roof on, as it was closed and had no windows. Two of these students did conclude that they had felt mildly claustrophobic in physical life situations.

> I think the only one that I actually disliked was the M208 classroom with the roof on. It just felt very weird, it was like going down into a cellar it was very closed in. It was just, er, I just found it quite unpleasant. It reminded me ... that I'd just sort of gone down into a dark cave. Once you removed the roof, once you got into the corridor it was pretty much the same as the others. ... I don't like small spaces without light, so that probably had an effect on it. (Student 3)
>
> I didn't like when we had the roof on, I think it was the M208 one, it was a bit claustrophobic ... and my favourite one was the SchomeBase tree-house, just because it was quite open. The classroom was definitely better with the roof off. (Student 4)

However, it is important to note that when the participant was queried further with the question "are you claustrophobic in real life" the student concluded *'Yeah'*. In contrast the other students were positive about the whole experience, although one student was mainly negative, and more affected by the different environments than the others.

> Where we had the tutorial in the tree-house we kept falling off the platform, and so everything had to stop in the middle of the tutorial to fetch someone back from wherever they'd fallen to. Although entertaining that kind of thing was distracting from the actual tutorial itself. ... I felt the actual surroundings were distracting, and detracted from the lesson considerably. I mean they were very pleasant surroundings. It would have been nice to have been there in person ... (Student 2)

It is important to note that when the roof was removed from the closed classroom it was then possible to move the camera controls and look at the avatars in the classroom from a distance. However, apart from this one detail there were no differences in the lighting conditions between the closed and open classroom. This factor highlights some interesting issues about the claustrophobic reaction to this situation.

In conclusion, it should be highlighted that despite the students stating there was little difference between the environments, they still used very emotive language when describing them. Comments continued to be made, which were not recorded, that included students comparing the bandstand to places they had visited in the past, or talking about seasons such as being outdoors in the summer. Students' sensory memory triggered by these environments is clearly a starting point for further research. Ultimately it could be concluded from this research that there are interesting points relating to the research questions for situated identity, practice and their impact on elearning. In particular the findings highlight how an environment and a student's interaction with that environment have a direct impact on a student's attention. This can relate to a student's motivation to learn through engagement and a feeling of presence in that environment. However, this study highlights how emotive these environmental encounters are. Although a 3D world interaction can positively increase a student's motivation to learn through empathising with the environment, it can also trigger negative memories of similar situations and environments. These situations and the students emotive responses relate strongly to how they see themselves (e.g. as a student, as claustrophobic). What is interesting is how these concepts of self then impact not only on abstract concepts of learning and professional development but also on practical concepts of attention.

14.5 Conclusion

Unlike previous studies relating to physical world situations within which students develop identities these studies focused totally on the reformation of digital virtual world identities. These studies identified how strongly a student's digital identity is bound to situations and previous experiences in physical world equivalents. However, despite virtual world's immersive removal from reality, identity issues did not relate primarily to digital identities but strongly to students' physical world identities. Regardless of how a student represented themselves within the world (e.g. changing sex, species or into fictional characters) physical world identities and social norms had a strong impact on their interactions.

Within the language learning study the findings identified the value of situational placement of objects, dialogue and scenes. Students appeared to empathise with these scenarios and relate them to personal needs. Although the study did not seek to review social interactions but situated simulation interactions, there was a strong impact of social norms and acceptable behaviour impacting on the students' behaviours. These behaviours had an impact on the comfort or discomfort the students felt in developing and changing their identities within virtual worlds. Static avatars for information and game playing roles were utilised within the simulations and tutorial settings. Established virtual world users were comfortable with real and artificial avatar constructions. New virtual world students were disturbed by this mixture of human-operated virtual world identities and artificial identities. However, the obvious artificial nature (e.g. some presented as card-board cut-outs) of some of these characters did support an ease of interaction according to changed perceptions of themselves. Gaming and role playing can often support us in extending our concepts of self through playing with versions of ourselves and reformulating our identities. Within this world it was decided that the concepts of self should be played with to support developing and extending the students through their learning. However, concepts of our identity as students are tightly interwoven with our perceptions of what it is to learn and what this should involve. Ultimately across all these findings stereotyped perceptions of what a student is and how learning should be had the strongest impact on their comfort and adaptability within the environment. Even some of those students who were motivated and enjoyed being within the environment perceived it more as fun than learning.

Within the second situated learning study participants were found to concentrate primarily on their environments and situations. Interestingly participants were found to relate powerfully to their physical world concepts of social self within social interactions. Although this wasn't the main focus of this study, social norms governing eye focus, space between people conversing and privacy still impacted strongly on social interactions. Finally personal concepts of comfort, fun and fear that often govern our physical world identities were found to translate directly into students' avatar identities. Students who were claustrophobic in the physical world found virtual world closed spaces unnerving. Environments (e.g. woodland) that reminded students of previous experiences were found to distract them from focusing on elearning studies. In contrast, a socially accepted construction of a classroom increased attention levels. Ultimately, when designing elearning contexts we need to understand the strong links that remain, although hidden, between virtual world identities and physical world identities.

Virtual environments have the potential to distort the assumptions that guide our behaviour (Sweeney and Adams 2009). They also have the potential to increase our sense of attention and of place thus making it more akin to those within face-to-face interactions. While the nature of the environment within a virtual world does not have as much effect as in the physical world, the findings detailed in these studies clearly show that virtual environments can still affect learning, which is more evidence that there is a genuine 'sense of presence' and 'genuine identities' in virtual worlds. The students' perceptions of 'claustrophobia' within a specific virtual context, their feelings of 'embarrassment' at opening a virtual bathroom door on an avatar on the toilet, or the ability of situations to spark memories of old places visited and establish empathy with specific scenarios in those settings – these all highlight an emotive level of immersion both within that situation and their virtual identity within that situation.

Concepts of ourselves are routed in situations both social and physical. We present sides of ourselves for different situations and often avoid developing and changing those concepts of self. As have been identified by the research detailed here reformation of identity can be supported or inhibited by different virtual world contexts. Within both studies there was a continuing notion of virtual worlds allowing easier adaption of realistic situations and identities. The ability for these to tap into students' physical world identities, memories and concepts of self was identified throughout both studies. However, within both studies students concepts of self and thus their identity was displaced by the flexibility of situations and representations of themselves and others. For some the resultant disorientation was a positive feeling whilst for others it was negative. What these studies reveal is the relationship between virtual world identities and experiences with those in the physical world. Our emotive responses to virtual world identities and experiences appear to be linked to the changing nature of these situations, out of our control, which we simply love or hate. This occurs in many immersive physical world situations which are out of our control. A roller coaster physically and continually changes our perceptions of the world around us. Theatre and films can unsettle concepts that we have of ourselves and our world. Many people, according to individual differences, can find these physical world experiences, as they find the virtual world experiences as emotively positive or negative. Understanding how emotive these situations can be will help us design learning situations more effectively. However, the worrying issue that the language learning project identified was the participants' stereotyped perceptions of student identities and learning experiences. Ultimately, without us challenging these biases towards what learning is, we cannot support students to advance and gain the most from education.

This chapter has identified several potential barriers to virtual world identity reformation based on the study evidence. The evidence has highlighted the socio-cultural underpinnings behind these obstacles frequently related to physical world identity norms and a fear of identity reformation. An over-riding concept throughout were the tensions between individuals' fluidity in identity formation and reformation in contrast to the rigidity of physical world professional, regulatory and some academic concepts of identity. Ultimately this leads to concepts of 'game-playing' to fit with expected and accepted identity norms. Part of learning is to understand the limits of these norms and how to play the identity game. It should be an 'identity game' that we seek to support students in playing. As such there are players, goals, rules and forfeits. Some of the goals and rules are understood well within elearning courses as well as teaching and learning objectives. However, we don't understand the unwritten rules, alternative goals, the players and the forfeits. More importantly as the game is continually changing, and as academics are frequently not active players, should our role be to support students in the official rules or support their understanding of how the game is currently being played? However, the next major problem in virtual world learning is the tension between changing concepts of the academics identity and role in learning. Academics don't understand their own identities and roles within these learning situations, let alone that of the students who are changing their identities. Ultimately, we need to have a better understanding of changing pedagogical models within online environments and academics new identities in student learning before we can seek to support students in their identity reformation through elearning.

References

Adams, A.: Situated elearning: empowerment and barriers to identities changes. In: Warburton, S. Hatzipanagos, S. (eds.) Digital identity and social media. IGI Global, Hershey (2011)

Alvesson, M., Wilmott, H.: Identity regulation as organisational control. Institute of economic research working paper series (2001). 2001:2 Accessed from http://www.lri.lu.se (1/2/10)

Augoustinos, M., Walker, I.: Social Cognition: An Integrated Introduction. Sage Publications, London (1995)

Bernstein, B., Solomon, J.: 'Pedagogy, identity and the construction of a theory of symbolic control': Basil Bernstein questioned by Joseph Solomon. Br. J. Sociol. Educ. **20** (2), 1999 (1999)

Bowker, G.C., Star, S.L.: Sorting Things Out: Classification and Its Consequences. MIT Press, Cambridge (2000)

Brna, P., Aspin, R.: Collaboration in a virtual world: support for conceptual learning. In: Dicheva, D., Stanchev, I. (eds.) Human-Computer Interaction and Education Tools, Proceedings of IFIP WG3.3 working conference, pp. 113–123. VirTech, Sophia (1997)

Cairns, P., et al.: Quantifying the experience of immersion in games. Cognitive Science of Games and Gameplay workshop at Cognitive Science 2006, Vancouver, July 2006

Delwiche, A.: Massively multiplayer online games (MMOs) in the new media classroom. Educ. Technol. Soc. **9** (3), 160–172 (2006)

Fluckiger, F.: Understanding Networked Multimedia Applications and Technology. Prentice Hall, London (1995)

Foster, A.: Second life: second thoughts and doubts. Chronicle of higher education (serial online), 21 Sept 2007, **54** (4), A25–A25. Available from: Library, Information Science & Technology Abstracts, Ipswich. Accessed 21 Sept 2008

Giddens, A.: Modernity and Self Identity, Self and Society in the Late Modern Age. Polity, Cambridge (1991)

Giles, H., Johnson, P.: Ethnolinguistic identity theory: a social psychological approach to language maintenance. Int. J. Sociol. Lang. **68**, 69–99 (1987)

Goffman, E.: The Presentation of Self in Everyday Life. Penguin, London (1959)

Guile, D.: Access learning and development in the creative and cultural sectors: From 'creative apprenticeship' to 'being apprenticed'. J. Educ. Work **19** (5), 433–53 (2006)

Harrison, R., Dourish, P.: Re-place-ing space: The roles of place and space in collaborative systems. In: Proceedings of the Conference on Computer-Supported Cooperative Work (CSCS'96), pp. 67–76. ACM Press, New York (1996)

Kaur, K.: Designing virtual environments for usability. In: Howard, S., Hammond, J., Lindgaard, G. (eds.) Proceedings of Human-Comptuer Interaction (INTERACT'97), pp. 636–639. Chapman & Hall, London (1997)

Kehily, M. J.: What is identity? A sociological perspective. In: ESRC Seminar Series: The educational and social impact of new technologies on young people in Britain, London School of Economics, London, 2 Mar 2009

Latour, B.: Pandora's Hope. Essays on the Reality of Science Studies. Harvard University Press, Cambridge (1999)

Laurel, B.: Computers as Theatre. Addison Wesley, New York (1993)

Lave, J., Wenger, E.: Situated Learning: Legitimate Peripheral Participation. Cambridge University Press, Cambridge (1991)

Oishi, L.: Surfing second life: what does second life have to do with real-life learning? (virtual world). Technol. Learn. **27** (11), 54(1) (2007) (June)

Peachey, A., Withnail, G.: A sociocultural perspective on negotiating digital identities in a community of learners. In: Warburton, S., Hatzipanagos, S. (eds.) Digital Identity and Social Media. IGI Global, Hershey, (2011).

Reeves, B., Nass, C.: The Media Equation: How People Treat Computes, Television and New Media Like Real People and Places. Cambridge University Press, Cambridge (1996)

Rousseau, J-J.: *Émile*. Dent, London (1911 edn.) (1762). (Also available in edition translated and annotated by Allan Bloom (1991 edn.), Penguin, London)

Savin-Baden, M.: Changelings and shape shifters? Identity play and pedagogical positioning of staff in immersive virtual worlds. Lond. Rev. Educ. **8** (1), 25–38 (2010)

Schroeder, R., Axelsson, A.S.: Trust in the core: a study of long-term users of activeworlds. Paper presented at the digital borderlands, A cybercultural symposium, Norrköping, 12–13 May 2000

Smets, G.J.F., Sappers, P.J., Overbeeke, K.J., Van Der Mast, C.: Designing in virtual reality: perception-action coupling and affordances. In: Carr, K., England, R. (eds.) Simulated and Virtual Realities Elements of Perception. Taylor & Francis, London (1995)

Star, S.L., Griesemer, J.R.: Institutional ecology, 'Translations' and boundary objects: Amateurs and professionals in Berkeley's museum of vertebrate zoology, 1907–1930. Soc. Stud. Sci. **19**, 119–128 (1989)

Suchman, L.A.: Plans and Situated Actions: The Problem of Human-Computer Communication. Cambridge University Press, New York (1987)

Sweeney, B., Adams, A.: Virtual world users evaluated according to environment design, task based and affective attention measures. In: People and Computers XXIII – Celebrating people and technology, Proceedings of BCS, HCI'09 Cambridge HCI 2009, pp. 381–387. British Computer Society, Salford, 1–5 Sept 2009

Tajfel, H.: Social identity and intergroup behavior. Soc. Sci. Inf. **13**, 65–93 (1974)

Tajfel, H.: Social stereotypes and social groups. In: Turner, J.C., Giles, H. (eds.) Intergroup Behavior, pp. 144–167. Basil Blackwell, Oxford (1981)

Tuomi-Gröhn, Engeström, Young: Between School and Work: New Perspectives on Transfer and Boundary-Crossing. Pergamon, Amsterdam (2003)

Vygotsky, L.S.: Thought and Language. MIT Press, Cambridge (1962)

Vygotsky, L.S.: Mind in Society: The Development of Higher Mental Processes. Harvard University Press, Cambridge (1978)

Wadley, G., Gibbs, M.: Speaking in character. In: Bainbridge, W.S. (ed.) Online Worlds: Convergence of the Real and the Virtual. Springer, London (2010)

Workman, T.A.: The real impact of virtual worlds. Chron. High. Educ. **55** (4), 12 (2008)

Chapter 15
Virtual Worlds and Identity Exploration for Marginalised People

Jon Cabiria

Abstract The recent rise in the use of virtual worlds as alternative spaces for social gatherings has increased people's access to identity role-play and redevelopment options. By being able to explore repressed facets of their identities in virtual safe harbours such as Second Life™, marginalised people may be able to benefit from positive experiences that can be transferable to their physical world lives. Social construction approaches and the broaden and build theory of positive emotions are used to support the claim that marginalised people, using virtual world interactions, are able to reformulate how they perceive and are perceived by others, leading to positive psychological effects. Online behaviours, such as deindividuation and disinhibition, coupled with anonymity, replace missing sensory informational cues in virtual world environments. Social evaluation theory and social identity theory aid in explaining how people relate to each other in these spaces and the effects on identity development.

15.1 Introduction

The introduction of the Internet and the World Wide Web has completely changed the dynamics of human relationships, putting to test the carefully evolved process of human interactions. People no longer have to be in one another's physical presence to communicate, nor does the communication have to be in real time. While letters and telephones were the standard means of distance communication for generations, computer communications advanced the concept of 'non-present' interactions to unimagined levels, even by the earliest developers. Not only have the dynamics

J. Cabiria (✉)
Walden University, Minneapolis, MN, USA
e-mail: jcabiria@verizon.net

A. Peachey and M. Childs (eds.), *Reinventing Ourselves: Contemporary Concepts of Identity in Virtual Worlds*, Springer Series in Immersive Environments,
DOI 10.1007/978-0-85729-361-9_15, © Springer-Verlag London Limited 2011

of interactions between people changed, but so, too, have people's relationships with themselves, especially when it comes to identity expression.

This new paradigm in connectedness not only addresses how we relate to each other, but how we relate to ourselves. In a constant search to discover "Who am I?" and "Who are you?" people are finding in various online social sites a means of self-exploration, emotional support, identity affirmation, belongingness, and strong communities that may have eluded them in physical life. In addition, researchers have found these same online social communities to be a vast research laboratory of human behaviour, from which negative and positive findings continue to emerge.

There is little formal research to date that has explored the benefits of virtual world societies for marginalised people. Furthermore, there is also little formal research that looks at the use of virtual world societies as a developmental enabler for marginalised people, as well as a safe harbour from which to explore identity deconstruction and reconstruction, or transportation of positive experiences gained in virtual worlds back into physical life.

This chapter presents information regarding the utility of social groups in virtual worlds for purposes of identity exploration and redevelopment in marginalised people. The investigation of these venues will include discussions about the paradox of living inauthentic physical world lives and finding authenticity in virtual world lives. In addition, because social construction addresses the effect people have on each other as they interact, this chapter will overview some of the ways in which people approach and respond to each other differently when online, including disinhibition effects, behaviour and anonymity, and deindividuation - all having important roles in nurturing emergent identities. Finally, the chapter concludes with a look at how positive benefits accrue while engaged in online activities and their transference back into physical world lives.

15.2   Social Construction and Identity Formation

In constructionist studies, the idea that there is an objectively identifiable truth about an individual and his or her social life gives way to other concepts about multiple identities that fluidly manoeuvre among various socio-cultural settings. This means that behaviours and values within certain social groups, such as sexual minorities, those with physical or mental challenges, or other attributes that society finds unacceptable, cannot be effectively studied by only comparing them with a more universal norm (Gergen and Davis 1985). Constructionism asks that we suspend belief about commonly accepted understandings and invites us to challenge the objective basis of conventional knowledge.

Social construction looks at the ways in which people account for who they are and how they interact with other people. It is concerned with how social phenomena evolve from the social environments in which they occur. A social construction will appear as a normal occurrence to those within a particular social group, but may appear as strange, or even perverse, to those not within that group. Social constructions are generally defined as artefacts of human activities and philosophies rather than as inherent natural laws (Wilson 2005).

If we accept that the self, one's identity, is the result of social pressures to conform, we should also consider that all societies also create "others" who are not accepted into the social mainstream and who are viewed as threats to the prevailing social order (Marmor et al. 1999, p 178). One function of the "other" is to help define for members of the dominant group that which is not deviant (Gross and Woods 1999).

It is not enough that a person or group be made out to be an "other." To be considered as an "other," society must first categorise those who behave, or appear to behave, outside of the norm and give them a name – society must construct an identity that describes the others so that members of the dominant group know how to think of them. While a behaviour is merely an action that is described as a part of a larger set of behaviours, an identity describes the combined set of behaviours. An "other" is more clearly defined and communicated as an identity than as a behaviour or trait.

15.3   Relationship Between Marginalisation and Identity

People are social beings who constantly make comparisons with each other. They create categories to help them organise each other, and everyone's place in the world. Behaviours are compared against a cultural norm to determine normalcy and deviancy. Social groups create deviance by making rules whose infraction constitutes deviance, and then categorise those who break the rules, labelling them as outsiders, others, deviants, and psychopaths (Becker 1963). The stages or processes of identity development for a person thus marginalised may become obstructed. The normal interactions with others in society, so important in the developmental process, may not be fully available or may be only available if the person assumes an inauthentic identity in order to fit in. It appears that efforts to conceal a marginalising condition can have a powerful, negative impact on an individual's daily life.

Loneliness and isolation are two more common issues faced by some individuals who are marginalised (Pachankis 2006). Research findings indicate that avoiding others is a common strategy to minimise negative effects of being viewed differently (Corrigan and Matthews 2003). One of the ways of coping with a marginalised status is by avoiding close relationships (Goffman 1963). This reduces the risk of rejection and negative evaluation, but also keeps one from developing support systems, a necessary feature for good mental health (Goldfried and Goldfried 2001). For marginalised people, the groundwork for loneliness, isolation, depression, low self-esteem, and pessimism often begins in childhood with the implicit and explicit social messages they receive through personal interactions and through various media, and is further exacerbated during the critical socialisation and identity-formation stages of adolescence. For those who acquire marginalisation status later in life, they may need to experience a redevelopmental process as part of their new position in society.

Marginalised people may seek out safe and accepting social venues where they might meet similar others. As will be discussed shortly, virtual world communities are near-perfect venues of identity exploration for marginalised people. Engagement in virtual world communities begins the process of self-acknowledgment and reso-cialisation. According to the research of Cohler and Galatzer-Levy (2000), marginalised people who find safe harbours from which to explore more authentic ways of interacting with others often report feeling more integrated and affirmed when they no longer feel the need to hide an important aspect of their lives. The great virtue of inhabiting a more authentic self is that one is simultaneously more alive and alert, and in both ways more available to others (Yoshino 2006, p 72). This would seem to indicate that the psychological and sociological damage of identity repression and fragmentation could be mediated if an outcast could find a nurturing community.

15.4 Developmental Obstructions in Marginalised People

Identity is typically understood as the central psychosocial issue of the adolescent or young adult who seeks to understand who he or she is and how he or she fits into the adult world (McAdams 1988, p 252). During the identity-forming stages of adolescence, any number of factors can influence how one's sense of self is formed. For the marginalised person, a sense of place in the world can be wrought with difficulties in the struggle to successfully deal with developmental stages and emerge with a more or less intact identity of self. Much of one's social development occurs as a result of direct interaction with others and engaging in group activities. Obstructed identity development, in some cases, requires finding and joining reference groups in order to obtain the skills and support needed to engage in the extra developmental steps that some marginalised people need to go through. It is through these groups of like-minded people that they can begin to explore identity transformation.

15.5 Media and Identity Formation

Research suggests that media have important socialisation benefits, including acting as an aid in the search for self-identity (Padilla-Walker 2006). For those who are starting to realise that part of who they are may include the label of a marginalised person, the role of media in their search for self and for a place in society becomes an important tool. Media depictions of marginalised people can cause skewed self-views (Gross and Woods 1999) and alter perceptions of the self by others (Gergen and Davis 1985). People can become unable to discuss their marginalised status, at least initially with those with whom they are close. To rectify this, various forms of media provide opportunities to find similar others and to explore identity formation while, at the same time, shedding an inauthentic façade that may have been created to help 'fit in' with mainstream society.

There has been on-going debate with regard to the influence of entertainment media on American culture. According to Putnam (2000), time spent with passive media, such as television, has come at the expense of time spent on vital community-building activities and there are now similar conversations about the effects of the Internet on culture and social communities. Some scholars have argued that online, Internet-based media are exceptions (Steinkuehler and Williams 2006). The evidence is mixed, with some arguing that the Internet's capacity for connecting people across time and space fosters the formation of social networks and personal communities (Wellman and Gulia 1999) and bridges class and racial gaps (Mehra et al. 2004); yet other scholars argue that the Internet functions as a displacer (Nie and Erbring 2002; Nie and Hillygus 2002) enabling little more than "pseudo communities" (Beniger 1987; Postman 1992).

Whatever the resulting effects of media use can be, it seems clear that people turn toward media for satisfaction and fulfilment of private needs: It has the power to ease loneliness, lift moods, provide important information, entertain, transmit culture and heritage, and cause people to somehow feel connected to a social community, even if only to a virtual one (Merrill et al. 1990).

15.6   Media Use and Social Identity Theory

People use media as a means to project identity, as well as to feel part of a larger community. The types of media that are used become a source of bonding with others through discussions of mutual experiences and shared interests. Social identity theory (SIT) focuses on "the group in the individual" (Hogg and Abrams 1988, p 3) and makes an assumption that self-concept can be partially defined through membership in social groups. Tajfel defines social identity as "that part of an individual's self-concept which derives from one's knowledge of one's membership of a social group (or groups) together with the value and emotional significance attached to that membership" (1978, p 63). According to Tajfel and Turner (1979), people categorise themselves and others as belonging to different social groups and evaluate these categorisations. Their membership in these groups defines their social identity (Trepte 2006, p 255). The goal of such strong affiliations with others, whether in physical groups or in mediated ones, is to achieve positive self-esteem and self-enhancement (Hogg and Abrams 1988, p 3). Thus, positive social identity is based on favourable comparisons between the members inside a group which are often solidified by highlighting their differences from other groups (Allport 1954; Trepte 2006). The most important idea behind the SIT model is that people not only select the media to fit their identities and to deliver identity-related satisfaction, but also that media functions as a source of information about groups and their legitimate status (Reid et al. 2004, p 22). In his early work, Tajfel (1969) stated that the motivation underlying positive social identity is to preserve one's self-image and that the main drive is to reach self-enhancement.

15.7 Virtual Worlds and Finding Communities

Virtual worlds have come into prominence in recent years although various forms of virtual worlds have been around for decades. Of particular note, Second Life has received quite a bit of attention from researchers. It might be accurate to think of a virtual world as simply a next-generation telephone; a mediated communication device that has advanced functionality like visuals, conferencing, and enhanced human-abilities, such as allowing for simulated flight. The basic intent is to allow people to communicate in real time through media devices that enable sound, sight, and motion.

Second Life is of particular interest for psychological and sociological research because it offers several interesting research amenities, including (a) providing parallel spaces (physical life and virtual life) in which to discover comparisons and contrasts of two environments by the same participant; (b) providing safe harbours for marginalised people to explore identity formation in ways that physical life may not have afforded them; and (c) offering potential for networks and resources that may aid in dealing with less-than-ideal physical life issues.

Virtual world social communities succeed by allowing people to experience the presence of others in a mediated environment. Presence is based on how the content in the virtual space is designed, and is enhanced by how the user perceives the space, allowing her or him to be oriented in space and understand the orientation of virtual objects in the same space (McMahon 2003, p 72, 75). A more apt term for presence in a mediated environment is *telepresence*, which is the extent to which one feels present in the mediated environment, rather than in the immediate physical environment. It is the experience of presence in an environment by means of a communication medium; in other words, presence refers to the natural perception of an environment, and telepresence refers to the mediated perception of an environment (McMahon 2003).

Building upon the sense of presence and telepresence is copresence, as can be found in virtual communities. Goffman (1959) described copresence as the sensory awareness of an embodied other, though it can also refer to feelings of spatial presence with another and/or a sense of mutual awareness. His seminal work emphasises the role of the human senses and social interaction and makes this approach applicable to media experiences by extending the senses to bodily representations (Biocca 2003), as seen in the avatars of online worlds (Tamborini and Skalski 2006). Recent advances in information and communication technologies have enabled people to share stories, via their avatars, in a mediated, copresence-producing environment. The creation and sharing of stories aid in the formation of community.

By providing spaces for social interaction and relationships beyond the home and workplace, virtual communities can function as a new kind of space of socializing for marginalised people, similar to the "third space" as described by Putnam (2000). Putnam noted how third spaces are disappearing from modern society. However, the arguable decline in physical third spaces appears to be replaced by a rise in virtual third spaces as a means of group identity creation. Virtual communities

are particularly efficient at socialising their members into group identity and articulating group categorisations (Jenkins 2000), taking on the role of traditional socialising venues. The virtual social venues appear well-suited to the formation of
creating social capital through ease of interactions and by creating social relationships that expose the individual to a diversity of worldviews (Steinkuehler and
Williams 2006).

People join virtual world communities for a variety of reasons, including having
access to information (e.g. Jones 1995; Wellman et al. 1996), which is also a reason
for group membership cited often by social psychologists (e.g. Hagel and Armstrong
1997; Watson and Johnson 1972). Virtual world communities are unique in that
most of their content is member-generated, as opposed to other Internet information
which is typically produced by the site provider (with some notable exceptions,
such as Wikipedia). This makes the quality of virtual worlds' content an important
factor in their success (Filipczak 1998). Due to the ability to remain pseudonymous,
a virtual community, such as Second Life, can be an ideal place to ask relative
strangers for information (Baym 2000; Wellman and Gulia 1999) and to access
social support in dealing with marginalising physical world factors. Social support
may also be linked with individual motivation to join groups because of the sense of
belonging and affiliation it entails (Watson and Johnson 1972) and the way it
addresses the need for self-identity (Hogg 1996). House (1981, p 26) offers a more
specific definition of social support: "it is a flow of emotional concern, instrumental
aid, information, and/or appraisal (information relevant to self-evaluation) between
people". Consistent with this definition, research suggests that virtual worlds are
places where people go to find emotional support, sense of belonging, and encour-
agement, in addition to instrumental aid (Hiltz and Wellman 1997; Sproull and Faraj
1997; Smith and Kollock 1999).

15.8   Virtual Worlds and Identity Redevelopment

Of special interest is the life-cycle stage where identity development is strong, such
as during adolescence. One place that adolescents now spend a considerable amount
of time is in online settings, and these online venues have been linked to identity
exploration (Huffaker and Calvert 2005; Turkle 1995). Identity is often characterised as one's interpersonal characteristics (Calvert 2002) and involves a sense of
continuity of self-image over time (Grotevant 1998). For Erikson (1993), a sense of
identity is constructed after a successful search for who one is in the world. However,
other perspectives of adolescent development view the construction of one's identity as involving multiple selves that are presented according to the situations in
which one finds oneself (Harter 1998). While physical constraints such as the body,
biological sex, race, or age can have a profound effect on self-definition and self-
presentation (Collins and Kuczaj 1991), these attributes become flexible in virtual
worlds. In fact, the pseudonymous nature of virtual environments allows people
who feel marginalised more flexibility in exploring their identity through the

personae they assume in the form of a self-constructed avatar (Calvert 2002; Huffaker and Calvert 2005). In the physical world, there is often no respite from the societal pressures to conform. For some people, it becomes a matter of hiding from others, physically and/or psychologically. However, in a virtual world, marginalised people may feel more comfortable expressing themselves and in exploring other facets of their identity. Studies concerning virtual worlds have found such worlds to have great significance to players for identity and community (Turkle 1995). In fact, it appears that a virtual world, such as Second Life, can function as a therapeutic tool. Research to date has shown that those with few friends in physical life feel happier as they spend more hours in Second Life (Cabiria 2008a; de Nood and Attema 2006).

15.9   Virtual Worlds as Safe Harbours

Social support is an important source of positive well-being and is needed to cope effectively with stressors. Studies have found that the effects of stressors on well-being were buffered by perceived social support, which either reduced the effect of the stressor or enhanced self-esteem, and which served to evoke stress coping mechanisms (Komproe et al. 1997; Lazarus and Folkman 1984; Sagiv et al. 2004).

A hallmark attribute of social support is that the context in which the support is being offered is perceived to be safe. Communities perceived to be safe help people become more comfortable. People may even change their own value system, internalising the values and goals of the group of which they wish to be a part in order to achieve a state of well-being. They may also help reshape the group environment to align with their own personal existing values and goals (Sagiv et al. 2004). Sagiv and Schwartz (2000) note the impact of environments on people's ability to attain their values and goals. Environments that are compatible with one's values and goals provide them with opportunities to achieve well-being. However, incompatible environments do not provide these opportunities (Sagiv et al. 2004). The ability to operate within an environment in a manner that increases one's sense of well-being can be described as an ability to cope.

Researchers who explore coping mechanisms have begun to investigate the usefulness of positive emotions in stressful contexts. A review of coping research findings indicates that positive emotions help buffer against stress, are related to the occurrence and maintenance of positive affect (Folkman and Moskowitz 2000), and serve to benefit psychological well-being (Affleck and Tennen 1996). These findings indicate that positive emotions are valuable tools for providing beneficial outcomes (Tugade and Fredrickson 2004).

Marginalised people under stress use a range of personal coping mechanisms, resilience, and hardiness to withstand stressful experiences (e.g. Masten 2001; Ouellette 1993). However, positive group-level factors can also provide further mental health benefits (Peterson et al. 1996). It is the group-level benefits that are of particular interest in this chapter. For example, Jones et al. (1984) noted that aligning one's self with similar others provides two important coping functions: (a) it allows one to exist within a non-marginalising environment, and (b) provides support against the negative effects of the marginalising external society. Social evaluation theory (Pettigrew 1967) proposes another way of looking at coping skills. Marginalised people who seek out and actively participate in welcoming and supportive groups, and who develop a strong sense of community as a result of this participation, evaluate themselves in comparison with those in their group who are like them rather than with those of the dominant and marginalising culture. The group validates and normalises what the general society would consider to be deviant behaviours or traits (Thoits 1985), providing the marginalised person with a new perspective on his or her place in the world and, thereby, allowing the possibility of increased self-esteem (Garnets and Kimmel 1991; Meyer 2003). It would appear that what is most important is that one surround her- or himself with supportive others, regardless of the formal nature of the group.

15.10   The Psychology of Virtual World Identity Formation

The reasons that compel people to interact with each other appear to be the same, whether they are offline or online – people need each other for support, companionship, love, safety, attaining goals, and for some, spiritual fulfilment. They also need each other to affirm a sense of self-view – a desire to have others see the value in who one is and what one does (Cabiria 2008b). Sometimes, the physical world does not provide these values and affirmations and people turn to online communities in search of fulfilment; however, something happens in the way some people conduct themselves when in the online environment. It is proposed that the lack of the informational and sensory cues, so important in physical world interactions, leads to adjustments in the way people interact with each other when online (Chayko 2002).

15.11   Informational Cues

We are what others perceive of us to be. That is, people use their sensory abilities, combined with past experiences, to create an impression of who other people are. They then relate to the other person based on those impressions, constantly adjusting perceptions as the other person responds back. At some point, hopefully, the perception of one person melds with the other person's self-concept to create a relationship that, more-or-less, functions well. A great deal of the formation of relationships rests upon each person's ability to 'read' the other person. Using physical nuances, people create meaning from a wide variety of cues, such as vocal tone, body posture, hairstyle and clothing, use of language, and more. With these, people add historical context, cultural interpretations, and mood. These social cues, as Goffman (1959) called them, are critical to our ability to understand and relate to each other. It is fair to say that social cues are just as much language as is the spoken word.

In the online world, people lose many of these cues (Golman 2007) and attempt to compensate for these losses, sometimes to good effect and sometimes with disastrous results. In a largely text-based world often found in online virtual world communities, relating to others is largely independent of the subtleties of social cue generation. Advances have been made in some respects, such as the ubiquitous use of emoticons and typefaces to express emotion. Certainly, the creation of avatars, essentially cartoon-like placeholders used to represent the self in virtual spaces, have provide limited return of the lost cues. The introduction of voice into formerly text-based spaces also helps improve on relationship-building, with notable exceptions (see for example Chapter 9 this volume).

This is not to say that the lack of social cues is always a negative. For some people, crippled by inescapable physical world judgments of them, the online environment can provide respite and the opportunity to be known for something other than their perceived deficits (Joinson 2001). Marginalised people, in using virtual worlds for identity discovery or reformation, can make use of several online social effects to further their goals. Among these are anonymity, deindividuation, and disinhibition.

15.12   Anonymous/Pseudonymous

In virtual world environments, people often leave their physical world lives behind. Many, while they may adopt virtual identities, remain anonymous by creating pseudonymous identities and do not allow physical world information to cross over into their virtual world activities. The pseudonymous nature of virtual world behaviours can lead to role-playing behaviours, such as children might do, in an attempt to 'practice' new identities without fear of compromising physical world relationships (Suler 2004). For some, it is a temporary activity used to relieve the stress of maintaining an inauthentic physical world identity; for others, it is a means to replace a perceived unhealthy identity with a more robust and authentic one (Cabiria 2010).

15.13   Deindividuation

Jung (1946, p. 561) described individuation as "the development of the psychological individual as a differentiated being from the general, collective psychology. Individuation, therefore, is a process of differentiation, having for its goal the development of the individual personality". Conversely, losing one's individuality or uniqueness can be described as deindividuation. We can look at deindividuation as something one experiences within one's self, or something one does to another.

Classic theorists such as Jung (1948), Rogers (1954), Allport (1955), and Maslow (1968) all note the drive of people to be regarded as unique individuals, and that the inability to be perceived as such can lead to unusual personality shifts. In fact, these concepts have been tested for decades, noting that deindividuation can lead to impulsive behaviour and atypical actions (Festinger et al. 1952; Zimbardo 1969). Later researchers agree with the proposals that deindividuation can be an explanation for abnormal and uninhibited behaviour (Siegal et al. 1986).

In a virtual world environment, it can be postulated that deindividuation, the process of identity loss, is a beneficial precursor to identity discovery. When a person enters a virtual world environment, there can be a period of disequilibrium as she or he seeks to establish who she or he is with the few social cues available. For the marginalised person, this disequilibrium can be used as a way to process out negative behaviours and affects rooted in physical world social constructions and replace them with more positive ones (Cabiria 2010). To borrow from organisational change psychologist, Kurt Lewin (1947), the marginalised person who is exploring virtual worlds has the opportunity to unfreeze engrained attitudes about one's self, transition to more beneficial behaviours, and then freeze the new identity in place. This strongly relates to Lewin's formula which states that behaviour is a function of the person and their environment (Lewin 1947). In short, deindividuation, it is proposed, can benefit the marginalised person seeking to use virtual worlds as a means to revise or recreate an identity by using the weakened identity inherent in virtual spaces, as a result of deindividuation, to release one's self of portions of the unwanted identity, transition to a new one, and then formalise it.

15.14 Disinhibition

Disinhibition can be described as behaviour that shows diminished concern for one's self-presentation to others, or for the judgment of others, than might otherwise occur in social interacitons (Joinson 1998; Coleman et al. 1999). This has also been coined as the 'disinhibition effect' when discussing online behaviours (Golman 2007; Suler 2004). Suler (2004), noted that disinhibition in online environments could arise out of several psychological factors, including anonymity, the asynchronous nature of many online communications, and the lack of strong socially-constructed boundaries that tell us when we are out-of-line. This disinhibition effect is, in itself, a neutral effect that takes on a value depending upon its use. For example, a marginalised person who enters a virtual space might feel free from the shackles of repression and explore relationships in new and positive ways. For them, disinhibition can be used as a means of self-discovery and self-expression that promotes psychic healing (Cabiria 2010). Disinhibition can be related to deindividuation, in that, when one feels a loss of uniqueness, she or he is motivated to explore atypical behaviours as a means to recapture a sense of identity (Coleman et al. 1999).

15.15 The Influence and Effects of Virtual World Communities on Identity Redevelopment

Virtual worlds offer marginalised people some very distinct advantages, including the ability to maintain relationships. One's online personal history and profile equate to offline informational cues, helping people to create identities and to have access to the identity information of others (Tajfel and Turner 1986). Online, marginalised people can choose how they wish to be seen in a way that places their marginalising attributes on par with their other attributes rather than in the forefront. Their physical world labels no longer need to dominate how others perceive and relate to them. Virtual world communities can provide marginalised people much needed safe spaces in which to explore identity issues, especially in the formative adolescent and young adult years. These communities can offer a variety of groups in which aspects of one's identity can be spotlighted and explored in ways that might not be possible in their offline environments (Cabiria 2008a). One's psychosocial development can benefit greatly from exposure to information and people with similar interests. However, online social network activities are not always positive. In fact, the utility of these sites for beneficial psychological and social development is continually explored and debated (Kraut et al. 2002; Shaw and Gant 2002; Valkenburg et al. 2006). Still, it is apparent that people who create social affiliations through online engagement are likely to behave in more positive ways that lead to better psychological health and development (Cabiria 2008b; Helliwell and Putnam 2004; Morrow 1999).

Over the past several years, a number of studies have come out on the subject of Internet use and psychological and social well-being (e.g. Kraut et al. 1998). While the results of these studies are not conclusive, it appears that frequent Internet use was associated with increased measures of depression and loneliness (e.g. Valkenburg and Peter 2007; Kraut et al. 2002; Nie 2001). Conversely, studies in which Internet use included frequent participation in online social communities indicated increases in self-esteem and overall well-being (e.g. Valkenburg et al. 2006; Shaw and Gant 2002). It can be assumed that people with poor physical world social networks could see an increase in positive affect once they have found an virtual world community of similar others with whom they could frequently interact (Cabiria 2008a).

Our self-esteem and identities emerge from social interactions (Owens et al. 2006). We can draw from this that when people have positive experiences in virtual world communities, the positive meaning that they give their experiences can increase their positive feelings about themselves. When people feel positive about their relationships, their interactions continue to increase, strengthening their social network ties and social capital accounts, thus leading to higher self-esteem and opportunities for increased positive interactions (see Fig. 15.1).

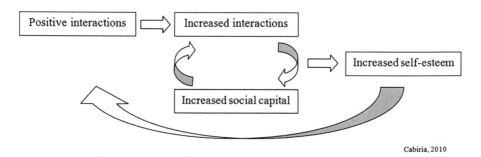

Cabiria, 2010

Fig. 15.1 The influence and effects of virtual world communities on identity redevelopment

15.16   A Case Study

In 2008, the author conducted a series of studies within Second Life that explored the positive benefits of virtual world activities for marginalised people, and the transference of those benefits into the participants' physical lives (see boxed insert). One of these studies, a grounded theory qualitative study, looked at a group of lesbian and gay people who had indicated through a series of questionnaires and interviews that they felt marginalised in their physical world lives. This study explored both their physical world lives and their subsequent virtual lives to discover if changes in behaviour and affect occurred. The purpose of the physical world study was two-fold: (a) to see if the participants' experiences as lesbian or gay people were similar to those reported in various studies conducted over the past few decades, and (b) to establish a point-of-reference in comparing physical and virtual world experiences. The results of the physical life portion of this study indicated that the participants' experiences were consistent with prior accepted studies, and that these experiences led to the expected emerging themes of loneliness, isolation, depression, low self-esteem, withdrawal, lack of authenticity, and lack of useful information. Specifically, the results indicated the causes of these affects to be developmental obstruction, negative psychological effect of being marginalised, the power of hetero-normative forces, and identity compartmentalisation, to name a few. While not every participant indicated all emergent themes, each participant experienced multiple effects in meaningful ways, as demonstrated by the representative excerpts from the interview transcripts and the questionnaire responses.

A Second Life: Online Virtual Worlds as Therapeutic Tools for Gay and Lesbian Cabiria (2008c)

In this particular study, I identified gay and lesbian people who felt marginalised in their physical world lives. I wanted to discover whether there was meaningful opportunity for, and support of, change in affective states for gay and lesbian people in a virtual world space, and if this led to positive emotions that could be transferred to the physical world. The goal was to suggest ways in which psychologists, educators, and social website developers could help marginalised people, such as gay and lesbian people, discover ways in which they might explore healthy identity formation.

This study utilised qualitative research methods to bring to light the value experience that a social outlet like Second Life provides. It sought to uncover the meaning that could be derived from the virtual world experiences of the participants. A grounded theory approach guided the analysis utilising software analysis tools (SPSS for Text) and manual coding for category creation.

(continued)

A Second Life: Online Virtual Worlds as Therapeutic Tools for Gay and Lesbian People (continued)

From a respondent pool of 32 potential participants, 17 participants were chosen for the study, based on their demographic survey responses. Fourteen completed the entire process. The data were collected from three questionnaires, two semi-structured interviews, and follow up conversations as needed. The analysis of individual questionnaire responses helped to shed more light on the meaning that participants gave to the intersection of their real and virtual world lives, and content analysis of the interviews and the questionnaires' open-ended responses helped me to discover emerging themes during the process of comparing and contrasting participant responses. The results of hand-coding and software coding were compared and contrasted as the analysis progressed in the search for emergent themes and theories between physical and virtual world lives (see Table 15.1 Emerging themes).

To help deal with the possibility that participants would not be who they said they were, I sought out groups within Second Life that were known to have an established reputation. These groups consisted of other researchers and academicians, as well as those from marginalised classes who formed inworld groups for mutual support. It was assumed that the chances of misrepresentation would be lower than soliciting from the general Second Life population. In addition, the questionnaires were designed to capture irregularities in responses, and the interview transcripts were compared to the questionnaire responses as well. Any participant information that raised red flags was not used in the study.

Due to the pseudonymous nature of Second Life, all research was conducted in the virtual world. The physical world identity of the participants remained unknown to the researcher. The participants were interviewed through my Second Life avatar in my Second Life office.

Table 15.1 Emerging themes

Physical life	Virtual life
Loneliness	Belongingness
Isolation	Connectedness
Depression	Improved well-being
Low self-esteem	Higher self-esteem
Withdrawal	Optimism
Lack of authenticity	Authenticity
Lack of useful information	Carry over effect of positive benefits

(continued)

A Second Life: Online Virtual Worlds as Therapeutic Tools for Gay and Lesbian People (continued)

The words of the participants can best describe the benefits derived from their virtual world engagements:

Billy: No one can hurt me [in Second Life] so I don't care what they think. In my real life, I have to be careful because the repercussions could be significant.

Freda: It is hard not to dislike yourself to some degree when you believe everyone else dislikes you because of this one thing ... I think I would have been happier sooner. I would not have felt alone, isolated, and confused.

Karen: I like how I act in Second Life and I wouldn't change it. I feel really more like myself even if it feels strange to be myself because I'm not used to it.

Vito: When good things happen in Second Life, I am bound to learn how to make those same good things happen in real life. And I know that I will get stronger about being an out gay person in real life because I am really enjoying being an out gay person in Second Life and it is getting harder to go back in the closet every time I leave Second Life.

Justin: I noticed a month or so after entering the Second Life gay community that my attitude/bearing/general sense of well-being had taken a significant boost ... I noticed that I'd gone from a feeling of chronic exhaustion, to a sense of almost euphoric energy and started to connect that feeling to my time in Second Life.

Rory: I am thinking more about coming out in real life. I almost did a few times. I am happier in Second Life but it is making me happier in real life too ... I am more like who I want to be in Second Life and I am working on being that same person in real life and getting rid of my phony real life self. So my sense of identity is getting stronger in both ... I pretend in real life and I don't pretend in the pretend life.

If I think of Second Life and the physical life as one-life, then what we are really looking at, for the purposes of this study, is simply a location in which positive benefits can be gained and which can positively influence other aspects of our lives. The word "virtual" carries a connotation of something not real, something artificial. Perhaps, as some participants indicated, the concerns of the realness of their virtual lives would not need to be considered if they were to think in terms of one-life, regardless of how it is mediated.

The purpose of the Second Life portion of the study was also twofold: (a) to see if there was any difference between stated physical and virtual experiences with regard to being lesbian or gay, and (b) to see if the broaden-and-build theory of positive emotions had applicability. According to Fredrickson's broaden-and- build theory, positive emotions broaden people's "momentary thought-action repertoires" (Fredrickson 1998, 2001; Fredrickson and Joiner 2002). This theory corroborates research that demonstrated the social benefits associated with positive emotions (Isen 1990). It appeared from the analysis that there were several differences between physical and virtual experiences, and that seven virtual world themes emerged from the data, namely belongingness, connectedness, improved well-being, higher self-esteem, optimism, sense of authenticity, and evidence of transferable positive benefits. While further exploration of this study is outside the scope of this chapter, it is worthwhile noting that all participants in this particular study experienced positive benefits as a result of their activities within virtual worlds, and that most developed stronger positive identities which they then transferred over into their physical world lives (Cabiria 2008b).

More than anything else, it appears that having access to similar others through virtual world interactions, and a sense of belonging, provides marginalised people with the tools they needed to redirect their developmental paths and to reform their identities. Second Life provides the place, safety, and relationship opportunities for that development to occur. This ground-breaking study showed that participants who had few friends in physical life had many friends in Second Life. There were also participants who socialised more in Second Life than in physical life. There were indications of higher levels of comfort with being lesbian or gay, a greater sense of belonging and connection, and hopefulness of a better physical life as a result of Second Life experiences.

The data appeared to show some very compelling evidence that there were significant changes in affect when many of the participants were discussing their physical world lives versus their virtual lives. Part of the reason for this appears to stem from a sense of personal authenticity that seemed to be missing in their physical lives. In fact, it was a major emerging theme throughout the research data. The theme of authenticity can be seen as the instigator for the other emerging themes, such as sense of belongingness, connectedness, higher self-esteem, and better sense of well-being. Participants noted, at various points in their narratives, the words and phrases that were implicit or explicit in meaning with regard to acting inauthentically or authentically. Even those who had heavily compartmentalised their lives in order to achieve some level of comfort with their marginalised status expressed how authentic they felt in Second Life.

Along with this expression of authenticity were the positive effects some of the participants indicated as a result of their Second Life experiences. Not only were the participants acknowledging positive effects and making explicit remarks about how these effects were not present in their physical lives, there were indications of comparisons between their physical and virtual lives, including a few very telling statements that seem to juxtapose the physical and the virtual. The participants' expressions of authenticity, positive benefits, and juxtaposition of physical and virtual affects also conveyed their desire to experience virtual worlds not as a unidirectional source of physical life improvement (e.g. from Second Life into physical life), or as a unidirectional source of physical life escape (e.g. from physical life into Second Life), but as a bidirectional experience in which there is constant transference of benefit from and to each.

It is important to note that the merger of the concepts of physical and virtual world, and the carry-over effects of positive benefits, seem to implicate permeability as an attribute of virtual worlds. It would seem that initial, positive experiences by marginalised people in virtual worlds offered them the ability to make substantial changes in their physical world lives. The various positive experiences were not only transferable into physical life, they caused some people to reflect further upon their unsatisfactory physical life situations with the goal of making further substantial positive changes in their physical world lives.

Many research studies and discussions about virtual world activities focus on negative effects. They note findings that deal with addictive behaviour, anti-social engagements, violence, sexism and racism, distraction from other learning opportunities, the decline of meaningful social interactions, and concern about the blurring of physical and virtual, to name just a few. While this study presents some initial conclusions to the contrary, it is by no means definitive. There is further need for more research that approaches the same issues from a variety of perspectives and methodologies.

15.17   Physical Life and Virtual Life Merged

The positive benefits that marginalised people gain as a result of their virtual world experiences, and which has been shown to carry over into their physical lives, indicates the possibility of an artificial construction of "here versus there". The concept of thinking about physical and virtual lives as two unconnected places creates a concept that places an artificial membrane between the two. Perhaps, due to the potential for high permeability, consideration should be given to dissolving this construct and thinking of physical and virtual as simply "one life" that exists along a continuum. After all, is a virtual world really anything more than an iteration of the telephone that has added sensory functionality? Certainly, we are not in a virtual world when speaking on the telephone. Does the potential for role-play and identity exploration make virtual world activities any less real?

15.18   Conclusion

With virtual online interactions come special considerations when attempting to build and maintain relationships. Due to the lack of various cues, people engage in behaviours that can be perceived as dysfunctional in the physical world, but which have utility in the virtual world. Disinhibition and deindividuation, paired with anonymity, can provide a means of avoiding physical world labelling and establishing a new identity framework.

It is clear that research into the psychological effects of engaging in online social communities requires more data. While it is now obvious that the potential for identity redevelopment and beneficial positive effects exists, research into the negative effects captures much of the public attention. Additionally, as these online social communities and related technologies evolve, and our online interactions become more textured and nuanced, we can expect to see stronger online parallels to our physical world behaviours.

From its earliest beginnings, the Internet was envisioned as a mass communications tool capable of keeping people connected and providing a platform for the sharing of information. Our needs and desires for more robust means of interaction spurred technological innovations that continue unabated. Even as we marvel at the proliferation of online social communities over the past few decades, and the recent prominence of virtual worlds, with increased abilities to replicate social and sensory cues, even more immersive possibilities are already visible on the horizon. Augmented reality technologies, which overlay digital images onto physical life spaces and were once only in the imaginations of science fiction writers, will be able to project the real-time digital images of people from distant locations into a physical world common space. In essence, we become the avatars. It will be interesting to discover the psychological implications of easily placing one's self, fully representative, into a new environment of one's choosing and how marginalisation effects are demonstrated to be a matter of environment.

References

Affleck, G., Tennen, H.: Construing benefits from adversity: adaptational significance and dispositional underpinnings. J. Pers. **64**(4), 899–922 (1996)

Allport, G.W.: The Nature of Prejudice. Addison Wesley, Reading (1954)

Allport, G.W.: Becoming: Basic Considerations for a Psychology of Personality. Yale University Press, New Haven (1955)

Baym, N.K.: Tune in, Log on: Soaps, Fandom and Online Community. Sage, Thousand Oaks (2000)

Becker, H.: Outsiders: Studies in the Sociology of Deviance. Free Press, New York (1963)

Beniger, J.: Personalization of mass media and the growth of pseudo-community. Commun. Res. **14**(3), 352–371 (1987)

Biocca, F.: The evolution of interactive media. In: Green, M.C., Strange, J.J., Brock, T.C. (eds.) Narrative Impact: Social and Cognitive Foundations. Erlbaum, Mahwah (2003)

Cabiria, J.: Benefits of virtual world engagement. Media Psychol. Rev. **1**(1) (2008a)

Cabiria, J.: Virtual world and real world permeability: transference of positive benefits. J. Virt. World Res. **1**(1) (2008b)

Cabiria, J.: A Second Life: Online virtual worlds as therapeutic tools for gay and lesbian people. Ph.D. dissertation, Fielding Graduate University, United States – California. Retrieved from Dissertations & Theses @ Fielding Graduate University. (Publication No. AAT 3310397). (2008c)

Cabiria, J.: Idle conversations: mundane discussions that create strong social connections. (unpublished). (2010)

Calvert, S.L.: Identity construction on the internet. In: Calvert, S.L., Jordan, A.B., Cocking, R.R. (eds.) Children in the Digital Age: Influences of Electronic Media on Development, pp. 57–70. Praeger, Westport (2002)

Chayko, M.: Connecting: How We Form Social Bonds and Communities in the Internet Age. SUNY Press, Albany (2002)

Cohler, B.J., Galatzer-Levy, R.M.: The Course of Gay and Lesbian Lives: Social and Psychoanalytic Perspectives. University of Chicago Press, Chicago (2000)

Coleman, L.H., Paternite, C.E., Sherman, R.C.: A reexamination of deindividuation in synchronous computer-mediated communication. Comput. Hum. Behav. **15**, 51–65 (1999)

Collins, W.A., Kuczaj, S.A.: Developmental Psychology: Childhood and Adolescence. Macmillan, New York (1991)

Corrigan, P.W., Matthews, A.K.: Stigma and disclosure: implications for coming out of the closet. J. Ment. Health **12**, 235–248 (2003) de Nood, D., Attema, J.: Second Life: The Second Life of Virtual Reality, vol. 1. EPN – Electronic Highway Platform, The Hague (2006, October)

Erikson, E.H.: Childhood and Society. W.W. Norton & Company, New York (1993)

Festinger, L., Pepitone, A., Newcomb, T.: Some consequences of de-individuation in a group. J. Abnorm. Soc. Psychol. **47**, 382–389 (1952)

Filipczak, B.: Trainers on the net: a community of colleagues. Training **35**(2), 70–76 (1998)

Folkman, S., Moskowitz, J.T.: Stress, positive emotion, and coping. Curr. Dir. Psychol. Sci. **9**, 115–118 (2000)

Fredrickson, B.L.: What good are positive emotions? Rev. Gen. Psychol. **2**, 300–319 (1998)

Fredrickson, B.L.: The role of positive emotions in positive psychology: the broaden-and-build theory of positive emotions. Am. Psychol. **56**(3), 218–226 (2001)

Fredrickson, B.L., Joiner, T.: Positive emotions trigger upward spirals toward emotional well-being. Psychol. Sci. **13**, 172–175 (2002)

Garnets, L.D., Kimmel, D.C.: Lesbian and Gay Male Dimensions in the Psychological Study of Human Diversity. American Psychological Association, Washington, DC (1991)

Gergen, K.J., Davis, K.E.: The Social Construction of the Person. Springer, New York (1985)

Goffman, E.: The Presentation of Self in Everyday Life. Doubleday Anchor, Garden City (1959)

Goffman, I.: Stigma: Notes on the Management of Spoiled Identity. Simon & Schuster, New York (1963)

Goldfried, M.R., Goldfried, A.P.: The importance of parental support in the lives of gay, lesbian, and bisexual individuals. J. Clin. Psychol. **57**, 681–693 (2001)

Golman, D.: Flame first, think later: new clues to e-mail misbehaviour. The New York Times (2007, February)

Gross, L., Woods, J.D. (eds.): The Columbia Reader on Lesbians and Gay Men in Media, Society, and Politics. Columbia University Press, New York (1999)

Grotevant, H.D.: Adolescent development in family contexts. In: Damon, W., Eisenberg, N. (eds.) Handbook of Child Psychology. Social, Emotional, and Personality Development, vol. 3, 5th edn, pp. 1097–1149. Wiley, New York (1998)

Hagel, J., Armstrong, A.G.: Net Gain: Expanding Markets Through Virtual Communities. Harvard Business School Press, Boston (1997)

Harter, S.: The development of self-representations. In: Damon, W., Eisenberg, N. (eds.) Handbook of Child Psychology. Social, Emotional, and Personality Development, vol. 3, 5th edn, pp. 553–617. Wiley, New York (1998)

Helliwell, J.F.K., Putnam, R.D.K.: The social context of well-being. Philosophical transactions of the royal society. Biol. Sci. **359**, 1435–1446 (2004)

Hiltz, S.R., Wellman, B.: Asynchronous learning networks as a virtual classroom. Commun. ACM **40**(9), 44–49 (1997)

Hogg, M.A.: Group structure and social identity. In: Robinson, W.P. (ed.) Social Groups and Identities: Developing the Legacy of Henri Tajfel, pp. 65–94. Butterworth Heinemann, Oxford (1996)

Hogg, M.A., Abrams, D.: Social Identifications: A Social Psychology of Intergroup Relations and Group Processes. Routledge, London (1988)

House, J.S.: Work Stress and Social Support. Addison-Wesley, Reading (1981)

Huffaker, D.A., Calvert, S.L.: Gender, identity, and language use in teenage blogs. J. Comput. Mediat. Commun. **10**(2), article 1 (2005)

Isen, A.M.: The influence of positive and negative affect on cognitive organization: Some implications for development. In: Stein, N., Leventhal, B., Trabasso, B. (eds.) Psychological and Biological Approaches to Emotion. Erlbaum, Hillsdale (1990)

Jenkins, R.: Categorization: identity, social process and epistemology. Curr. Sociol. **48**(3), 7–25 (2000)

Joinson, A.: Causes and implications of disinhibited behavior on the Internet. In: Gackenbach, J. (ed.) Psychology and the Internet, pp. 43–60. Academic, San Diego (1998)

Joinson, A.N.: Self-disclosure in computer-mediated communication: the role of self-awareness and visual anonymity. Eur. J. Soc. Psychol. **31**, 177–192 (2001)

Jones, S.G.: Understanding community in the information age. In: Jones, S.G. (ed.) CyberSociety: Computer-Mediated Communication and Community, pp. 10–35. Sage Publications, London (1995)

Jones, E.E., Farina, A., Hastorf, A.H., Markus, H., Miller, D.T., Scott, A.S.: Social Stigma: The Psychology of Marked Relationships. Freeman, New York (1984)

Jung, C.G.: Psychological Types or the Psychology of Individuation. Harcourt, Brace, New York (1946)

Jung, C.G.: The Undiscovered Self. Routledge & Kegan Paul, London (1948)

Komproe, I.H., Rijken, M., Ros, W.J., Winnubst, J.A., Hart, H.: Available support and received support: different effects under stressful circumstances. J. Soc. Pers. Relationships **14**, 59–77 (1997)

Kraut, R., Patterson, M., Lundmark, V., Kiesler, S., Mukhopadhyay, T., Scherlis, W.: Internet paradox: a social technology that reduces social involvement and psychological well-being. Am. Psychol. **53**, 1017–1031 (1998)

Kraut, R., Kiesler, S., Boneva, B., Cummings, J., Helgeson, V., Crawford, A.: Internet paradox revisited. J. Soc. Issues **58**(1), 49–74 (2002)

Lazarus, R.S., Folkman, S.: Stress, Appraisal, and Coping. Springer, New York (1984)

Lewin, K.: Frontiers in group dynamics 1. Hum. Relat. **1**, 5–41 (1947)

Marmor, J., Bieber, I., Gold, R.: A symposium: should homosexuality be in the APA nomenclature? In: Gross, L., Woods, J.D. (eds.) The Columbia Reader on Lesbians and Gay Men in Media, Society, and Politics. Columbia University Press, New York (1999)

Maslow, A.H.: Toward a Psychology of Being, 2nd edn. Van Nostrand Reinhold, New York (1968)

Masten, A.S.: Ordinary magic: resilience processes in development. Am. Psychol. **56**, 227–238 (2001)

McAdams, D.P.: Power, Intimacy and the Life Story. Guilford, New York (1988)

McMahon, A.: Immersion, engagement, and presence. In: Wolf, M.P., Perron, B. (eds.) The Video Game Theory Reader. Routledge, New York (2003)

Mehra, B., Merkel, C., Bishop, A.P.: The Internet for empowerment of minority and marginalized users. New Media Soc. **6**(6), 781–802 (2004)

Merrill, J.C., Lee, J., Friendlander, E.J.: Modern Mass Media. Harper Collins, New York (1990)

Meyer, I.H.: Prejudice, social stress, and mental health in lesbian, gay, and bisexual populations: conceptual issues and research evidence. Psychol. Bull. **129**, 674–697 (2003)

Morrow, V.: Conceptualizing social capital in relation to the well-being of children and young people: a critical review. Sociol. Rev. **47**, 744–765 (1999)

Nie, N.: Sociability, interpersonal relations, and the internet: reconciling conflicting findings. Am. Behav. Sci. **45**, 420–435 (2001)

Nie, N.H., Erbring, L.: Internet and society: a preliminary report. IT Soc. **1**(1), 275–283 (2002)

Nie, N., Hillygus, D.S.: The impact of internet use on sociability: time-diary findings. IT Soc. **1**(1), 1–29 (2002)

Ouellette, R.: Management of Aggressive Behavior: A Comprehensive Guide to Learning How to Recognize, Reduce, Manage, and Control Aggressive Behavior. Performance Dimensions, Powers Lake (1993)

Owens, T.J., Stryker, S., Goodman, N.: Extending Self-Esteem Theory and Research. Cambridge University Press, New York (2006)

Pachankis, J.E.: The psychological implications of concealing a stigma: a cognitive-affective-behavioral model. Psychol. Bull. **133**(2), 328–345 (2006)

Padilla-Walker, L.M.: Peers I can monitor, it's media that really worries me. J. Adolesc. Res. **21**(1), 56–82 (2006)

Peterson, J.L., Folkman, S., Bakeman, R.: Stress, coping, HIV status, psychosocial resources, and depressive mood in African American gay, bisexual, and heterosexual men. Am. J. Community Psychol. **24**, 461–487 (1996)

Pettigrew, T.F.: Social evaluation theory: convergences and applications. Nebr. Symp. Motiv. **15**, 241–311 (1967)

Postman, N.: Technopoly: The Surrender of Culture to Technology. Knopf, New York (1992)

Putnam, R.D.: Bowling Alone: The Collapse and Revival of American Community. Simon & Schuster, New York (2000)

Reid, S.A., Giles, H., Abrams, J.: A social identity model of media effects. Z. Medienpsychologie **16**, 17–25 (2004)

Rogers, C.: Psychotherapy and Personality and Change. University of Chicago Press, Chicago (1954)

Sagiv, L., Schwartz, S.H.: Value priorities and subjective well-being: direct relations and congruity effects. Eur. J. Soc. Psychol. **30**, 177–198 (2000)

Sagiv, L., Roccas, S., Hazan, O.: Value pathways to well-being: healthy values, valued goal attainment, and environmental congruence. In: Linley, P.A., Joseph, S. (eds.) Positive Psychology in Practice. Wiley, Hoboken (2004)

Shaw, B., Gant, L.: In defense of the Internet: the relationship between Internet communication and depression, loneliness, self-esteem, and perceived social support. Cyberpsychol. Behav. **5**, 157–171 (2002)

Siegal, J., Dubrovsky, V., Kiesler, S., McGuire, T.: Group processes in computer-mediated communication. Organ. Behav. Hum. Decis. Process. **37**, 157–187 (1986)

Smith, M., Kollock, P. (eds.): Communities in Cyberspace. Routledge, London (1999)

Sproull, L., Faraj, S.: Atheism, sex and databases: the net as a social technology. In: Kiesler, S. (ed.) Culture of the Internet, pp. 35–51. Erlbaum, Mahwah (1997)

Steinkuehler, C., Williams, D.: Where everybody knows your (screen) name: online games as "third places." J. Comput. Mediat. Commun. **11**(4), article 1 (2006)

Suler, J.: The online disinhibition effect. Cyberpsychol. Behav. **7**(3), 321–326 (2004). June

Tajfel, H.: Cognitive aspects of prejudice. J. Soc. Issues **25**, 79–97 (1969)

Tajfel, H. (ed.): Differentiation Between Social Groups: Studies in the Social Psychology of Intergroup Relations. Academic, London (1978)

Tajfel, H., Turner, J.C.: An integrative theory of intergroup conflict. In: Austin, W.G., Worchel, S. (eds.) The Social Psychology of Intergroup Relations. Brooks-Cole, Monterey (1979)

Tajfel, H., Turner, J.C.: The social identity theory of intergroup behavior. In: Worchel, S., Austin, W.G. (eds.) The Psychology of Intergroup Relations, 2nd edn, pp. 7–24. Nelson-Hall, Chicago (1986)

Tamborini, R., Skalski, P.: The role of presence in the experience of electronic games. In: Vorderer, P., Bryant, J. (eds.) Playing Video Games: Motives, Responses, and Consequences, pp. 225–240. Lawrence Erlbaum Associates, Mahwah (2006)

Thoits, P.A.: Self-labeling processes in mental illness: the role of emotional deviance. Am. J. Sociol. **91**, 221–249 (1985)

Trepte, S.: Social identity theory. In: Bryant, J., Vorderer, P. (eds.) Psychology of Entertainment. Erlbaum, Mahwah (2006)

Tugade, M.M., Fredrickson, B.L.: Resilient individuals use positive emotions to bounce back from negative emotional experiences. J. Pers. Soc. Psychol. **86**, 320–333 (2004)

Turkle, S.: Life on the Screen: Identity in the Age of the Internet. Simon & Schuster, New York (1995)

Valkenburg, P.M., Peter, J.: Preadolescents' and adolescents' online communication and their closeness to friends. Dev. Psychol. **43**, 267–277 (2007)

Valkenburg, P.M., Peter, J., Schouten, A.P.: Friend networking sites and their relationship to adolescents' well being and social self-esteem. Cyberpsychol. Behav. **9**, 584–590 (2006)

Watson, G., Johnson, D.: Social Psychology: Issues and Insights. J. B. Lippincott, Philadelphia (1972)

Wellman, B., Gulia, M.: The network basis of social support: a network is more than the sum of its ties. In: Wellman, B. (ed.) Networks in the Global Village: Life in Contemporary Communities, pp. 83–118. Westview, Boulder (1999)

Wellman, B., Salaff, J., Dimitrova, D., Garton, L., Gulia, M., Haythornthwaite, C.: Computer networks as social networks: Virtual community, computer-supported cooperative work and telework. Annual Review of Sociology, **22**, 213–238 (1996)

Wilson, D.S.: Evolutionary social constructivism. In: Gottshcall, J., Wilson, D.S. (eds.) The Literary Animal: Evolution and the Nature of Narrative. Northwestern University Press, Evanston (2005)

Yoshino, K.: Covering. Random House, New York (2006)

Zimbardo, P.G.: The human choice: individuation, reason, and order vs. deindividuation, impulse and chaos. In: Arnold, W.J., Levine, D. (eds.) Nebraska Symposium on Motivation, pp. 237–307. University of Nebraska Press, Lincoln (1969)

ERRATUM

Erratum to: Chapter 13
What Is My Avatar? Who Is My Avatar?
The Avatar as a Device to Achieve a Goal:
Perceptions and Implications

Marc Conrad, Alec Charles, and Jo Neale

In this chapter on page 263 Tables 13.5 and 13.6 were not displayed correctly. They should be displayed as hereafter:

The online version of the original chapter can be found at
http://dx.doi.org/10.1007/978-0-85729-361-9_13

A. Peachey and M. Childs (eds.), *Reinventing Ourselves: Contemporary Concepts
of Identity in Virtual Worlds*, Springer Series in Immersive Environments,
DOI 10.1007/978-0-85729-361-9_16, © Springer-Verlag London Limited 2011

Table 13.5 Avatars chosen by male respondents in relation to user ethnicity

	White	Black – African	Black – Caribbean	Black – other	Asian – Indian	Asian – Chinese
	5					
	6				2	1
		5	1	1		
	1					
	3					

Table 13.6 Avatars chosen by female respondents in relation to user ethnicity

	White	Black – African	Asian – Pakistan
			1
	1		1
			1
		1	

Glossary

This list defines terms used within the book that may be unfamiliar to some readers, or may be used in an unfamiliar way. These are offered as only general guidance; the meaning of these terms will depend on the writer, and on the context, and few are used consistently within the wider community. Where authors have used these terms in a way that differs from the meaning listed below, they have given their own definition within the chapter.

Alt Most virtual worlds permit users to maintain more than one avatar within the virtual world. These alternative avatars are referred to as "alts".

Anonymity and pseudonymity Many virtual worlds enable people to interact without revealing their physical world identities. However, when participating most require that participants take on a persistent identity, with which they are always identified when inworld. They are therefore often said to be pseudonymous rather than anonymous.

Avatar and character A representation of the user within the virtual world, operated by that user. The word "avatar" implies that the representation is to some extent an extension of the identity of the user; "character" implies a greater element of role-play. A single avatar may take on many different types of appearance or forms, but can be identified as the same avatar through being ascribed the same avatar name and profile.

Bling The effect caused by scripts in Second Life objects causing them to blink or flash. In some circles much admired, in other circles considered to be very camp. The use of these particle effects is sometimes restricted due to the extra processing power (or "rendering cost") they place on the servers running the virtual world.

Build Either the process of creating something 'physical' inworld, or a description of the finished item or set of items – the build.

Camping 1. In action role playing games and first-person shooters: staying on the same spot waiting for mobs to respawn. 2. In Second Life used to increase traffic

A. Peachey and M. Childs (eds.), *Reinventing Ourselves: Contemporary Concepts of Identity in Virtual Worlds*, Springer Series in Immersive Environments, DOI 10.1007/978-0-85729-361-9, © Springer-Verlag London Limited 2011

to (and thus popularity ranking of) regions by paying people a tiny sum per hour to have their avatar sitting there.

Chat/local chat Local chat is a means of public text-based communication between virtually collocated groups of two or more avatars.

Copresence The experience of "being there with others" within the virtual world.

Flow Flow is a concept originated by Csíkszentmihályi[1] and describes a state in which attention is heightened, and goals, action and the environment are all aligned.

Game world A virtual world where tasks and activity are primarily driven by a game narrative imposed by the environment.

Griefing A term used in virtual worlds to describe vandalism and/or deliberately aggressive or intimidating behaviour.

Instant Message/IM An instant message within Second Life is sent as a private communication between two or more individuals. IM means the same across most other virtual worlds.

Inworld Occurring inside the virtual world environment.

Lag Delay in processing information inworld, such as chat or movement, often due to high demand on the server.

Linden Linden Research, Inc./Linden Lab own the social world Second Life. The employees that operate within the virtual world have avatars with the surname Linden. "A Linden" can describe one Linden dollar (Second Life's currency) or a person employed by the company.

Linden Dollar The currency used within Second Life, which can be bought and transferred in and out of the virtual world. The exchange rate varies according to the trade market. On average, 1 US dollar is equal to 260 Linden dollars

Machinima A contraction of machine + cinema. Machinima have the appearance of animated films, but are actually recordings of the movement of avatars as they perform within the virtual world.

MMORPG/MMOG Massively Multiplayer Online Role-Playing Game/Massively Multi-player Online Game

MOO Object Oriented MUD. A text-based virtual world in which objects can be created, acted upon and persist within the text-based environment.

MUD Multi User Dungeons (or sometimes Domains) are text-based virtual worlds that create metaphorical virtual spaces despite being entirely text-based.

MUVE Multi-User Virtual Environment, covering any online environment with very large numbers of users.

Newb(ie)/Noob Term for a new player or user. "Newb" is usually used in a non-derogatory sense and simply indicates inexperience. "Noob" (or "n00b") is derogatory and indicates someone who is not just inexperienced but also behaves foolishly or inappropriately because they have not yet learned the conventions of the virtual world.

---

[1]Csíkszentmihályi, M. (1991). *Flow: The Psychology of Optimal Experience.* Perennial (HarperCollins).

Open Sim An open source environment that can be used to create a world very similar to Second Life, or adapted instead to meet individual requirements.

Open world A virtual world that is not defined by a set of game rules, meaning users can create their own content seemingly without limits and all activity is primarily socially driven.

Prim Short for Primitive – a building block in Second Life. Each area of land has a prim limit on the volume of items it can hold.

Render The display of the virtual world on the monitor of the person viewing the virtual world. Because of delays caused by bandwidth and the processing power of the user's computer, objects may exist within the virtual world (rezzed) but may not yet be rendered, and so are invisible to the viewer.

Resident A user of Second Life

Rez(z) To create or make 'physical' an object inworld

Sandbox An area in a virtual world where unrestricted building is allowed, with built items being automatically returned to the owner within a set period of time

Second Life An open, social world owned by Linden Research, Inc.

SLURL Second Life Universal Resource Locator: A link from a web URL that will take you direct to a location in Second Life, as long as you already have an avatar inworld.

Social world A virtual world that could be a game world or open world, but is predominantly social in nature.

Spawn point Place or area in a game or virtual world where characters (player or non-player) appear or "spawn".

Teleport To instantly transfer from one location to another within a virtual world

Telepresence and virtual presence These terms are used inconsistently within the literature. Some take "telepresence" to mean specifically the sense of "being there" at a remote physical location (e.g. through webconferencing), in which case the term "virtual presence" is then applied to the sense of "being there" within a computer-generated environment. Others take telepresence to represent either of these experiences. Within this book we have taken the latter of these definitions of telepresence.

Virtual world A persistent online environment, either text based or richly graphical, that users navigate for social or game purposes using an avatar.

VLE and LMS These terms are used inconsistently between US and UK educators. In the UK a VLE, or virtual learning environment, is an institutional web-based environment used for storing learning resources and communicating with students. In the US, this is described as an LMS (learning management system) and a VLE is a virtual world. In this book we have adopted the UK nomenclature.

World of Warcraft A game world that is the world's most successful virtual world when measured by user numbers.

Index